SUBVERSIVE
TRADITIONS

SUBVERSIVE TRADITIONS

REINVENTING THE WEST AFRICAN EPIC

Jonathon Repinecz

MICHIGAN STATE UNIVERSITY PRESS | *EAST LANSING*

♾ The paper used in this publication meets the minimum requirements
of ANSI/NISO Z39.48-1992 (R 1997) (Permanence of Paper).

Michigan State University Press
East Lansing, Michigan 48823-5245

This book was made possible by a Helen Tartar Memorial First Book Subvention
from the American Comparative Literature Association.

Printed and bound in the United States of America.

28 27 26 25 24 23 22 21 20 19   1 2 3 4 5 6 7 8 9 10

LIBRARY OF CONGRESS CATALOGING-IN-PUBLICATION DATA
Names: Repinecz, Jonathon, author.
Title: Subversive traditions : reinventing the West African epic / Jonathon Repinecz.
Other titles: African humanities and the arts.
Description: East Lansing : Michigan State University Press, 2019. | Series: African humanities and the arts
Identifiers: LCCN 2018059367| ISBN 9781611863345 (pbk. : alk. paper) | ISBN 9781609176136 (pdf)
| ISBN 9781628953763 (epub) | ISBN 9781628963779 (kindle)
Subjects: LCSH: Epic poetry, African—History and criticism. | Oral tradition—Africa, West.
| African fiction (French)—21st century—History and criticism. | Oral tradition in literature.
Classification: LCC PL8010.4 .R47 2019 | DDC 809.103209896—dc23
LC record available at https://lccn.loc.gov/2018059367

Book design by Charlie Sharp, Sharp Designs, East Lansing, MI
Cover design by Shaun Allshouse, www.shaunallshouse.com
Cover art is Lat-Dior and the Battle of Dékheulé, detail of mural by Papisto Boy along a factory wall
in Bel-Air, Dakar. Photograph, 2008, used by permission of Ji-Elle/Wikimedia Commons.
Title page art is Lat-Dior and Faidherbe. Mural by Papisto Boy at the Centre culturel français, Dakar.
Photo © Catherine and Bernard Desjeux.

Michigan State University Press is a member of the Green Press Initiative and is committed to developing
and encouraging ecologically responsible publishing practices. For more information about the Green
Press Initiative and the use of recycled paper in book publishing, please visit www.greenpressinitiative.org.

Visit Michigan State University Press at *www.msupress.org*

CONTENTS

CONTENTS

ACKNOWLEDGMENTS

This book is the product of years of collaboration with teachers, friends, and colleagues in North America, Africa, and Europe. I first became interested in the idea of an African epic through discussions with scholars at the University of Dakar, who have produced numerous books and theses documenting particular Senegalese oral narrative traditions. From there I became acquainted with the wider field of studies in West African oral traditions, particularly Mande studies, from which the *Sunjata* epic is never absent.

It would be impossible to name everyone who is deserving of my thanks, but there are a few elders and peers whose support deserves special acknowledgment. Many colleagues have contributed comments, readings, rebuttals, and discussions as my writing unfolded. The faculty of the French departments of UC Berkeley and Reed College, and of the Department of Modern and Classical Languages at George Mason University, have my eternal gratitude. GMU has provided valuable sabbatical and summer research time to support this research in its later stages. I have been fortunate to count on friends at these institutions for intellectual stimulation and collaboration, as well as support of all kinds, both big and small. David Conrad's generous feedback has been especially encouraging. My brother, Martin Repinecz, a Hispanist, deserves thanks for being my toughest critic.

This work owes a great deal to my Wolof teachers, especially Paap Alsaan Sow and Assane Diallo, whose linguistic expertise and patience have enabled me not only to read *Doomi Golo* and the Epic of Kajoor in the original, but also to have a real sensitivity toward the nuances of other African languages, all of which I unfortunately cannot learn. I have also benefitted enormously from the razor-sharp feedback of the Wolof Literature Working Group, funded by a Mellon grant through the UC Humanities Research Institute, including Tobias Warner, Ivy Mills, Cullen Goldblatt, and Fatoumata Seck. *Jërë ngeen jëf.*

I write these words with special affection for the memory of Mathieu Hilgers, a rising star in Africanist anthropology from the Université Libre de Bruxelles, who left us too soon. He was not only the most demanding collaborator I have ever had, but a mentor and friend. His influence on my work is inestimable. He is sorely missed.

Finally, I am grateful to the American Comparative Literature Association, who enabled the publication of this book by awarding it the Helen Tartar Memorial First Book Subvention.

To all those who have given me a hand along the way, whether by scribbling in my margins, hosting me during my endless peregrinations, or telling me to start over: Thank you.

NOTE ON THE TEXT

This book uses many terms borrowed from West African languages. In order to help the reader get her or his bearings, I offer a few clarifications here.

Spelling

Many West African words, both proper and common, have passed into English or French in more than one spelling. In addition, a number of West African languages have their own standard orthographies, though these are generally only respected in restricted settings. For the sake of ease, I follow whatever the most common convention is in English scholarly writing, to the extent possible. Thus I write "Lat-Dior Diop" rather than "Lat Joor Jóob," "Sunjata" rather than "Soundjata" or "Son-Jara," etc. When quoting other writers, I keep their spellings.

Translations

I have opted to include both original text and English translations for Wolof, French, and German. An exception has been made for epigraphs, most of which are in English only. In the case of titles, formatting indicates whether the English translation is from me or from a published work. For example, *L'Etrange destin de Wangrin* (*The Fortunes of Wangrin*) exists in a published English translation, whereas *Le Jujubier du patriarche* (The Patriarch's Tree) does not. The same goes for in-text quotations. In the following cases, the first citation references a published English translation, whereas the second merely offers my rendering of the original, since a published English version is unavailable:

> "dieu bizarre," "à la fois bon et mauvais, sage et libertin," "le grand confluent des contraires" ("weird divinity," "both kindly and ill disposed, chaste and libertine," "confluence of all opposites") (A. H. Bâ 1992: 20–21; 1999: 8)

> "l'amazone à l'allure de guêpe et au cœur de lion" (the Amazon with the speed of a wasp and the heart of a lion) (Sow Fall 1993: 29)

In the case of indented block quotes, I always indicate parenthetically whether an English rendering is mine or from a published work. All translations are my responsibility alone, though I was graciously helped with the German by Justin Ward.

Ethnolinguistic Terminology

This book undertakes a transethnic exploration of West African epic. As such, it regularly references the region's major ethnolinguistic groups: the Mande, the Fulbe, the Bamana, the Wolof, the Songhai, and so on. For the most part, each of these terms designates both an ethnic identity and a language. However, two of these terms, Mande and Fulbe, warrant some clarification.

The Mande heartland is the area along the Mali/Guinea border, once home to the great Mali Empire (thirteenth to sixteenth centuries). Because the medieval empire's influence spread far and wide, Mande languages are spoken in a culturally linked space that reaches from Mali to Liberia. Following established scholarly usage, I use the term "Manden" to refer specifically to the heartland, "Maninka" to refer to the language that is spoken there (note that it is typically called *malinké* in French), "Mande" to refer both to the wider family of languages to which Maninka belongs and to the West African sociohistorical world where these languages are spoken, and "Manding" to refer to the narrower continuum of more or less mutually intelligible Mande languages: Maninka, Bamana (Bambara), Jula, and Senegambian

Mandinka. See Durán and Furniss (1999: xi); Traoré (2000b: 36–48); and Conrad (2004: xxxii–xxxiv).

"Fulbe" is an umbrella term for linguistically related groups of historically nomadic peoples, spread between Senegal and Chad, who in some cases became sedentary and formed several important empires over the centuries. These include Futa Toro along the Senegal River, Futa Jallon in central Guinea, and Masina in southeastern Mali, to name a few. I use "Fulbe" as a noun to refer to these people collectively, "Fula" as an adjective, and "Fulfulde" to designate this people's language. "Pular" refers to the dialect of Fulfulde spoken in the Futa Toro region.

The nomenclature for this people is especially confusing, as it varies geographically, and different writers have their own conventions. Among the authors I cite, my reader will encounter the Wolof word "Peuls," which has passed into French, used to designate the Fulbe in general, as well as "Toucouleur" and "Halpularen" used to specify the Fulbe of the Futa Toro. See Kane and Robinson (1984: 2).

ALTERNATIVE TRADITIONALITIES

Lying in bed that night, after Toumani [Diabate]'s concert, I thought about the griots' power to keep West Africans in the thrall of a heroic past, to evoke feelings that have not changed in seven hundred years. Despite our attempts to catch up with the modern world, they have trapped us in a narrative of return, a permanent identification with the heroes of old griot songs: Sundiata, Mansa Musa, and Samory Touré.

—Manthia Diawara, "The Song of the Griot"

"Cosaan" se meurt. [Tradition is dying.]

—Aminata Sow Fall, *L'Appel des arènes*

The desire to become modern and the lament for the loss of tradition are two sides of the same coin. Across the world, the association of traditionality with times of old and nostalgic longing has become a powerful motif, perhaps as universal as the notion of tradition itself. The sentiment underlying it is profoundly human, often bound up with the exile's longing for home. Even so, in West Africa, this narrative runs the risk of obscuring the boundless creativity of artists and thinkers who continue not only to draw inspiration from "the heroes of old griot songs"—that is, the region's famous oral epic traditions, passed down by word of mouth from generation to generation—but to rethink them. Traditions, as relatively recent scholarly consensus teaches us, should not be understood as fossils or relics from another age, but as dynamic objects and texts that are, and have always been, in a constant state of renegotiation.

As I will argue in this book, the distinction between tradition and its so-called opposite, modernity, not only was invented by colonialism but has remained entrenched in certain currents of francophone West African thought in the post-colonial era. Whether construed as tradition, primitivism, or the Dark Ages—or, as Achille Mbembe has argued, Africa itself (2001a)—a backwards Other has historically been necessary in order for modernity, inevitably associated with European and later American influence, to define itself. Modernity is now a completely inescapable notion in every academic discipline, and African studies are no exception. For decades, scholars have debated what Africa's "place-in-the-world" is, that is, whether and how it fits into the worldwide category of modernity (Ferguson 2006: 6).

To take the example of Dakar, my adopted home in West Africa, I am struck by the city's visible progress each time I visit. Since my first stay in 2008, numerous highways have been built or rebuilt, and pedestrian bridges, intended to discourage people from crossing traffic at their peril, have become more numerous. Official strategies abound to reduce electricity and water cuts, which were everyday occurrences in 2008 but have become less frequent today. The changes aren't limited to infrastructure. In culture, the winds are blowing toward empowerment of youth, and in politics, away from oligarchic rule. The Senegalese hip-hop industry is not only bursting with creativity, but wielding political influence. The Y en a marre ("Fed up") movement gained international attention in 2012 for its democratic activism and its role in preparing then president Abdoulaye Wade's peaceful cession of power to his opponent and successor, Macky Sall. The reaction to Macky Sall's time in power is mixed, with many accusing him of having betrayed his promises. Yet this will to national and urban progress constitutes an aspiration to modernity.

What is the place of the old oral traditions in this globalized world? Is nostalgia for dying genres and ways of life merely a social anesthetic for the growing pains of Afromodernity? Or should we only remember, with the occasional shudder, various African nations' co-optation of vernacular knowledges as political capital: L. S. Senghor's romantic nationalization of Wolof and Serer stories and tam-tam rhythms into a state ideology of Negritude, Sékou Touré's pantheon of anticolonial heroes in Guinea, Mobutu Sese Seko's aesthetics and politics of *authenticité* in Zaire?

From Shakira to Sunjata

I would like to begin this book, which offers a fresh answer to the above question by exploring the potential for subversion common to oral and written texts, with a reflection on three visual expressions of African aspirations to inclusion in global modernity. All three expressions are "realms of memory" located in Dakar and centered, more or less, around the year 2010. This reflection on simultaneous but diverse imaginations of modernity in an urban setting will set the stage for the interdisciplinary, hybrid rereading that I propose of the issue of traditionality in francophone West African writing. The first object is the (in)famous African Renaissance Monument, a 49-meter (160-foot) statue that was completed in 2010 as one of then president Abdoulaye Wade's crowning aesthetic achievements; the second is Shakira's music video "Waka Waka/This Time for Africa," the theme of the World Cup from the same year, which was ubiquitous in Dakar and around the world as the tournament was unfolding that summer; and third is a mural painting of Lat-Dior Diop, one of the last kings of the Wolof precolonial kingdom of Kajoor, a figure remembered as an anticolonial resister, protagonist of an oral epic, and Senegalese national hero canonized by Senghor. The image is part of a 200-meter (650-foot) long mural by Papisto Boy (Pape Samb) in the Bel-Air neighborhood of Dakar.

Mamadou Diouf describes Afromodernity as "une entreprise de désorganisation qui est aussi une aventure de réorganisation et de recomposition de plusieurs héritages historiques" (an undertaking of disorganizing that is also an adventure of reorganizing and recomposing several historical heritages) (2002: 262). All three figures illustrate this definition, but in different ways: whereas the Renaissance Monument and Shakira represent an Afromodernity imposed from above, that is, by government and corporate interests and served to the public without much democratic input, the mural by Papisto Boy is a form of popular, pedagogical street art generated by and for the streets of Dakar. It is the most organic illustration of Diouf's notion of recomposition of historical heritages, given its palimpsestic juxtaposition of historical and religious figures in a wall mural that was constantly revised until the artist's death in 2014. In contrast, rather than analyzing the

FIGURE 1. The African Renaissance Monument, Dakar.

FIGURE 2 (*opposite, top*). Lat-Dior and the Battle of Dékheulé. Detail of mural by Papisto Boy along a factory wall in Bel-Air, Dakar.

FIGURE 3 (*opposite, bottom*). A longer section of the same mural, Bel-Air, Dakar. Note the pink slave house of Gorée Island and its "door of no return" (far left). Mural by Papisto Boy.

Renaissance Monument and "Waka Waka" as aesthetic creations in themselves, what interests me about them is the controversies they generated. The public reactions that I observed in Dakar to these objects during the summer of 2010 parallel the commentary on nationalist discourses undertaken by Papisto Boy in the Bel-Air mural. This reflection is meant to invite the reader to think about what different Afromodernities look like in Senegal and beyond. By moving from these figures of modernity to a discussion of traditionality—from Shakira to Sunjata, West Africa's most famous epic hero—I hope to show that the seemingly contradictory aspirations to modernity and to so-called traditional authenticity have more in common than we might think.

The giant African Renaissance Monument overlooking the Atlantic from the capital's western corniche, completed in 2010, was criticized in public opinion as a narcissistic monument by Wade to himself (Quist-Arcton 2010). This bronze statue, a rival to the Statue of Liberty, consists of an enormous muscle-bound man emerging dramatically from a mountain, lifting a baby aloft in one arm and flanked by a woman set slightly behind them. Her gaze is fixed on the baby, whose finger points forward, toward the future—and the west—while the man stares distantly out to sea. In addition to an assortment of Muslim and feminist objections to the project, denizens of Dakar mocked the scene in Wolof as representing *Góor gi, soxna si, ak doom ji*, that is, "the old man, the lady, and the son," in reference to the president, his wife Viviane, and their son Karim. During and after construction, speculations swirled that Abdoulaye Wade was grooming Karim, named a cabinet minister in 2009 after a humiliating performance in municipal elections, to replace him in the nation's highest office. But even the resentment felt toward the monument bears the marks of an aspiration to modernity: Why, people asked, were 15 billion CFA francs ($27 million) being spent on a statue instead of on schools, hospitals, or decent housing projects in Dakar's overcrowded suburbs? The same criticism was leveled at some of the infrastructural improvements made in Dakar under Wade, as well. Why focus so much on beautifying the capital to impress foreign visitors—such as myself?

This question was all the more urgent since scholarship on African cities, including on Dakar, is far from optimistic. A great deal of it has been devoted to the phenomena of "urban crisis" or "disorderly urbanization" (Abdoul 2005: 235–36). The precariousness of urban life has fueled a crisis of the family and reproduction, as young people find themselves unable to found or sustain families of their own (Comaroff and Comaroff 2004: 336–39). Longing for a future, young men from across the continent emigrate massively, often clandestinely, in an attempt to escape entrenched poverty and unemployment. And then there are the more spectacular dangers facing Africa. Thanks to the international news media's breathless reporting, the whole world is kept up to date on the continent's woes: Islamic terror in all its forms, Ebola, AIDS, pirates, refugee camps, the specter of genocide, the list goes on. In Senegal, the erosion of French-style *laïcité* or secularism seems to parallel a crisis in the state's own legitimacy (Havard 2013). In Dakar, while it is true that some live well, or at least decently, a walk in any major thoroughfare reminds one that many do not. The 2005 law banning forced child begging is poorly enforced. Koranic school pupils, or *talibés*, and other mendicants roam the streets today as they did when I first visited in 2008.

It is thus debatable how exactly Dakar—or Senegal, or Africa—may be said to fit within the seemingly inevitable worldwide condition of modernity. It is difficult enough to pin down the idea of modernity itself: the term simultaneously signifies "one thing," an aspiration to liberation through rationalism and science produced by the thought of the European Enlightenment, and many different things, produced by the same Enlightenment's underside of violence, oppression, and exclusion in a myriad of particular contexts (Comaroff and Comaroff 2004: 330–33). James Ferguson's famous anecdote about a villager in Lesotho wanting to replace his beautiful, ecologically friendly one-room hut of stone and thatch with an ugly steel-roofed house containing two or three rooms remains illustrative. One common symptom of modernity is that people seek to emulate Western models perceived as superior (Ferguson 2006: 18–21). Meanwhile, Arjun Appadurai's description of cultural aspirations in 1960s Bombay fleshes out this desire in an urban context: modernity was something he "saw and smelled" as a boy, whether in *Life* magazine, B movies, or the bite of "the American bug" (1996: 1–2). Manthia Diawara, whom I quote in the first epigraph to this introduction, writes that in 1970s Bamako, "We tried to look like our black American heroes. We walked tall, in packs, and pretended we couldn't speak French" (1997: 16).

Appadurai's argument that modernity is a work of the imagination engendered by the twin pillars of mass media and mass migration has been extremely influential. The role of Shakira's "Waka Waka" in Dakar offers a supporting anecdote from my own experience. In the summer of 2010, only a few months after the completion of the Renaissance Monument, in a city ebullient with excitement over Ghana's qualification for the quarterfinals, I couldn't go an hour without hearing "Waka Waka" blasting from a shop, out a car window, or over the rooftops. Everything about this scenario seemed emblematic of an up-and-coming "place-in-the-world" for Africa: much of the continent was celebrating fifty years of independence from colonial rule; the biggest sports event on the planet was being held there for the first time; an African team had beaten the United States and still had hope of advancing; and Shakira's proclamation that "We're all Africa" was being overplayed not only in the host country, but around the world. Teresa Barnes offers the following recollection of Cape Town from June and July 2010, though the scenes she describes could just as easily have played out in Dakar:

> For the month, the song that hummed up through people's feet was the tournament's bouncy theme song called Waka Waka, which featured, for some reason, Shakira, a blonde Colombian belly dancer, with backing vocals from South Africa's favorite pop group (once a group of college students), Freshly Ground. You couldn't get away from it, you had to Waka. We Waka-ed in the supermarket and Waka-ed buying gas for the car and Waka-ed on the radio and TV. "This time for Africa!" declared Shakira, and wiggled winsomely. South African friends had "Football Fridays" at their workplaces, wore the shiny jerseys of different national teams and tried to learn a new dance, diski, at lunchtimes. You stuck one leg in the air, wiggled, and Waka-ed. (2011: 104)

That song, and its accompanying music video, were the source of public controversy. Why was Shakira chosen to represent the tournament to the world, with South African artists playing second fiddle (Dugger 2010)? And why didn't Shakira, or the world for that matter, give credit to Zangaléwa (formerly the Golden Sounds), the Cameroonian group who had recorded the original version of the song in 1986? Did the global public need a well-known nonblack face to make the unpleasant brand of "Africa" palatable? Or was the very message of "This time for Africa" somehow condescending, insinuating that the continent remains, or ought to remain, on the margins of global pop culture?

As well founded as these criticisms may have been, no one whom I talked to in Dakar in the summer of 2010 appeared to care. My friends were happy that "Africa" was being included in global pop culture and, by extension, the world consumerist economy. "Most Africans," Ferguson writes, "can hardly feel that they are being dominated by being forced to take on the goods and forms of a homogenizing global culture when those goods and forms are, in fact, largely unavailable to them" (2006: 21). It seemed to me that everyone I spoke to—or under whose window I passed—in

Dakar during that summer could see their aspirations for a better place-in-the-world reflected in the fact that the world's attention was riveted on a positive image of Africa, via FIFA and Shakira. As Cameroonian journalist Mohamadou Houmfa wrote for France 24, "The Cameroonians are actually very proud of the remake. In cybercafés you see both versions of the song," that is, Shakira's and Zangaléwa's, "playing on repeat. . . . It's also something positive for the Cameroonian players, who will be proud to think that the song comes from their country" (2010). The same was true in Dakar: the major hip-hop artist Didier Awadi had made his own cover, "Zamouna," in 2006, and his version could be heard alongside Shakira's all over town. In fact, Zangaléwa's original had been a global hit of sorts in its own right, covered dozens of times over the years, from Senegal to Suriname to the Dominican Republic to Liberia. Some scholars, and Shakira's agents, in response to South African criticism, emphasized the artist's and song's deliberate global appeal: with her Lebanese-Colombian background and international renown, Shakira has long marketed herself as a transnational phenomenon; and the tune's popularity showed that it was not just addressed to "Africa," but to the whole world (Gontovnik 2010: 153). Meanwhile, a former member of Zangaléwa announced an agreement with Shakira in July 2010 that included compensation for use of the tune (Houmfa 2010). Appadurai's and Ferguson's arguments seemed to be perfectly demonstrated: a deterritorialized public longed for the modernity offered to it in a globally televised soccer tournament and the infinitely mobile mass-media genres of a pop song and video. Rather than seeing themselves as located in Dakar, or Yaoundé, or Barranquilla, fans across the continent and the globe celebrated the insertion of "Africa"—which, as many scholars have noted, is more an imaginary category than a place, but a powerful one—into global consciousness.

It is true that this imagination of Africa was conveniently flattened, packaged, and stripped of historical depth. Few people outside Cameroon remembered Zangaléwa, let alone the original music video's satirical tone, or the song's use as a rousing tune for the Cameroonian military, or its adaptation from martial songs of colonial African troops conscripted to fight for France in World War II (Mackey 2010). But never mind all that: when Shakira crooned "This time for Africa," people sensed that it might really mean something now. When Ghana lost to Uruguay in the quarterfinals, the bartender at the tiny Dakar watering hole where I had watched the game was so distraught that she refused to take anyone's money. Customers placed their bills and coins on the counter and left. "A quand notre tour?" she asked through her tears, her head in her hands. "When will our turn be?"

If the desire for recognition on the world stage, or for an elsewhere full of opportunity, form one side of Afromodernity's coin, then "the epidemic sense of crisis in contemporary Africa" is on the other side (Comaroff and Comaroff 2004: 330). As I have already suggested in the case of cities, an omnipresent sense of postcolonial disorder subtends the desire for upward mobility on the continent. Crisis, for Jean Comaroff and John Comaroff, is always part of modernity, which, in turn, is always theorized through a logic of rupture: even in its least spectacular iterations, "modernity, *sans* italics, in its mundane, everyday workings, describes a process of creative destruction that lays waste as it develops, building its continuities on *dis*continuity" (2004: 329–30). But discontinuity from what? The European colonial project may have needed a primitive Other against which to define itself, but contemporary thinking on modernity has tried to eschew such facile binaries. For one, the scholarly emphasis on such topics as "creative destruction," "creative adaptations," the economy of getting by (*débrouille*), arts of citizenship, and modes of self-writing signals a will to recognize the agency of African and other non-Western subjects responding in different ways to the exigencies around them, rather than being mere imitators of Western modernity, victims of one crisis or another, or effects of a Dark Continent's never-ending chaos.[1] Indeed, the call to restore the agency of the African subject has set the agenda of African studies for the last three decades. Much of this work has tried to imagine modernity in nonexclusively Western terms. Dilip Gaonkar helpfully theorized the concept of "alternative modernities" (2001). For him, the West's "unforgettable figures of modernity"—the Enlightenment faith in reason, the emergence of secularism, democratic forms of government, and the legacy of thinkers like Karl Marx, Charles Baudelaire, Walter Benjamin, Max Weber, and Friedrich Nietzsche—are now unavoidable to any theorist working on the subject. And yet, these figures cannot simply be posed *tel quel* as a telos toward which the rest of the globe must be expected to tend: "Still, many of the aforementioned cultural forms, social practices, and institutional arrangements do surface in most places in the wake of modernity. But at each national and cultural site, those elements are put together (reticulated) in a unique and contingent formation in response to local culture and politics" (2001: 3 and 16). This diversified view of modernity allowed provocatively titled monographs in African studies, like Peter Geschiere's *The Modernity of Witchcraft* and Charles Piot's *Remotely Global: Village Modernity in West Africa*, to become classics. And, to return to Manthia Diawara's example of the Bamako music scene in the 1970s: "The fusion of African American and Mande music in Soriba

[Kouyate]'s performance had blown me away: it was as if, at long, last, African music was unafraid of becoming modern" (1997: 22). Modernity encompasses, then, not only the visible and symbolic progress of metropolises like Dakar or Bamako, but also their peripheries, the marginalized realms of the remote, the rural, the superstitious, as well as the traditional. As these examples show, if such a thing as Afromodernity exists, it is not only thanks to the emergence of a Pan-African diasporic consciousness, in opposition to the West's belief in its own superiority, but also because, across Africa, what Gaonkar calls contingent reticulations of globalized networks of power are set in the context of a continentally shared experience.[2] Unhealed postcolonial wounds are coupled with newer forms of imperialism, especially that of the "neoliberal world order," which extends the logic of international capitalism to biopolitics and the lifeworld at large.[3]

That brings us to Papisto Boy's mural image of Lat-Dior. It glorifies the antico-lonial hero's last stand against the French at the Battle of Dékheulé, where he was killed on October 27, 1886, along with his famous horse Malaw. It is set in a gallery of images that celebrated the recognizable theme of resistance through portraits of local and international figures like Jimi Hendrix and Bob Marley, Aïda Souka and Coumba Gawlo;[4] religious figures like Cheikh Amadou Bamba, a staple of Dakar wall art particularly favored by the artist, but also Christ crucified and John Paul II, in deference to Senegal's Catholic minority; and American presidents like Jimmy Carter and the Kennedy couple (Leduc-Gueye 2016: 7–8). In the Bel-Air mural's bust of Lat-Dior, the hero's head surmounts a black-and-white sketch titled "La Bataille de Dékheulé," in which a miniature Lat-Dior mounted on a rearing Malaw occupies center stage as the battle rages around them. The composition is clearly palimpsestic, with traces of previous black markings visible through the white background of the battle scene. The bust of Lat-Dior is framed by two rifles that are outlined in a pattern evoking smoke and gunfire, but also lightning amid clouds and tree branches amid leaves. A resting black panther, a coiled cobra, Yasser Arafat in a checkered headscarf, and Blaise Diagne with his name inscribed on a book provide a further company to the icon of the hero. On the one hand, this constellation clearly offers a pedagogy of resistance: Lat-Dior's opposition to the French conquest is echoed by Yasser Arafat's struggle against Israeli occupation and the Black Panthers' fight for justice in the civil rights era; the book invites the viewer to learn about Blaise Diagne's push for Senegalese representation in the French colonial state; and the cobra is a recurring motif that signifies "the mortal dangers of treachery" (Roberts and Roberts 2000b: 77).

At first glance, this arrangement of images might elicit a strongly patriotic, patriarchal reading, one rooted in Senegalese and global stories of (mostly male) resistance against Western oppression. Indeed, Lat-Dior has been commemorated in many nationalist iconographies ranging from postage stamps to the theatrical stage to a TV miniseries to stadiums and schools bearing his name. Cullen Goldblatt reads the twentieth-century heroization of Lat-Dior as a foundation of the paternalist, heavy-handed Senegalese state under Senghor and his successor Abdou Diouf, a form of "enforced" memory:

> The historical imaginary of the Senghorian state cast Senegal as a free, unified, masculine nation, born of two nineteenth-century fathers, one African and one European, Lat Dior and Faidherbe.[5] . . . Under the administration of Senghor's successor, Abdou Diouf, Faidherbe's paternity was quietly neglected in favor of a single resistant national father; the 1986 centenary of Lat Dior's death became a state occasion and an important way in which Diouf sought to legitimize his authority. (2015: 106 and 105)

In slightly different ways, the memory of Lat-Dior helped cement the narrative of state legitimacy under Senegal's first two presidents. The mythologized Battle of Dékheulé, even though it pitted Lat-Dior against Faidherbe, seems to encapsulate Senghor's view of a "dual paternity" of the nation: through the clash of valiant hero-warriors, a new country, born of the encounter of Negritude and Francophonie, was forged. This perspective is all the more visible in another mural by Papisto Boy, on the wall of the Centre culturel français in downtown Dakar, that depicts Lat-Dior and Faidherbe in a stylized face-off (see title page spread). Compared to this scene, which juxtaposes the two fathers-of-the-nation in a Senghorian union of geniuses, the Bel-Air version might easily be read as eclipsing Faidherbe's paternity in favor of Lat-Dior's, following the representation favored by the Abdou Diouf regime.

And yet, such a reading would be reductionist. What is unique about the Bel-Air mural as a whole is not so much its choice of heroes but their democratization: whether religious or secular, political or pop-cultural, local or foreign, they are displayed at equal scale, in haphazard order, on a single, universally accessible visual plane; images blend and yield to each other as they are palimpsestically replaced over time; and now that the artist has passed, sadly, they are subject to neglect and erosion. (If one visits either the Bel-Air or the downtown mural today, one will find both significantly faded and damaged.) The sheer marginality of the site, its unauthorized use of a factory wall in an otherwise bleak industrial zone of Dakar, reflects its embeddedness in the economic realities of the local community: "through it he hopes to give courage to the hardworking people of Dakar's informal economy," that is, to "ceux qui n'ont pas les moyens d'acheter des toiles, qui ne se rendent pas dans les galeries ni les expositions, comme il avait coutume de le souligner" (those without means to buy canvases, who don't go to galleries or exhibits, as he liked to emphasize) (Roberts and Roberts 2000a: 288; Leduc-Gueye 2016: 7). Both the construction and the composition of this mural reflect the aesthetics of "getting by," of *débrouille* in French or *góorgóorlu* in Wolof, of making do with available scraps in the context of neoliberal state disinvestment in education, housing, and the arts (Seck 2018: 263–68). The work invokes the disorganized multiplicity of the collective Senegalese imaginary for the casual passerby to contemplate as he or she strolls along the length of the wall. This plurality is reproduced not only in the banner effect of the mural as a whole, but in the juxta- or superposed effect that unites individual portraits to their immediate neighbors. In direct contradiction to the rigidly paternalist reading outlined above, Leduc-Gueye notes that Senghor is not represented in the mural as a father-of-the-nation, but joined with one of his political adversaries, Omar Blondin Diop, "figure emblématique de la contestation de la fin des années 1960" (an emblem of the contestations of the late 1960s) (2016: 7): both fatherly authority and youthful rebellion find a place in the tableau. Similarly, the artist is known to have transformed, at one point, the likeness of then opposition politician Abdoulaye Wade into that of Che Guevara simply because he felt inspired to do so (Roberts and Roberts 2003: 91–92). Oppositionality is as important a theme as the state's claim to legitimacy. As a last example, although Papisto Boy was a profoundly committed Murid artist, and the Murid saint Cheikh Amadou Bamba is a recurring figure in his art, the heterogeneity of portraits chosen for inclusion at Bel-Air complicates the scholarly emphasis on Murid wall art as an expression of public piety (2002: 200–201). Although the artist described his work as an act of devotion inspired by Bamba, it nevertheless indexes the multiplicity of Senegal's founding fathers and heritages, including their increasing diversification over time, rather than a single-minded glorification of any one (or pair) of them.

This rearticulation of the national imaginary offers a certain creative potential. The nation's generators are not only presidents, *cheikhs*, epic heroes, or other figures from the history books, but all of these and more, springing from diverse and dissimilar mythologies. Seen from this perspective, the portrait of Lat-Dior need not only be read as legitimizing the state, but as one piece in the ever-evolving collage of a collective memory that the viewer is invited to imagine differently in turn. Such a reading is all the more plausible when we remember that the hero's legacy in the Wolof landscape predates his co-optation by Senghor: his story, particularly the episode of the Battle of Dékheulé, had already passed into the oral epic tradition. Documented performances of this epic in Wolof are readily available.[6] Presidential political baggage is not the only important aspect of this hero as a realm of memory. The epic of Lat-Dior is a primary material that is readily usable not only by politicians, but by artists interested in dis- and reorganizing hybrid historical heritages.

This fact has three important consequences that this book will explore at length. First, the oral epic tradition still matters. Contrary to interpretations of West African epic that relentlessly frame it as an object of nostalgia or relic of an "absolute past," the traditions associated with this umbrella genre still inspire reformulations and reinventions that make them pertinent today. While Lat-Dior is the emblematic epic hero in Senegalese nationalist discourse, Sunjata, reputed to have founded the Mali Empire in the thirteenth century, is the most famous of all West African epic heroes. These figures and others will be major recurring reference points in this study, both in terms of their co-optation by political discourses and in terms of their stories' capacity to serve as models of resistance. Indeed, even though Manthia Diawara writes that "Mande heroism," as incarnated in *Sunjata*, is "a discourse which, together with the caste system and the subordination of women through polygamy, sustains the power of the clans that constitute the main barrier to the creation of a democratic society in Mande West Africa" (1997: 30), there is a long history of interpreting *Sunjata* and other iterations of West African heroism precisely *as* models for democratic society, and even as sites from which to invert gender roles and noble–slave relations—and to imagine an entirely casteless society. This exemplifies my second point: that all cultural monuments, including the African Renaissance, "Waka Waka," and the epic tradition, are subject to dialogization in public discourse. Regardless of what they were "intended" to mean, and whether they were imposed from above or spontaneously generated from below, their significance to society is determined by the ongoing conversations that people have about them and, especially in the case of epic heroes, the creative rearticulations that result from those conversations. Finally, just as there are normative and alternative configurations of modernity, the same is true of traditionality. Traditionalizing registers can be deployed not only to enforce authorized or authoritarian ideologies and social norms, but to critique them and, as we shall see, to formulate liberating alternatives to them.

Alternative Traditionalities and the West African Novel

Within his continuing work on hybrid expressions of urban modernities, Mamadou Diouf has spoken of a "désertion de l'espace scriptural," that is, a decline of the culture of writing and the book among young people in Senegal, who he says have turned to other urban cultural forms to express themselves, especially hip-hop, *mbalax*, iconography, and fashion (2013: 88). Expressions of modernity no longer seem to need book culture. Manthia Diawara highlights the turn to African-American music—*away* from the "Francité" of Senghor—as his generation's claim to modernity in Bamako (1997: 21). The apparent shift away from the francophone canon of the past—the poetry and essays of Senghor, the classic writings of Bernard Dadié, Cheikh Hamidou Kane, etc.—correspond with the decline of the French school as a motor for social ascent and of the francophone state bureaucracy as a source of reliable careers. The three monuments that I analyzed above seem to illustrate this point. All three represent the potential for expressing African aspirations to a better "place-in-the-world" without resorting to writing. Indeed, the book identifying Blaise Diagne on the Bel-Air mural, titled *Qui était Blaise Diagne? 1872–1934*, seems to point precisely toward the memory of a francophone bureaucracy that has lost its prestige. Nevertheless, Papisto Boy frequently described his work as "literature" and "poetry," captioned his murals here and there with poetic fragments in French, and even wrote poetry in French about his own art; this quasi-literary dimension has been noticed by scholars, who describe his work as a "visual literature" with a "grande force narrative" (great narrative force).[7] While the symbolic capital of francophone writing may no longer be what it was in the 1930s or 1960s within West African societies, it continues to be associated in some way with the power of storytelling, which, regardless of medium, remains as fundamental to human expression today as ever. Rather than dismissing literature outright, it is important to realize that the francophone literary field has played a huge role in shaping the storytelling force that Papisto Boy tried to capture. Incontestably, francophone literature has helped open up a crucial space for social critique in West Africa, including, as I argue here, by theorizing alternative traditionalities.

In the context of literature, tradition generally means oral tradition, that is, discursive genres such as tales, songs, or epics whose content or form is passed down, or is said to be passed down, over generations by word of mouth. African oral traditions are examples of oral literature, that is, "utterances that show artistic characteristics of accurate observation, vivid imagination, and ingenious expression" (Nandwa and Bukenya 1983: 1). The role of this ancient heritage in shaping "modern" African literature is itself a vast subject of scholarly study, located at the heart of what it means, or not, for African literature to be African. From the 1960s on, literary scholars, including many Africans, have made the argument that the African novel ought to be seen as an outgrowth not of the European novel, but of oral tradition, usually understood through the lens of "traditional values" that first persisted, then *fell apart* as colonial modernity imposed itself on the African continent. The work of Mohamadou Kane (1982) and Amadou Koné (1985 and 2004) is emblematic of this vein of scholarship. Eileen Julien's disagreement with Kane over the issue of African "specificity" marked a sea change in the discussion. Whereas Kane argued that African writers' inevitable borrowings from the oral tradition, conscious or not, are precisely what makes African literature African, Julien's analysis of "the question of orality" laid out the ideological stakes and pitfalls of agreeing or disagreeing too rigidly with his position (1992). We risk rehashing old stereotypes of diffusionism and primitivism if we understand literature, particularly the novel, as a Western export that African writers fill with their own content or local color, but we also risk essentialism and naive romanticism if we declare, with Kane, that the oral tradition is the "real" source of all literary inspiration in Africa (Julien 2006: 673–75). Julien argues for an approach between "the Scylla of tradition and the Charybdis of empire" (Apter 2007: 2), based on a more or less explicit textual choice: some works written by African authors choose to engage with oral forms, and some do not. Individual cases should be treated as such, not as fodder for conclusions about the specificity or authenticity of African literature as a whole. It is insufficient for scholars to "identify a Euro-language text's authenticating traces of orality or local languages . . . without examining the transformations and uses of oral genres and forms in specific, historical contexts" (Julien 2006: 676–77). By examining these transformations, she suggests, we can avoid the "*bien pensant* platitudes" of connecting African literature "to some generalized roots in 'the oral tradition'" (Austen 1999b: 82).

Thus, I am intervening in a debate that is already old. Scholars have been debating the kinship between African traditions and novels for the better part of a century. But the conversation has stagnated because of a slowness to question the terms on which it is based: orality vs. writing, tradition vs. modernity, epic vs. novel. It is taken for granted that "oral tradition," including the "traditional epic," morphed into the "modern novel" because "tradition" has been replaced, in whole or in part, by "modernity." Thanks to this entrenched paradigm, far too much ink has been poured into the so-called great divide between oral and writing societies, and to the long-lamented decline of the ways of old. These overdetermined concepts need to be resituated as constructs. All were, in large part, invented by colonialism and are therefore subject to reinvention. Indeed, all have been subject to incredibly creative reinventions by later artists and thinkers. Given advances in social science and humanities research in recent decades—specifically, in studies of folklore, performance, invented traditions, colonial and postcolonial ethnography, and history—as well as the appearance of new literary contributions, the moment is right to rewrite this calcified literary history. In doing so, we can better grasp the interplay of "alternative modernities" and "alternative traditionalities" in a region whose creative vibrancy and dynamism deserve renewed attention. It is time for a fresh look.

This new approach to the relevance of traditionality requires some ground clearing. First, it is necessary to think about the colonial enterprise. Both "tradition" and "modernity" were constructed by colonialist thinkers in Africa and elsewhere in order to justify Europe's own fantasy of cultural superiority and its project of economic exploitation of the globe. Whether in the fields of colonial anthropology, literature, folkloristics, or law, a knowable, reified, traditional Other was made legible both as a governable subject and as a foil against which modernity could be conceived: "The modern not only invented tradition, it depends upon it" (Dirks 1990: 27). The progress associated with modernity was then intimately linked with the concept of racial superiority, specifically with the project of violently bringing inferior races out of the bog of traditionality and up to speed with the rest of humanity. Meanwhile, scholarship on "invented traditions" has emphasized the roles played by, for example, colonial governance or local communities in the creation of cultural forms that are said to be old but that in fact are recent. This research, which has come so much into its own that some critics now focus on the problems of what we might call excessive inventionism, has nevertheless helped shift the emphasis from essence to construct in tradition studies.[8] Today, the pair colonialism/modernity is well established among literary theorists; but postcolonial literary studies have not yet reckoned with the pairing of colonialism/tradition, which is well established in its own right in the social sciences.

The melancholic posture of nostalgia for a dying traditional life, according to which ancient African cultural genres or practices are always being lost in the modern world, was a favorite trope of early twentieth-century colonial thought. In European folkloristics, scholars have traced this sentiment far beyond the nineteenth century, to the Enlightenment and the seventeenth-century colonial expansion, both of which also depended on a binary of primitive and civilized.[9] Curiously, however, the "savage" from a far-flung continent was far more likely to be mythologized by Enlightenment writers as belonging to the "noble" variety, while the peasants from Europe's own backwaters passed for ignorant, superstitious, and morally corrupt. In Africa, colonial-era amateur ethnologists and folklore collectors, perhaps most famously the German Leo Frobenius, resurrected the Enlightenment myth of the noble savage in new iterations, evoking great black civilizations in ruins and romantic scenes of storytelling around the moonlit palaver tree. Beginning in 1904, Frobenius undertook numerous expeditions across the continent searching for "Atlantis," the legendary lost civilization described by Plato, and published voluminous tomes describing his voyages and summarizing legends that his informants helped him collect.

The cliché of nostalgia for a lost traditionality, which serves as a constant distraction from the violence or mediocrity of colonialism in the writings of Frobenius, permeated later writings as well. It is hard not to remember the Dogon of central Mali as "the group immortalized in French anthropology," especially by Marcel Griaule, "as quintessential 'traditional' Africans, who have resisted Islamization" (Soares 2014: 35). One could also cite Birago Diop's *Contes d'Amadou Koumba* (*Tales of Amadou Koumba*) (1947), which are still read as an authoritative presentation of Senegalese folklore for posterity. The preface frames the whole collection of tales as a moment of "nostalgie tenace" (tenacious nostalgia): the author writes the tales down while feeling alienated by the dark gray skies of his exile in France, whereas the wholesomeness he attributes to oral storytelling strikes him as a fleeting memory, the lost paradise of childhood (B. Diop 1961: 10). In an absurdist twist on the same theme, Fama, the hero of Ahmadou Kourouma's classic novel *Les Soleils des indépendances* (*The Suns of Independence*) (1968), quixotically clings to the privileges associated with his noble rank in the ancestral homeland of Horodogou, despite the fact that all around him, in a metropolis resembling Abidjan, the New Africa is utterly indifferent to him, his noble privileges, and his hopeless nostalgia for the old ways.

That novel is most often read as a Voltairean return to reason, a resolute facing-up to the violence of modernity, and an abandonment of the nostalgic obsession with tradition, which is equated, by many readers of Kourouma, to a utopian African fantasy of times gone by.

As a last example in this quick survey, Aminata Sow Fall's novel *L'Appel des arènes* (The Call of the Arena) (1982), which I quote in the second epigraph to this introduction, extols the world of traditional Senegalese wrestling, attended by its rituals and oral traditions, as an antidote for the self-hating Europhilia of the urban bourgeoisie. The panegyric genre of *bàkk*, historically sung to wrestlers by griots or women in order to prepare them for combat, connects it to the praise genres sung for epic heroes. Instead of paying attention to his dreary grammar lessons in the French school, twelve-year-old Nalla daydreams of visiting his grandmother's village where the older, simpler ways are still alive:

> Là-bas, chez Mame Fari qui était tout à la fois mère, père, frère et compagnon de jeux, la solitude lui était inconnue. Et certains jours, à l'ombre du flamboyant en fleurs, le bruyant [griot] Mapaté ressuscitait les acteurs de la merveilleuse épopée des Ndiogou, et Nalla se voyait héros parmi les héros, brandissant un sabre fulgurant dans le tumulte des champs empourprés de Lambaay, de Gille, et de Déquele. (Sow Fall 2012: 22)

> Over there, with Mame Fari, who was simultaneously mother, father, brother, and playmate to him, loneliness was unknown. And on some days, in the shadow of the flame tree in flower, the raucous griot Mapaté resurrected the characters of the marvelous epic of the Ndiogou, and Nalla saw himself among the heroes, brandishing a lightning-swift saber amid the tumult of the blood-stained fields of Lambaay, Guilé, and Dékheulé. (my translation)

As in Birago Diop's *Contes*, the reference to oral traditionality is framed in the context of memory, of a desire to go back to better times. Nalla remembers a warmer, more wholesome kind of childhood in the village, which he wishes could replace the sense of loneliness and dissatisfaction he feels with his parents and schoolteacher. His memory of the village immediately slips into a time of "resurrected" heroes—ancestors of his father Ndiogou—and their "marvelous epic." My reader will immediately recognize the reference to the Battle of Dékheulé; that of Guilé refers to another real battle between heroic protagonists that has passed into the Wolof epic tradition, while Lambaay refers to the capital of the precolonial Wolof kingdom of Baol.[10] *L'Appel des arènes* summons up these epic memories as romantic glimpses into a time of courageous heroes and of a more authentically African village life—in short, into better times gone by. The rest of *L'Appel* sets out to demonstrate that the wrestling arena is the one place where these heroes still fight out their epic battles, and still speak to the African soul. While reproducing a modified image of a lost paradise of childhood, the above passage shows that the nostalgic posture is not limited to folktales that usually serve the education of children: it also applies to the adult world of epic, with its proud heroes and warlike attachment to honor and courage.

These examples begin to show how the trope of traditions as authentic, romantic, and untainted by the corruption of Western influence was invented by colonialism but has persisted in postcolonial thought. The goal of this book, which will further analyze this trope throughout its chapters, is to examine how the notion of tradition, a construct once organized by colonialism, has constantly been, and continues to be, reinvented by modern writers in francophone West Africa, specifically through the lens of epic—against colonialism and nostalgia, of course, but also, in many ways, in constant dialogue with them.

In highlighting the inventedness of some traditions, or of the connections between traditionality and colonialism, my goal is in no way to diminish the importance, or to denigrate the aesthetic qualities, of oral traditions themselves. Rather, my objective is to highlight the necessarily political aspect of particular articulations of traditionality in specific contexts. To perform or write in a traditionalizing register has its own politics, just as the colonial act of collecting and classifying did. How can social critique be voiced through the deployment, criticism, and rethinking of traditional epic forms in francophone writing? Because innovation—the "play interest of the artist"—is intrinsic to oral traditional discourse, the capacity for oral epics to incorporate innovation and newness became a major mechanism upon which writers like Amadou Hampâté Bâ of Mali, Ahmadou Kourouma of Ivory Coast, and Aminata Sow Fall (elsewhere than in *L'Appel des arènes*) and Boubacar Boris Diop of Senegal have seized, in order to reinvent traditional genres to speak to the needs of modernity (Okpewho 1979: 2). This work of adaptation and reinvention is not limited to writing, but already present in the oral setting. While some specialists of the *Sunjata*, for example, have emphasized that narrative's stability, even "immutability," over time, plenty of room for idiosyncrasy remains in performances by individual bards (Jansen 2001: 15–16). Certain performers are known to have changed their performances of the *Sunjata* over the course of their careers: as they matured and traveled, they heard different versions of the epic and incorporated new influences (Innes 1973: 118). In some cases, as Boubacar Boris Diop in particular shows, the line between an innovative tradition and an invented one is blurry.

It is here that I part ways from other recent theorists of the "modern epic" in world literature, who always frame epic as a genre of antiquity on which the novel acts, rather than a living tradition that can work with the novel by reflecting critically on recent history and contemporary events.[11] Over the course of the twentieth and early twenty-first centuries, African writers have consistently used oral epic as a tool for thought because of its intrinsic capacity for innovation, not just as a monument to be disassembled and reinvented. By insisting that the category of tradition is intrinsically dynamic, and that our relationship to this category is shaped by colonialism, this study attempts to offer an alternative to prescriptions regarding how African literature ought to be written or read in some authentically African way. Its genealogy of West African writing in French is sensitive to indigenous oral genres and histories, while freely interrogating them, rather than lionizing them. Is it possible for tradition to persist in modernity, or for orality to persist in writing, other than in a nostalgic mode? What other uses and transformations of traditionality does West African literature undertake, and what do they have to offer readers in the context of a world aspiring to, or trapped in, modernity?

In ways that move beyond the nostalgia illustrated in the examples above, the reinventions of tradition and epic in postcolonial writing produce effects similar to those that I discussed above as symptoms of Afromodernity. On the one hand, the worldwide recognition of the epic genre stokes the African continent's hunger for symbolic capital and upward mobility; and on the other, ubiquitous postcolonial crises demand that African oral traditions be infinitely reinventable in order to remain pertinent. By tracing these aspirations from the modern to the traditional, from Shakira to Sunjata and back, I argue that some West African writers have fashioned their own alternative traditionalities, and modernities, against the colonially influenced norm of nostalgia for tradition.

A Brief Overview of West African Epic: Genre, History, Region

Since the 1970s, the professional academic debate over "the African epic" has engaged historians, anthropologists, folklorists, and literary scholars, not to mention literary writers. A few key moments in this debate are usually remembered: Africans used to be considered too primitive to produce great poetry that could be compared to European masterpieces—a point that I will challenge in chapter 1; D. T. Niane's publication of *Soundjata, ou l'épopée mandingue* (*Sundiata: An Epic of Old Mali*) in 1960 marked a major discursive shift by popularizing that text as an epic in the same right as the *Iliad* or *Gilgamesh*; and Ruth Finnegan, a British scholar of African oral literature, famously argued in 1970 that "epic hardly seems to exist in sub-Saharan Africa," triggering a wave of rebuttals that has made her original position, which she has since reversed, impossible to hold anymore.[12] Nevertheless, there has been some resistance to all this epic talk. Senegalese historian Mamadou Diouf argued in 1991 that literary scholars at the Cheikh Anta Diop University of Dakar, a prolific source of scholarship on West African epic, had constructed, even invented, this genre as an object of study by relentlessly highlighting its perceived proximity to the poems of Homer. Jan Jansen and Henk Maier also suggested in 2004 that the word "epic" is overused by academics as a publicity stunt to attract attention to the oral narratives that they collect.[13] Overriding these objections, a generation's worth of scholarly work has proposed lists of criteria to define the African epic, including universalizing lists of rules for the epic worldwide, or the "hero," or lists of features that are limited to specifically African data without reference to Greek models. Over the course of the twentieth and early twenty-first centuries, increasing attention has been paid not only to the textual but also to the cognitive, musicological, and performance aspects of epic in Africa. It is clear that the conversation has not yet ended: debates continue over what African narratives should or should not be counted as "epics."[14]

The region of francophone West Africa, by chance, largely coincides with a zone or "belt" identified as rich in historical epics, that is, oral traditional heroic narratives that claim to recount historical subject matter.[15] *Sunjata*, the narrative of the founding of the Mali Empire in the thirteenth century, is the best known of these narratives, both within West Africa and abroad. D. T. Niane's publication of it in French prose, still popular among literate audiences as the definitive presentation of the story in easily readable form, signaled a turning point in Africa's entry into world literature—a foreshadowing, one might venture, of Africa's aspiration to global inclusion in pop culture as expressed during the 2010 World Cup. While the totality of local genres, narratives, and performances considered to be part of "the African epic," as represented in several anthologies and surveys, is limited neither to the western part of the continent nor to French-speaking countries,

I nevertheless propose that this set of general limitations is a useful one for my study.[16] It demarcates a historically coherent area that has produced an abundant set of discourses on what the nature and significance of epic narrative might be.

I argue for this historical coherency for several reasons. First, because of the influence of the three celebrated medieval empires, Ghana, Mali and Songhai, that successively dominated sub-Saharan West Africa between the ninth and sixteenth centuries and that left their marks on the cultures of the Sahel region even after their breakup: a proliferation of centralized states and empires, many of which lasted until the European conquest; the frequent retention of a hierarchical system of hereditary statuses or castes, particularly based on the oppositions of noble vs. commoner and free vs. slave; and the tendency to maintain, within the rank of free commoners, endogamous artisanal groups like blacksmiths, woodworkers, and bards, the last of which are commonly referred to in English and French as griots.[17] Of course, these criteria are far from universal across all the region's peoples. But for many of the transethnic explorations I undertake in this book, these shared traits are pertinent because they correspond to the tendency of West African epic narratives to recount precolonial state formation (or tragic last stands), to be sung in praise of patrons of noble status, and to be performed by a specialized caste of bards or griots. Second, the sub-Saharan West African region shares a religious experience: today it is mostly Muslim, thanks to a combination of complex factors that gradually unfolded over the *longue durée*, beginning with trans-Saharan traders who "brought Islam to the Saharan nomads and sowed its first seeds in the Sudan" as early as the eighth century (Levtzion 1971: 124). Islam only spread beyond "quarantine" or "minority" status to "majority" status by fits and starts, as it was imposed upon, or adopted by, peasants in the countryside in a myriad of specific circumstances (Robinson 2004: 28–32). Among the best-known instigators of Islam's proliferation among the masses were the series of reformist and expansionist holy wars that shook West Africa between the seventeenth and nineteenth centuries, upending many established political equilibriums. Most famously, the West African jihads gave rise to Usman dan Fodio's Sokoto caliphate in Hausaland and Umar Tall's theocracy in Masina at the beginning and middle of the nineteenth century, respectively; Samori Touré's empire-building "Jula revolution" followed those holy wars at the end of the same century (Person 1968). The latter two of these military campaigns opposed the encroachment of the colonial French army and were eventually defeated by it. Both of their commanders are sung in epic oral tradition as anticolonial resisters. During the colonial period, increased mobility of people and goods further accelerated the spread of Islam. In what is today Mali, for example, the late nineteenth and first half of the twentieth centuries "witnessed the rapid spread of Islam in new areas and among groups that had historically not been Muslim"—including the Dogon, whom, as we saw above, Griaule had praised as un-Islamic, therefore "traditional" in an untainted and pure sense (Soares 2004: 208).

That point brings us to the last important commonality that the region shares, namely, an experience with Europe. The French dotted the West African coast with trading posts from the seventeenth century onward, following the earlier example of the Portuguese and setting the stage for the Atlantic slave trade. Reaching its apogee in the eighteenth century, the trade sowed human misery and political disorder far and wide. In the 1880s, the European "scramble for Africa" sought to replace this fraught commercial relationship with formal administrative jurisdiction. The subsequent French military penetration of the West African interior at the end of the nineteenth century succeeded at incorporating most of the region, from Senegal to Niger and from Mauritania to Benin, into a single federation, colonial French West Africa, which I refer to in this book by its French abbreviation, the AOF (Afrique Occidentale Française). The colonies federated under the AOF umbrella would become independent in the late 1950s and early 1960s, as the winds of liberation blew across the continent. Since then, the nations of the ex-AOF (plus Togo, which was awarded to France after Germany's defeat in World War I, but administered separately) have shared French as a common language of government, education, and written literature. They have also shared a continuing and often tense political relationship with the former colonial power, France. For this reason, the influence of oral epic in written literature has been especially pronounced in francophone contexts. That is why all of the writers I study in this book work in French—although, importantly, Boubacar Boris Diop works in Wolof, too.

For all these reasons, which I have sketched out extremely briefly, literary texts and oral traditions from very disparate locations across this wide region bear strikingly similar features and concerns. In the oral tradition itself, the presence of epics or long heroic oral narrative is widely documented, as the scholarship on "epic belts" has shown. Generally speaking, the epics from this region tend to claim to recount historical subject matter.[18] That is, they sing heroes who really lived, like Umar, Samori, and Lat-Dior of the nineteenth century, or heroes who performers claim really lived, like Sunjata, associated with the thirteenth. These heroes' feats are full of magical exploits, and the stories themselves may owe more to borrowed traditional patterns than to historical accuracy. Nevertheless, the recurring claim to historicity is important because it not only patently belies the cliché that Africans had no history before the arrival of Europeans, but it also paves the way for a certain literary vision of the present as rooted in a lineage of past heroes. This narrative structure of shuttling between past and present enables critical reflexivity, the ability to self-consciously criticize current social realities, which, I argue, is a central feature of the continuity between oral and written literary forms. Given the context of slavery, political turmoil, jihad, and the colonial conquest in the eighteenth and nineteenth centuries, oral narratives about those periods offer a fascinating window into their ideological transformations, as epic heroes staked out a variety of often ambivalent political positions, notably with regard to Islam and to European activity. Bassirou Dieng's work on the gradual Islamization of pre-Islamic epic themes in Senegambia during the eighteenth and nineteenth centuries, and the use of Islam in epic to articulate militant resistance to colonialism, has been especially productive. By showing the capacity of epic tradition to adapt creatively over time, and to express within its own forms and constraints the ideological conflicts of successive generations, Dieng's work also rebuts the nostalgic colonial search for an authentic Africanness that was supposed to have remained intact from Islamic or other corruption (1993b). Islam can be incorporated into tradition, and vice versa. Thanks to the common colonial experience and a shared postcolonial language, written discourses in French about these heroic narratives and their interactions with changing times are also extremely rich. It is these, in the end, that this study attempts to tease out: how francophone West African literature of the twentieth and twenty-first centuries rewrites the heroic genres of the oral tradition, both with and against colonial-era studies of it.

Even within these limitations, however, it would be impossible to cover every relevant written text, oral narrative tradition, or even country, given the vastness of "francophone West Africa." By necessity, the trajectory I propose is partial and selective, but hopefully thought-provoking and representative. The writers I study in depth in the following chapters—Yambo Ouologuem, Amadou Hampâté Bâ, Ahmadou Kourouma, Aminata Sow Fall, and Boubacar Boris Diop—hail from Mali, Ivory Coast, and Senegal. The oral narratives I discuss recurrently include those of *Sunjata* and *Samori* (originally from the Mande heartland along the Mali/Guinea border, but known far beyond) and *Samba Gelajo Jegi* and *Bubu Ardo* (Fula heroes sung from Mauritania to Niger). They also include the epics of the Wolof state of Kajoor (present-day central Senegal) and the Bamana state of Segu (present-day southern Mali). A number of writers, oral performers, and other oral heroic narratives from these and other countries, especially Guinea, come up along the way. For example, Amadou Hampâté Bâ's years in colonial Upper Volta (today Burkina Faso), recounted in his memoirs, and Ahmadou Kourouma's particular attention to Togolese politics inspired by his years working in Lomé give those countries a significant presence in this study. Though no one can possibly undertake to represent "francophone West Africa"—let alone "Africa"—in any exhaustive way, I have nevertheless attempted to select case studies that represent the region's breadth, while remaining attentive to the specificities of historical and political context.

Certainly, these five writers—Ouologuem, Bâ, Kourouma, Sow Fall, and Diop—are not the only ones who could have figured as major foci of this study. A number of other artists could have been included or treated in greater depth. Laye Camara of Guinea, Massa Makan Diabaté of Mali, Dani Kouyaté of Burkina Faso, and Cheikh Aliou Ndao, and Ousmane Socé Diop of Senegal all come to mind, as do Tierno Monénembo of Guinea and—why not?—the two volumes of *Ségou* (*Segu*) (1984) by Maryse Condé of Guadeloupe. Some of these artists' works serve as important points of reference in various chapters, but none is the subject of an individualized, in-depth study. I have ultimately limited the scope of this book, partially for reasons of pure feasibility, and also because any attempt at exhaustiveness would have been foredoomed to failure. As it stands, the selections I have made bring my argument into sharp enough focus on their own: certain West African writers channel the critical reflexivity of oral epic in their writing. If this argument offers an insight or way of reading that can be applied to texts beyond those studied here, then it will have been successful.

Orality, Performance, Text

Given the complex literary history of the idea of an African epic, I use the words "epic," "epic narrative," and "heroic narrative" synonymously and in a generally inclusive sense throughout this study. While I discuss a number of ways in which scholars have sought to delineate what ought to be included and excluded in the term "African epic," it is not my goal to offer a rigorous generic definition of this term myself. Rather, I describe how the genre concept of epic was imported into Africa, how it has been put to use in discussions about Africa's place in world literature, and what is at stake in those discussions. For me, African epic refers to oral traditional narratives of heroic subject matter. In analyzing the relationship between epic and a set of francophone novels, I refer to novels' use of or reliance on these kinds of oral narratives through a variety of literary strategies. In a similar way, my use of the term "tradition" also focuses on the constructedness of this category as an ambiguous and contested act of interpretation rather than as an intrinsic and undisputed quality of cultural objects. My reflections on the inseparability of transmission and innovation in traditional discourse, a theme that recurs in every chapter of this study, is indebted to Karin Barber's anthropological approach to text and genre (2007).

By putting my readings in dialogue with studies from anthropology and folklore studies, I hope, in a gesture echoing Christopher Miller's in *Theories of Africans* (1990), to clarify the eminently dialogical work that heroic narratives perform, both as items of oral tradition and when they are called upon in francophone writing. Miller, along with many others, has already indicated the problematic nature of using anthropology to understand African literature, given the former's long history of attempting to produce a knowable, colonizable Other (1990: 24). My own turn to ethnography is, on the one hand, constantly aware of that discipline's historical complicity in colonial governance and in the invention of politically useful categories—like "epic," which allowed administrators to understand African cultures in terms of a hierarchy of civilizations in which Europe was always located at the top, and even "tradition," which colonial thought imagined as static and in opposition to the light of its own modernity. At the same time, my recourse to anthropology is intended precisely to remedy overly simplistic accounts of the epic/novel divide in literary studies. Anthropology need not serve only to objectify an exoticized Other—to look at Africans "as if we were insects," as the Senegalese filmmaker Ousmane Sembène famously said (Busch and Annas 2008: 4). Instead, anthropology can help question and complicate literary understandings of how oral and written genres interact with each other.

The dialogical turn in folklore studies and anthropology in recent decades has helped alleviate many of these concerns. The field now emphasizes that ethnographic knowledge is produced in the dialogue between scholar and informant, and that classic anthropologists' representations of themselves as all-knowing authorities ought to be read as literature rather than as science. Furthermore, meaning in an utterance is shaped by any number of variables in performance, making simplistic accounts of the "traditional worldview" moot.[19] While deeply influenced by these findings, my own engagement with oral tradition, which I have undertaken in the context of a broader study of written literature, is admittedly limited by its bookishness. This study depends on documentation—transcriptions and translations—as opposed to fieldwork and direct observation, as would have been the case in a truly anthropological or folkloristic study. Far from conflating or flattening written and oral narratives into a single kind of literary object for reasons of expediency, I have elected to focus on ways in which such narratives align, overlap, and work together, while acknowledging their differences. An explicit methodology of "reading" oral and written literary forms together can be productive, and indeed is needed, since the specificity of the oral has already been studied at voluminous length. One of the longest and most impressive monuments to orality in recent years is Mamoussé Diagne's *Critique de la raison orale* (Critique of Oral Reason) (2005), which attempts to build a philosophical framework for understanding orality, while rescuing it from colonial paternalism or dismissals of it as "primitive." The very title evokes Immanuel Kant and Jean-Paul Sartre. And yet, Diagne's elaboration of *la raison orale* in opposition to *la raison graphique* (oral reason and graphic reason) is not only reminiscent of Jack Goody—no doubt the most famous theorist of orality, conceived as fundamentally opposed to writing—but explicitly indebted to him (2005:18). In this regard, it is worth recalling that Goody's critics had an important point: no matter how much Goody tried to escape the ethnocentric great divide of primitive vs. modern, he reproduced that dichotomy through sweeping claims regarding intrinsic differences between oral and writing cultures (C. Miller 1990: 105–6). What Goody calls "the consequences of literacy," one of which is supposedly fiction itself, distinguishes the complexity of writing cultures from the limited scope of oral ones.[20] "Goody sees literacy as the factor that, almost unaided, made possible science, philosophy, and empire" (Barber 2007: 68). Diagne, even in seeking to recuperate the category of the oral by aligning it with the rational, reproduces this great divide by constantly distinguishing between so-called civilizations of orality and civilizations of writing.

Rather than further widening the great divide, I follow other scholars in contending that oral narratives, like written ones, can be studied from a literary point of view. The fact that writers often espouse a literate relationship to both orality and tradition supports this approach. The Malian Amadou Hampâté Bâ, though his interest in oral tradition sprang from listening to the stories of his elders as a child, spent much of his career collecting, translating, and publishing oral narratives of different kinds. While it is well known that Laye Camara of Guinea wrote a "novelized" version of the *Sunjata* epic in his book *Le Maître de la parole* (*The Guardian of the Word*) (1978), it is little remembered that he collected and translated an academically rigorous performance of that epic as part of a doctoral dissertation at the University of Dakar in the 1960s (1971). Ahmadou Kourouma, famous for his "Africanization" of the French language, imbued himself with Louis-Ferdinand Céline's strategies for writing the sounds of oral French by rereading *Voyage au bout de la nuit (Journey to the End of the Night)* before writing each of his books (Calmettes 2003); he also admitted his love and dependence on "livres de proverbes africains" or books of African proverbs (Chemla 1999: 29). In one striking case that this book does not study in depth, the Malian writer Massa Makan Diabaté, a griot by birth, saw his multiple published translations into French of songs from the *Sunjata* as fulfilling his inherited duty to preserve the Mande traditions and spread their glory (Keïta 1995: 60–77). Finally, to end this far from exhaustive list, Senegalese writer Boubacar Boris Diop's Wolof-language novel *Doomi Golo* (literally "Children of the Monkey") (2003), adapted into French as *Les petits de la guenon* (2009), self-consciously intervenes in a Wolof literary canon that is simultaneously written and oral, inclusive both of Moussa Ka's Islamic poetry and of many oral legends and heroic episodes. Moving in the other direction, Diop has recently made the original Wolof version of his novel available in an audio format on the radio and online in hopes of reaching the enormous Senegalese public who cannot read it in a book.

The fact is that the oral, the traditional, and the written move in and out of each other. Though they are not the same thing, we must ask not only how oral tradition and written literature are different, as so many authors have done, but how they can overlap as literary objects. Oral and written texts may be analyzed alongside each other as texts—that is, units of discourse marked as detachable from their context:

> Paul Ricoeur spoke of textual "autonomy"—the establishment of textual forms that in some sense have an independent existence—as being above all the achievement of writing [Ricoeur 1976]. . . . A study of the entextualisation of oral genres, however, suggests that writing is only an extension of processes already well established and flourishing without it. Fixing words, attaching them to material objects, making them object-like in themselves, making a mark, constructing vast networks of linked and mutually-suggestive formulations, creating forms that others can recognize, appropriate and inhabit, are what "oral cultures" do. (Barber 2007: 100–101)

The ability to study oral performances not only as events, in which an extremely variable set of dynamic, emergent processes are unfolding in time, but also as fixed, marked texts suggests a common space of textuality that is shared by written and oral forms, thereby opening the door to a practice of reading written and documented oral texts side by side. It is true that studying an oral performance as text, especially in the goal of comparing it to other texts, may lose some of the emotive aspects of the total performance event. And yet, a text-focused methodology is appropriate here, since I am not trying to make claims about total performance events, but rather, looking for common ground between the oral and the written. The term "critical reflexivity," which draws on Andrew Apter's study of "critical agency" in African performance traditions via the methodologies of ethnopragmatic analysis and of reading transcribed oral performances, seeks to carry his insights into dialogue with written literature (Apter 2007). Rather than directly heeding Apter's call for further explorations in Africanist pragmatics of performance, I want to understand—indeed rethink—how writers working in French choose to explore the critical potential of West African heroic narrative.

It makes sense, then, to excavate the shared space of textuality that both oral and written modes of expression produce. Critical reflexivity is articulated in individual performances of a traditional narrative, often depending on nuances in a performer's use of a known episode that help it reflect problems in society—just as an author's nuances of word choice help a written narrative refer critically to the outside social world in complex ways. This concurrent study of oral and written forms necessarily uses the referential dimension of language—and therefore, text—as its primary object of study, highlighting, for example, such moments as when a performer is criticizing a ruler while seeming to praise him, or moments in an epic narrative that work to problematize gender or religious norms.

This book's title, *Subversive Traditions*, applies to every chapter of this book. The work done by literature, both written and oral, is to conduct thought: about many things, but here, especially, about politics and identity. This work is subversive—dangerous—because it interrogates the Big Men and ideological paradigms of West African historical experience, rather than merely monumentalizing them. As such, this book is not another story of subver*ted* traditions, but of subver*sive* ones. More precisely, it shows how traditions are interpreted and reinvented in subversive ways. This fundamental creativity runs across the divides of oral and written, traditional and modern. It is captured as a key theme by the African writings I study here, which lay out in detail what is at stake in the acts of recalling, confronting, and reinventing heroes and traditions. Therefore, this study looks both backward to the colonial construction of an African epic and forward to the postmodern reinvention of it signaled by Boubacar Boris Diop. In doing so, it aspires, in some small and admittedly incomplete way, to help theorize an African literary modernity that is critically aware of its own uses of the past, as figured in traditions and epics. Such a theory might even serve as an alternative to the cultural icons with which I began: an introspective Afromodernity, highly informed by traditionality, one that does not simply erect itself as a heroic monolith demanding homage, like Abdoulaye Wade's statue in Dakar, or efface its dependence on the creativity of its forbears, like Shakira's seductive refrain, "This time for Africa."

PART ONE

Epic and Race

CHAPTER ONE

The Half-Black Iliad

African Epic and the Racialization of Comparative Literature

> For a pedigree is something imaginary and devoid of reality. Its usefulness consists
> only in the resulting connection and close contact.
>
> —Ibn Khaldūn, *The Muqaddimah*

There is more at stake in the idea of epic than disinterested commentary on literary forms. Africanist theorists of the epic genre had to confront, and often repudiate, the great amount of European literary baggage associated with the term. Their work had a sense of urgency: to reject the word "epic" in the context of Africa, when it is taken for granted in other parts of the world, risked implying that Africa's history and heroes are somehow not as admirable as those of other places. And yet, what is less commonly realized is that the issue of Africa's comparability to Europe was not just a major concern of the postcolonial period; it was one of the French colonial project's key obsessions. This chapter excavates the history of the idea of an African epic before the beginning of the professional academic debate over its existence that erupted in the 1970s. It shows that epic was not universally denied to the African continent in the decades before Niane's publication of *Soundjata* in 1960 or the fracas over British folklorist Ruth Finnegan's famous statement that "epic hardly seems to exist in sub-Saharan Africa" (1970:108).

The idea of epic as a worldwide genre—a product of nineteenth-century comparative literature—was applied to West Africa long before 1960 or 1970, but in ways that were closely intertwined with colonial and precolonial ideologies of race, especially the Hamitic myth, a now discredited notion of racialized diffusionism known to both European and Islamic historiography. Generally speaking, according to this legend, the descendants of an ancient migration of light-skinned peoples from the Middle East formed at some point in history a superior race among the primitive blacks of Africa. These light- and dark-skinned races were often said to descend from the sons of the biblical patriarch Noah, who cursed the descendants of his son Ham, while the descendants of his son Shem included Abraham, the people of Israel, and, later, the Arabs. (The name "Shem" is, for this reason, the root of the modern word "Semitic.") In both Christian and Muslim thought, the Hamitic curse was connected to black skin and its connotations of unbelief or divine disfavor. These connotations were advanced in both religions as a justification for slavery. Colonial ethnography used various articulations of this myth in combination with the term "epic" in West African colonies in an effort to determine who was superior to whom: If ethnic group A possessed epic, with its attending tropes of heroism and nobility, then was it whiter or blacker, closer to or farther from the supreme standard of European civilization, than ethnic group B?

After reviewing the notion of African epic as contributing to a worldwide genre, this chapter will examine how racialized constructions of this genre were imagined by white writers in colonial French West Africa around the turn of the twentieth century, focusing on Maurice Delafosse, François-Victor Equilbecq, Leo Frobenius, and Henri Lanrezac. Finally, it will explore the connections between colonial and precolonial ideologies of race in West Africa. These connections will be key to understanding the critique and reinvention of epic formulated by black writers. My overarching goal here is to situate the notion of "African epic" as the product of a certain kind of comparative literature deeply rooted in French colonialism. This argument will take us on a journey through multiple racisms from distinct cultures and time periods: European and African; "Arab" and "black"; Muslim and Christian; colonial and precolonial. In excavating the colonial and racialized roots of the notion of an African epic, my intention is in no way to discredit this genre or the generation of professional scholarly work on it that has matured since 1960. Rather, I hope to set the stage for how West African artists rewrite their oral epic heritage in ways that wrest it away from, without ever quite forgetting, the crisscrossing racisms that haunt it.

The Worldwide Epic

The concept of an epic genre is, at its origin, a European one. Until the nineteenth century, the term was only applied to the Homeric poems and sometimes other European texts thought to be modeled on them; but with the discovery of comparable genres elsewhere in the world, some of which predate the *Iliad* and the *Odyssey*, European literary critics hypothesized that disparate genres of heroic narrative poetry had originated independently of each other, yet might have some fundamental traits in common (Derive 2002: 5–7). As such, today's commonly understood notion of the epic as a worldwide genre marked by universal rules and found in a great many countries is a product of comparative literature. It was propelled by a desire to explain the perceived proximity of texts from Mesopotamia—and eventually, Japan, India, Central Asia, and various parts of Europe—to the long-known Greek points of reference. The burning question that would evolve over the course of the twentieth century is, "Does Africa have anything to contribute to this transworld genre?"

That question is, of course, itself problematic. It imposes a category theorized by Western scholarship going back to Aristotle's *Poetics* on peoples and practitioners who do not themselves identify with it. David Conrad highlights this nonequivalence between Western and local genre concepts: in the case of terminologies for the *Sunjata* narrative, "it is to the Arabic derivative tariku (Ar. *tarikh*)"—which Conrad translates as "the book, the chronicle, the story of the Manden"—"and not to the French épopée that has, for the Mande people, accrued the mystery and power conveyed by the indigenous phrase *kuma koro* (ancient speech)" (1999: 189). This overlap, which causes different audiences to prefer either the Western label "epic" or the locally familiar labels *tariku* and *kuma koro* to refer to the same performance object, is all the more noteworthy since other theorists of the epic explicitly try to define it in opposition to the genre of the "chronicle"—a possible equivalent of *tariku* (Seydou 1983: 51). Lilyan Kesteloot and Bassirou Dieng, who themselves propose a distinction between epic and chronicle, are nonetheless aware of the difficulty of such a gesture:

> Plusieurs langues africaines où fleurissent des épopées ne séparent pas ces textes des autres genres narratifs historiques: c'est le cas du peul, du manding, du wolof, du songhaï-zerma, etc., où les chroniques, voire les mythes, seront rangés sous le même vocable: *jaloore, cosaan, daarol, fasa, maana, masalia*. . . . Il y a quelque

chose d'artificiel à vouloir "plaquer" sur les civilisations étrangères, les concepts européens, et singulièrement la taxinomie. En fonction de ce principe, on ne devrait parler des genres qu'en utilisant la taxinomie locale propre à l'ethnie concernée . . . mais ce serait l'arrêt de mort de la littérature comparée! (Kesteloot and Dieng 1997: 29)

Several African languages where epics flourish do not separate these texts from other narrative historical genres: such is the case of Fulfulde, Maninka, Wolof, Songay-Zerma, etc., where chronicles, or even myths, are categorized under the same term: *jaloore, cosaan, daarol, fasa, maana, masalia*. . . . There is something artificial about wanting to "paste" European concepts, especially taxonomy, on foreign civilizations. Following this principle, we should only speak of genres according to a given ethnic group's own local taxonomy . . . but that would be the death warrant of comparative literature! (my translation)

On the one hand, the question of terminology might seem trivial, given that oral genres have always been studied from a transcultural point of view. One has only to think of the folktale, which is assumed to be everywhere, in spite of the fact that both the notion and the word have a history rooted in eighteenth-century German romanticism. But the case of epic is more vexed, since it comes with different, and contradictory, connotations. It is the noble genre of Aristotle; for centuries, the Homeric texts have been canonized as the founding texts of Western literature, and, as though in imitation, romantic movements in various European nation-states have also consecrated epic poems as the founding texts of their national literatures.

In effect, while it may be somewhat artificial to debate the applicability of the word "epic" outside of European literary history, to reject the question altogether on particularist grounds is to exclude Africa from comparative literature and, by extension, to deny it the symbolic capital associated with the heroic feats, relatively advanced civilization, and general prestige associated with the genre for many centuries, now taken for granted in a number of other parts of the world. Because Africa's historiography is replete with denials of its historicity, or even of its full humanity, and because the epic genre is always tied up in issues of comparability between different civilizations, the question of the epic's existence in Africa has necessarily become entangled with larger struggles over what Kesteloot elsewhere calls "the dignity of the African" (1993a: 11). Dan Ben-Amos's take on the subject illustrates this problem:

Consequently, the possession of epic poetry had a value in itself, as it testified to the antiquity of both literary creativity and ethnic self-definition of a nation and, thus, enabled a society to take its place as an equal member in the literary-political round table of nations. From such a romantic perspective it is possible to appreciate the severity of the wound that Ruth Finnegan inflicted upon proud Africans and Africanists. Fortunately, like the body cells that rush to heal, scholars have been fast to correct the damaged image, and the research that has followed her remarks has proved her wrong. (1983: 278)

What is at stake is not merely impartial dissection of literary forms, but a desire to prove the cultural equality of Africa with other parts of the world—not only for the sake of Africans themselves, in this account, but for "proud Africanists" as well.

To be fair, Finnegan originally intended her doubt of the African epic's existence "to stimulate debate and not cut it off" (Johnson 1980: 308). Decades later, she addressed the controversy she had ignited in a second edition of her book, *Oral Literature in Africa*:

> One of the most famous passages in my original work was its short two-page note, extending from pages 108 to 110, on what turned out to be the uncontrollably emotive subject of epic. This, incredibly, has attracted more debate, criticism, and, dare I say it, misunderstanding than the rest of the book put together. . . . Much has happened since then. Multiple epics have been collected—or at least lengthy poetic texts that can be so described—from many places in Africa, most notably ex-French West Africa.[1] Collections, anthologies, translations and annotated texts abound. Epic now has its place in the corpus of recognized African literature. (Finnegan 2012: xxxi–xxxii)

The Finnegan case demonstrates how charged the subject of African epic is. This charge invites us to re-pose the fundamental question of genre studies: Is a genre something "in here" or "out there"? That is, is it a set of innate criteria that structure a literary or performance object and allow it to exist, located "in authorial intention, in the work's historical or literary context, [or] in the text itself," or rather something that "readers and their conventions assign to texts" (Beebee 1994: 3)?

One influential Africanist answer to this question has been that that epicness is something an audience feels: it engages a subjective sense of intuition that we try to explain in terms of objective certainty. Kesteloot and Dieng point out that specialists of Swahili, Fulfulde, and even the French *chansons de geste* express having the same gut feeling that they are in the presence of epic in all three cases (1997: 33–34). Put simply, they know it when they hear it. From that gut feeling scholars search for an internal logic of commonalities that unite such disparate literary objects. Christiane Seydou describes this reaction succinctly:

> While an epic text is fairly easy to discern, it is difficult to define the genre itself. The ability to recognize an epic is developed principally through a certain emotive quality inherent to the genre. When attempting to define that quality however, one is hampered by preconceived ethical, esthetic, and emotional associations which impede objective analysis. . . . [I]nstead of trying to avoid the emotive quality of the epic, we should, on the contrary, recognize it as a distinguishing feature. It is perhaps the affective, esthetic and cultural impact of the epic which best reveals its function and justifies its form. (1983: 47)

Here, the desire to discover the rules that govern the epic's form and function across distant cultures springs from an emotional reaction that one needs to account for in a meaningful way. The approach of Seydou and others is, under the premise that something in the text triggers the reaction, to figure out what elements constitute an epic—sung vs. spoken, written vs. oral, "the epic" (*l'épopée*) vs. "the epic-like" (*l'épique*), ideological content, exultant tone, social function and setting, type of performer, etc.—giving rise to a rich and voluminous scholarly discussion.

But, returning to Beebee's question, it is necessary to ask how the meaning of the term "epic" has changed over time. That is, we might look at genre in this case less as a set of formal conventions or criteria that can be observed at work in a given text or context, and more as a series of readings and reinterpretations over time that different commentators have attempted to mobilize according to their own vested interests. In the colonial era and its immediate aftermath, genre in this sense became an object of contention as parties disagreed over whether Africa could, or ought, to be compared to Europe in "epic" terms, and what the consequences of such a comparison might be. A sense of the need to preserve an African authenticity thanks to the oral tradition, especially through epic, has persisted to this day. I propose to look at this change historically. How have European commentators shaped this object—the "extroverted African epic," to adapt a phrase—whose existence we can no longer doubt today (Julien 2006)? A study of how the idea of epic changed among observers of Africa will allow us to see how the politics of genre have been appropriated, questioned, and put to use in colonial and postcolonial contexts over time.

Epic in the AOF

European discussions of African epic grew from interest in collecting oral narratives, which can be traced back at least to the eighteenth century (Masonen 2000: 436). From the early nineteenth century, collections of tales were published and circulated in Europe. Kesteloot and Dieng suggest that the interest in tales, and especially the ability to frame them as naive, childish, and ultimately primitive, prevented the earliest collectors from recognizing epic (1997: 10). However, we must not exaggerate the colonial era's ignorance or rejection of the possibility of an epic in Africa. The existence of narratives we now call epics was well known among the mostly amateur ethnologists and linguists who labored in French West Africa, or AOF, on a day-to-day basis. Administrators and military personnel often collected oral traditions in their spare time, sometimes even as a matter of official policy, and the educational system encouraged African pupils and teachers to collect and analyze their own traditions.[2] These efforts would become instrumental in shaping the colonial historiography of Africa. Contributors debated how such venerable narratives as the *Sunjata* of the Mande and the *Samba Gelajo Jegi* of the western Fulbe were to be classified and, perhaps more importantly, what their significance could be for understanding African history and cultural accomplishments.

Joseph Miller describes the "perplexed respect" of colonial invaders for "African military power, political leadership, and even monumental architecture, the litmus tests of progress" (1999: 4). Among these litmus tests, we must include literature: not just the existence of writing, a well-known and ancient criterion for recognizing someone as civilized, but also the existence of recognizable oral genres like epic. Epic formed the point at which the colonial interest in empire intersected with the interest in collecting oral traditions. Indeed, colonial historiography was fascinated with the formation of complex states in Africa, liberally using the word "empire" and delving with enthusiasm into detailed description of great historical states (Triaud 1998: 218). Many of these states, along with their related cultural accomplishments, were attributed by French writers to foreign, especially "white" influence—a loose but charged notion, as we shall see. In the case of West Africa, the medieval empires of Ghana, Mali, and Songhay became the source of endless inquiries and speculation during the colonial period.

Sunjata is the most visible example of the epic–empire intersection, since its subject is the founding of the Mali Empire in the thirteenth century. But it was far from the only narrative discussed in epic terms. Other heroic narratives were judged as evidence of the superiority of a given ethnic group or, alternatively, of its inability to separate historical fact from myth. While it is true that a few Western scholars denied outright the existence of an African epic in the decades before the independence era, the term was readily applied by writers in the AOF during the late nineteenth and early twentieth centuries.[3] With the help of diffusionist and evolutionist anthropological theories, epic in West Africa would come to be intimately associated with a more advanced level of political organization and intelligence and, by extension, overall civilization.[4] The idea of an oral literature with a strong, recognizable heroic element that could be described according to more or less universal generic and political terms became one signpost among many along the path to civilization. And colonial interpretations about the natives' location on the scale of evolution helped shape theories of colonialism itself.

In any case, rather than claiming that the epic was suddenly recognized in Africa in 1960 thanks to Niane, or established as a scholarly field in reaction to Ruth Finnegan, we can examine how their understanding of the genre was mediated through older colonial debates. These debates, whose details seem obscure today, are known to contemporary specialists of African heroic narratives who have attempted to document the earliest written versions of specific texts like the *Sunjata*.[5] They merit a second look, so that we can gauge the extent to which the epic genre that we study today is derived from those stereotypes, and how it continued to take shape in their aftermath. By highlighting the relationship between epic and colonial thought, I hope to fill a gap that has remained nearly empty so far in studies of this genre in Africa.

The towering figure in French colonial efforts at understanding and codifying African history is Maurice Delafosse, who produced many ethnographic and linguistic studies while holding different posts in the colonial administration between 1894 and 1918, as well as teaching posts in Paris after his return to France. His three-volume *Haut-Sénégal-Niger* (1912), while not the first serious European attempt at reconstituting precolonial African history, was considered definitive by many, and long remained influential thanks to its coherent, confident, date-filled narrative of nearly two thousand years of events leading up to the French conquest.

Delafosse's choice to focus the history of the Sudan colony around a neatly organized succession of empires and periods of domination, among which his fascination with the great states of Ghana and Mali stand out, had two important consequences. It contributed in no small way to the "invention of the Sudanese Middle Ages" (Masonen 2000); that is, it packaged the history of Africa in terms familiar to the study of medieval Europe, so well that some readers have seen through Delafosse's work a grand entry of Africa into world history. Jean-Louis Triaud argues, for example, that *Haut-Sénégal-Niger* is

> placé sous le signe de l'histoire, d'une histoire qui confère au Soudan un privilège sur toutes les autres colonies subsahariennes et place cette terre, même en position périphérique, au sein de l'oecumène civilisé. (1998: 213)

> placed under the sign of history, a history that confers on the Sudan a privilege over all the other Sub-Saharan colonies; it places this land, albeit in a peripheral position, at the heart of the civilized ecumene. (my translation)

Oral tradition holds a special place in Delafosse's thought, not only for the historical information it offers, but also for the "extraordinaire richesse" (extraordinary richness) of the literary production that it represents (Delafosse 1912, 3:380). In addition to providing a summary of the *Sunjata* narrative itself (1912, 2:162–84), he refers to the genre of the "épopée" with a certain, albeit limited admiration:

> Cette littérature [orale] n'est pas seulement riche; elle est variée et aborde tous les sujets. L'histoire et l'épopée y sont représentées par de très curieuses traditions relatives à l'origine des peuples et des tribus, aux faits et gestes des héros ou des guerriers célèbres. (1912, 3:380–81)

> This [oral] literature is not only rich, but diverse, covering a wide variety of subjects. History and epic are represented in it through quite curious traditions about the origins of peoples and tribes, and about the deeds and feats of famous heroes and warriors. (my translation)

At one level, this promotion of an elevated view of African history and culture makes Delafosse an ambiguous character among his contemporaries, whose notions of primitivism often precluded such enthusiasm. He is known, for example, to have been a proponent of associationist rather than assimilationist policy, believing that Sudanese political systems were worthy of respect and should be incorporated into French rule (Bulman 1999: 239). Nevertheless, it is clear that the progressivism attributed to him only goes so far: the second interesting consequence of his work is that his packaging of precolonial African history seems to point not toward questioning but toward justifying French colonialism. Since the greatness of African empires is generally framed as arising from conquest, the overarching narrative he produced of Sudanese history can be read as a succession of episodes in which one group dominates another, giving rise to an evolutionist scheme of increasingly complex state forms from the *case* or hut to the *empire*.[6] The French conquest fits neatly into this narrative, superseding the African empire thanks to its inevitable superiority and crowning all previous conquests with itself.

The prime example of Delafosse's racialized theory of conquest is his argument in favor of a version of the Hamitic myth. In Delafosse's version of the myth, the light-skinned race is the *Judéo-Syriens* or Judeo-Syrians, who migrated from the Middle East across the Sahara and whose original "white" descendants founded ancient Ghana in West Africa before being conquered and subsumed by black races. As evidence for this great migration's origin in the "white race," Delafosse cites the *Tarikh es-Sudan*, a seventeenth-century Arabic manuscript attributed to Abd al-Rahman Al-Sa'di, according to which the kingdom of Ghana's first forty-four kings "étaient de race blanche, mais nous ignorons d'où ils tiraient leur origine" (were of white race, but we do not know where they originated from) (Sa'di 1900: 18). Or, at least, that is how the translation prepared by Delafosse's father-in-law, Octave Houdas, read. John Hunwick's English translation, prepared a century later, is more cautious: for him, the kings "were *bīḍān* in origin" (Sa'di 2003: 13), where *bīḍān*, literally "white" in Arabic, refers to Berbers and Arabs and has "cultural rather than skin-colour connations" (Hunwick in Sa'di 2003: 13 n. 5). Whereas Delafosse was happy to exploit the colonialist meaning of the French word *blanc*, insinuating a long-lost white heritage in West Africa that it was the destiny of the French to restore, Hunwick is careful to remind us that the Arabic *bīḍān* meant something quite more circumspect in West African history. With a confidence anathema to later, more skeptical historians, Delafosse goes on to trace his Judeo-Syrian migration from biblical Palestine to ancient West Africa, via Cyrenaica (eastern Libya), and asserts that it established colonies in the Sahara all the way to Morocco.[7] Among their mixed-race descendants are, in this narrative, the modern Fulbe, usually called Peuls in French—an umbrella term englobing a number of linguistically and culturally related ethnic groups, now scattered across a huge region from Lake Chad in the east to the Futa Toro region along the Senegal/Mauritania border in the west.

However hasty, and politically convenient, Delafosse's use of the word *blanc* may have been, the notion of nonblack origins among certain West African peoples neither began nor ended with his intervention. Delafosse was not the first European writer to connect the Fulbe to Jewish origins.[8] The Fulbe themselves refer to Middle Eastern origins in their oral traditions, as I discuss below, and are reputed even today in some areas to have a lighter skin color than other groups. Amadou Hampâté Bâ describes them as "blancs parmi les noirs, et noirs parmi les blancs" (whites among blacks and blacks among whites) due to their light eyes and tan complexion (1966a: 23), while Nehemiah Levtzion insists that their nomadic populations have "non-negroid traits" (1971: 137). In addition to this reputation for light skin, Delafosse's and other versions of the Hamitic myth caused the issue of nonblack Fula origins to be extensively debated over the course of the twentieth century (see Lam 1993). The issue has been more or less abandoned by contemporary anthropology because of its obvious racist undertones. By revisiting the discursive construct of Fula origins in Delafosse and his followers here, my goal is not to revive the question of where the Fulbe came from—or other African peoples reputed to have hybrid Semitic origins, such as the Soninké, or the Tutsi!—or whether any particular group is more white or less black than anyone else. Rather, my goal is to trace the entanglement between colonial racisms and the construction of the West African epic genre.

Delafosse's fixation on a connection between so-called white influence and complex state formation among blacks, with special emphasis on the Fulbe, hints at the French claim to legitimacy in its colonies and would be made perfectly explicit by one of his most eager readers. That disciple was François-Victor Equilbecq, a fellow, though far less known, administrator and amateur Africanist. The importance of race, conquest, comparability to medieval Europe, and colonial politics for Delafosse becomes clear when we turn to Equilbecq's work. Having served in a number of administrative posts in the colonies of Senegal, Guinea, and French Sudan between 1902 and 1916, he is remembered today mainly as a folklorist, thanks to his three-volume collection of folktales *Contes indigènes de l'Ouest-Africain* (Native Tales from West Africa) (1913–16), which bears a preface by Delafosse.[9] Equilbecq was the first French commentator to discuss the idea of an African epic at significant length. *Contes indigènes* glosses quickly over the genre at various moments, discussing a "mentalité chevaleresque, analogue à celle de notre moyen âge" (chivalrous mentality analogous to our Middle Ages) among Pular-speakers in the Futa Toro, and even referring to the *Samba Gelajo Jegi* narrative as a "veritable *chanson de geste*" and a "chanson épique comme on les concevait au Moyen Age" (epic song like those conceived in the Middle Ages) (Equilbecq 1972: 60, 160–61). While these labels already make clear Equilbecq's interest in comparing Africa to medieval Europe, a far more developed discussion of the topic can be found in a different work of his, *La Légende de Samba Guélâdio Diêgui, Prince du Foûta* (Legend of Samba Gelajo Jegi, Prince of Futa). This book was written in 1914 but was published only in 1974, thanks to the efforts of another colonial administrator-turned-scholar, Robert Cornevin, who saw in his elder colleague an unsung genius.[10]

Here, Equilbecq first expresses surprise at the presence of an epic form in Africa that is recognizable to him, a Frenchman, and comparable to European heroic narrative, by wondering if these kinds of narratives actually come from European authorship and are merely imitated by African copycats. But after reassuring us that there are too many sources of the narrative for copycatting to actually be the case, Equilbecq recognizes the need to explain such a surprising discovery. The explanation he gives is taken directly from Delafosse's version of the Hamitic myth:

> Les traits chevaleresques y abondent et l'on jurerait d'autant de pastiches—heureux d'ailleurs—des faits de notre histoire nationale ou de celle d'autres pays européens.
> … D'ailleurs il ne faut s'étonner qu'à demi de la parenté de la légende indigène avec nos épopées médiévales. Les premiers auteurs de cette légende, les Déniankôbé, étaient des Foulbé, c'est-à-dire des Sémites à peine métissés. Quant aux Tôrobé, qui l'ont adoptée en la modifiant légèrement, ils ont une forte dose de sang maure ou poular dans les veines. Ce sont encore des métis et non des nègres au sens absolu du mot. (Equilbecq 1974: 15)

> Chivalric traits abound in it, and one would swear that it amounted to as many pastiches—fortunate ones, at that—of the achievements of our national history or that of other European countries. . . . Moreover, one must only be halfway surprised at the kinship that the native legend bears to our medieval epics. The first authors of this legend, the Deniyanke, were Fulbe, that is, Semites who have only barely mixed with other races. As for the Torobe, who adopted it while modifying it slightly, they have a strong dose of Moorish or Pular blood in their veins. They are still half-castes, not Negroes in the absolute sense of the word. (my translation)

This statement needs some unpacking. Let us take "Pular" and "Fulbe" to be near-synonyms, where "Pular" means the present-day speakers of the dialect of Fulfulde in the Futa Toro, along today's Senegal/Mauritania border. Pular-speakers in the Futa are the result of many centuries of ethnic mixing, but consider themselves to be part of the larger "Fulbe" people because of linguistic and cultural proximity (Kane and Robinson 1984: 1–2). Equilbecq notes that the plot of *Samba* takes place during the Deniyanke dynasty, which dominated the Futa from the sixteenth to the eighteenth century. The jihad that overthrew it in 1776, led by a class of clerics known as the Torobe, established a theocracy in the Futa that remained in power until the French conquest in 1861. Scholarly consensus today places the historical Samba Gelajo Jegi on which the epic is based in the early eighteenth century: he was among the last kings of the Deniyanke dynasty before its fall (Belcher 1994: 76–77). Equilbecq's attribution of "Semitic" origins to the Deniyanke dynasty directly recalls Delafosse's Judeo-Syrian migrations, while the "Moorish," that is, Berber or Hassaniyya Arab, influence on the Torobe guarantees, in the author's eyes, the continuing influence of "whiteness," that is, advanced light-skinned civilizations, in more recent times. For Equilbecq, the Deniyanke were, at any rate, only "à peine métissés," barely contaminated by blackness at all.

Thus, the presence of epic as noble genre, as well as the ability to compare Africa with Europe, is explainable because the genre's inventors were thought to be not really black. They had Semitic blood through which the high sentiments necessary for epic were made known and transmitted to them; that is, they were at least partially "white," in the sense of *bīḏān*, and by extension, for Equilbecq, in the sense of *blanc*, for purposes of comparison to Europe. Hence Equilbecq's telling choice of epithet for the *Samba* epic that encapsulates the rest of his commentary and gives this chapter its title: "cette Iliade demi-nègre" or half-black Iliad (1974: 132). The role of this white ancestry in guaranteeing future progress makes explicit the racist agenda of his evolutionist-diffusionist theory, as well as of the conflation of the terms *blanc* and *bīḏān*:

> La proportion relativement forte de sang de Blancs dans les veines des Tôrobé et la supériorité intellectuelle manifeste de cette race sur les autres races dites noires nous est un précieux enseignement quant aux moyens d'assurer et même de précipiter l'évolution de ces races. . . . [L]e progrès mental des races africaines est lié, non à leur métisation proprement dite, mais à leur éthiopianisation, c'est-à-dire—qu'on me permette cette expression de viticulteur—au mouillage de leur

sang par un certain mélange du sang des races plus claires avec retour, subséquent mais incomplet, vers le type noir. Il va de soi que, lorsque je parle de progrès, j'envisage tout d'abord le progrès intellectuel. Pour le moral, ce sera l'affaire du gendarme et du pouvoir fortement constitué. (1974: 86)

The relatively high proportion of whites' blood in the veins of the Torobe, along with the manifest intellectual superiority of this race over other races typically called black, offers us a precious lesson on how to guarantee and even speed up the evolution of these races.... The mental progress of African races is linked, not to their hybridization as such, but to their Ethiopianization, that is—if I may use a winemaker's metaphor—to the dilution of their blood by a certain mix of blood from lighter-skinned races with a subsequent but incomplete return toward the black type. It goes without saying that, when I say progress, I am thinking above all of intellectual progress. As for moral progress, that will be the affair of the gendarme and of power, vigorously constituted. (my translation)

Equilbecq sees the Judeo-Syrian and Moorish influence among the western Fulbe as making them superior to their peers and as precedents to French colonization. This assertion is carefully nuanced in such a way as to avoid encouraging officially sanctioned *métissage* or miscegenation in the AOF, which would no doubt have stirred up a ruckus. For Equilbecq, the biological contribution of whiteness has already been made—and weakened, thanks to a "subsequent but incomplete" return toward blackness over the course of the post-Judeo-Syrian centuries. Now, he says, it is up to a muscular French domination, particularly including the ability to punish, to do the rest of the civilizing mission's work.

After Delafosse and Ecquilbecq, the third colonial commentator I would like to introduce is Leo Frobenius. He is something of a unique case. For one, he was German, not French, and unlike his fellow collectors, he was not directly involved in any colonial administration. A self-taught ethnologist who eventually held teaching and curating posts in Germany in the 1920s and 1930s, he remains a figure of special importance in the history of black literature, given his well-known influence on the Negritude generation. A number of Frobenius's prolific writings, though nowhere near all of them, were translated into French and well placed to have an effect on, or at least provoke a reaction from, French colonial ethnography. For example, Charles Monteil, a more typical example of the French administrator-ethnographer type, blasted Frobenius for having written no less than eighteen books on Africa before setting foot there for the first time in 1904, as well as for his farfetched theories and failure to learn a single African language (1953: 367–68). Later views of Frobenius, while occasionally more generous, are in agreement on his shortcomings: his extreme beliefs are seen not only as unscientific, but as fawning and sentimentalist. Jahnheinz Jahn suggests that he tried to compensate for his intellectual shallowness by overcollecting (1974: 12), an effort that found its culmination in an untranslated twelve-volume collection of African stories, *Atlantis* (1921–28).

The title of that collection captures the heart of Frobenius's intellectual quest. Frobenius believed in and spent his numerous expeditions across Africa searching for "Atlantis," the legendary lost civilization described by Plato. Certain that this country had been historically located in Africa and inhabited by nonblack people, Frobenius hoped to prove a link between Africa and the "high" cultures of the Mediterranean, especially ancient Greece, and, in a gesture similar to the Hamitic hypothesis, to attribute the memory of African greatness to foreign, nonblack influence. The idea of epic plays an interesting role in this grandiose vision. Recounting a performance by a bard named Korongo of a narrative now known as the Wagadu tradition[11]—the fall of Wagadu due to the rescue of a maiden from the serpent to whom she was supposed to be sacrificed—as a preface to the events of *Sunjata*, Frobenius constructs a fantasy world that is strikingly similar to the European medieval imaginary:

Dazu Korongo—wie er dies vortrug! Die Stimme modulierte, die Gesichtszüge mimten in zierlichen Nuancen einzelne Worte und Gesten, der Vortrag, zögerte oder schnellte, senkte sich und schwoll. Wahrlich ein gewaltiges Heldentum, eine lebendige Epik, und ein naturgeborner Künstler, dieser Korongo! . . . Jetzt spricht er mit voller Stimme, erzählt von Burgen und Helden, von Kämpfen und Minne, von edlen Frauen und kunstfähigen Barden. Ein Leben warm und voller Blut, an Stil klar und rein wie Quellwasser; Formate und Dimensionen. Und nichts von dichterischer Flausenmacherei, sentimentalem Schwindel und schmierigen Überschwenglichkeiten! (1924: 63–64)

And so Korongo—how he sang it! His voice modulated, his facial features mimed with delicate nuances individual words and gestures; his speech, paused or hastened, sank and rose. Truly a tremendous heroism, a living epic, and a natural-born artist, this Korongo! . . . Now he speaks in full voice, tells of castles and heroes, of battles and love, of noble women and artful bards. A warm and full-blooded life, a style clear and pure as spring water; with its forms and dimensions. And no trace of poetic nonsense-making, sentimental humbug, or greasy mawkishness! (my translation)

This account of an oral performance reveals more than a fascination with heroic feats and tropes; it represents an idealization of these, hinting at an exoticized, nostalgic escape from the less lively routine of everyday European life. The epic (*Epik*), a "living" genre, is associated with life itself, particularly a mythologized past when life was more "warm and full-blooded" than in modern times.

Frobenius uses the German words *Epos* and *Epik* quite freely to describe these narratives. He says of Korongo's performance that "Das Epos ist großzügig gebaut" (The epic is generously built), praising its sense of chivalry and honor (1924: 63). But elsewhere, he makes the rather farfetched conclusion that the *Sunjata*'s pre-Islamic content is Libyan in origin:

Die Namengebung und Thronfolge ist libysch, die Königsbezeichnung die einer libyschen Dynastie. Wir werden sehen, daß die ganze Ausgangsidee des Sanges libysch ist, und das ist so wichtig, weil wir uns ja klar machen wollen, wie der Islam sich auf den Wegen, mit den Machtmitteln und im Sinne der vorislamischen Kulturwelt im Sudan einnistete. (1912: 461)

The nomenclature and the line of succession are Libyan. The dynastic title is Libyan. The basic idea of the Epos [epic] will be proved to be originally Libyan, and the latter fact is of the greatest importance, because it is desirable to determine the way in which Islam insinuated itself into the Soudan by following the lines, the methods of acquiring influence and the political intentions adopted by a pre-Mahommedan civilization. (1968, 2:466)

The supposed Libyan origin of the *Sunjata* is "of the greatest importance" because of North Africa's connection to the world of Mediterranean antiquity—a connection that Frobenius regularly emphasizes and that, for him, is the source of noble literary sentiments and forms south of the Sahara. This antique Mediterranean influence allows him to minimize the influence of Islam, which he denigrates.

In an earlier text, Frobenius racializes the noble genre of epic even more explicitly. After listening to the performance of an unspecified Fulfulde narrative—by a memorably ugly, thieving, and drunk bard named Alleï in Mopti (present-day Mali)—he exclaims, "Mopti! Ritterleben! Königspracht!" (Mopti! Life of chivalry! Royal splendor!) (1911: 220). He goes on to tackle the apparent similarity between the African and European ages of chivalry by again relying on the racial myth of the Fulbe:

> Und wie kann jemand, der nur den landläufigen typus des heutigen Negers kennt, es ohne weiteres verstehen, dass in meinen Akten ebensoviel von Mannheit, Turnierkunst, Waffenklirren, Knappentreue und Frauenschönheit verzeichnet ist, wie in jedem Werke über Rittersagen unseres eigenen Altertumes! . . . Gelbe und rote Leute wohnten hier, und ihre Art hatte nichts Negerhaftes am körper und im Wesen. Uber nach Süden hin wohnten die Neger in Ländern, die reich waren an korn und Gold. . . . Mischvolk entstand. Immer mehr schlug das Negerblut durch. Der Sudan vernigerte, immer Schwärzer ward das Volk. Nur wenige "reinere" Familien hoben sich allerorts vom vorherrschenden Gesamttypus ab, und die waren dann nicht nur dem Namen nach, sondern auch in der Tat die Vornehmen, die Adligen (1911: 220–21).

> And how can someone who knows only the common type of the modern Negro easily understand that in my files are recorded just as many examples of virility, the art of the tournament, the clangor of arms, squirely fealty, and feminine beauty as in every work about the chivalric legends of our own antiquity! . . . Yellow and red people lived here, and their kind had nothing Negro-like in body or in character. To the south, the Negroes lived in countries that were rich in grain and gold. . . . A mixed race was born. Negro blood penetrated ever deeper. The Sudan blackened, the people became ever blacker. Only a few "purer" families set themselves apart from the predominant type everywhere, and were then not only in name, but in fact, the high class, the nobles. (my translation)

Once again, we get a sense of Frobenius's idealization of kings, knights, and damsels in distress that cannot but remind him of European medieval literature. But in order to make such a comparison thinkable, or palatable, he must cast the link he fantasizes between high culture (courtly and chivalric themes) and high class (aristocracy) in Africa as a racial vestige from less dark-skinned races: his "yellow and red" peoples clearly indicate a nonblack origin for things like "virility," "fealty," and chivalry, which would otherwise have been unknown on the dark continent.

Like Equilbecq, he then theorizes a return to blackness through back-cross-breeding: the hybridized red/yellow/black population "blackened" over time, generating the population of Masina as he saw it in the early twentieth century. For both men, literary genre must be racialized in a way to accommodate the apparent cultural sophistication of blacks who ought to have been primitive. Nonetheless, Frobenius goes farther than either Equilbecq or Delafosse in his implications for everyday black-skinned people, making clear the contrast between the "common type of the modern Negro," which he disdains, and the rarefied, less-black nobility celebrated in his romantic view of epic.

As has become clear, colonial comments on the literary potential of African cultures were inevitably tied up with the issue not only of how to represent Africans, but of how to treat them. In the case of Equilbecq, epic became a specific means of answering the question of how to shape colonial governance, and Delafosse based his view on that subject at least in part on his respect for African political complexity. Another rich discussion of epic and governability comes from the pen of Henri Lanrezac, a military lieutenant whose series of articles from 1907 on "Légendes soudanaises"—a source for both Equilbecq and Delafosse—oscillates conspicuously between describing oral genres and prescribing policy for colonial government.[12] On the one hand, like Equilbecq, Lanrezac compares Sudanese and European oral forms with the intention of showing that they are more similar than different. He argues, for example, that Charles Perrault, Jacob and Wilhelm Grimm, and Hans Andersen, all famous publishers of European folktales, can each be found in Africa by way of their themes and motifs, yet African tales remain authentically African (1907b: 163–64). Recognizable genres such as "épopées" and "chants épiques" (epics and epic songs)—which include the legends of "Soundgata" and "Samba-Galdji," narratives familiar to us by now (1907a: 296 and 430)—ought to be classified at the top of the hierarchy of oral genres, above, for example, improvised war songs, which he disdains (1907c: 215). The prestige of epic enables intercultural generic comparisons that often lead Lanrezac to sound like a universalist and a humanist. Specifically, *Samba* moves him to declare:

> On y sent palpiter l'âme héroïque d'un peuple qui aime les combats et honore les mâles vertus de l'homme de guerre. Cette poésie nationale valait bien la peine d'être connue, puisque grâce à elle l'âme soudanaise nous révèle ses beautés, ses grandeurs. . . . J'espère seulement avoir démontré, en parlant de ces peuplades soudanaises, que nous n'avons pas affaire à de véritables sauvages, mais à des êtres

humains ayant véritablement une âme vibrant sous les mêmes joies, sous les mêmes douleurs que celles qui émeuvent notre coeur. (1907d: 618–19)

In it, one feels the throb of a combat-loving people's heroic soul, a people who honors the manly virtues of the warrior. This national poetry deserved to be known, since, thanks to it, the Sudanese soul reveals to us its beauty, its grandeur.... I only hope to have demonstrated in my account of these Sudanese tribes that we are not dealing with real savages here, but with human beings who truly have a soul, one that quivers under the same joys, the same sorrows as those that move our own heart. (my translation)

The recognizability of epic has provoked this dramatic declaration of humanism. In addition to the cliché of revealing the native soul, the idea that a "national poetry" could exist in precolonial Africa is itself indicative of the effort to dress African culture up in European political terms and, by doing so, to facilitate its entrance into world history. But the vague idea of a "nation," with its potential connotations of autonomy, is left incomplete here, as though to avoid letting the favorable comparison to Europe go too far.

Among the paradoxes that this balancing act generates, the most interesting is perhaps Lanrezac's interpretation of the epic value of "energy" as evidence of Africans' laziness. While oral literature is full of "leçons d'énergie" (lessons of energy), he nevertheless laments the "état d'indolence et de paresse dans lequel vivent les noirs . . . depuis la disparition des grands Empires (Songhai, Mali, Berbères) jusqu'à nos jours" (state of indolence and laziness in which the blacks have lived... from the disappearance of the great empires [Songhai, Mali, Berber] until today) (1907a: 430). Thus, the discourse of epic and empire is mobilized to prefigure, rather than to contest, French hegemony, implying that colonial rule has merely occupied the space formerly held, and long left vacant, by imperial greatness. Carefully eliminated is the case of Umar Tall, the Muslim theocratic warrior who declared jihad against the French encroachment in the mid-nineteenth century, and whose empire and "légendes historiques" (historical legends) Lanrezac had been discussing only a few pages earlier (1907a: 423–24). Epics and empires can only be signs of "energy" when they are too distant in the past to be explicitly anti-French. Lanrezac's notion of human equality, made manifest through the universal sentiments expressed in epics from different cultures, is calibrated in just the right way to defend French colonialism while giving it a veneer of enlightenment. One particular digression away from the subject of oral literature is especially revealing in this regard:

> pendant un temps, les coloniaux se sont partagés en deux écoles: les amis des noirs, qui prétendaient que les Africains devaient un jour profiter de nos droits, être soumis aux mêmes lois (particulièrement au point de vue électoral et judiciaire) et les ennemis des nègres, qui les considéraient comme des animaux à peine supérieurs aux singes. Les uns soutenaient l'assimilation complète, les autres le principe de la domination sous un joug inflexible. Entre ces deux théories extrêmes il y en a une troisième bien française: celle qui consiste à juger les Soudanais tels qu'ils sont, en les considérant comme des auxiliaires dont on peut faciliter l'évolution morale sans chercher néanmoins à effacer les différences essentielles qui existent entre eux et nous, différences, qui, il ne faut pas l'oublier, ne tiennent nullement à la valeur morale des individus, mais seulement aux agents extérieurs qui, autant que l'ancestralité, modèlent l'homme. (1907a: 426–27)

> For a long time, colonials were divided into two schools: the friends of the blacks, who claimed that Africans should one day enjoy our rights, be subject to the same laws (especially electoral and judicial ones), and the enemies of the blacks, who considered them to be animals barely higher than monkeys. The former called for total assimilation, the latter for a principle of domination under an inflexible yoke. Between these two theories is a third one, a truly French one: it consists of judging the Sudanese as they are, seeing them as auxiliaries whose moral evolution we may facilitate without trying to erase the essential differences that exist between us—differences that, let us not forget, have nothing to do with the moral value of individuals, but only with exterior agents that, as much as ancestry, shape man. (my translation)

Like Delafosse and Equilbecq, Lanrezac has let his admiration for historical African accomplishments shape his theory of colonialism, though his opinion seems closer to the former than to the latter. Rather than leaving the natives' moral evolution to the "gendarme" and to colonial institutions of "power, vigorously constituted" (Equilbecq 1974: 86), he suggests that historical circumstances require both a mission to facilitate civilization in Africa and a respect of cultural difference, echoing Delafosse's rejection of assimilation in favor of association. The interpretation of literary forms, and the comparability implied by epic in particular, is brought directly to bear on the nature of the civilizing mission.

Besides the collectors mentioned so far, a number of other colonial administrators in French West Africa dealt with epic material and tried to classify its genre. Most, especially those interested in historical reliability, were less enthusiastic about the significance or worth of oral literary forms than Frobenius or Lanrezac. The above-mentioned Charles Monteil, known for his study *Les Empires du Mali* (Empires of Mali) (1929), which was seen by some as updating Delafosse's *Haut-Sénégal-Niger*, begrudgingly acknowledged the importance of oral tradition for historical research in West Africa. Though he recognized the "caractère épique" or epic character of some material and presented summaries of narratives that are still used by scholars today, he generally considered oral literature to be ephemeral, fragmented, contradictory, and incoherent, and always remained convinced of its very limited historical usefulness.[13] Jean Vidal, in a summary of *Sunjata*, describes the "prouesses épiques" of the "héros national des Malinkés" (epic prowess of the national hero of the Maninka) (1924: 317), but nevertheless takes a condescending tone toward the narrative before him, removing "certains détails par trop puériles et enfantins qui ne pourraient qu'allonger inutilement le récit sans rien ajouter à sa clarté" (certain excessively puerile and childish details that would only lengthen the story needlessly without adding to its clarity) (1924: 318). Notice here that as soon as epic's recognizability is obscured by details whose meaning is unclear to the collector, its comparability to the European Middle Ages is abandoned, and the genre is demoted from one of chivalry to one of childishness. Robert Arnaud also finds an infantile quality, commenting upon the *Wagadu* and *Sunjata* narratives that in terms of their historical content, "le Noir bouscule avec naïveté les époques" (the black naively mixes up time periods), while he himself "prenai[t], à les entendre, le plaisir du gosselet aux contes de nourrice" (took, upon hearing them, the pleasure of a child listening to his nurse) (1912: 144). The colonial historian Georges Hardy takes a somewhat more generous view of the historical value of oral tradition. For him, in spite of the fact that historical traditions lose their connection to reality over generations and take on a "tournure d'épopée" or epic dimension, nevertheless, the pleasure of studying great African empires is comparable to that of studying kingdoms and empires in Europe (1929: 95–96). Even though epic narratives are inferior to historical fact, being full of invention and low on reality, they remain important tools for expanding historical research beyond the shores of the Mediterranean (1929: 96). Gilbert Vieillard, a linguist of Fulfulde, adds a dimension of nostalgia to the idea of epic: writing at a time when the French conquest was long complete, he presents his collection of four narratives on "héros païens" (pagan heroes) as part of "un véritable cycle épique, très abondant, que déclament, en s'accompagnant sur la guitare, chanteurs et musiciens peul, pour le plaisir mélancolique des chefs de guerre, devenus 'chefs de canton'" (a true epic cycle, very abundant, performed by Fula singers and musicians, with accompaniment on the guitar, for the melancholy pleasure of the war-chiefs, now turned into *chefs de canton*) (1931: 137). A tinge of Frobenius-like romanticization here colors the memory of the warriors of old, now transformed into agents of the humdrum colonial bureaucracy.

But even in earlier generations of French colonial writing, there is evidence of the possibility of conceiving an African epic. Alfred Le Chatelier, a specialist of French policy toward Islam in North and West Africa, refers to Sunjata and his nemesis Sumaoro as "deux héros d'épopée" (two epic heroes) (1899: 86–87). This is in the context of a discussion of the place of Islam in popular culture, with Le Chatelier's ultimate goal being to help craft the French response to this religion's influence. And while Jean-Baptiste Raffenel, an explorer admired by Equilbecq, never quite uses the word "epic" in either of his two travel narratives on West Africa (1846 and 1856), he does compare the Fula hero Samba to Ulysses (1856, 2:329)—an allusion that the aforementioned Georges Hardy might have resisted, given his criticism of the common practice among colonial writers of using facile labels such as the "Joan of Arc of Sudan," the "Louis XIV of Morocco," or a "Charlemagne in Africa" (Hardy 1921: 30–31). For Hardy, such facile prepackaged comparisons actually obscured historical study in the colonies; but his complaint remains a revealing indicator of the general tendency in colonial letters to depend on such comparisons in order to make Africa legible and to locate it on the hierarchy of civilizations. In colonial thought, the idea of an African epic, an "Iliade demi-nègre," fit right into that desire for comparability and legibility. But the comparison inevitably supported Europe's assertion of its own superiority.

Crisscrossing Racisms: Black and White Before the Colonial Era

At first glance, the colonial packaging of epic as a racialized genre is offensive to twenty-first-century eyes, merely one more crazy European fantasy of racial superiority, a blatant attempt to justify oppression and to explain away African accomplishments as products of foreign influence. It is that. And yet, before we turn to militant black reactions to this discourse, it is necessary to recall that ideologies of race in West Africa predated the colonial era. As we shall see, the essence of Yambo Ouologuem's critique of Negritude and other racial self-retrieval movements was that they depended on the same racist premises as the colonial project itself, which, in turn, was indebted to racial ideologies already present among its African subjects. The specific example of the origins of the Fulbe is especially enlightening in this regard. If we return to Delafosse's and Equilbecq's treatment of the Fulbe as partially "white," we can open up an important intersection of racial ideologies—not just colonial European, but also precolonial African. Equilbecq's argument that the Fulbe are *métis* rather than blacks, following Delafosse's own hardened racialism and obsession with the "white" kings of ancient Ghana, certainly says more about colonial racism than it does about the history of African migrations. However, we must recognize that these claims to white origins do, in fact, overlap with precolonial West African ideologies of race. Two separate, but intersecting, ideological tendencies characterize a broad swath of West African genealogical traditions: First, the specific belief in a foreign, pre-Islamic lost homeland—perhaps Middle Eastern, or Egyptian, or Jewish—has been documented in Fula (and other ethnicities') oral traditions from different parts of West Africa. Second, the absorption over time, following the spread of Islam in the Sahara and farther south after the eighth century CE, of Arab ideas of their own racial superiority to "blacks" (Ar. *sūdān*) caused many ethnic groups, of various skin colors, to rework their genealogies in such a way as to trace their origins back to heroic Arab—therefore Semitic rather than Hamitic—ancestors. These ancestors especially included companions of the Prophet Muhammed (Hall 2011: 40–68; O. Kane 2004: 515 n. 40). As Bruce Hall has brilliantly shown, in many such cases, African claims of familial connection to early Islamic heroes constitute claims to nonblack origins, where, more than skin color per se, "black" is understood to correspond with paganism or "diluted" Islam, while "white" is understood to mean Arab, and therefore "pure" Islam. Historically, from at least the seventeenth to the nineteenth centuries, such claims had bearing upon how West African Muslims determined who was enslaveable or not.

The crisscrossing of these racisms—Muslim and Christian, African and Arab and French—is important not only because it allows us to destabilize and historicize the terms "white" and "black," but because it contextualizes the racial hierarchy that the French colonial administration sought to mobilize as it debated the significance of the African epic genre. Just as the possession of epic located an African people somewhere on a scale from primitive to civilized in European eyes, African uses of genealogy also located various African peoples on a distinct but ultimately very similar hierarchy between blackness and whiteness. While Delafosse's conflation of the French colonial notion of whiteness (*blanc*) with the Arabic term for religious and ancestral legitimacy (*bīḍān*) was both too easy and politically motivated, we must recognize that both terms are opposed, in their own contexts, to a lesser blackness (*noir* or *nègre* in French, *sūdān* in Arabic). Equilbecq saw in *Samba* a "chivalrous mentality" that reminded him of the white heroes of European *chansons de geste*; in a parallel way, lists of descent of the kind celebrated in oral African epics became a way by which some Africans gave themselves imaginary "white" (*bīḍān*) ancestries, which could then be mobilized to prove nobility for one's lineage, superiority over one's peers, or the right to keep another person enslaved. As we shall see, this parallel is important because it would help Yambo Ouologuem define the West African epic as a discourse of the masters, of racial hatred and class warfare.

The belief in a nonblack or hybrid origin of the Fulbe runs far and deep, both in oral traditions and in interpretations of them. It was not just a colonial invention, nor did it die with the colonial era.[14] Lam (1993) traces an impressive number of colonial and later views on the subject, dividing arguments into "fantastic," "Asiatic," and "Nilotic"; Delafosse's Judeo-Syrian narrative falls into the second category. While this outline is helpful, Lam's own view follows that of Cheikh Anta Diop, the renowned mid-century Senegalese physicist-turned-linguist who argued for an Egyptian origin of the Fulbe as part of his broader revisionist Afrocentrist historiography (C. A. Diop 1959: 114). For Diop, still an intellectual icon credited by his admirers with rescuing African history from European arrogance, the Egypt–Fulbe connection was a small piece of his larger, controversial attempt to claim ancient Egypt as a "black" African civilization (C. A. Diop 1959 and 1979). It goes without saying that Diopian Egyptology is problematic, and its issues are beyond the scope of this book. Suffice it to say that in claiming Egypt as a black civilization, Diop was attempting to decapitate the long-standing colonial cliché that everything worthwhile in black Africa must be attributable to nonblack influence.

In spite of scholars' reticence to resuscitate the subject now, an apt example of the persistence of the notion of Fula origins in a mythical east can be found in Guinean novelist Tierno Monénembo's historical novel *Peuls* (2004), a romanticized but well-documented narration of seemingly endless Fula migrations, dispersions, and diasporas across West Africa over the centuries. The novel begins with a traditional account of the people's common origins:

> Cela commence dans la nuit des temps, au pays béni de Héli et de Yôyo entre le fleuve Milia et la mer de la Félicité. C'est là-bas, dans les fournaises de l'est, sur les terres immémoriales des pharaons que l'Hébreu Bouïtôring rencontra Bâ Diou

Mangou. Le Blanc vit que la Noire était belle, la Noire vit que le Blanc était bon. Celui-ci demanda la main de celle-là.[15]

It begins in the depths of the past, in the blessed country of Heli and Yoyo between the River Milia and the Sea of Happiness. There, in the crucibles of the east, in the immemorial lands of the Pharaohs, the Hebrew Bouitoring met Ba Diou Mangou. The white man saw that the black woman was beautiful, and the black woman saw that the white man was good. He asked for her hand. (my translation)

The author's footnotes tell us that Héli and Yôyo are substitutes for the forgotten, true name of the lost Fula homeland, somewhere in the east, and that the "River Milia" refers to the Nile while the "Sea of Happiness" is the Red Sea (Monénembo 2004: 13 nn. 1 and 2). This mythical Egyptian geography and reference to a "white" Hebrew ancestor match up surprisingly well with the oral traditional sources from which Delafosse derived his Judeo-Syrians. A further footnote from Monénembo makes his own theory of original Fula *métissage* even more explicit:

> Les Peuls seraient nés d'un métissage entre des Noires d'Egypte et des Hébreux de la tribu des Fout qui, avant de pénétrer l'Egypte, avaient longtemps séjourné à Tôr dans le Sinaï. (2004: 14 n. 1)

> The Peuls are said to have descended from a mixing of black women of Egypt and Hebrew men of the tribe of Put who, before penetrating Egypt, had long sojourned in the land of Tor, in Sinai. (my translation)

This statement recalls with striking exactness Delafosse's statement that, from Syria, the biblical tribe of "Fout" or Put (cf. Gen. 10:6), that is, the Fula ancestors,

> toujours depuis les traditions indigènes, . . . seraient venus d'abord dans le pays de *Tôr* (presqu'île du Sinaï), puis du pays de Tôr dans celui de *Missira* (Egypte), et de l'Egypte dans le pays de *Soritou* (sans doute Sort ou Syrte, Cyrénaïque), d'où ils auraient, longtemps après, gagné le pays de *Diaka*, Diaga ou Dia (Massina occidental), où nous les retrouverons un peu plus loin. (1912, 1:211–12)

> still according to native traditions, . . . are said to have come first to the land of Tor (Sinai peninsula), then from Tor to *Missira* (Egypt), and from Egypt to *Soritou*

(no doubt Sort or Syrte, Cyrenaica), from where, much later, they are said to have reached the land of *Diaka*, Diaga or Dia (eastern Masina), where we will find them again later on [in this work]. (my translation)

Such stories of Fula ancestors sojourning in Egypt and the land of Tor, at least, were not made up by Delafosse himself. As referenced above, his great Judeo-Syrian theory linking biblical patriarchs to ancient Ghana and the modern Fulbe was influenced by myths of eastern origin that really did, and do, circulate among people who identify as Fulbe. Should we take this as evidence that maybe he was on the right historical track with this theory in spite of his blatantly racist agenda; or should we see here just another example of an overeager colonial historian's penchant to fabricate connections between data points for the sake of creating a smooth narrative?[16] I tend to agree with the fourteenth-century Arab historian Ibn Khaldūn's skepticism of pedigree, quoted in the epigraph to this chapter. Regardless of the "objective truth" of who migrated where and what color their skin was, the French colonial claim to a nonblack origin for certain African peoples became eminently politically charged.

The second tendency in West African genealogical traditions that is important for this discussion is the desire among some sub-Saharan communities to connect their lineages to Arab heroes or the companions of Muhammed. This desire spread through the region over the centuries through contact with Saharan and Arab ideas about race. Bruce Hall's work (2011) is key here: while he is not the first scholar to study Islamically influenced manipulations of West African genealogies, he is the first to frame them thoroughly in terms of racial hierarchy. In medieval North Africa, to be "white" (*bīḍān*) was to be Arab and Muslim. The historian Ibn Battuta excluded the Berbers from this term in the fourteenth century because he saw them as culturally too different from himself (Hall 2011: 34). But, especially beginning in the seventeenth century, the gradual Arabization of Berbers meant that Berbers followed Arabs in seeing themselves as superior to their black neighbors. Clerical clans claimed heroic ancestors including Ali, companion of the Prophet, and Uqba, who began the conquest of the Maghreb (Hall 2011: 61–65). Thirteenth- or fourteenth-century romances of the Sanhaja Berbers describe the exploits of a great Himyarite (Yemeni Arab) ancestor and conqueror, Dhul-Qarnayn (Ar. *ḏū al-qarnayn*), who had to face "the greatest obstacles and hazards to spread the faith" in Africa, "the place of warfare against the Sons of Ḥām," that is, blacks (Norris 1972: 53). Dhul-Qarnayn is named as a pre-Islamic hero and apocalyptic figure in the Koran (18:83–101). He is often identified by commentators as Alexander the Great, although his appropriation as a Berber ancestor shows that this is not always the case. The point is that belief in racial superiority was expressed in pedigree: whereas "genealogical claims made by virtually every significant Arabic- or Berber-speaking 'noble' group in the Sahel invoke an Arab Muslim origin," the "absence of genealogical connections to Arab Muslim ancestors was what rendered one black" (Hall 2011: 59 and 68). This invocation of an Arab origin allowed groups defining themselves as "white" to assert religious authority through proximity to the Prophet, and even to enslave "blacks" (*sūdān* or *zanj*) who could not connect themselves to an Arab origin, even if they practiced Islam. Although Islamic law theoretically only allows the enslavement of non-Muslim prisoners of war or people already born into slavery (cf. Koran 47:4), thereby forbidding the enslavement of freeborn Muslims, a number of West African fatwas or religious opinions from the seventeenth century on worked around that obstacle by ruling that the descendants of people who were converted by force or in raids, that is, "blacks," could be kept in permanent servility, regardless of their current religion (Hall 2011: 69–74 and 80–87). Once again, the ambiguous position of the Fulbe makes this hierarchy especially legible. It was not only Berbers or Arabs who traced themselves to Arab heroes; Fula traditions evoke descent from Uqba and Ali as well: "If the Arabic-speaking scholars in the Sahel made a dichotomy in their writings between themselves and the blacks by the pairing 'the whites and the blacks' (*'al-bīḍān wa-l-sūdān'*), Fulbe scholars arrived at a similar distinction between 'the Fulbe and the blacks' (*'al-fulān wa-l-sūdān'*) that did exactly the same thing."[17]

Complicating Hall's narrative somewhat, however, is the well-documented tendency of a number of West African "black" genealogies to trace themselves not to Arab Muslim heroes, but to Bilal, another companion of the Prophet, who was a freed black slave and the first muezzin. Sunjata's ancestry is most often traced to this figure in Mande epic discourse, as is that of some Senegambian royal families in their own genealogies.[18] These genealogical claims seem to invoke the Islamic ideal of racial egalitarianism, according to which faith and piety make all believers equal, regardless of culture or skin color. By elevating as its founder a figure who was both a black-skinned African and irreproachably Muslim, Bilalian ancestry represents a claim to the legitimacy of blackness within the racial hierarchy of the West African Muslim world, even as it upholds the notion that a connection to the founders of Islam makes one's lineage superior to non-Muslim lineages.

Interestingly, the story of Bilal does nothing to challenge the institution of slavery itself. Bilal was manumitted as a reward for the strength of his belief, and manumission as an act of mercy remains a recommended but nonmandatory option for slave owners in Islam more generally.[19] As such, Bilalian genealogies represent something of an exception to the tendency of dynastic or epic genealogies to claim nonblack origins. Nevertheless, even they participate in claims to religious authority and legitimacy via proximity to the Prophet—the very same kinds of claims that were otherwise intimately bound up with racial identity as expressed in *bīḍān* origins. The attribution of Sunjata's ancestry by Mande bards to Bilal thus creates a particularly ambiguous grey zone: To what extent should we read it as a racialized rhetorical move? Is it a true vindication of blackness in West African genealogical thought? Or does it merely repeat the implication that other "black" lineages are less genuinely Muslim, and therefore tainted—enslaveable—because they are less connected to so exceptional an ancestor?

Whatever the case may be, allusions to the racial hierarchy were not limited to the genealogical traditions of Fula or Berber kings and heroes. References to Himyarite, or Yemeni Arab, origin can be found elsewhere in sub-Saharan traditions as well. In particular, Dhul-Qarnayn, associated with Himyarite origin in Berber traditions, shows up as a known figure in a variety of contexts. In D. T. Niane's version of the *Sunjata*, performed by the Maninka bard Mamadou Kouyaté, he is a point of reference, but not an ancestor: Sunjata's exploits are said to be *even greater* than those of "Djoul Kara Naïni" (Niane 1960: 10), whom a footnote identifies as Alexander the Great (1960: 10 n. 2). But the Maninka bard Wa Kamissoko—precisely in an attempt to criticize manipulation of Maninka genealogy in the name of Islamic piety—accuses the Sise (Cissé in French) clan of claiming descent from "Dyulu Kara Nayni" (in Farias 1993: 18), which seems to evoke the Koran and Sanhaja romances of a Himyarite conqueror of the Sahara, even though, the bard claims, Mande lineages clearly predate Islamic influence by many centuries. Meanwhile, the (admittedly Fula) genealogist Sirê-Abbas Sôh's *Chroniques du Foûta-Tôro*, written in Arabic and translated by Delafosse, make the Deniyanke hero Samba Gelajo Jegi a descendant of the great Maninka hero Sunjata, that is, "[le] roi du Manden *Sundyata* fils de Mohammadu fils de Kinānata, d'origine himyarite" (*Sundyata*, king of the Manden, son of Mohammadu son of Kinānata, of Himyarite origin).[20] The upshot: even Sunjata, the most famous of all West African epic heroes, can have a "white" ancestry.

World Masterpieces, a Racial Problem

The notion of an African epic comes with a complex cultural baggage. Focusing on the French West African context, this chapter excavated the racialized dimensions of that baggage. Contrary to typical views of the region's literary history, colonial writers throughout the early twentieth century recognized the presence of "epic" in their midst, but drew on long-entrenched genealogical and Islamic notions of Semitic, Arab, or eastern origins—always, at the end of the day, signs of black inferiority—in order to explain it. While contemporary scholars have problematized the idea of world literature at great length, the specific connection between African epic, colonialism, and ideas about race has never been made. Professional Africanists in the second half of the twentieth century attempted to decolonize literature, and rehabilitate the continent in the world's eyes, by erecting African epic as a monumental cultural accomplishment. But this kind of challenge to colonial dismissals of African cultures still depends, in some ways, on the highly racialized discourse that already surrounded the genre well before the independence era. Ralph Austen's criticism of the "Proust of the Papuans" paradigm makes this paradox perfectly clear:

> In a much-publicized response to demands for multicultural revision of college humanities programs, the Nobel prize novelist Saul Bellow rhetorically demanded that he be introduced to "the Tolstoy of the Zulus? The Proust of the Papuans?" If students of Africa ever took up Bellow's challenge, the most obvious candidate for such monumental status would have to be the *Sunjata* epic. . . . Most specialists on African history or oral literature would, however, reject the very terms in which Bellow poses his question.[21]

This gesture manages deftly both to answer Bellow's question on its own "great books" terms, then to reject those terms as implying an unsuitable approach to literature. Epic, and the great imperial past that goes with it, continue to be counted as African contributions to the "civilized ecumene" or "literary-political round table of nations," even as we dismiss such notions as romantic fictions, and even as we remember that the idea of civilization is haunted by its opposite: the racialized, uncivilized Other.

CHAPTER TWO

The Suns of Independence

Anticolonial Heroisms and Their Limits

I concede that whatever proof there is of a once mighty Songhai civilization
does not change the fact that the Songhais today are undernourished, illiterate,
abandoned to the skies and water, with a blank mind and glazed eyes.

—Frantz Fanon, *The Wretched of the Earth*

Frantz Fanon, an icon of African anticolonial thought, begins his classic essay
"Sur la culture nationale," chapter 6 in *Les Damnés de la terre* (translated as
"On National Culture" in *The Wretched of the Earth*) (1961), with a reflection
on the need to rehabilitate precolonial cultures in the independence era. In
spite of the material uselessness of the project, he argues that African intellectuals
have a political and psychological imperative to reclaim glorious histories that will
help legitimate their fledgling nations:

Cette recherche passionnée d'une culture nationale en deçà de l'ère coloniale tire
sa légitimité du souci que se partagent les intellectuels colonisés de prendre du
recul par rapport à la culture occidentale dans laquelle ils risquent de s'enliser. Parce
qu'ils se rendent compte qu'ils sont en train de se perdre, donc d'être perdus pour
leur peuple, ces hommes, la rage au cœur et le cerveau fou, s'acharnent à reprendre

contact avec la sève la plus ancienne, la plus antécoloniale de leur peuple. . . . Le colonialisme ne se satisfait pas d'enserrer le peuple dans ses mailles, de vider le cerveau colonisé de toute forme et de tout contenu. Par une sorte de perversion de la logique, il s'oriente vers le passé du peuple opprimé, le distord, le défigure, l'anéantit. Cette entreprise de dévalorisation de l'histoire d'avant la colonisation prend aujourd'hui sa signification dialectique. (Fanon 1991: 255–56)

This passionate search for a national culture which existed before the colonial era finds its legitimate reason in the anxiety shared by native intellectuals to shrink away from that Western culture in which they all risk being swamped. Because they realize they are in danger of losing their lives and thus becoming lost to their people, these men, hot-headed and with anger in their hearts, relentlessly determine to renew contact once more with the oldest and most pre-colonial springs of life of their people. . . . Colonialism is not satisfied merely with hiding a people in its grip and emptying the native's brain of all form and content. By a kind of perverted logic, it turns to the past of the oppressed people, and distorts, disfigures and destroys it. This work of devaluing pre-colonial history takes on a dialectical significance today. (Fanon 2005: 37)

To research the great empires and their ancient traditions is, for Fanon, to attempt to undo the brainwashing of colonialism. And yet, as we have seen, colonial representations of precolonial West African accomplishments were actually quite varied; they were not only "devaluing." While it is clear that Maurice Delafosse, for example, wrote *Haut-Sénégal-Niger* (1912) with an agenda of legitimating the French conquest, his work also advanced precolonial African history as an object of inquiry and field of study. Contrary to "Heart of Darkness"-type perceptions of the continent, colonial writers struggled to make sense of their own wonder at African civilizational accomplishments while fitting them into available schemes of thought through now discredited mechanisms like the Hamitic myth. Fanon may be right that works like *Haut-Sénégal-Niger* "distort" and "disfigure" West African history in many ways, but we must admit that colonial discourse was more nuanced, variegated, and influential on later generations than his militant critique allows.

The Guinean historian Djibril Tamsir Niane's *Soundjata, ou l'épopée mandingue* (*Sundiata: An Epic of Old Mali*) (1960) illustrates this ambiguity. At first glance, this text, now recognized as an African classic, seems like it should have been a key example of the nationalist intellectual project of rehabilitation that Fanon names.

And yet, a number of paradoxes in Niane's position must be acknowledged. First, Niane's *Soundjata* bears a certain resemblance to *Haut-Sénégal-Niger*: its accessible packaging of a complex oral tradition into easily readable French reasserted a recognizable African contribution into universal world history and literature, "answering the . . . Hegelian dismissal of the peoples of Africa as without history" (Belcher 1999b: 89). Indeed, Niane, the father of African epic studies, expressed deep admiration for Delafosse's work, rather than programmatically opposing it:

> Nous devons une dette de reconnaissance à ces pionniers et dans cette galerie coloniale il nous plaît de citer entre autres le Gouverneur Maurice Delafosse qui . . . donna une vigoureuse impulsion à la recherche historique en lançant plus d'un administrateur sur le terrain. (Niane 1975: 8)

> We owe a debt of recognition to these pioneers, and within this colonial gallery, we are pleased to cite, among others, the Governor Maurice Delafosse who . . . gave a vigorous drive to historical research by sending more than one administrator into the field. (my translation)

Niane was not the only West African writer to acknowledge such a debt. The colonizers' work on precolonial culture played a significant role in shaping the independence generation's knowledge of it. L. S. Senghor and Aimé Césaire famously held Leo Frobenius in high affection, while Birago Diop's favorite reading material is known to have included F.-V. Equilbecq and Henri Lanrezac, both of whom were major commentators on West African epic during the colonial period (S. Camara 2002: 102).

Nevertheless, there was an air of Fanonian urgency surrounding Niane's research on oral traditions, which were unfolding at the height of anticolonial fervor. But—and this is the second paradox—as his rocky relationship with Guinea's vehemently anti-French president, Sékou Touré, would demonstrate, the nationalist project had its pitfalls, too. Fanon, who praises Sékou Touré throughout *Les Damnés de la terre*, and includes an epigraph from him at the beginning of "Sur la culture nationale," died in 1961; he did not live to see how mortally dangerous Touré's dictatorship became for Guinean intellectuals, including Niane (Conrad 2010: 356–61; C. Miller 1990: 51–60). Imprisoned from 1961 to 1964, Niane escaped Guinea in 1972, only returning after Touré's death in 1984; Fodébo Keita, the one-time minister of Internal Affairs whose poetry Fanon celebrates as an expression of a

Touréist anticolonial awakening, was not so lucky. He was executed by Touré in 1971. The final paradox is that *Soundjata* appeared in the middle of Sékou Touré's 1959–61 demystification campaign:

> In an effort to create a new national identity, traditional religious practices were declared illegal, public manifestations of indigenous ritual were forbidden, and masks, songs and dances were destroyed or appropriated by the state. . . . If 1960 marked the mid-point of the demystification campaign, the release of *Soundjata* in the same year meant it also marked the appearance of an oral narrative that vividly reflects the Guinean people's pervasive involvement in the supernatural world through sorcery, divination and ritual sacrifice. (Conrad 2010: 356)

Read today, Fanon's chapter "Sur la culture nationale" seems tragically short-sighted. He may have been right that African intellectuals were "in danger of losing their lives and thus becoming lost to their people," but, in Guinea as elsewhere, the danger was often more from their own governments than from France. The dialectical opposition that Fanon tried to establish between colonialist and anticolonialist thought blurs under closer scrutiny: as the example of Niane and Delafosse shows, the two could overlap and echo each other significantly. Furthermore, in its most despotic expressions, anticolonial fervor could, in fact, stifle the traditional knowledge that was supposed to form the basis of Fanonian national cultures.

And yet, Fanon was right that many black African writers sought to revalue oral traditions as a way of countering colonial alienation. This chapter examines a series of West African thinkers who called upon epic heroes in order to counter colonial arrogance and assimilationism. While these writers often express hostility toward the French presence in Africa, they nevertheless rely upon the work and assumptions of colonial collectors, ethnographers, and historians. Beginning in the 1930s, and accelerating after World War II, this effort to reclaim a sense of pride in African cultural accomplishments through epic increased in intensity. At the same time as a new canon of African anticolonial heroes from the nineteenth-century resistance was being constructed, comparison with Europe remained a key stake. It was not only necessary that these heroes be convincing within Africa, but that their legacy be recognizable to the rest of the world. This created a certain political ambiguity that Fanon was unwilling or unable to recognize. Colonial and anticolonial approaches to the study of precolonial culture shared significant resemblances and common assumptions. Moreover, celebrators of the anticolonial epic often colored their work in tragic hues: great last stands by nineteenth-century resisters like Samori Touré were inexorably defeated by the French conquest. This, combined with the disappointments of independence incarnated by Sékou Touré himself, led a number of anticolonial writers to focus not so much on the hope that heroic resistance was supposed to engender, but on its tragic limitations.

After reviewing anticolonial tropes of heroism, and their limits, in the work of Niane and several Negritude-influenced models of nationalist epic-writing from West Africa—notably Abdoulaye Sadji and Cheikh Aliou Ndao of Senegal and Laye Camara of Guinea—this chapter will turn to the notorious "antiepic" of the Malian Yambo Ouologuem, *Le Devoir de violence* (*The Duty of Violence*) (1968), which relentlessly and harshly satirizes the epic heritage. Ouologuem seizes on the racial hierarchies explored in the last chapter to depict West African tradition and history as a seemingly never-ending cycle of racist, sadistic violence. Drawing particular inspiration from the Songhai and Kanem-Bornu empires, the novel lampoons West African historical memory as the creation of elite classes claiming some form of "whiteness"—especially African aristocracies referring to the Hamitic myth—who use this supposed racial superiority as an excuse to oppress the "black" masses. Precolonial aristocracies and colonial oppressors are, in this vision, more alike than they are different. If anything, the former are crueler than the latter, because they are less naive and incompetent. Ouologuem's view serves as a dark but important alternative to Fanon's militant progressivism, even as it recalls his reflection on the contradiction between the "once mighty Songhai civilization" of yore and the "undernourished, illiterate" masses of today, quoted in the epigraph to this chapter. Ouologuem foregrounds the ambiguous connections between colonial and anticolonial thought, rather than effacing them; it is this thread of ambiguity that I want to trace in anticolonial approaches to epic leading up to him. This study will clear the ground for subsequent chapters of this book, which will demonstrate how epic can be used as a critical tool for thought, rather than a racialized tool within an anticolonial dialectic, as is the focus here.

From Sunjata to Samori

Before turning to anticolonial writers in earnest, it is necessary to recognize that the very idea of an African epic or African hero was, by the middle of the twentieth century, a contested space. Outside of the examples studied earlier, when the words "épopée africaine" appear in French colonial discourse, they often refer not to oral performances of any sort, but to the heroic exploits of the French conquest of Africa. Both the hagiographers of the French conquest and the defenders of the nineteenth-century African resistance imagined their respective champions as heroes of a great African epic. Indeed, when we remember Charles-André Julien's observation that "l'histoire coloniale est le triomphe de la biographie" (colonial history is the triumph of biography) (1946: 5), it is easy to realize how the image of the fearless (white) adventurer, explorer, and conqueror came to be crowned with a heroic aura. The publishing house Plon printed the popular series *Grandes figures coloniales* from 1930 to 1932, of which each edition covers a different French conquistador: Louis Faidherbe, Joseph Gallieni, and Pierre Savorgnan de Brazza each have a volume dedicated to them. In this vein, colonial historiography used the term "epic" for decades, from Albert Corbie's 1908 collection *L'Epopée africaine*, which describes in classical alexandrines a romantic vision of the French penetration of the continent from Napoleon's landing in Egypt onward, to Albert Duboc's military history of the conquest entitled *L'Epopée coloniale en Afrique occidentale française* (1938). As the expression "épopée coloniale" became commonplace, it was used regularly in all kinds of propaganda; suffice it to cite, as a last impressive reference, Léon Poirier's film *Brazza ou l'épopée du Congo* (1939). In contrast to this self-aggrandizing cliché, the great empires and epic heroes of West Africa were crucially symbolic for black writers in the AOF and its successor states to redefine their sense of their continent's place-in-the-world. This historical material not only represented the greatness of an African past but, with a bit of subversive interpretation, also came to glorify resistance to colonization itself. Indeed, while colonial writers were, with few exceptions, overwhelmingly interested in epic and empire as a relic of Africa's distant history, a number of black writers held up nineteenth-century anticolonial resisters like Umar Tall, Lat-Dior Diop, and especially Samori Touré, each of whom had become the subject of heroic narratives in the oral tradition, alongside the older heroes like Sunjata and Samba Gelajo Jegi. The crucial question of the epic genre changed from, "How can we classify and govern primitive peoples?" to, "What models can we hold up for a new Africa?" As a response to this question, Sunjata attracted nationalist, anti-French readings, while Samori, whose heroic status depended on opposing colonial rule, became a "Sunjata of modern times." The conflict of competing heroic periods is striking: the African hero advanced by African intellectuals is not only a rewriting of older colonial debates over oral literature, but of colonialism's history of itself. While D. T.

Niane's now-famous prose adaptation *Soundjata* draws on a fascination with epics and empires that was already old by 1960, it also participates in the effort to replace the most famous men of the colonial épopée africaine—the Louis Faidherbes and Louis Archinards—with a set of authentic African heroes, ancient and recent.

But the importance of *Soundjata* in early 1960s Guinea was not so much its status as world, or anti-French, classic as its ambiguous role in national politics. It quickly took on the role of political allegory in which Sékou Touré occupied the role of either hero or villain. Mohamed Saidou N'Daou, once a student of Niane's, explains how *Soundjata* was eagerly read by the Guinean political elite during this period as the story of the president: "During this time, the epic story metaphorically identified Sunjata and the anti-colonialist struggle against Soumaoro's domination with the nationalist Ahmed Sékou Touré and the Guinean heroic resistance against French colonization, respectively" (N'Daou 2007: 172). The fact that Niane's prose rendering of *Soundjata* appeared serially in *Horoya*, the official newspaper of the ruling Parti démocratique de Guinée (PDG), in 1961 suggests that the text lent itself quite easily to a propagandistic, proregime interpretation.[1] Christopher Miller's research confirms that a pro-Touré reading of Niane's *Soundjata* was practiced at least as late as 1983; but he adds astutely that when we consider the book in retrospect, in particular given Niane's personal suffering at Touré's hands, it is nearly impossible for critically minded readers not to invert the early nationalist paradigm, such that the despot becomes the nemesis rather than the hero (C. Miller 1990: 98). For better or for worse, Niane's *Soundjata* was immediately read by the Guinean elite as being "about" Sékou Touré, the man at the center of the young country's madness.

The case of the writer Laye Camara, who himself had been forced to flee Guinea in 1965 as a political exile, provides a counterpoint to the proregime reading invited by *Horoya*. Camara includes a barely veiled attack on the dictator in his introductory essays to *Le Maître de la parole* (*The Guardian of the Word*) (1978), another French prose rendering of the *Sunjata* that is typically said to be more thoroughly "novelized" than Niane's. In these essays, Camara launches into a tirade that is clearly directed against Touré but does not explicitly name him. He contrasts the toxicity of "our politicians" to the serene heroism of the *Sunjata*:

> [Cette légende] peut-être aussi incitera-t-elle les cadres africains à venir s'asseoir auprès des Anciens, pour puiser la sagesse, la science, l'histoire du Continent noir, à sa source la plus authentique, le griot traditionaliste. . . . Nos hommes politiques

d'aujourd'hui, à l'exception de quelques-uns, sont-ils de grands hommes? C'est douteux: ils font de la politique une entreprise sanglante. Ils affament nos peuples, exilent nos cadres, sèment la mort! Ils ne font pas la politique pour le progrès des peuples africains mais pour la régression de ces peuples. Ils ne servent pas l'Afrique; ils se servent de l'Afrique, ils ne sont pas précisément des bâtisseurs, des organisateurs, des administrateurs de cités, mais des geôliers qui se comportent avec les femmes, les hommes, les enfants de nos peuples, comme avec du bétail. Ils sont des apparitions périphériques de l'Afrique; ils sont ces mauvais intermédiaires qui laissent nos peuples sur leur soif de vie et de progrès. (L. Camara 1978: 34–35)

Perhaps also [this legend] may persuade African peoples to sit at the feet of the Ancients, to draw the wisdom, the knowledge, the history of the Black Continent from its most authentic source, namely, the traditionalist griot. . . . Today, are our political leaders really great? Apart from one or two, it is really doubtful whether they are; they turn politics into a bloody massacre. They starve our peoples, exile our tribes, sow death and destruction! Theirs is not a politics for the advancement of the African peoples, but for their regression: They do not serve Africa: they make Africa serve themselves. They are far from being builders, organizers, city administrators, but are rather gaolers who deal with the men, women and children of our peoples as if they were cattle. They are peripheral apparitions over Africa; they are agents of evil who will not quench our peoples' thirst for life and progress. (L. Camara 1980: 32)

What a difference from Fanon's encomium of the same man! While Camara exemplifies Fanon's judgment of the necessity of precolonial culture for nation-building, he uses this culture precisely to illustrate how alienated the likes of Touré are from it. For Laye Camara, such politicians are ghastly "apparitions" from the continent's periphery, rather than manifestations of its cultural soul.

This declaration is all the more striking since it does not appear in the first draft of this essay, which Camara had written between 1963 and 1971 under the title "Epopée et legendes: Critiques générales" (Epic and Legends: General Criticisms), the introduction to his thesis, "Le Haut Niger vu à travers la tradition orale" (The Upper Niger Seen through Oral Tradition) (L. Camara 1971). This thesis was prepared at the University of Dakar based on fieldwork at Fadama, in northern Guinea, in March and April 1963.[2] It consists of a series of transcribed and translated performances by Babou Kondé, a Maninka griot famous throughout Guinea in his day, covering first the life and feats of Sunjata, then those of Samori. The *Sunjata* narrative collected here forms the basis of the "novelized" story in *Maître de la parole*, while the *Samori* narrative transcribed by Camara has remained unpublished and largely forgotten. Both the thesis and *Maître de la parole* open with very slight variations on the following statement:

> Quand des peuples vivent depuis des années en peuples libres ou sous une influence, dans la féodalité ou sous la domination coloniale . . . il est naturel que ces peuples se cherchent, qu'ils se reportent dans leur passé, et que, creusant ce passé, ils y recherchent passionnément les traits des êtres et des choses qui ont guidé leur destin. (L. Camara 1978: 11)

> When people live for years in freedom or within some sphere of influence, either in a feudal state or under colonial domination . . . it is natural that such people should return to their roots, should investigate their past, and, delving into that past, should enter upon a passionate quest for traces of those beings and those things that have guided their destiny. (L. Camara 1980: 15)

This opening echoes Fanon's diagnosis of the need for precolonial inspiration. But whereas the thesis focuses only on the possibility for postcolonial liberation, *Maître de la parole* in its final form bitterly denounces the disappointments that followed the hope of Guinean independence. Sékou Touré, as of 1978, did not live up to the values of the African soul reflected in *Sunjata*, in Camara's eyes. Camara's and others' interpretations of *Sunjata* as reflecting their opinions of Sékou Touré are complemented by Mohamed Saidou N'Daou's own opinion: for him, the epic is specifically prodemocratic, recommending an exemplary form of parliamentary government—which the PDG abandoned soon after Guinean independence— since the hero Sunjata always respected the principle of shared governance.[3]

Thus, in spite of its seemingly ancient content, the *Sunjata* epic's literary incarnations in French were subject to politicization from the beginning of the independence period. In a parallel way, the more recent, nineteenth-century hero Samori Touré attracted a growing amount of political and literary attention over the course of the twentieth century. The famous warlord built a mobile military empire through violent conquest while rallying opposition to the French penetration across large swaths of West Africa (present-day Mali, Guinea, Sierra Leone, and Ivory Coast) at the end of the nineteenth century. While Sunjata remains the most

FIGURE 4. Sections of Babou Kondé's Epic Historical Narrative

MANINKA TERM (KONDÉ'S)	FRENCH TRANSLATION (CAMARA'S)	ENGLISH TRANSLATION (KIRKUP'S)	CONTENT
Kuma lafoloo kuma	Histoire de la première parole	History of the First Word	Creation of the world
Kuma koro	Parole vieille	Ancient Word	From the descendants of Adam to Sunjata
Kuma korootoola	Parole vieillissante	Ageing Word	From the life of Sunjata to Samori
Kuma	Parole	Word	From the life of Samori to independence

L. Camara 1971, 1:112–14; 1978: 32–33; 1980: 30.

famous of all West African epic heroes, the oral tradition remembers Samori as a modern successor to the medieval founder. Laye Camara's thesis illustrates this juxtaposition beautifully. As shown in figure 4, the griot Babou Kondé's history is divided into four parts that make the connection between ancient and recent heroic cycles entirely explicit. The lives of Sunjata and Samori take up the vast majority of this material.

The oral epic form represents the many phases and changes of history, from the beginning of the world up to the time of writing, the "*Dépendan tele*" or "times [literally 'suns'] of Independence" (L. Camara 1971, 1:31)—a Maninka expression used by Kondé here, and made famous in French by Ahmadou Kourouma's novel *Les Soleils des indépendances* (*The Suns of Independence*) (1968). Babou Kondé shapes his performance in such a way as to make the most ancient traditions readily applicable in the modern world, while Camara exploits the parallels that this framing offers. Samori, the anticolonial warlord, is explicitly cast as a new Sunjata—a comparison that may actually have originated during Samori's lifetime—and the times of independence form a piece of history alongside both major heroes.[4] This narrative structure automatically poses the question of who will serve in the role of the next Sunjata/Samori: after the medieval Mande Empire and the anti-French resistance, who will be the hero of independence? To what extent do real-life African leaders embody, or fall short of, such an ideal? For Babou Kondé, performing in 1963, the answer seems clear enough: in one scene of his performance, a sage prophesies to Samori that an as-yet-unborn heir will restore his empire after sixty intervening years of European rule, seeming to suggest that Sékou Touré is the hero of independence (L. Camara 1971, 1:307–8). For Laye Camara, the answer changes over time, as we have seen: his reflections on liberation in his thesis turn to indignation in *Maître de la parole*. In all cases, the historical heroic narrative functions as a representation of the desire for liberation, including political liberation from the French, and, in the long run, from the disappointments of independence.

The question of whether Sunjata = Samori = Sékou Touré stems from a long-running desire throughout the twentieth century to clear Samori's memory of colonial stereotype. Defeated in 1898 after a sixteen-year struggle, Samori was represented by colonial authors as a bloodthirsty tyrant from whose cruelty France saved defenseless peasants. The French historian Yves Person, who was among the first of his generation to take African perspectives seriously in writing their history, wrote a magisterial three-volume study, *Samori: Une révolution dyula* (Samori: A Jula Revolution) (1968), documenting the Almami's military conquests and their accompanying social upheaval. He summarily, and pertinently, dismissed the likes of Albert Duboc's *Samory le sanglant* (Bloody Samori) (1947):

> Tous ces écrivains n'ayant d'autre dessein que de populariser quelques pages d'épopée coloniale, et n'attachant pas un intérêt particulier à la révolution samorienne, on comprend qu'ils n'aient pas songé à des recherches longues et ingrates (Person 1968, 1:7).

> Since all of these writers had no other intention than to popularize a few pages of colonial epic and since they held no particular interest in the Samorian revolution, it is understandable that they did not bother with long, tedious research. (my translation)

In Guinea, to refute the colonial stereotype of "Bloody Samori," Sékou Touré declared himself to be the Almami's direct descendent—note that they share a patronym—and the embodiment of his heroic anticolonial resistance; the dictator was all too happy to be seen as a latter-day Sunjata and Samori at the same time. Sékou Touré and the PDG transformed Samori into a national hero, a symbol of their partisan propaganda and the postcolonial struggle in general, all of which, of course, they saw as one (N'Daou 2008; Bertho 2015). The PDG elevated him to one of several official national heroes of the republic, in spite of the fact that some Guinean villages did indeed remember the Samorian conquest of their homes as a period of subjugation and oppression.

Indeed, paradoxically, perhaps the greatest twentieth-century monument to Samori, besides Person's opus, is a film that was never made. Ousmane Sembène, the Senegalese "father of African cinema," spoke in several interviews of a massive, six-hour film and multiepisode teledrama titled *Samori* that he described as the crowning achievement of his life's work (Bertho 2016b). Only the film's script was ever completed. It exists in three leather-bound tomes, dated 1962–85, numbering a total of 2,000 pages, filled with meticulous plans for 2,265 scenes. Although a few copies still exist, the only known (two) complete sets are in Sembène's own former office in Dakar. Envisaging the film as a Pan-African summa, Sembène collaborated with both Person and D. T. Niane in order to gather historical detail, although he intended to portray Samori rather unambiguously as a champion of the oppressed. A number of African heads of state, including Sékou Touré himself—for whom Sembène expressed admiration on a few occasions—promised funds for the project, but these apparently never materialized at the right time: "la réunion de tant de chefs d'États sur le long terme a été sans aucun doute l'une des causes de la faillite du projet" (getting so many heads of state together over the long term was no doubt one of the causes of the project's insolvency) (Bertho 2016b: 878).

In any case, Sembène's aborted film was only one manifestation of a long-running movement to vindicate Samori as a hero for the new Africa. Mamadou Dia, a Senegalese activist with a turbulent political career of his own, had made the link between Samori and political nationalism explicit much earlier. His memoirs describe the mid-1930s as a period of strong anticolonialism among his circles of friends:

> Nous revendiquions notre authenticité, l'identité nationale, l'identité africaine. Nous passions notre temps à écouter la kora, les hauts faits de Samory, de Sonndiata et les commentions avec [Abdoulaye] Sadji. . . . Nous commencions par réhabiliter des hommes comme Samory, en disant que Samory n'était pas le tyran, l'esclavagiste qu'on nous avait décrit. C'était un patriote, un africain, qui défendait son pays contre l'envahisseur. (Dia 1985: 36)

> We staked our claim to authenticity, to a national identity, to an African identity. We spent our time listening to the kora, to the heroic feats of Samori and Sunjata, and we commented on them with [Abdoulaye] Sadji. . . . We began by rehabilitating men like Samori, saying that Samori had not been the tyrant, the slave-trader who had been described to us. He was a patriot, an African, who defended his country against the invader. (my translation)

Dia's portrayal of a "patriot" who "defended his country against the invader" casts Samori's empire-building as primarily a move of collective self-defense, of heroic resistance to invasion.

But what, exactly, we might ask Dia and Sembène, is self-defense, or resistance: resistance to the French, or resistance to conquest? No intellectual or political effort to restore Samori's good name could escape the moral ambiguity of this figure who, by all accounts, was an imperial conqueror in his own right and was unafraid to use violence to crush resistance to him.[5] For example, Dia connects the recovery of Samori's reputation to his friend Abdoulaye Sadji, a Senegalese schoolteacher best known today for his novel *Maïmouna* (1958). Like Dia, Sadji had become a convinced nationalist and a partisan of the Negritude movement in Senegal by 1934.[6] His essay "Ce que dit la musique africaine" (What African Music Has to Say), first published in a journal for colonial schoolteachers in 1936 and to which Dia alludes in the quote above, presents a collection of heroic legends summarized from performances by a Kassonke griot named Bakary Diebaté.[7] It includes not only *Sunjata* and *Samba Gelajo Jegi*, but actually begins with *Samori*. Short, and intended for the colonial classroom, Sadji's summary hides neither the carnage of Samori's rule nor the conflict between him and the French. Sadji's Samori appears to be torn between the colonial image of a slave-trading tyrant and the nationalist image of a hero-resister:

> Les héros, de nos contrées africaines, faisaient voisiner les actes les plus glorieux, les plus héroïques avec ceux que la morale moderne considère comme barbares. ... La cruauté de Samory égala sa bravoure, et il fut surnommé le roi sanguinaire. (A. Sadji 1936: 159)

> The heroes of our African lands undertook the most heroic, glorious feats amid actions that modern morality would find barbarous. ... Samori's cruelty equaled his bravery, and he was nicknamed the bloody king. (my translation)

Like Dia, Sadji seems intent on glorifying the nineteenth-century anticolonial resistance alongside the feats of the distant epic past. However, Samori's defining characteristic is his moral ambiguity. The few Samorian feats that Sadji records from Bakary Diebaté's performance—such as disemboweling a pregnant woman and throwing two thousand children into a fire—are all related to this theme. One episode in particular, in which Samori has his son Karamoko executed, is particularly striking because it relates directly to the hero's military efforts against the French. It begins when Karamoko is captured by a French colonel and taken to France: "Et là on le fit monter sur un édifice très élevé (la tour Eiffel) du haut duquel il vit toute la puissance des Toubabs" (And there he was taken to the top of a very high building [the Eiffel Tower], from whose summit he saw all the power of the whites) (A. Sadji 1936: 120–21). The young Karamoko returns home, where he tells his father to cease fighting the French because their military and industrial power, which he has seen firsthand, are simply too great to be beaten. Samori, furious, declares this son incapable of ever heading the empire and puts him to death.

Bakary Diebaté's narrative, as recorded by Sadji, is based on a historical event: Karamoko really was Samori's son and really was taken to France as a guest of honor after the signing of peace treaties in 1886–87. (The accords would fall apart soon after due to disagreements over their terms.) Many colonial sources describe the profound impression that France made on Karamoko and the pop-culture sensation he caused during his visit. One Sudanese *tirailleur*'s memoirs recount:

> Karamoko fut, à Paris, l'objet d'une vive curiosité. Il rendit visite au Président de la République, au Ministre de la Marine et, enfin, au général Faidherbe, grand chancelier de la Légion d'honneur, dont le nom, parmi les indigènes soudanais et sénégalais, restera à jamais célèbre. Mais la visite la plus retentissante fut celle qu'il fit au général Boulanger, ministre de la Guerre. Le chef de l'armée, au milieu de tout son Etat-Major, le reçut avec une bienveillance marquée. Enfin, les reporters lui consacrèrent de nombreux articles, et il fut même mis en chanson dans quelques revues de fin d'année, sans la moindre méchanceté d'ailleurs. . . . Parmi tous les spectacles qui lui furent offerts au cours de son séjour en France, la revue du 14 juillet fut celui qui produisit sur Karamoko l'impression la plus profonde. Il avait peine à s'imaginer tant d'hommes sous les armes, manœuvrant avec un ensemble aussi parfait, et une si surprenante correction. Les cuirassiers surtout, par leur charge finale, lui laissèrent de notre armée une vision éblouissante. (Sy 1931: 26)

In Paris, Karamoko became the object of burning curiosity. He visited the president, the minister of the Navy, and finally General Faidherbe, chancellor of the Legion of Honor, whose name will be forever famous among the Sudanese and Senegalese natives. But most momentous was his visit to General Boulanger, minister of war. The head of the army welcomed him into the heart of his headquarters with remarkable goodwill. Finally, reporters penned many articles about him, and he was even sung about in end-of-year variety shows, though without meanness.

. . . Of all the spectacles offered him during his stay in France, the review of the troops ceremony on July 14 made the deepest impression on Karamoko. He could hardly imagine so many soldiers maneuvering with such perfect togetherness and surprising accuracy. The cavalry especially, with its final charge, left him dazzled by what he had seen of our army. (my translation)

Though visibly colored with colonial stereotype, this account gives a general idea of the Karamoko phenomenon in Paris. We might note that the prince could not have surveyed the city from the top of the Eiffel Tower, as Sadji indicates, since construction on that monument was still under way when Karamoko left France in September 1887. (Of course, the symbolic point stands.) The French strategy of persuading the enemy to put down arms through a show of might worked too well: upon his return to his father's side, Karamoko was convinced of the absolute military and technical superiority of the French and was unafraid to say so in public. After several years of apparently unwavering francophilia and defeatism, he was executed by Samori in 1894 through immurement and forced starvation in a walled-off hut (Person 1968, 2:695 and 3:1505–6).

This tragic end is counted by several colonial sources as an example of a heartless warlord's savagery (Person 1968, 3:1505). But it is important to remember that the story passed into African epic tradition as well, as documented both by Sadji through Bakary Diebaté and by Camara through Babou Kondé:

Après la signature du traité, l'Almamy fut invité en France
par les toubabs. Il y délégua à sa place son fils bien-aimé, le prince
Diaoulen Karamo. Ce Diaoulen Karamo, à son retour de France prit
peur de la force des toubabs, de leur puissance. Il ne put se retenir
de faire des remontrances publiques à son père, l'empereur, lors
des pourparlers devant aboutir au traité de Bissandougou. Pour
des raisons d'état, l'Almamy le condamna à mort. Le prince
Karamo fut enfermé dans une case sans porte ni
fenêtre, et mourut de faim, de soif et d'asphyxie. (Kondé in L. Camara 1971, 1:292–93)

After the signature of the treaty, the Almami was invited to France
by the whites. There he delegated his place to his beloved son, the prince
Diaoulen Karamo. This Diaoulen Karamo, upon his return from France, was
frightened by the whites' strength and power. He was unable to stop himself

from making public remonstrances to his father, the emperor, during
the negotiations leading up to the treaty of Bissandougou. For
reasons of state, the Almami condemned him to death. The prince
Karamo was locked in a hut with no door or
window, and he died there of hunger, thirst, and asphyxiation. (my translation)

The end of Karamoko marked African minds as much as French ones. The fact that
it survived in the oral tradition until at least the 1960s indicates its importance in
the historical memory of Samori's actions.

In another literary example, Cheikh Aliou Ndao's play *Le Fils de l'Almamy*
(1985) takes this conflict between father and son as its main subject. Both men are
cast as tragic heroes. Karamoko feels he must follow his conscience by revealing
to common soldiers the inevitability of their defeat; but in Samori's eyes, his son's
cowardice is sabotaging the army's morale, and in any case, yielding to one's feelings
is incompatible with running an empire.

Finally, Yves Person, Samori's great defender for the historical record, deals
with the problem of the warlord's reputation for cruelty by dedramatizing it. Once
colonial propaganda is brushed aside, we must, Person argues, see his use of terror
as a tactical necessity responding to specific crises, rather than as a personal lust for
blood (1968, 2:824). Person, who does not deny Karamoko's persistent and public
francophilia following his return from France, attributes his execution to a very
specific betrayal of his father in 1894, namely, two unauthorized offers of military
surrender by Karamoko to the French (1968, 3:1505–6). And yet, it is harder for
him to justify to a modern audience how the Almami condemned two of his own
daughters to death in 1887—erroneously—for losing their virginity, in an attempt
to enforce adherence to Islamic law in his state by example:

> Deux de ses filles, confiées à l'une de leurs belles-mères, furent accusées à cette
> époque d'avoir accordé leurs faveurs à des bilakoro—jeunes captifs élevés par
> l'almami dans le métier des armes. Ne pouvant admettre que sa propre famille
> bafoue la virginité prescrite par le Coran, Samori condamna à mort les coupables.
> Or, il apprit trop tard que la marâtre, femme vieillie et jalouse, les avait accusées
> faussement. Cette "erreur," ressentie douloureusement par Samori, lui fut très
> longtemps reprochée. Ses ennemis, dont les Français, étaient heureux de dénoncer
> la "cruauté" de l'almami. En fait, sans vouloir minimiser l'horreur de ces morts
> innocentes, il faut comprendre que Samori sentant la révolte gronder ait cru devoir,
> même un peu trop vite, faire un exemple. (Person 1976: 78)

Two of his daughters, having been sent to live with one of their mother's cowives, were accused at that time of having granted their favors to *bilakoro*—young captives being trained in the use of arms. Hardly in a position to allow his own family to scoff at the virginity prescribed by the Koran, Samori condemned the guilty parties to death. However, he learned too late that the old stepmother, wrinkled by age and jealousy, had accused the girls falsely. This "error," which Samori suffered with deep pain, was long held against him. His enemies, including the French, were eager to denounce the Almami's "cruelty." In fact, without wanting to minimize the horror of these innocent deaths, we must understand that Samori, sensing a swell of revolt, must have thought it necessary to make an example, albeit too quickly. (my translation)

The professional historian's attempt at a dispassionate, empiricist defense responds as effectively as possible to colonial propaganda, but it does little to settle the midcentury debate over whether and how Samori should be seen as an inspiration for a new Africa.

In sum, both *Sunjata* and *Samori* were interpreted by anticolonial activists as allegories of the African liberation movement. However, such readings were soon forced to contend with the failures, disappointments, and ambiguities of decolonization. *Samori*, in particular, came to embody a sense of the anticolonial African intellectual's dilemma: the "return to the roots" effort to reframe African history could and did serve nation-building purposes, but the violence required for nation building seemed in many instances merely to repeat the violence of colonialism.

Resistance, Tragedy, and the African Soul

Abdoulaye Sadji and Laye Camara were both caught in this dilemma, in different ways. Each writer paints oral epic in tones strongly reminiscent of Senghorian Negritude, evoking notions like the "black soul," the "call from the depths," and transcendent black aestheticism. Yet, as we have seen, both of their idealisms are compromised by the violence of their heroic models. For Sadji,

Considérer ces histoires comme des légendes ou comme des contes indignes d'attention et de créance, c'est laisser dans l'ombre quelques-uns des éléments essentiels à la connaissance profonde de l'âme nègre. . . . Et d'ailleurs, ce n'est pas la vérité historique toute nue qui pourrait éclairer la vérité psychologique de l'âme

nègre, c'est plutôt l'action mystique de cette âme sur le canevas offert par la vie
des héros. . . . On dirait que nous ne sommes jamais satisfaits de la stricte vérité et
qu'au-dessus des banales réalités, nous sentons autre chose de plus grand, de plus
beau; que nous voulons identifier le donné à cet idéal inaccessible. (A. Sadji 1936: 119)

To consider these stories as mere legends or folktales, unworthy of attention and
credence, would be to leave in the shadows some of the elements that are essential
for deep knowledge of the black soul. . . . Moreover, it is not naked historical truth
that can illuminate the psychological truth of the black soul, but rather, this soul's
mystical action on the canvas offered by the lives of heroes. . . . It would seem
that we are never satisfied with strict truth, and that beyond banal reality, we feel
something else, something greater and more beautiful; as though we wanted to
assimilate a given element to this inaccessible ideal. (my translation)

The idea of revealing native psychology through folklore was already a well-estab-
lished colonial trope. But Sadji conceives this psychology as a fount of wonders,
of creativity and imagination; through it, the black soul conquers the dreariness
of the everyday and of "mere" history, not to mention dull European rationalism.
The African soul derives its uniqueness from its experience of the marvelous as
represented in heroic narrative. This interpretive framework makes Samori's cruelty
legible: the hero may have been cruel, but even his cruelty is a kind of romantic,
tragic ideal because it rises above the tedium of the everyday.

Laye Camara, for his part, builds on this romanticization by insisting on the
membership of oral heroic narrative in the category of art:

En vérité, le griot, un des membres importants de l'ancienne société bien hiérar-
chisée, avant d'être historien, détenteur par conséquent de la tradition historique
qu'il enseigne, est, avant tout, un artiste et, en corollaire, ses chants, ses épopées
et ses légendes, des œuvres d'art. La tradition orale tient donc plus de l'art que de
la science, elle relève de l'art plus que de la science. (1978: 21)

In truth, the griot, one of the important members of that ancient, clearly-defined
hierarchical society, is above all—preceding his status as an historian and consequently as the custodian of the historical tradition he teaches—is above all an artist,
and, it follows, his chants, his epics and his legends are works of art. Therefore the
oral tradition is more of an art than a science. (1980: 25)

Camara's insistence on art demands that works of the African marvelous should be rescued from the analytical realms of history and ethnography favored by colonialism. The act of communication is above all an aesthetic one, rather than a reaffirmation of community identity, or the expression of a worldview. The African experience of art is comparable to, and perhaps more intense than, its European counterpart: while a European might feel an instant of communion with a work of art, the African mind experiences this communion constantly.[8] And yet, this high praise of African epic as art has its limits. Camara never questions the noble aesthetic of Samori as hero, but the doubts he expresses in Sékou Touré as Samorian successor hint at the tragic possibility that the heroic cycle has ceased to regenerate itself.

Even more than Camara or Sadji, Cheikh Aliou Ndao also hints at tragic limitations to an idealized epic form. All of his plays about anticolonial resistance portray tragic heroes who suffer the inevitable fate of defeat. In addition to *Le Fils de l'Almamy*, two other plays by Ndao take inspiration from nineteenth-century resistance narratives: *L'Exil d'Albouri* (Alburi's Exile) (1985), probably his most famous work, and *Du sang pour un trône, ou Gouye Ndiouli un dimanche* (Blood for a Throne, or the Sunday of Guy Njulli) (1983). Both stage the tension between internal rivalries among precolonial Senegalese kingdoms—Jolof in the former, Saalum in the latter—and the need to oppose the French conquest with a united front. Both are centered on heroic figures of the Wolof epic tradition.[9] Making the epicness of their content perfectly explicit, *L'Exil*'s preface, written by Bakary Traoré, declares that "le théâtre africain sera épique ou ne sera pas" (African theater will either be epic or it will not be). And Ndao, in his prologue to the same play, writes:

> Une pièce historique n'est pas une thèse d'histoire. Mon but est d'aider à la création
> de mythes qui galvanisent le peuple et portent en avant. Dussé-je y parvenir en
> rendant l'histoire plus "historique." (Ndao 1985: 17)

> A historical play is not a history thesis. My goal is to help create myths that galvanize
> the people and move it forward. Even if I must do so by rendering history more
> "historic." (my translation)

This prefatory material emphasizes the epic dimensions of Ndao's theater. The plays desire to "galvanize the people" and spur it toward progress. Collective memory and heroic themes help make history be more than just history: the author must grab the audience's attention and serve a national purpose beyond the simple documentation of facts. On the other hand, the plots of the plays turn this heroic dimension into tragedy. In each case, the hero must choose between duty and sentiment, an unhappy dilemma that always benefits the French in the end. The European conquest always looms in the background as the inexorable aftermath of each play's plot. *L'Exil* ends with the defeat of Segu, Jolof's last hope for an alliance against the French, and the dispersion of Jolof's citizens across the Sahel; and *Gouye Ndiouli*, like *Le Fils de l'Almamy*, turns royal father against royal son in a conflict between filial piety and patriotic duty, as well as between local rivalries and the need for unity. Instead of the Senegalese kingdoms forming an alliance against the French, the king of Saalum kills his own father—who, after having been ousted from the thrones of Kajoor and Baol, had tried to promote such an alliance by usurping his son's crown—and declares eternal war on the Futa Toro, the Muslim theocracy to the north that he sees as his mortal enemy and the ultimate cause of his patricide. In all three cases, the audience knows all along that the brave but flawed heroes will be unable to put aside their differences in order to stop the greater evil of colonial encroachment. This contrast between framing and content reveals two contradictory gestures in Ndao's theater. On the one hand, they seek to move modern audiences to sentiments of patriotism and nation building based on the courage of African heroes of the not-so-distant past. But on the other hand, these works radiate an air of uncertainty, if not despair, about the possibility of ever really accomplishing the task. In spite of the inspirational ambitions of their framing, Ndao's vision of epic, even more than Camara's or Sadji's, is inextricably tied to the tragic.

The theme of the inexorable downfall faced by nineteenth-century hero-re-sisters animates several other West African tragedies written for the stage: the falls of Lat-Dior and of the women of Walo, in a Senegalese context, and of the citadel of Sikasso in a Sudanese/Malian one, inspired plays by Thierno Bâ (1987), Alioune Badara Bèye (1990), and D. T. Niane (2009), respectively. The celebration of these heroes' courage in the face of defeat colors this strain of West African dramatic literature an unmistakably tragic hue.

The Art and Farce of Racial Hatred: The Special Case of Yambo Ouologuem

One West African novel stands out from everything else this in this chapter. Yambo Ouologuem's *Le Devoir de violence* (*The Duty of Violence*) (1968), sometimes referred to as an "antiepic," radically rejects both colonial and anticolonial mobilizations of an African heroic past.[10] Unlike the militant writers surveyed in this chapter, it finds no reason, tragic or otherwise, to glory in ancient or recent heroes. Nor does it try to redeem the continent's supposed ahistoricity in the eyes of European readers. On the contrary, its multigenerational saga of a fictional West African dynasty portrays a centuries-long "tableau d'horreurs" or "gallery of horrors": oppression, sadism, sexual abuse, and racial hatred define the region's history from the period of the great empires to modern times.[11] Drawing, among others, on oral narratives and written chronicles of the Songhai Askia kings, the novel's beginning covers the fictional Saif dynasty of the "Empire of Nakem" between the fifteenth and nineteenth centuries. But the bulk of the text focuses on the deeds of the family's last member, Saif ibn Isaac al Heit, between 1898 and the advent of the West African "Republic of Nakem-Ziuko" in the mid-twentieth century. More of a villain who takes pleasure in cruelty than a hero, Saif ibn Isaac al Heit alternately resists, accommodates, and manipulates the French, while always making the *négraille* or "black-rabble" victims to their and his own atrocities. The interpretative schemes we have seen so far are both repeated and inverted: at one level, Saif ibn Isaac al Heit resembles another literary incarnation of Samori, the figure of the cruel but heroic resister, and especially of the colonial stereotype of him as a bloodthirsty tyrant; but in Ouologuem's universe, no liberation is possible, whether from Saif ibn Isaac al Heit or through him. Unlike African mobilizations of Samori, he cannot possibly be seen as a liberator standing against the French, a "Sunjata of modern times." Both the French conquest and the African resistance are cast as manifestations of an ancient, never-ending history of violence. As in the writings of the Marquis de Sade, the only roles that seem to exist besides that of criminal are those of victim and accomplice.

This reading of Ouologuem as a perverse, "murderous antidote to a nostalgia for [Alex Haley's] *Roots*" is already well documented (Appiah 1999: 59). What I would like to offer here is a new investigation of the *Devoir*'s intertextuality in the light of my arguments in this chapter and the preceding one. As we have seen, French colonial views on epic and empire drew on older, precolonial racisms: the fixation on the part of French historians and ethnographers with "white," that is, Arab, Mediterranean, or Middle Eastern, influences on ancient and medieval sub-Saharan Africa—as exemplified by Delafosse's *Haut-Sénégal-Niger*—must be read in the context of older claims by Islamized noble classes on the southern edge of the Sahara to Arab or Middle Eastern ancestries. Subsequently, many militant writers from francophone West Africa reappropriated the heritage of the great Sudanic empires and heroes for anticolonial and nation-building purposes, but in terms that often recycled those of colonial historiography. As the culminating point of this two-part itinerary, I will close this chapter by arguing that the *Devoir*'s view of African history—according to which European colonialism is simply an imperfect repetition of a much deeper pattern of racial oppression on the African continent—cannot be fully appreciated unless we read it intertextually with Delafosse; the precolonial racial ideologies, transmitted through Islam and oral tradition, that inspired him; and the tragic turn in nationalist epic-writing explored in the last section. By exposing West African epics and heroes as founded on centuries of racial thinking from the medieval empires to the AOF, the *Devoir* ridicules the ability of heroic ideological models to serve as a foundation for twentieth-century political liberation. The reading I present here explores an underappreciated aspect of this novel: while the *Devoir* has long been recognized as a cynical satire of "return to the roots"-type celebrations of African heritage, it is also a carefully researched polemical pamphlet on the continuity between precolonial and colonial ideologies of race.

Indeed, the misfortunes of Ouologuem's career and the sheer shock value of the text have prevented the reading public from taking the *Devoir* as seriously as it deserves. Ouologuem was among the first anticolonial writers—perhaps *the* first—to realize how deeply racist thinking was embedded in West African history before colonization. He saw how indebted French colonial racism was to Islamic notions of whiteness and blackness, and how both of these racisms were entangled with the slave trade, the defining driver of West African history between the fifteenth and nineteenth centuries. And yet, the *Devoir* remains best known not for this brilliant and profoundly painful insight, but for the plagiarism scandal it caused soon after its publication:

> Comparison of *Le Devoir* with other texts, from the Bible to André Schwarz-Bart's *Le Dernier des justes* (1959) and Graham Greene's *It's a Battlefield* (1934), revealed a fabric of quotation, translation and incorporation, which, depending on your point of view, constituted either a freewheeling exercise in intertextuality or a cynical act of plagiarism. (C. Miller 1999: 111)

I will return to the plagiarism controversy later. For now, I would like to delve into the text, focusing on an entirely different intertextuality, namely the role of Delafosse, as well as Delafosse's sources, in the *Devoir*'s treatment of "Afro-Jews." This theme, which is central to Ouologuem's depiction of race relations, has remained underexplored by critics. In the novel, the Saif dynasty uses a supposed Jewish heritage to claim superiority over slaves and the *négraille* or "black-rabble." By repeatedly emphasizing this claim, Ouologuem exploits the allusions to ancient Jewish influences in Delafosse's theories of Semitic migration to Hamitic lands, as well as the many oral traditions across North and West Africa in which this theme can be found, in order to expose colonial and precolonial racisms as two sides of the same coin. This claim of otherwise "black" aristocracies to Semitic or white origins is more than a passing theme in the *Devoir*. It is part and parcel of received West African memory about nobility, as Ouologuem sees it, which is in turn central to his rejection of epic and heroes as possible sources of national consciousness. White supremacy, he shows, has been part of African genealogical thinking for centuries, in the form of sub-Saharan African claims to nonblack origins that are supposed to demonstrate racial superiority to neighboring people who do not share them.

Scholarly commentary on Ouologuem's Afro-Jews has missed the profoundness of this critique. It has mostly limited itself to remarking that the *Devoir* suggests a kind of "African Holocaust" based on its structural and other borrowings from *Le Dernier des justes* (*The Last of the Just*) (1959), André Schwarz-Bart's multigenerational novel of a persecuted European Jewish family from the Middle Ages to the twentieth century.[12] In this comparison, the African occupies the position of victim being led to the slaughterhouse of history, in a way that parallels the victims of Hitler's genocide. However, the role of Jewishness in West African historical memory is more ambivalent and multifaceted than such a comparison allows. A claim to Semitic origin actually signifies a claim to a higher place on the racial hierarchy in West African contexts. On a few occasions, scholarly readers of the *Devoir* have begun to pick up on this thread, but have not pursued it far enough. They note that "the Judaic ascendancy of the African chiefdom shows how blacks were 'colonized' well before the era of European colonialism"; how Saif's "heirs will exploit this [Jewish] birthright in order to lord it over the *négraille*"; and that the "link with Jews invites interpretations that stress both the higher status of a people with a such a long and richly documented past as well as identification with the suffering that they have undergone."[13] Hale goes on to assert that the notion of a partially Jewish origin for a Sahelian empire's rulers is historically plausible. Yet he dismisses

Sandra Barkan's (passing) observation of a certain proximity between Ouologuem's Afro-Jews and Delafosse's theory of Judeo-Syrian migrations on the grounds that the Frenchman's "theory of the origin of the Fulani people" is "now-discounted" (Hale 1999: 166). Barkan, for her part, had simply supposed that "by drawing upon Maurice Delafosse's history of the migration of [Judeo-Syrian] peoples into the West African territory which would roughly correspond to the fictional Nakem empire, Ouologuem succeeds in linking apparently disparate peoples" (1985: 107). In other words, while Barkan detects the intertextuality between Delafosse and Ouologuem, she does not make much of it. Hale ignores it outright.

Only Christopher Wise, whose biographical research on Ouologuem is extremely thorough, has stated firmly that "Yambo Ouologuem savagely parodies the Peuls' claim to racial privilege as the 'black Jews' of West Africa" (in Ouologuem 2008: ix). He attributes Ouologuem's malaise with racialized African genealogies to the author's own mixed Toucouleur-Dogon ethnic background (2008: ix–x). Wise is right to focus on the example of the problem of Fula origins, but, as I will show, the *Devoir*'s critique is far more wide-reaching. It lambasts not only twentieth-century Fula claims to white ancestry, but precisely the fact that such claims are so deeply rooted and ancient, so widespread across West African ethnicities and landscapes, and so inspirational to colonial historiography. In what follows, I will pick up on the threads identified by Sandra Barkan and Christopher Wise—namely, Ouologuem's indebtedness to Delafosse, and his interest in legends of white ancestry among West African peoples—in order to more fully unpack the profoundness of his critique of racial thinking.

In fact, Barkan had uncovered something important in the connection to Delafosse. The narrative of Judeo-Syrian migrations in *Haut-Sénégal-Niger* exercises a clear and direct influence on the *Devoir*'s imaginary Afro-Jews, regardless of whether Semitic-origin theories are "now-discounted" or not. Compare the three passages in figure 5. The first two are from Delafosse, the third from Ouologuem. I have put repeated and other significant elements in bold.

The juxtaposition demonstrates that Ouologuem was not only a reader but an active borrower of Delafosse. The former's "black Jews" follow exactly the same migratory itinerary as the latter's Judeo-Syrians, down to the same place-names ("Cyrénaïque," "Touat," "Aïr"), ordered, spelled, and even punctuated the same way: in quotes 2 and 3, "Kénana" is followed by an explicative "Chanaan" in parentheses. It can no longer be disputed that Ouologuem's black Jews are literary reincarnations of Delafosse's Judeo-Syrians. Just as Delafosse tried to explain the origins of the

FIGURE 5. Comparison of Passages from Delafosse and Ouologuem

(1) Mais vers 320 avant J.-C. à la suite de la prise de Jérusalem par Ptolémée Soter, de nombreux **Juifs** furent déportés en **Cyrénaïque**. Sans doute ils y trouvèrent, plus ou moins mélangés d'éléments berbères, les descendants, devenus nombreux et puissants, des fractions israélites ou hyksos venues d'Egypte longtemps auparavant, et il se forma là une population fort importante, d'origine judéo-syrienne dans son ensemble et pratiquant des religions diverses qui, toutes, devaient dériver plus ou moins du culte des Hébreux primitifs ou culte d'**Abraham**. C'est à cette population que je crois pouvoir faire remonter l'origine ethnique des Peuls ou du moins de celles de leurs fractions qui n'ont pas été **trop transformées par des unions avec des Noirs**. (Delafosse 1912, 1:211)	(1) But around 320 B.C., following the fall of Jerusalem to Ptolemy I Soter, many Jews were deported to Cyrenaica. There, no doubt, they found the descendants—now numerous and powerful, and mixed to greater or lesser extents with Berber elements—of Israelite or Hyksos fractions who had come from Egypt much earlier; and a very significant population formed there, mainly of Judeo-Syrian origin, but practicing diverse religions, all of which must have derived more or less directly from primitive Hebrew religion or the religion of Abraham. This is the population to which I believe the ethnic origin of the Fulbe can be traced—or, at least, the populations whose fractions have not been too greatly transformed by unions with Blacks. (my translation)
(2) [Le Pharaon], jaloux du nombre, de la puissance et de la richesse en troupeaux des *Banissiraïla*, les accabla d'impôts de toutes sortes; les Israélites—ou plutôt les Judéo-Syriens—s'enfuirent alors de l'Egypte. Une partie d'entre eux regagna le **Kénana** (**Chanaan**, Palestine) et le Sâm (Syrie) sous la conduite d'un chef nommé Moussa (Moïse). . . . [Les Judéo-Syriens] vinrent se fixer dans le pays de *Soritou* (**Cyrénaïque**) et prirent, dès ce moment, "en souvenir de leur fuite," le nom de *Foudh* ou *Fouth*. Plus tard, une fraction d'entre eux, prenant la route du Sud-Ouest, se rendit au **Touat**; mais une fraction se dirigea vers le Sud et gagna le **Bornou** (ou plutôt **l'Aïr**, comme nous le verrons plus loin). (Delafosse 1912, 1:215)	(2) [The Pharaoh], jealous of the number, the power, and the wealth in livestock of the "People of Israel," overwhelmed them with taxes of all kinds; the Israelites—or rather the Judeo-Syrians—thus fled Egypt. A part of them returned to Kenana (Canaan, Palestine) and the Land of Shem (Syria), led by a chief named Moussa (Moses). . . . [The Judeo-Syrians] settled in the land of *Soritou* (Cyrenaica) and assumed, from that moment, "in memory of their flight," the name of *Foudh* or *Fouth*. Later, a part of them, heading southwest, went to *Tuat*; but another part headed south and arrived in *Bornu* (or rather the Aïr mountains, as we shall see). (my translation)
(3) Le Seigneur—saint est·Son Nom—nous a accordé la faveur de faire apparaître, à **l'origine de l'Empire nègre Nakem**, la splendeur d'un seul, notre ancêtre le **Juif noir Abraham** El Héït, métis né d'un père nègre et d'une mère juive d'Orient—de **Kénana (Chanaan)**—descendant des Juifs de **Cyrénaïque** et du **Touat**, qu'une migration secondaire à travers **l'Aïr** aurait porté au **Nakem**. (Ouologuem 1968: 12)	(3) The Lord Almighty—holy is His Name—granted us the mercy of bringing forth, at the founding of the Black Nakem Empire, our illustrious ancestor the Black Jew Abraham al Heit, born of a black father and an Oriental Jewish mother from Kenana (Canaan), descended from Jews of Cyrenaica and Tuat, late-coming migrants to Nakem who traveled across the Aïr mountains. (Ouologuem 2008: 8)

light-skinned Fulbe by connecting them to a Jewish migration from the Middle East, Ouologuem explains the claims to legitimacy and power of his fictive Nakem aristocracy through claims to Jewish ancestry.

However, this connection still does not fully account for the Saif dynasty's claim to nonblack origin in the *Devoir*. Delafosse's reference to Bornu in quote 2 is not repeated verbatim by Ouologuem in quote 3: rather, it is recoded in the name of the Saifs' fictional empire, "Nakem." Thomas Hale has pointed out that Nakem is an anagram of Kanem (1999: 157). Together, these clues—Delafosse's Bornu being replaced by Ouologuem's Nakem, an anagram of Kanem—suggest a clear reference to the historical Kanem-Bornu, an important precolonial empire in the region of Lake Chad (present-day Nigeria, Cameroon, and Chad). Having lasted in various forms from the eleventh to the nineteenth century, Kanem-Bornu is credited as possibly "the empire with the longest history in Africa" (Hiribarren 2017: 37). Whereas in quote 2, the Judeo-Syrians move from the Saharan oasis of Tuat (present-day Algeria) across the Aïr mountains to Bornu, on the western side of Lake Chad, Ouologuem's Afro-Jews follow the same path but end up in "Nakem"—that is, Kanem, on the eastern side of the same lake, an area united to Bornu under a single ruling dynasty for many centuries. Although Hale notices the anagram, he does not follow the trail, preferring to see in Ouologuem's Nakem a re-creation of the Songhai Empire, the heartland of which was much farther west, along the bend in the Niger River (present-day Mali).

But the link to Kanem-Bornu is significant because its longtime dynasty, the Sayfawa, claimed ancestry from a Himyarite (Yemeni Arab) hero named, of all things, *Sayf* ben Dhi Yazan, "an Arab king of the Jewish faith (recast as a Muslim in the [Arab folk epic]), who lived in the sixth century A.D., prior to the rise of Islam, and who is viewed as one of the first genuine Arab heroes" (Jayyusi 1996: xxi). I posit that Ouologuem's fictional Saif dynasty is inspired by this Himyarite hero, still sung today in the Arab world and claimed as ancestor south of the Sahara, where he served as badge of legitimacy for the historical Sayfawa dynasty of Kanem-Bornu. Here the labyrinth of Ouologuem's literary borrowings begins to lead us beyond Delafosse himself, since *Haut-Sénégal-Niger* does not talk about Kanem-Bornu, the Sayfawa, or their claimed heroic ancestor. Yet the theme of genealogical claims to Arab, and specifically Himyarite, origins among Saharan peoples and sub-Saharan nobilities dovetails perfectly with Delafosse's invention of a great Judeo-Syrian migration across Africa, since the Frenchman did, after all, imagine this monstrous brainchild on the basis of actual genealogical traditions. Ouologuem's mixing of racist French colonial history with highly racialized precolonial genealogical traditions makes perfect sense. His great insight, and the source of much of his bitterness, is that the two are, uncomfortably, aligned.

The legends of Sayf ben Dhi Yazan are very ancient, beginning with tenth-century Arabic historians and evolving over the centuries via numerous books and oral traditions into a *sira*—a folk-epic or romance "composed in Middle Arabic during the Egyptian Mamluk period, that is some time between the thirteenth and sixteenth centuries," and that is still performed by oral storytellers throughout the Arab world, particularly, in this case, in Egypt (Norris in Jayyusi 1996: ix). Sayf ben Dhi Yazan is celebrated for his defeat of Ethiopian Christians in the Arabian Peninsula, a feat that would take on, over the centuries, the marked and explicit allegorical meaning of the triumph of Arab Islam over black unbelievers—that is, of Semites over Hamites:

> In the twelfth century, Nashwan ben Sa'id al-Himyari, in *Shams al'Ulum* and the ode of *al-Qasida al-Himyariyya*, was one of those who transformed the record of the rule and achievements of Sayf into a national folk epic and Arab saga, albeit markedly Yemeni in its national loyalties. By that date, Sayf's exploits were no longer limited to the Arabian Peninsula; he had sailed to Ethiopia to wage war. The conflict had become ethnic between the sons of Shem and Ham, the "red" Arabs, and the "black" peoples of Ethiopia and the Sudan. . . . Hence, the Berbers of North Africa, who claimed to have originated from the Yemen in pre-Islamic times, took Sayf as the model for their heroic fight against the blacks (pagan and nonpagan) to the south of the Sahara, while the Somalis, who saw themselves as "Yemenis," regarded both Dhu Nuwas and Sayf as heroic fighters against their traditional enemy, the Ethiopians. (Norris in Jayyusi 1996: xiii–xiv)

The Himyarite Sayf became an emblem of racial difference in Africa centuries before the arrival of the French. Celebrated by the (real) Sayfawa dynasty of Kanem-Bornu, he is a natural source for the (literary) black, "Jewish-yet-Muslim" Saifs of Nakem. Ouologuem could have easily learned of this heroic figure from Yves Urvoy's *Histoire de l'empire du Bornou* (History of the Bornu Empire) (1949).

With all of this context in mind, we can finally appreciate the depth and breadth of Ouologuem's critique of racial thinking, both via his vision of ages-long, shape-shifting iterations of white supremacism and in his antipathy toward Negritude's celebration of blackness. Negritude, Ouologuem argues, is hypocritical because it conveniently effaces centuries of Africans trying to claim "white" origins in order to exert political advantage over their "black" neighbors, that is, fellow Africans. This argument is at the heart of the biting satire to which Negritude and its forbear Frobenius are subjected in the *Devoir*. The novel mocks its daft character "Shrobenius" as an

> écrevisse humaine frappée de la manie tâtonnante de vouloir ressusciter, sous couleur d'autonomie culturelle, un univers africain qui ne correspondait à plus rien de vivant. (Ouologuem 1968: 102)

> human crawfish who was possessed by the desire to resuscitate an African universe that no longer corresponded to anything that actually existed, all in the name of cultural autonomy. (Ouologuem 2008: 104)

This acid humor actually makes a profoundly Fanonian point: Fanon, in the epigraph to this chapter, laments that the descendants of medieval Songhai are now "undernourished" and "illiterate" like the rest of the wretched of the earth. What Fanon calls their "once mighty . . . civilization" "no longer correspond[s] to anything that actually exist[s]." But Ouologuem goes farther: Frobenius and Negritude's desperate mania for resuscitating African epics and empires does not just represent a desire to combat, or escape, the misery of the postcolony; it is wishful thinking altogether. The movement to celebrate African "cultural autonomy" is nullified, for Ouologuem, in the light of centuries' worth of African emperors, nobles, and peoples claiming nonblack origins in order to prove themselves superior to blacks. He reasons: if Sayf ben Dhi Yazan is the stuff of the marvelous African imaginary—a hero-ancestor, a peer of Sunjata and Samori—then that imaginary is grotesquely racist. If the African marvelous is what is to be celebrated by "le romantisme nègre" or "black romantics," then what is really being celebrated is an Africa where people spanning the whole range of light and dark skin colors—not just the Sayfawa and their descendents, but innumerable branches of Berbers and Fulbe—have, for centuries, held on to legends of Semitic, Himyarite, or otherwise "white" origins in order to prove religious legitimacy and perpetuate slavery.[14]

The *Devoir* makes this point totally explicit in its account of a meeting of Saif ibn Isaac al Heit's notables to plot against the French. The scene is dated 1902:

> Et voici que le froid envahit les cœurs:
> Car soudain l'on vit s'avancer à pas tricotants El Hadj Ali Gakoré, quinquagénaire

idéaliste, ramassé sur lui-même tel un vautour en sommeil. . . . "S'il est vrai, ergote-t-il d'une voix dialecticienne, s'il est vrai que le peuple de Cham dont parlent les Ecritures est le peuple maudit, s'il est vrai que nous sommes partie de ce peuple nègre et juif, descendant de la reine de Saba, comment donc expliquez-vous que nous puissions lutter contre l'homme blanc?" (Ouologuem 1968: 59)

A cold dread filled the hearts of all:

> For suddenly, they saw that al Hajj Ali Gakore, a well-known idealist of advanced years, had now arisen from his seat, ambling before the Saif like a drowsy vulture. . . ."If it is indeed true," he argued with the voice of a dialectician, "that the children of Ham, of whom the Scriptures speak, labor under a curse, and if it is true that we are indeed the descendants of Black and Jewish peoples, born in the lineage of the Queen of Sheba, why then should we revolt against the white man?" (Ouologuem 2008: 56)

Gakore's question reveals the fundamental contradiction in African resistance to the racist premises of European colonialism. As we have seen, the Saif dynasty's belief that it constitutes a mixed black-Jewish race suggests that the denigration of blackness is embedded in some African genealogies themselves. In this passage, Gakore's evocation of the Queen of Sheba only serves to reconfirm the connection of West African racial hierarchy to a Middle Eastern, and specifically Jewish, lineage, through this famous figure's connection to King Solomon.[15] Through Gakore, Ouologuem puts his finger on what he sees as hypocrisy at the heart of anticolonial thought. The message is clear: black anticolonial resistance is impossible as long as African peoples carry traces of white supremacy in their own religiously and ethnically inherited ideologies and collective memories.

This argument has been, unsurprisingly, controversial. Completely aside from the plagiarism issue that obsessed the worlds of publishing and academia, Ouologuem's text sabotaged African attempts to turn to Islam, or precolonial glory, as a source for authentic identity. In the *Devoir*, Jewishness functions simultaneously as a metonymic substitute for Islam, with its historical institutionalization of Semitic Arab origins as superior to black ones, and for Delafosse's theory of Judeo-Syrian migrations, which canonized the cliché of Semitic/Hamitic difference in French colonial historiography. Indeed, Ouologuem's Afro-Jews could further be read as a metonymy for West African ideologies of nobility and caste, with their system of innately hierarchical statuses, some of which are founded on claims to racial difference among members of a single ethnic group.[16] The most inflammatory object of this criticism is Islam itself: as Wole Soyinka writes, "a sanguinary account of the principal rival to the Christian mission in Africa cannot be anything but provocative. Ouologuem pronounces the Muslim incursion into black Africa to be corrupt, vicious, decadent, elitist and insensitive" (1999: 22). This denunciation of West African Islam's racial baggage ridicules, and undermines, a whole series of African and African-American attempts to rescue precolonial genius from colonial stereotype. "Shrobeniusology" includes not just the sentimental romanticism of Frobenius and his acolyte Senghor, but Cheikh Hamidou Kane's "transcendentalist apologia for Islamic spirituality," as well as Malcolm X's celebration of Islam as authentically African and antiracist, in opposition to the Christianity of white slavers (Soyinka 1999: 19). In effect, Ouologuem's diatribe may seem, to some readers, to make resistance to colonialism, or to racism, look altogether futile.

Ouologuem and Intellectual History

The central thrust of Ouologuem's contention, including its potentially negative implications for black resistance, was clear from the moment of the novel's publication. What I have tried to do here is to shed new light on the author's sources in order to elucidate the sweeping breadth of his critique. This critique is not limited to the history of Islamization, or to Fula origins, or to chronicles of precolonial empires, or to traditions of precolonial heroes, or to European colonial stereotype, but encompasses all of these, and likely more. Still less are the novel's concerns limited to a single geographical area or historical period: rather, the text lays out a complex network of allusions that leads the close reader from the classic empires of the bend of the Niger River and Lake Chad north and east toward legendary ancestral homelands in the Middle East. Finally, I have sought to reframe this critique in the light of contemporary research on Islamic racial ideas in West Africa as well as francophone intellectual history from the same area. This chapter has followed threads of tragedy and cynicism that run through depictions of anticolonial heroism—in counterpoint to Fanon—from the critics of Sékou Touré to the defenders of Samori and the theater of Cheikh Aliou Ndao. Seen in this light, Ouologuem's *Devoir* seems to give voice, however uniquely and forcefully, to an awareness of the tragic limits of anticolonial heroism that was already quite well established among other twentieth-century writers.

What, then, is the *Devoir*'s place in West African letters? Ralph Austen's dismissal of the novel as "heartlessly satirizing the past" does not do it justice (1999b: 84). Soyinka, somewhat more productively, sees it as a ground-clearing, if ultimately insufficient, call for new explorations of the precolonial past:

> At the least such a work functions as a wide swab in the deck-cleaning operation
> for the commencement of racial retrieval. The thoroughness of its approach—total
> and uncompromising rejection—can only lead to the question already posed: what
> was the authentic genius of the African world before the destructive alien intrusion?
> And the question can today be confidently asked, backed as it is by findings from
> the labor of ethno-scientists.... A social condition in which Semites (though black
> and pre-Islamic) are overlords and negro-Africans the slaves still leaves the basic
> curiosity about black historic reality unsatisfied. (1999: 22)

Soyinka is right that the *Devoir* does not offer much to the reader searching for the "authentic genius of the African world." It clearly harbors no such ideals. However, the "labor of ethno-scientists" has shown that there is something more to the *Devoir* than a cynical rejection of precolonial heritage. Such historical research has demonstrated that ideas about Semitic superiority did permeate religious treatises and dynastic genealogies, including epic ones, from the region before the advent of European colonialism. These racialized religious hierarchies were inextricably tied to the slave trade, for they made claims about which Africans were enslaveable by Muslims and which were not. Why should Ouologuem, writing during the "suns of independence," not have criticized this massive historical complex as hypocritical?

In fact, Ouologuem is not alone in this skepticism. Since the *Devoir*'s publication, a number of scholars have lamented the classism and violence underpinning West African epic, including its connection to slavery. Boubacar Barry, the historian of Senegambia, singles out the narrative of *Samba Gelajo Jegi*—Equilbecq's "half-black Iliad"—as emblematic. He argues that its constellation of heroic traits—"delight in risk-taking," "dauntless courage," and "larger-than-life exploits"—really ought to be read as a chilling glorification of slave-raiding violence (Barry 1998: 89–90). Samba, the Deniyanke ruler, was one of the "leading stars in [the] firmament" of eighteenth-century *ceddo* warlords whose "organized, massive manhunts" generated a self-perpetuating "reign of violence" across Senegambia (1998: 81). For Barry, the heroic imperative to prefer death to shame, associated with noble rank and sung in epic, emanates from a time of generalized violence, when aristocrats raided their own populations to feed the inhuman trade in human bodies. Although *Samba* "is still chanted with marvelous grace in the Futa Toro," Barry writes, "sadly, these days the epic of Samba Gelaajo Jeegi is recalled with no awareness of its real historical context. That context was dominated by the violent slave trade, which was the real reason behind the emergence of this type of warlord, steeped in the *ceddo* ethos" (1998: 90). At its core, *Samba* is "a celebration of the macabre," of "the virile themes of death and violence" (1998: 90). The eminent historian's critique adheres, with uncanny closeness, to the so-called heartless satire that Ouologuem is variously accused of having fabricated or plagiarized.

The Malian scholar Shaka Bagayogo also unmasks epic heroism as depending on slavery. As though in response to Fanon's directive to anchor national culture in precolonial heroes, Bagayogo cautions against elevating

> au rang de culture nationale la geste des guerriers pillards et esclavagistes qui ont dominé pendant des siècles le Soudan. Cette geste, extraite de son contexte, n'est nullement présentée comme l'expression d'une oppression passée, mais comme un des fondements culturels de l'affirmation de l'identité nationale. (1987: 107)

> to the rank of national culture the gest of pillaging and slave-mongering warriors who dominated the Sudan for centuries. This gest, removed from its context, is never presented as the expression of a past oppression, but as one of the cultural foundations for the affirmation of national identity. (my translation)

Finally, Claude Meillassoux, author of the seminal *Anthropology of Slavery*, draws the logical Marxist conclusion from these findings:

> Dans la lutte maintenant séculaire que mènent les Africains pour leur libération, la tentation est grande de se tourner vers la geste épique pour y reconnaître les champions de cette croisade. ... Cette démarche me paraît fausse et dangereuse, car si le héros soudanien est fondamentalement distinct du héros chrétien, comme lui, cependant, il est l'expression non pas du peuple mais de la classe ou d'une fraction de la classe au pouvoir. Il ne peut être l'inspirateur d'une libération radicale. (in Meillassoux and Sylla 1978: 371–72)

In the now age-long struggle that Africans have led for their liberation, there is a great temptation to turn toward the epic gest in order to recognize the champions of this crusade.... This approach seems false and dangerous to me, for if the Sudanese hero is fundamentally different from the Christian one, nevertheless, like him, he is the expression not of the people but of the class in power, or a fraction of the class in power. He cannot be the inspiration of radical liberation. (my translation)

These arguments make it clear that Ouologuem was not a lone voice in the desert. I would even suggest that they make visible the possibility for liberation that so many readers have missed in his work. At the end of the day, however bitter it may taste, the *Devoir* might be thought of as a kind of unpleasant but potent medicine. Rather than an exercise in Afropessimism, it is like a pill, or shock treatment, whose intended effect is to purge the West African mind of centuries of racist thinking. It leads us to understand that African liberation cannot be based on the claims to race-, class-, and caste-based difference that were so foundational to precolonial dynasties and their vested interests in perpetuating slavery—certainly via the Atlantic trade of the fifteenth to nineteenth centuries, as Barry emphasizes, but also via the trans-Saharan trade that preceded it. Liberation may be outside the reach of the *Devoir*'s characters, but if it is to arise, it must originate among the despised masses: the blacks with no claim to whiteness, the non-Muslims, the casted subjects, the slaves. This *négraille* must cast off the *négritude* imposed on it by self-serving others and replace it with the universal recognition of common humanity.

Ouologuem's impassioned cry of outrage is not the last word on West African traditions. We should see it, with Soyinka, as a "deck-cleaning operation." More directly and thoroughly than any other twentieth-century text, the *Devoir de violence* attacks the racialization of West African epic heritage that had begun under the influence of Islam and continued under French colonialism. This book will investigate other, more positive intellectual approaches to this heritage. While its association with noble status and racial difference will not disappear entirely, my overarching argument is that other West African writers turn away from hierarchies of race and status in order to locate a liberating potential in the critical reflexivity of epic discourse, that is, its ability to challenge, rather than authorize, the status quo by reflecting critically on the crises of the present.

Epic and Thought

Against Bakhtin

African Misadventures of "Epic and Novel"

[Bakhtin's] vision of the epic world . . . adds up to an oppressive anthropological interpretation of preliterate culture as Oriental despotism.

—Christopher Miller, *Theories of Africans*

In spite of newer research, many literary critics continue to associate heroic narrative with a flat, bygone era of premodernity. This is especially true in the case of African texts and traditions. Scholarship on written literature still relies on the vision of epic constructed by theorists of the European novel, notably the hugely influential Mikhail Bakhtin, whose classic essay "Epic and Novel," first written in Russian in 1941, claims that

tradition isolates the world of the epic from personal experience, from any new insights, from any personal initiative in understanding and interpreting, from new points of view and evaluations. . . . Thanks to this epic distance, which excludes any possibility of activity and change, the epic world achieves a radical degree of completedness not only in its content but in its meaning and its values as well. The epic world is constructed in the zone of an absolute distanced image, beyond the sphere of possible contact with the developing, incomplete and therefore re-thinking and re-evaluating present. (2002: 17)

Bakhtin's epic world is untouchable by the present and functions only as an unreachable model of stable values and meaning that people in the present can gaze upon with awe; any critical reflexivity or reinterpretation of this world must come from outside it—from a "modern" perspective, embodied in the *always* rethinking and reevaluating genre of the novel.

Although Bakhtin had nothing to say about African material, or living epic discourse, literary scholars have frequently applied his model to African contexts. Bakhtin, along with other classic theorists of the "birth of the novel" in the European context, has historically wielded outsized influence in literary approaches to African texts.[1] In an exemplary manner, Amadou Koné's study of African epic and novel seems to transpose "Epic and Novel" into Africa:

> En effet, la société que nous avons appelée traditionnelle et qui est, dans sa forme la plus pure, antérieure à la Traite des esclaves, est une société "close" dominée par la collectivité et dont l'effort le plus important consiste à sauvegarder la cohérence du groupe. Dans cette société, les questions essentielles sont résolues d'avance par une métaphysique exprimée dans les mythes auxquels l'on croit fermement.... Ce héros ne présente pas une grande densité psychologique. Dans ce monde "clos et parfait," la question fondamentale n'est pas de savoir s'il faut "être ou ne pas être" mais plutôt comment être le plus en conformité avec les valeurs considérées comme les meilleures. Le héros ne porte en lui aucun abîme. (Koné 1985: 137)

> Indeed, the society that I have called traditional and that, in its purest form, dates from before the slave trade, is a "closed" society dominated by the collectivity and whose most important effort consists in safeguarding the coherency of the group. In such a society, the essential questions are resolved in advance by a metaphysics expressed in myths that are firmly believed. . . . This hero does not have much psychological density. In this "closed and perfect" world, the fundamental question is not whether "to be or not to be" but rather how best to conform to the values considered best. The hero bears no abyss within himself. (my translation)

Koné traces the persistence of such traditional values in certain historical African novels, but sees a progression away from such epic-inflected tropes toward the ever-increasing alienation of the modern hero, whose psychological density is born of his individualism. Koné makes no room for epic as a living, multilayered, or changing genre. Its relation to the novel is essentially one of slow death and replacement. Koné is hardly alone in this vision. His "closed and perfect" traditional world, along with the Bakhtinian absolute past from which it is derived, is emblematic of how African literature is, all too often, read and taught.

In spite of the fact that the Bakhtinian vision has been replicated so many times by scholars working on West Africa, his equation of epic and the absolute ought to be an easy target from an Africanist perspective. For one, he relied uniquely on the canonized, written Homeric poems as models. And it is clear that even from a European point of view, the object of study that he really cares about is the novel, against which Greek epic is contrasted to provide a foil (Sherman 1995: 184). This chapter, notwithstanding its deliberately polemical title, will apply Bakhtinian concepts—especially dialogism and heteroglossia—to the West African epic, in spite of the fact that Bakhtin cast them as the very opposite of epic character. This argument is important not only because it challenges the literary application of Bakhtin to African texts, but also because even anthropologically informed analyses of oral epic often tend to overemphasize their functions as signifiers of "collective ideology" or "worldview." Such ideological flattenings of epic performances run the risk of rehashing Bakhtin's absolutist interpretation of epic as monological. Oral epic is readily seen as a conservative force in societies that possess it, favoring a dominant model of class and gender roles, and of ethnic or religious identity.

But what happens when each performance of a genre is precisely about the crisscrossed processes of negotiation and reevaluation that must take place between the heroic models of the past and the cloudy conundrums of the present? I argue that the crucial contribution of epic narrative to West African intellectual activity is its present-ness—that is, its constant and complex engagement with the present through a critical negotiation with the past. This perspective moves away from all too frequent definitions originating in European literary studies according to which epic sings an "absolute past" or otherwise nostalgic identity of wholeness that has been lost to the alienation of modernity. The complexity of West African heroic narrative itself, as many scholarly analyses have shown, belies such a facile opposition. After reviewing literary and anthropological approaches to the relationship between epic and ideology, I will turn to some important examples of what I call ideological thickness in historical epic discourse: the theme of the androgynous woman warrior that runs throughout several narratives from across the region; ambivalence toward Islam in the unique Fulfulde narrative *Bubu Ardo*; the intertwinement of praise and criticism of national politicians in epic discourse; and, finally, the self-reflexivity of one especially well-known Maninka bard, Wa Kamissoko, whose idiosyncratic performances scholars have found particularly perplexing. These examples of ideological thickness demonstrate the possibility of critical reflexivity in epic discourse, setting the groundwork for the overarching goal of this chapter, which is to offer an explicit reevaluation of the relationship between oral traditional discourse and written literature—epic and novel—in the West African context. Setting aside literary theories that have imagined, for too long, an abyss between these genres, epic and novel should be seen as aligned. Both are capable of expressing critical perspectives on the ideological structures in which they are embedded.

Genre and Ideology

When we remember a certain strain of anthropology's focus on group identity in the study of oral literary production, it becomes easy to understand why the African epic heritage is portrayed in literary scholarship as one-dimensional, conservative, or monological, rehearsing the "worldview" approach that Isidore Okpewho had decried (1979: 1–2). For Christiane Seydou,

> Anyone who has witnessed a performance of the African epic cannot remain insensitive to either the communal character or to the specific features of this cultural manifestation: its engaging vitality, and its capacity to unite an audience through intense excitement. To a great extent, this excitement or exaltation is created by the specific manner of performing recognized ideological themes and elements of the group's collective knowledge. (1983: 53)

Seydou emphasizes here and throughout her work how epic discourse is meant to interpellate the listener into a preexisting ideology of belonging, through its key trait of exaltation or intense excitement. In a similar vein, Mamoussé Diagne labels this function of epic as an "idéo-moteur" (ideo-motor), that is, a provocation to celebrate group identity (2005: 291). While these authors are certainly right to a certain degree, their emphasis on this aspect of epic forecloses alternative

FIGURE 6. Comparing Five Definitions of African Epic

	OKPEWHO	SEYDOU	KESTELOOT AND DIENG	JOHNSON	BELCHER
Music	Usually accompanied by music	Must be tied to a specific musical instrument	Rhythm marked by cadence and pause; music not always necessary	Poetic meter determined by music	Most often has musical accompaniment; poetic meter is closely tied to music
Performance	Narrated or sung by a bard, with or without a group of accompanists		Specialized performers; performance happens in specific contexts; epic may be written	Ritualized context	Specialized performer; performance is public (as opposed to narratives told in private)
Narrative	Applies criteria from Homeric scholarship to African context	Plot motivated by the transgressions of an exceptional hero	Long narrativity	Great length; narrative composed of themes and episodes; multigeneric	Extended narrative, distinct from panegyric
Subject Matter	Superhuman deeds in extranormal context; significance to the development of a people		Human war or supernatural struggle. May have historical or mythological emphases	Heroic and legendary content; specifically African heroic patterns	Subject can be historical, mythical, or "historicized myth"; notion of heroism is questionable
Tone/Style	Performance is shaped by individual artistry of the bard	Paroxysm and intense emotion	Elevated tone	3 poetic modes (narrative, song, praise-proverb)	Different narrative traditions can be more or less serious
Function	"Basic play interest of the artist"; entertainment; not blind expression of collective ideologies and deep structures	Ideology of identity: listeners are excited to belong to the group	Epic "character" signaled in other criteria is more important than ideological function of cementing identity	"Multi-functional" ideology of identity; *Sunjata* models relations between social groups and symbolizes Mande nationhood	Different narrative traditions can weight entertainment value and collective ideology differently

Sources: Okpewho (1979), drawing on Lord (1960), Parry (1971), and Nagler (1974); Seydou (1983 and 1988); Kesteloot and Dieng (1997: 29–49); Johnson (1980: 312–21; 1999; and 2003: 30–57); Belcher (1999a: xi–xxii and 186–92). Johnson's criteria are drawn exclusively from *Sunjata* (which he spells *Son–Jara*) but aspire to have wide applicability: he states that his purpose is "to describe the characteristics of African epic as exemplified by the epic of *Son–Jara*" (2003: 30). This list is not exhaustive: Biebuyck (1976), Boyer (1982), and, no doubt, others have been excluded from this table for mere reasons of space. Regarding epic subject matter, Belcher states in his introduction that he will not use heroism as an analytical criterion because it is too culture-bound (1999a: xiv). But in his conclusion, he discusses relationships between African heroic models and worldwide heroic patterns (189–90).

approaches, especially explorations of moments of ambiguity, contradiction, and self-reflexivity in a performer's narrative. The "worldview" emphasis further serves Diagne's too neat typology of civilizations of orality and civilizations of writing, which continues to serve as a widely unquestioned premise in Africanist literary criticism: the very notion of "traditional values" that the modern African novel "subverts" is ubiquitous in scholarship. Critical or individual reflection, in this view, always seems to belong to the alienated world of modernity, not to the value system of epic, the vestige of a world from before the time when *things fell apart.*

Other scholarly definitions of African epic have expressed a range of views on ideology and identity. All of the definitions summarized in figure 6 have been particularly influential in the field. There is, of course, a great deal of overlap in these definitions, but we can also highlight some trends that make them distinct. Belcher is probably the most hesitant to generalize of all the scholars in the figure, insisting on the specificity of individual narrative traditions and arguing that any understanding of "the African epic" must necessarily remain loose. Whereas Seydou gives pride of place to ideology of identity, Okpewho does just the opposite, criticizing "worldview" approaches to epic studies in favor of the creativity of each individual performer. Johnson's extremely thorough description of the structure of *Sunjata* asserts that this epic, which permeates Mande cultural life, reflects certain aspects of group identity, yet cannot be read as straightforward ethnographic information since "some of the narrative is undoubtedly employed only for literary purposes" (2003: 51–52). Okpewho engages with Homeric and other European material to prove that African epics really are epics; other scholars resist this temptation entirely, relying only on African data. Kesteloot and Dieng reject Seydou's emphasis on collective ideology because, they point out, it is impossible to know everything about a group's ideology, especially when an oral text represents times gone by (1997: 34–35). Belcher is also critical of this tendency:

> Further, especially in Francophone scholarship, there is a sense that the performer or informant is an essentially passive vehicle for a communal burden of historical knowledge. Personal control of the information is thus secondary to the larger, collective charge, although the traditionalist, as a possessor of knowledge, is still imbued with some reverence. An American folklorist might observe that such a conception was exploded some generations ago; it is impossible to separate the transmitter from the knowledge. (1999a: xx)

Belcher goes on to qualify this objection on the grounds that "faith in the content of historical oral tradition has remained a cornerstone of modern national consciousness throughout Francophone West Africa and beyond." And yet, his objection reminds us that any attempt to extract a coherent, consistent ideology of identity out of African epic discourse is subject to problematization. The utterances of individual performers necessarily have a complex, dialogical relationship to collectively held ideas. Pascal Boyer's theorization of African epic as a subgenre of tradition—itself a genre of discourse with its own rules and constraints, not a set of beliefs or collective knowledge—follows this line of thought by arguing that every performance adds something to the shared body of collective knowledge, rather than merely expressing or repeating it (1982: 24 and 1984: 234).

This diversity of thought in African oral tradition studies offers a wealth of alternatives to Bakhtin's absolutist vision of epic. At the level of world literature studies, some comparatists have also moved away from Bakhtin's binary, redrawing the line between epic and novel in the context of contemporary Western culture. For Franco Moretti and Wai Chee Dimock, modernity ponders the lost sense of totality that the hero embodies, or endlessly rewrites the great genre of Eurasian antiquity.[2] Both critics' fascination with the updating of ancient epics—particularly *Gilgamesh* in Dimock's case—whose concerns continue to thrive and circulate globally today is a welcome relief from the hegemony of the Bakhtinian model in the critical landscape. And yet, for all their big-picture scope, neither critic's theories of the genre address living epic traditions, or African material, at all. Moretti's notion of the modern epic depends on an act of reinvention that is entirely located within a Euro-modernist practice, as exemplified by James Joyce's *Ulysses*. This argument is provocative insofar as it bypasses the metanarrative of loss and alienation. So does Dimock's notion of an "epic DNA" that is constantly decomposing and regenerating through the ages (2013b: 27). And yet, both scholars' approaches ignore issues like orality, traditionality, and colonial legacy that require attention, and a different set of critical tools, in the West African context.

Indeed, we need not just to bypass the Bakhtinian separation of epic and modern, but to remember how central it was to Euro-modernity's conception of itself:

> One of the ways that modernity legitimizes itself is by emphasizing discontinuity and creating myths of an absolute past. The same obsession has driven efforts to establish a mechanical equivalence between the epic and orality in "primitive"

cultures, an equivalence that has been downplayed or rejected in the latest anthropological studies. (Fusillo 2006: 39–40)

The issue at stake in equating epic with the nonmodern—whether we call it an absolute past, an ancient heritage fixed by tradition, or a pillar of civilizations of orality—is that of time. The nonmodern subject is either trapped in the present and has no history, or else is trapped in the past and has not yet caught up to the present of modernity. This kind of claim represents a literary incarnation of what Johannes Fabian calls the "denial of coevalness" in anthropological discourse (1983 and 1991): the relegation of the Other to another regime of time. My argument is that West African epic discourse, contrary to the colonial discourses that were articulated around it, interacts with, represents, and helps produce the present. It seeks both to define the present in terms of the past and to reinterpret the past in light of the present—all while commenting on political and social realities like religion, gender, and the nation-state.

Theoretical work in folklore studies and linguistic anthropology in the last few decades has opposed both of the above negations, namely the denials of critical potential and of coevalness in oral performance genres. Studies now emphasize just the opposite: that performances contain many tools for reflecting critically on a community's history and official discourses while remaking its social relations, and that the student of Africa should allow the "intersubjective time" of communication and fieldwork to penetrate her or his scholarship.[3] Karin Barber and Paolo de Moraes Farias have called for a greater attention to the side of oral texts that is "evasive and ambiguous[,] their capacity not only to take on radically different significances from one historical moment to the next, but also to accommodate at the same moment incompatible significances, with an effect of dynamic ambiguity" (1989: 1). If oral narratives are able to provoke different interpretations both diachronically and within a single utterance, it is because they reflect both changing times and the complexity of any given moment. That is, they are always in a self-reflexive dialogue with the present. This conclusion is the result of an increasingly clear awareness among scholars that any traditional repertoire must constantly renew itself in order to remain pertinent in light of present concerns and contexts (Vansina 1965: 78). Pragmatics- and performance-based approaches in linguistic anthropology have further theorized this phenomenon by describing the multiple variables that shape meaning in a single performance event (Bauman and Briggs 1990). This stress on specificity complicates any simple view of "group ideology" or "worldview," since the interactions between variables, and between participants in the event, dynamize the social creation of meaning and the production of social relations, rather than merely constituting a one-way transmission of message from speaker to listener.

This increased complexity has been bolstered by a redefinition of what traditional discourse is. Instead of an ensemble of knowledge or practices that bears objective transmission from past generations, we now tend to see tradition as an interpretive designation that is always applied in the present (Handler and Linnekin 1984). The interpretive act of *traditionalization* takes place in a historical present and is inevitably tied to strategic goals; it is "seen less as an inherent quality of old and persistent items or genres passed on from generation to generation, and more as a symbolic construction by which people in the present establish connections with a meaningful past and endow particular cultural forms with value and authority" (Bauman 1992: 128). Such a focus on construct rather than essence has opened up a wide field of study in the area of tradition studies. Like modernity, tradition is a constructed category, subject to differing meanings attributed to it by different social actors. An object is "traditional" not so much because it comes from the ancestors, but because people *say* it comes from the ancestors. Paradoxically, these kinds of analyses are heavily indebted to Bakhtin, who emphasizes the dialogism of all discourses in society, and for whom the novel constitutes a laboratory par excellence for studying this reality at work.[4] Studies of verbal performance draw Bakhtinian dialogism away from the novel and into the arena of oral genres, thus including living traditions of epic or heroic narrative, which Bakhtin himself had not considered in "Epic and Novel."

The consequence of these various areas of anthropological and sociolinguistic inquiry—performance studies, traditionalization, and dialogism—is that specific performances of epic narrative can be studied in all their complexity, that is, as sites where a diversity of social discourses and interests intersect, rather than as transparent articulations of a group's ideology. While a sense of the epic genre's unifying function of celebrating identity and expressing social norms has not been lost, the importance of this has been relativized by a greater awareness of all the other factors shaping meaning in a performance. Rather than expressing only a monological worldview or a single official discourse, these messages are traversed by a multitude of other concerns.

Transgender Warriors and Upside-Down Heroes

Even for Christiane Seydou, there is a certain incongruity within heroic narrative. While she always maintains her underlying view that African epic enforces a normative ideology of identity, she suggests that it must represent these norms in terms of exceptions that prove the rule. Epic heroes are

> excessive, outside of the norms, and essentially inimitable (without which they would undoubtedly lose their epic stature). It is evident that epic does not present model characters or behavior patterns to emulate, nor does it illustrate the exemplary and pedagogical aspects of the tale. Rather, the epic seeks to inspire an awakening of intense consciousness and sustained will as much by the content of the text as through mediums for expressing it. (1983: 63)

Significantly, therefore, epic narrative creates a space where social norms do not apply, where thought can happen outside of them, where contradiction and ambiguity are possible. This view echoes David Conrad's analysis of potentially contradictory traditional utterances in his study of gender in Mande epic. Discussing the recurring figures of the femme fatale and the heroine, he explains,

> The men whom these women serve and the jeliw [griots] who tell the story (it is basically all the same one) express their own attitudes toward the femme fatale through variations of such sentiments as "never trust any woman," "all heroes who perish, do so as victims of woman's treachery," and "if you see men fighting it is women who make us fight."
>
> Proverbs reflecting female marginalization on the one hand and epic discourse exalting heroines on the other demonstrate the ambiguous position of women in Mande society. . . . On the positive side [of this ambiguity] are episodes of epic discourse containing implicit acknowledgement that females, however dangerous they may be, lay the foundation of male success. (Conrad 1999: 193)

Conflicting views on gender roles and the importance of women can be encapsulated within traditional speech, and even within individual performances. For Conrad, the griots' and heroes' stated mistrust of women are one and the same, for their use of misogynistic proverbs is conflated into a single male discourse shared by performer and character—a discourse that is contradicted by figures of women who help deliver victory to male heroes, or take on warlike heroic traits themselves in a given episode. Any attempt to analyze such a performance must take into account both of these narrative components, one of which asserts male superiority and admonishes against female malice, while the other mitigates these claims. This leads us to a paradox: epic presents itself as both imposing and resisting normative readings, both (centripetally) enforcing social norms and (centrifugally) inviting us to question or reinterpret them. This double potential, at the same time pragmatic and reflexive, takes form concretely in the fact that a performance can reflect or challenge the concerns of those participating in it.

Indeed, the motif of transgender warriors, which recurs in heroic narratives both from within and outside Mande cultural areas, can be revealing here. Conrad gives an example from a *Samori* variant, where "One-Breasted Denba" organizes a vengeful battle against the hero precisely because he did not trust her. She not only bares the formidable occult power of the female sexual organ, but demands to wear her brother's trousers, thus appropriating male power as well; her one-breastedness serves to underline her androgynous might (1999: 209–10). In one variant of the Fulfulde epic of *Bubu Ardo*, the hero's wife Wela-Takaade fights to the death with a jinn who has blinded her husband (Dieng et al. 2004: 78–79). In the Wolof heroic legend of the "Tuesday of Nder," the women of the Walo kingdom's capital village ride into battle against the Moors of Trarza, dressed as men, because their husbands are away. And yet, all of these same narratives of heroines doing battle like men also contain scenes of misogynistic disdain or worse: in *Samori*, innocent women are disemboweled and untrustworthy ones beheaded; Bubu Ardo both is manipulated by a deceitful old lady and sends one to betray his enemies; and the Moors, realizing the threat of a humiliating emasculation at the hands of women, finally rally to defeat the heroines of Nder, who nobly commit suicide to avoid capture.[5] These examples demonstrate the clash between the social norm of male domination and the female capacity to transgress it. In another evocative episode, Sunjata's mother Sogolon uses sorcery to resist the sexual intercourse necessary for the hero to be conceived, using, in some versions, "a variety of defensive weapons including lion-like claws, porcupine-quill pubic hair, and spikes from her breasts"; but she is eventually tamed, thus paving the way for the hero's birth and the reproduction of male-dominated order.[6] Female power, including the occult forces of sorcery and the body, is immense and dangerous, capable of violently checking or appropriating male power and being violently checked by it.

Bubu Ardo is especially fraught ideologically. Epic narratives about this hero celebrate his refusal to submit to Islam—indeed, his and others' blasphemous mockery of the religion—as an expression of political resistance to the nineteenth-century theocratic state known as the Dina, founded by Amadu Lobbo (also referred to as Seku Amadu) at Hamdallahi in Masina in 1818. In one version, Bubu, under pressure from the Dina to convert, insults the Koran, declaring that a book's place is on a shelf, not in the law (Seydou 2010: 164–65). His griot encourages him to spurn ablutions and latrines, and to refrain from banging his head on the ground like a demented person, in comedic reference to the rituals of Muslim prayer; Bubu himself retorts, elsewhere, that to bow toward the east in prayer would be to expose his rear end to the winds of the west. Perhaps most poignantly, in a recurring episode, Bubu asserts his intention never to convert, or to apostatize after having superficially converted, upon seeing the repulsive sight of a woman being flogged for adultery.[7] His defiance is rooted in a desire for freedom: he refuses to do anything that is imposed upon him by an outside power (Seydou 2010: 160–61). However, his thrilling rebelliousness eventually ends in defeat. Usually with the help of intervention from a jinn, Bubu is killed by the Dina's men; and, in two published variants, his head is brought back to Amadu Lobbo, who expresses remorse at his death and pardons him.[8] This surprisingly frank heroization of resistance to Islam continues to be performed in the profoundly Muslim West African region, from Mauritania to Niger (Seydou 2010: 11). Seydou, who collected and translated six narratives about this hero from five different performers, interprets Bubu's defiant actions as incarnating the *pulaaku*, an idealized system of values specific to the Fulbe, even though ordinary people listening to his feats today could never be expected to imitate his conduct. And yet, even this cohesive interpretation of *Bubu Ardo* must account for the obvious ideological tension at the heart of this narrative: the epic

autorise de la sorte l'apologie d'un héros qui va au plus haut point à l'encontre des normes d'une société à laquelle il sert pourtant de référence culturelle éminente; et la conscience de cette contradiction n'est pas sans ajouter à l'habituelle admiration provoquée par ce genre de récits, ce plaisir ambigu que savoure l'auditoire peul à l'écoute des insolentes provocations de Boûbou Ardo Galo. (Seydou 2010: 19)

thus authorizes the apology of a hero who contradicts, to the highest possible degree, the norms of a society for which he nevertheless serves as an eminent cultural reference; and the awareness of this contradiction adds to the habitual admiration provoked by this kind of narrative, the ambiguous pleasure that the

Fula audience savors while listening to the insolent provocations of Bubu Ardo Galo. (my translation)

What exactly is the nature of the "ambiguous pleasure" triggered by this narrative in a Muslim audience? For Seydou, it is rooted in the hero's exceptional and inimitable attachment to the traditional values of the *pulaaku*, in spite of their clear opposition to the tenets of Islam, the nearly universal religion of the region today. But Bassirou Dieng sees a certain ambiguity in the narrative itself: "La conscience narrative reste indécise sur le héros à glorifier" (The narrative consciousness remains undecided as to which hero to glorify) (in Dieng et al. 2004: 6). For him, the epic does not only glorify the *pulaaku*; it also celebrates Islam's triumph over it.

As though to further demonstrate this hesitation on which hero to glorify, the second of Seydou's six narratives makes Bubu Ardo the *enemy*, a despotic and arbitrary ruler who is flouted and upstaged by a person of slave status named Wordu Goro (Seydou 2010: 99–130). This slave transgresses the hierarchy of social statuses first by defying Bubu—taking one of his slaves as a bride while refusing to pay the dowry—then by appropriating the personal melody or *devise* reserved for Bubu and played by his griot (2010: 112–13). Bubu's wife even sings Wordu Goro's praises, as though she were a griot and he a noble, and gives him names reserved for princes (2010: 110–11). At the end of this episode, Wordu Goro dies at the hands of Bubu's men, having been tricked by an old woman indebted to his hospitality; his wife commits suicide in despair; and his house is pillaged and abandoned. Whereas Bubu himself is the heroic resister who meets a glorious death in most narratives, here that role is played by a captive, the lowest rung on the hierarchy of statuses. This reversal, which humiliates a noble and a known epic hero by having an inferior usurp his privileges and glory, is striking. While Wordu Goro can still be read as incarnating the heroic exceptionalism encoded in the *pulaaku*, what does this upside-down narrative structure say about the hierarchy of statuses that makes those codes possible?

Rather than forcing this rather complex narrative cycle into the expression of a single identity—whose contents are, at any rate, self-contradictory—it can be helpful to focus on its tensions and fault lines. I would argue, with Dieng, that— even setting aside the outlier story of Wordu Goro—the primary point of this epic is not just to celebrate the *pulaaku*, but also to commemorate and narrativize the ideological and political conflicts that shook the Fulbe, the Masina, and indeed much of West Africa in the eighteenth and nineteenth centuries, as waves of

Islamization swept over the region. *Bubu* embodies the clash of ideas whose explosive confrontation is only superficially smoothed over by the eponymous hero's death and pardoning. At the end of the cycle, each ideological system seems to highlight the other's ambiguities: Islam is associated with dishonor because it implies submission, while the *pulaaku*, which is supposed to be at the heart of Fula identity, must be bracketed into a performance genre outside of which it would threaten the Muslim order that reigns today. In appropriating Bubu's heroism after his death into the Islamic idiom of "pardon," "blessing," and "paradise," the epic signals the advent of a hybrid, profoundly heteroglossic society that remembers its roots both in Amadu Lobbo's theocracy and in resistance to it.[9] As such, multiple layers of conflicting values and power/authority structures sit uneasily together in a single text, each system inviting criticism of the other. This ideological complexity illustrates the multidimensionality of epic and opens up a space for questioning and reframing ideological norms within this supposedly monological genre. For, at its heart, *Bubu Ardo* not only tries to transform the hero's military defeat into glorious renown, or to legitimate Amadu Lobbo's moment of triumph, but also poses a question that would become crucial across nineteenth-century West Africa: To what extent must the new Muslim expansionism compromise, or coexist, with the non-Muslim cultural forms and practices that preceded it?

The Nation-State Revisited

These layers of ideological complexity in the West African epic are generated by forces that influence a performance's production of meaning in different ways. These forces are exercised not only at the level of content, as in the examples above, but also in the way epic, or other traditional genres, are deployed for political purposes: many scholars have remarked that oral tradition serves a praise function that can be directed toward anyone the performer wishes to flatter.[10] As we have seen, Sékou Touré co-opted *Sunjata* and *Samori* as representations of his anticolonial struggle and genealogical legitimacy as president of Guinea. Such comparison of epic heroes to national politicians enables people to legitimize any political agenda they choose by claiming it as traditional; but, at the same time, the epic heritage also provides a standard against which politicians can be judged. This critical potential can be subtle and ambiguous, but it is there. In a way reminiscent of the dynamic in 1960s Guinea, *Sunjata* has played an important role in Mali, where the Griots praised Modibo Keita, the country's first president, as the direct descendant of Soundiata Keita, Emperor of Mali. After the coup d'etat in 1969, however, the same Griots hailed the new president, Moussa Traore, as the savior of the country, a parallel to Tira Maghan Traore, one of Soundiata's chief generals who conquered Gambia. Evidently, Griots relate every event to The Epic of Soundiata. (Manthia Diawara 1992: 157)

The work of a number of Malian intellectuals, most notably Massa Makan Diabaté, lends support to this analysis.[11] At the same time, Shaka Bagayogo complicates the role of genealogy in the case of the despotic ruler, arguing that the despot both claims a heroic lineage and places himself above family ties altogether. Through this contradictory gesture, the ruler intends to connect himself to the hero's family even as he echoes the uncertainties and exceptionality of a hero's birth, removing both from their family histories so that he may pose as the universal leader with no interests but those of the nation (1987: 94–95). Much literary effort has been expended to link the contemporary Malian state to the ancient Mali Empire, and specifically the *Sunjata* epic, thus connecting statehood upward to a heroic age and downward to still current ethnic identities.[12] Mamadou Diawara suggests that the advent of radio and television actually encourages present-day griots to put traditional knowledge at the service of the nation-state, since getting on national or international radio exponentially magnifies their audience and prestige (1996). However, the relations between the state and the griot's art are not always straightforward or free of conflict. For one, the Malian state both needs and resists the power of griots: traditionality is an "indispensable" sign of legitimacy, yet it represents "an archaic social order anathema to the modern democratic state where citizens are all equal under the law and owe allegiance only to the state itself" (Roth 2008: 52). Conversely, griots are sometimes expected to maintain their independence from politicians. In one notorious case, Bakary Soumano, who had been recognized as the "chief griot" (*jelikuntigi*) of all Mali in 1992, was removed from this function in 1998 for being perceived as too much in cahoots with the government of President Alpha Konaré; the public, feeling that griots should be beholden to their local patrons rather than to politicians on the national stage, turned against him and sided with his usurper Jeli Baba Sissoko (Roth 2008: 39–49).

Yet the collusion between presidents and griots is by no means universally rejected. It is common practice for high-level West African politicians to hire griots for public occasions; in the case of Senegal, presidents have been known to choose official, personal griots to glorify them while recounting episodes in national history in traditionalizing or epic-like terms.[13] In spite of the uneasiness that may arise in such connivance between state and tradition, it is certain that each contributes to the other: griots confer legitimacy on the state, and the state claims traditional legitimacy for itself while conferring prestige and fame on fortunate griots.

We can thus adjust Manthia Diawara's formulation of politics and tradition under Mali's first two presidents. First, there are multiple, contradictory strategies of heroizing a political figure: the president is both descended from Sunjata and beyond family descent. Second, griot opinion is not universal, for traditionalizing speech may serve critical rather than purely sycophantic ends: "les faits et gestes serviront de supports pour expliquer, justifier, voire critiquer, la vie politique contemporaine" (the feats and gests will serve to explain, justify, or even criticize, contemporary politics) (Bagayogo 1987: 106). This insight is verified at least partially when we return to Guinea, where Sékou Touré claimed to be and was hailed as a descendent of Samori. David Conrad has collected fragments of the *Samori* epic narrative that alternately praise and criticize the dictator (2008: 179–81). A look at Seydou Camara's words in a Maninka-language *Samori* fragment, which I quote below in Conrad's English translation, nevertheless demonstrates the potential for criticism of power in griot speech:

> If you don't know politics, don't start a war. . . .
> Don't lead other people's sons into battles where they will disappear.
> Sékou Touré is a descendant of Toure ni Manjan [Samori]. (Conrad 2008: 181)

The griot's criticism is left implicit, phrased as a commentary on Samori's actions at the siege of Sikasso—which he lost; the allusion to Sékou Touré's behavior is only legible because his name is inserted as a descendent of Samori, ostensibly as a praise-line, but precisely during the description of one of the hero's failures. We are left to infer that Sékou Touré has committed the same mistake as his supposed ancestor Samori at the siege of Sikasso. Scholars have reflected on this double-sidedness of praise and panegyric in other African contexts, suggesting that beyond legitimation of a ruler's authority, praise also formulates "exemplary standards of conduct" against which his rule is to be judged, as well as a means of influencing his actions.[14] Ralph Austen explains the potential for veiled reproach in such a context: "The performed praise language may even be deliberately cryptic both to display the poetic skill of the performer and to convey in a subtle way sometimes discomforting messages to an incumbent ruler" (1999b: 71). This phenomenon seems to be exactly what we observe in the speech of Seydou Camara regarding Sékou Touré.

As such, if a comparison between African and European epic forms is to be made truly pertinent, the point of contact is to be found in the politicization of this genre for a multitude of particular agendas, as David Quint has shown for European literary history (1993). Isabel DiVanna has made this argument specifically in the context of the *Song of Roland*, which was politicized in various ways during France's mid-nineteenth-century vacillations between monarchy, republic, and empire (2011). What is universal is not necessarily the existence of a worldwide epic genre per se, but the use of prestigious oral and written texts to claim traditionality for power and authority. The past is glorified through cultural forms to simultaneously bolster and distract from a political present; but its refraction through different interests and interpretations illuminates the present with different hues.

Toward a Critical Use, or Open Reading, of Epic

Thus, epic fills different political needs. In addition to uniting its audience into a common sense of belonging, it offers a space from which to represent the various shapes that belonging has taken. It can reflect the political polarizations of the past, as in *Bubu Ardo*, and connect them to those of the present, as in the uses of *Sunjata* and *Samori* in Mali and Guinea. A close reading of any particular concern—whether gender, religion, or national politics—does not generate straightforward ideological tenets about these issues, but rather a range of possible interpretations that cultural arbitrators like griots, writers, and politicians can pull in the direction of their particular preferences. In the process, social actors inevitably have different intentions and interpretations when they perform or react to an epic narrative, complicating any attempt to identify the messages embedded in it as expressions of common values or beliefs. The fundamental characteristic of oral tradition—that it must be constantly reperformed and reinterpreted in order to remain pertinent in the present—is the source of this ambiguity. We can see the innumerable orally transmitted variations of epic narratives, as well as their innumerable reinterpretations in written literature, as related applications of this principle. Among the many ideological readings that can be, or have been, ascribed to such traditions—imperialist, democratic, monarchist, for or against a given president—I have tried to highlight their ability to problematize, rather than to just solidify, political and social norms, in order to show, against the paradigms that are still called upon in literary studies, that a space for critical thought is indeed possible in the epic tradition. While an epic text or performance may always include an element of exaltation that seeks to defend and reanimate normative categories, there is ample opportunity for this process of traditionalization to be mobilized by performers and listeners, writers and readers, toward critical ends rather than just groupthink.

Andrew Apter labels this potential in oral performance as *critical agency*, defined as "a speaker's self-conscious deployment of discourse to transform the sociopolitical relations within which he or she is embedded"; such agency is always "grounded in linguistic performance and reflexivity" (2007: 12 n. 11). Apter points out that agency can be directed toward any purpose the speaker intends, whether for claiming authority, exercising power, or both, "maximizing agentive power within the cloak of legitimate authority to make the desired difference" (2007: 6). But we can expand on this notion of agency by situating it not only in the pragmatics or metapragmatics of oral performance, but also in the unending dialogical process of interpretation that takes place in society. The moment of performance itself is already inscribed in this dialogical process, since it constitutes an interpretation of a wider, preexisting repertoire. The communal values, sense of identity, and claim to traditionality that epics transmit are always being discussed and reinterpreted by a variety of different speakers—sometimes in a way restricted to qualified participants such as elders, a court, or griots themselves, but also, especially in the democratized Africa of today, by citizens and writers at large.[15] In this increasingly scattered process of interpretation, there is a real potential for performers and other speakers to use epic, amid other kinds of traditional discourse, to question or reframe social norms rather than to merely assert them.

These two points—agency expressed in the pragmatics of an utterance, and the dialogical reinterpretation of the utterance's meaning in society—together constitute what I call *critical reflexivity*, understood, in an expansion of Apter's definition, as an ultimately dialogical deployment of discourse, whether at the scale of the individual speaker or of the ongoing conversation in society, that seeks to judge, question, historicize, or transform dominant sociopolitical relations. Indeed, the multidimensionality of African heroic narrative has always been able, to some degree, to invite both individual performances and wider discussions of them to reflect on and challenge political and cultural realities. But this is all the more true today, for the weakening of censorship imposed by ancient social institutions, coupled with the spread of new ideas and intellectual empowerment, enables people interested in traditional genres like epic to conduct increasingly "open" interpretations or readings of them—so much so that certain figures have been accused of reading modern concerns, like liberation of the individual, into discourses where they have no place.

Traditional Criticism? An Ambiguous Example

An interesting case of this tension between the "authentically ancient" and the "modern intrusion" within traditional discourse is that of an unusual griot from Mali, Wa Kamissoko—unusual both because he was recognized by his peers as a *nwara*, a griot of special talent and privilege, and as such was eventually buried with state honors, but also because his work has attracted a great deal of scholarly interest (Cissé and Kamissoko 2000: 1, 21). Not only was he extremely prolific in his knowledge of Mande traditions, but his performances of these were extensively documented and submitted to considerable scrutiny by academics. Paulo de Moraes Farias identifies Wa Kamissoko's critical perspective as a key aspect of his originality: his representation of Mande tradition offers criticism of past communities, of unfolding events in Mali, and of the historical formation of particular traditions themselves (1993: 15). This originality would be challenged by other scholars precisely because they saw it as too unique.

Beginning in 1959, Kamissoko became a close collaborator with the Malian ethnologist Youssouf Tata Cissé, with whom he traveled across the country on research trips until his death in 1976, and through whom he met such luminaries of French anthropology as Jean Rouch, Germaine Dieterlen, and Claude Meillassoux. A frequenter of this milieu, he also participated in two unconventional seminars of the Société commerciale de l'Ouest africain (SCOA) in Bamako in 1975 and 1976, attended by the above scholars and others, including Amadou Hampâté Bâ and D. T. Niane.[16] The idea behind these gatherings was that Kamissoko, as the griot, would participate fully: both by performing or providing recordings of traditional material, much of which was related to *Sunjata* and other aspects of precolonial history, and by accepting questions about his performances. This gave rise to lively, sometimes tense debate, since the authenticity of certain passages and themes of Kamissoko's repertoire was disputed by scholars as idiosyncratic; and, just as problematically from Kamissoko's point of view, the scholarly debate included issues of oral history, questioning the status of certain events that he recounted and their relation to what "really" happened. Farias identifies items that were especially controversial, such as Wa Kamissoko's assertion that Sunjata, upon conquering the Manden from his enemy Sumaoro, abolished a practice of the slave trade that had been current in the twelfth and thirteenth centuries. Because this narrative element had not been found elsewhere, scholars disagreed over whether it could reflect an accurate historical reality, or perhaps a projection of the nineteenth-century experience of slavery into medieval historical discourse; it was further unclear, in the latter case, whether such a projection constituted a theme that had actually been transmitted over a few generations, or was merely evidence of revisionism undertaken by Wa Kamissoko himself. This kind of intellectual skepticism, when expressed during the SCOA conferences, put Kamissoko in an uncomfortable position, leaving him torn between the role of griot—which he took extremely seriously, and through which he claimed authority and expected some degree of deference—and that of scholarly interlocutor, expected by at least some participants to dialogue openly with them as an equal.[17]

A second point of controversy was Wa Kamissoko's frequent formulation of critiques of Islam, especially of what he called the "nouveaux, petits musulmans" (new, petty Muslims), whose reformist rigor he saw as destructive of pre-Islamic Mande culture (Cissé and Kamissoko 2000: 5). He commented in particular on the artificiality of Mande traditional genealogies that claim Muslim founders, since the lineages in question clearly predate the arrival of Islam. I quote Cissé's French translation of Kamissoko:

> Quand l'islam prit au Manden le dessus sur la religion traditionnelle, "on" demanda à chaque clan de se trouver un ancêtre parmi les personnalités dont les noms figurent dans les "quatre livres descendus du ciel," autrement dit dans les quatre livres révélés par Dieu aux prophètes. C'est ainsi que *Djòn Bilali*, "Bilal, le serviteur" du prophète Mahomet devint l'ancêtre des Massalens. Sinon chacun sait que les ancêtres des Keïta, les Konâté, ont vécu longtemps au Wagadou avant d'émigrer au Manden où leurs descendants sont installés depuis plus de 2700 ans. (in Cissé and Kamissoko 2000: 26)

> When Islam gained ascendancy over traditional religion in the Manden, each clan was asked to find an ancestor among the figures whose names are mentioned in the "four books sent down from heaven," that is, in the four books revealed by

God to the prophets. This is how *Djòn Bilali*, "Bilal, the servant" of the prophet Muhammed, became the ancestor of the Massalens. Moreover, everyone knows that the ancestors of the Keita, the Konate, lived for a long time in Wagadu before emigrating to the Manden, where their descendants have been settled for over 2,700 years. (my translation)

This discussion by Wa Kamissoko of the origin of the Massalens-Keita, the lineage that gave birth to Sunjata and the Mali Empire, deserves special attention. On one level, it can be read simply as a critique of Islam that defends pre-Islamic culture and ideology. The expression "traditional religion" reflects the specifically non-Muslim valence that the words "tradition" and "traditional" have taken in the work of many Africanist scholars, who use these terms to refer to precolonial, pre-Islamic ideological systems with their own norms, and that are understood as being in competition with strict Islam. According to this reading, which would emphasize an ideological clash of "tradition vs. Islam," that is, "non-Islam vs. Islam," the griot attributes both authority and superiority to the former; for the fact of claiming a Muslim foundation narrative for the Massalens-Keita lineage can clearly be challenged on empiricist historical grounds, even if the specific figure of 2,700 years is unreliable. But at another level, Wa Kamissoko's discourse can be read as drawing attention to traditionalization as historical process. His comments highlight how discourses of authenticity can change over time as a function of particular ideological interests—in this case, how Keita genealogies were reinvented to accommodate Islam. As such, he has formulated a critique not only of Islam, but of traditionalization itself—understood as the process by which authority drawn from the past is attributed to a cultural item—for he portrays it as historically contingent and dependent upon the political needs of the moment. In this reading, the notion of tradition takes on a wider meaning than "pre-Islamic," for the essential criterion is that Mande genealogies still claim authenticity and authority from the past, even though they combine Muslim and non-Muslim elements.

This depiction of tradition as historically contingent is something of a risky business for a griot, because if taken too far, it could mitigate the authority of his or her own discourse, which is also influenced by present political needs that are projected into the past. For this reason, Jean Rouch remarks that "les traditionalistes ne veulent pas parler les uns devant les autres" (traditional specialists do not wish to speak in front of each other); any disagreement between their discourses could undermine the credibility of all (SCOA 1977: 257). Wa Kamissoko's allusion to the historical limitedness and inventedness of certain traditions, then, constitutes a remarkable sense of self-reflexivity and critical perspective. The question we must ask is whether to understand this reflexivity as something that is part and parcel of speech that claims traditionality, or whether it is something from elsewhere, the product of a "modern" or ethnological consciousness that this particular griot may have acquired during his travels or from contact with outsiders—especially ethnologists. For Rouch, the latter scenario is more likely:

> Pour moi, aujourd'hui, ce phénomène de Wâ Kamissoko est peut-être unique. Wâ est à la fois un traditionaliste et un érudit, capable de participer avec véhémenece et vigilance à des discussions comme celle-ci. Pour le moment, . . . nous n'avons pas rencontré de personnage de cette classe et de cette catégorie. Si c'est un cas unique, pourquoi? Ma seule hypothèse: c'est que cette érudition est le fruit d'une collaboration de plus de 15 ans entre Cissé et Wâ. (in SCOA 1977: 256)

> For me, today, this phenomenon of Wa Kamissoko is perhaps unique. Wa is simultaneously a traditionalist and a scholar, capable of participating with vehemence and vigilance in discussions like this one. For the moment, . . . we have not met anyone else of this class and category. If it is a unique case, why? My only hypothesis: that this erudition is the fruit of over fifteen years of collaboration between Cissé and Wa. (my translation)

Charles Bird echoes this recognition of Kamissoko's uniqueness while expressing a greater sense of doubt as to its cause:

> Bards like Wa Kamissoko could hold forth for hours explaining his interpretations of the things that he sang. Some of the things he would say were also said by others over a large territory; they were common knowledge. Other things that Wa would say were, to me, idiosyncratic. That is, I knew no other bards who said things like that. Did this mean that he was revealing things to outsiders that should be kept secret? I do not know the answer. My feeling is that he was a very original person. (Bird 1999: 280)

Paulo de Moraes Farias, on the other hand, sees Wa Kamissoko as most likely working within the conventions and limits of tradition, under the principle that "tradition and critique of tradition [are] not watertight compartments":

In spite of remaining a *jeli* [griot], he transgressed the roles conventionally ascribed to the informant/performer. He did so by weaving critical comments into his narratives, or parallel to them, and by re-expressing tradition in ways which risked being perceived as eccentric adulterations of traditional sapience. The substance of what he said can be shown to belong to the Mandenka pool of criss-cross traditions and counter-traditions, and can be attested from other oral sources. But inherited information was liable to be organised by him in new patterns (including new time patterns), and to be presented in the form of new narrative episodes, in the light of his personal interpretation of it. (Farias 1993: 22, 15)

Rouch's framing of the problem implies a certain incompatibility between tradition and modernity, authenticity and intrusion: Wa Kamissoko's praxis either is located within the strictures of tradition, or supersedes it somehow. Farias's approach is perhaps more productive in that it moves beyond this opposition. While he does not use the word "traditionalization," he hints at the reality that traditional discourse is not a given fact, but dependent on a process of interpretation, and as such has always been capable of incorporating new elements into preexisting material, or rearranging itself according to present-day concerns. Seen from this point of view, Wa Kamissoko's reorganization of ancient discourse according to "his personal interpretation" is what all performers have always done. Whether we choose to interpret Wa Kamissoko's idiosyncrasies as mostly "authentic" or mostly new, his intertwining of social criticism and self-reflexivity into traditional narrative offers us an inspiration to search actively for such criticism in the oral epic tradition. Was Wa, or are we, reading modern concerns into ancient traditions? Maybe to some degree; but he shows us that there is enough creative space in those traditions for such a reading to be possible.

Oral Epic and Writing Realigned

Wa Kamissoko illustrates the ability of traditional discourse—including epic, given the central place of *Sunjata* in his documented work—to adapt to new situations, to draw in new perspectives, and to reinterpret itself from a critical point of view. In doing so, he invites us to question the classic binaries that underpin anthropological thinking in general, and discourse about Africa in particular. Johannes Fabian expresses these binaries in a diagram, proposing the following analogy, where each term in the top row represents the speaker position of anthropological or colonial discourse.

civilized   *present*   *subject*

to   as   to   as   to

savage   *past*   *object*   (Fabian 1991: 195)

This (European) speaker reifies his Other as belonging to a different category from himself, a category that is stuck in the past and incapable of adequate representation or self-reflexivity, and against which the speaker's own exclusive category of subjectivity, presentness, and the ability to represent is defined. To this set of correspondences we might also add the following terms:

anthropologist   *modernity*   *novel*

to   as   to   as   to

native or *informant*   *tradition*   *epic*

The top-row alignment of the novel with modernity, as forcefully expressed by Bakhtin in "Epic and Novel," corresponds to the classic trope of the anthropologist, for it is only to these three figures that the ability to critique and interpret is said to belong.[18] Meanwhile, the native informant, the traditional, or the African epic are not represented as thinking, but as simply being, or at most speaking themselves, in as restricted and unreflexive a way as possible. Wa Kamissoko, in contrast, demonstrates the possibility that traditional speech can incorporate a critical consciousness that is both self-reflexive and in dialogue with outside ideas, potentially including professional anthropology—with its links to colonial legacy and mass education—into the process of performance, thus rendering the above binaries obsolete. Like the ideological thickness and dispersed processes of interpretation that I have highlighted, Wa Kamissoko allows us to envision epic as something dynamic, rather than flat.

Turning more specifically to the epic/novel problem, we can now move beyond the schema in which a dynamic novel form replaces a relatively static epic one. Locha Mateso argues that African literary criticism should be seen as continuous with critical capacity embedded in oral performances themselves. Against "une assertion qui présente la critique comme contemporaine de la civilisation de l'écriture" (an assertion that presents criticism as contemporaneous with the civilization of writing), traditional performances always translate "un travail 'réflexif' sur le langage'" or reflexive work on language:

> L'intervention de l'artiste consiste donc en une actualisation de la tradition (relecture). Celle-ci comporte nécessairement une critique. Il n'y a donc pas de différence irréductible entre l'œuvre et sa critique.... L'idée de "critique interne" ... est plus proche de la conception traditionnelle de la critique: toute œuvre, pour autant qu'elle est porteuse de réflexion sociale, est inévitablement chargée de critique. (Mateso 1986: 14–15, 30–31)

> The intervention of the artist thus consists of an actualization (rereading) of tradition. This necessarily includes criticism. As such, there is no irreducible difference between the work of art and its criticism.... The idea of "internal critique" ... is closer to the traditional conception of criticism: every work of art, insofar as it carries a social reflection, is inevitably charged with criticism. (my translation)

If every traditional utterance is, by its nature, a reactualization of a body of discourse, then the utterance is simultaneously part of the discourse while conferring upon it a specific meaning in the here and now. The speaker's ability to reentextualize the discourse implies a critical awareness of, and distance from, it.

What is needed, then, is a recognition that African traditional genres like epic and so-called modern ones like the novel work together, not separately. While traditional discourse's ability to reinvent itself may be more limited than that of written literature because of the generic and institutional conventions that it must respect—hence the debate on whether Wa Kamissoko's discourse can be considered truly "traditional"—it is clear that a certain amount of reworking must always be applied to a performer's repertoire in order to produce a performance. This process generates new opportunities for traditional speech to be pertinent in the present, and in some cases, endows it with entirely new themes, as the example of Sunjata's purported abolitionism may demonstrate. Seen from this light, the turn toward heroic material among certain African writers becomes not just an attempt to monumentalize the past—nor only an attempt to parody, reinvent, or lament it—but to mobilize those features of epic discourse that enable dialogue with the present, especially criticism of the present. Since the novel has long served as a platform for social criticism, it can thus be seen as continuous with epic in an important way. While the two genres are not the same thing, this continuity reveals an attention on the part of literary writers to details of orality, in particular to the timeliness of orality, that can shed new light on their work.

CHAPTER FOUR

Through Wangrin's Looking Glass

Politics of the Mirror in the AOF

> The bards of Negritude did not hesitate to reach beyond the borders of the
> continent. Black voices from America took up the refrain on a larger scale. The
> "black world" came into being, and Busia from Ghana, Birago Diop from Senegal,
> Hampâté Bâ from Mali and Saint-Clair Drake from Chicago were quick to claim
> common ties and identical lines of thought.... This historical obligation to racialize
> their claims, to emphasize an African culture rather than a national culture leads
> the African intellectuals into a dead end.
>
> —Frantz Fanon, *The Wretched of the Earth*

This moment in *Les Damnés de la terre* (*The Wretched of the Earth*) (1961) has always left me puzzled. Why does Frantz Fanon name Amadou Hampâté Bâ, the great Malian researcher and diplomat, as one of the "bards of Negritude"? Bâ was actually quite outside the Negritude circuit: he was given neither to French lyric poetry nor to affirming the unity of the black race; he expressed far less sweeping Pan-Africanist sentiment than many of his peers; and his published work has very little to say about African-Americans at all.[1] Indeed, his intellectual genealogy had much more to do with French Africanist ethnology, his mentor Tierno Bokar, and his exchanges with the Protestant pacifist Théodore

Monod than with L.S. Senghor or Aimé Césaire. All of this makes Fanon's reasons for lumping him in with the Negritude movement seem dubious. While the occasional title in the available lists of Bâ's voluminous works may have a Negritude-esque resonance—such as a lecture entitled "Pour un retour fécond aux sources de l'art nègre" (For a Fecund Return to the Sources of Black Art), given several years after Fanon's death—the vast majority of them are focused on rigorous documentation and ethnographic analysis of West African peoples, with a special focus on collecting and interpreting Fulfulde texts from Mali.[2]

Fanon's dismissal can perhaps be attributed to the fact that Bâ spoke of peace, tolerance, and ecumenical understanding—instead of the Algerian War. In any case, he is not the only reader to see in Amadou Hampâté Bâ a black romantic. The Senegalese historian Mamadou Diouf has criticized his "célébration toute romantique de la tradition" (totally romantic celebration of tradition) (in Afriques Créatives et al. 2012: 28). Indeed, Bâ is most often remembered as a "defender and illustrator" of dying traditions, the determined rescuer of African authenticity against modern alienation (Mariko 2005). His most famous maxim, "En Afrique, quand un vieillard meurt, c'est une bibliothèque qui brûle" (In Africa, when an old man dies, it's a library burning), is summarily taken to be a one-sentence condensation of his entire œuvre, an œuvre that included decades' worth of ethnographic and historical studies, documentation of oral tradition, and literary writing. The image of old men with libraries in their heads has taken on a proverb-like life of its own, to the point of becoming a cliché in African letters, embodying an attitude of reverence toward the past, incarnated in the elders, particularly in the grandfatherly figure of Bâ himself.[3] It also carries a tone of urgency, reiterating the metanarrative that traditional knowledge is on the verge of death and needs to be saved. Muriel Devey subtitled her biography of Bâ, rather unsubtly, "L'Homme de la tradition" (the man of tradition) (1993).

Bâ's supposed romanticism needs to be questioned. He began to repeat his famous aphorism only after 1960, when he worked as a representative of Mali to UNESCO, and especially after 1962, when he was elected to UNESCO's executive council, where he remained for eight years. Throughout this decade, he called for international aid to countries like his own for the purpose of preserving oral traditional knowledge. It is in this setting, for example, that he justified the creation of the Institut de tradition orale in Niamey by declaring that "l'exploitation des traditions . . . peu[t] aider à la connaissance profonde de l'âme africaine" (the exploitation of traditions can help foster a deep knowledge of the African soul) (A.

H. Bâ 1972: 36). That is to say, if Bâ expressed a romantic, Negritude-like affirmation of deep African culture in the form of oral traditions, it was a form of advertisement. Bâ's extroverted romanticism, an ideological interpretation of African traditionality that made it easily digestible for the outside world, was articulated for the specific purposes of institution-building, of attracting publicity and funding, of advancing research and conservation efforts—not because his approach to culture was fundamentally essentialist or racialized. This reading illustrates my overarching argument in this chapter: Bâ's philosophy of traditionality should not be reduced to, or dismissed as, romantic nostalgia. It is true that bits of evidence here and there would seem to justify Fanon's and Diouf's accusations, such as the essay "The Living Tradition," which compares oral tradition to a "sacrament" embedded in "a *religious view of the world*" (A. H. Bâ 1981: 171). Even so, such statements do not capture the totality of Bâ's thought, which was vast, "proteiform," and not always so reverent (Ekoungoun 2014: 11). Bâ was, among many other things, a strategist and tactician, constantly thinking about the political consequences of his work—especially after 1937, when his public support for the controversial Hamallist religious movement began to create problems for him with the colonial administration. His representations of African cultures and histories are permeated with a fine-tuned political consciousness and filled with calculating characters, of which his famous literary character Wangrin is the greatest, but hardly the only one. This is the hero of the work considered Bâ's masterpiece, *L'Etrange destin de Wangrin* (*The Fortunes of Wangrin*) (1973), a semifictional narrative, inspired by real people and events, about a shrewd black interpreter's money-making schemes across a number of AOF colonies from 1906 to 1932. Bâ's writing, whether ethnographic or literary, is eminently aware of traditional genres' usability and malleability. Traditions are one form of cultural code among others, all of which are constantly being put in the service of vested political interests in the colonial world of the AOF: the customary chiefs, the marabouts and imams, the colonial administration, and competing factions within each of these, not to mention all manner of intermediaries between them, all manipulate the cultural codes at their disposal in order to get ahead. For this reason, a more nuanced reading of Bâ's work is necessary, one that will allow us to rethink this important writer as offering not just a backward-looking defense and illustration of African traditions, but a celebration and critique of their inevitable politicization.

Wangrin offers the clearest demonstration of this argument about culture as a means to power. A speaker of perfect French as well as several African languages,

Wangrin's unparalleled ability to move between languages and cultural codes makes him the best player in the colonial world's games for money and influence. Of the text's multitude of characters, whether black or white, powerful or marginal, he alone is able to use all the languages and cultural codes at play in order to consistently advance his commercial and political interests. For this reason, the text characterizes him as a kind of modern epic hero: Wangrin's virtuosic abilities to deceive his enemies, combined with his specifically noble sense of honor, cause his deeds to be sung and recounted like those of a hero. The text even gives him a birth prophecy and a patron deity. Unlike Amadou Hampâté Bâ himself, both the character Wangrin and the historical person on whom he is based were ethnically Bamana, but they circulated within the same continuum of geographical and ethnic spaces in which Bâ spent much of his life.[4]

Wangrin's extremely pragmatic analysis of culture as a weapon in the battlefield of colonialist capitalism is echoed in the two volumes of its author's personal memoirs: namely, *Amkoullel l'enfant peul* (Amkoullel, Peul child) (1991), which covers his ancestry and childhood, and *Oui mon commandant!* (Yes Chief!) (1994), which covers his service in the colonial bureaucracy in the 1920s and early 1930s. Both volumes were published posthumously and are still untranslated. Bâ wrote a third volume about his career from 1937 onward, but it is not accessible to the public.[5] The two published volumes vividly illustrate the extent to which the colonial West African world in which both Wangrin and Bâ operated was the product of layered, competing histories and memories. *Amkoullel* begins in the nineteenth century, showing how the Sahel's political and religious crises produced the twentieth-century colonial universe familiar to Wangrin and Bâ. As Umar Tall's jihad conquered rival empires, especially Amadu Lobbo's Dina and Segu (both of which were headquartered in what is today Mali), clashes over religion, opposing alliances, and rival dynasties became more acute. The conflicts were first enflamed, then "pacified" by the French penetration of the West African interior in the century's last decade. As colonial political order was imposed in the early twentieth century, ethnic and religious rivalries continued to simmer in the background, maintained for decades through collective memories and oral tradition. It was in this context that Amadou Hampâté Bâ was born around 1900, descended from rival Fula lineages that had fought on opposite sides of Umar Tall's holy war; and it was in the fully fledged federation of the AOF, with the trauma of the nineteenth century still imprinted on collective memory, that Wangrin and Bâ circulated as colonial bureaucrats. Together, these three texts—*Wangrin* and the two available volumes of Bâ's memoirs—paint a rich portrait not only of daily life in the AOF, but of its historical thickness. They also illuminate the many personal connections between the historical Wangrin and Bâ. The two men crossed paths a few times before Bâ committed to writing down Wangrin's life story; as such, Bâ's memoirs constantly refer to episodes recounted in *Wangrin* and, in spite of the author's denials, give the distinct sensation of a kind of mirror image connecting the writer to his famous literary hero.

Importantly, Bâ's analyses of the politicization of traditions and other cultural codes cut across the barriers of the colonial world. This chapter will examine how *Wangrin* and Bâ's two volumes of published memoirs articulate a major cross-cultural analysis that encompasses both colonizer and colonized. Together, these three texts show that for all the boundaries that separate the inhabitants of the colonial universe—black and white, dominated and dominant, Muslim/animist and Christian/secular—both sides have in common the politicization of the cultural codes at their disposal, whether it be oral tradition, religious practices, law, or collective memory. *Contra* attempts to read Bâ as a bard of Negritude or nostalgic romantic, this constantly comparative, transracial critique suggests that the two major categories of human subjects in the colonial world are, in many ways, mirror images of each other. Bâ's writing emphasizes that similar political structures, fractures, and processes, as well as human desires, are repeated in all quarters of the colonial world and its past.

Epic Avatars, Hybrid Genres

Wangrin stands out from the rest of Bâ's work for a number of reasons. Not least of these is the controversy surrounding the author's claim that it is a work of pure nonfiction. Bâ always insisted that *Wangrin* was a nothing more than a faithful translation into French of the real Wangrin's autobiographical narrative as told to him in Bamana;[6] but scholarly readers have never stopped objecting that the story borrows significant elements from oral tradition, other writers, and Bâ's own life story, displaying elements of creative writing or rewriting—or genius—on his part, and constituting a kind of generic hybrid. Ralph Austen has submitted the text to historical scrutiny, concluding that "Wangrin is a historical figure who... 'inspired' what now must be called Hampâté Bâ's novel."[7] For Justin Izzo, *Wangrin* is an "ethnographic biography" because of its "rigorous documentation and explanation of oral traditions and indigenous customs, in addition to a rich portrait of everyday life under colonial rule in French West Africa" (2015: 2). Anna Pondopoulo (2010) sees *Wangrin* as borrowing from colonial literature, especially the novels of Robert Arnaud, an administrator whom Bâ knew personally and who appears in *Oui mon commandant!*

In addition, a number of scholars have seized on the notion that *Wangrin* combines the genres of novel and epic.[8] *Wangrin*'s epic dimensions are remarkable. The text of the story was ostensibly dictated to Bâ by (the real) Wangrin himself while a griot provided musical accompaniment in a manner evoking a traditional performance; it raises the protagonist to cosmological dimensions, beginning with a myth of origin of the hero's village and a prophecy announcing his great destiny; the account of Wangrin's coming-of-age is centered around his ritual initiation and consecration to a Bamana divinity who returns throughout the narrative as his particular patron; a multitude of proverbs and passages from oral tradition are woven into the main narration; and the historical context of the hero's birthplace in Masina (today, southeastern Mali) is explicitly situated in the aftermath of Samori Touré, Umar Tall, and the French conquest, that is, in the legacy of empire builders who had come to be remembered in epic terms. Adding to the text's claim to historical accuracy, Bâ constantly uses anagrams to refer to real places and persons in *Wangrin*, supposedly in order to protect the real-life identities of his characters. Masina becomes "Namaci" and Samori becomes "Yorsam." This practice was typical of colonial literature (Pondopoulo 2010). "Wangrin" itself is, as the author tells us, a pseudonym. Even when anagrams are not readily decipherable in *Wangrin*, the names they conceal are often given in correct form in the author's memoirs.

Eileen Julien and Susan Gorman suggest that these epic features of *Wangrin* essentially function as signifying their own past-ness, even obsolescence. The central drama of this text is, in these readings, the staging of a recent historical period as absolute past in Bakhtinian epic terms. For Julien, Wangrin's trickeries are heroic in the age of colonialism because "no other outlets for heroic action seem possible. ... The old heroism is gone, and in its new avatar, it can only work toward personal, material gain" (1992: 66). For her, this situation encapsulates a Bakhtinian shift from an "epic impulse" to novel, while Gorman sees *Wangrin* as occupying a "both-and" position, fulfilling Bakhtin's criteria for both epic and novel (2003: 141–46), but in which epic represents the past. Amy Wynchank reads Wangrin's epic-ness differently: for her, the "evolution of the epic" provides us a with an "adaptable" hero, "a witness of, and clear-sighted actor in, the metamorphoses of the times" (1991: 237–38). This view foregrounds a historical present that the epic genre helps stage and produce, rather than relying on a Bakhtinian past where the backdrop of the AOF is more or less contingent.

It is necessary to flesh out an understanding of *Wangrin*'s epic modalities as productive of a historical present, rather than an inaccessible, fossilized past. Harry Harootunian's notion of a "thickened" present, as an objective conjuncture in time where different subjective collective memories are at play, provides a useful paradigm for understanding connections between time, genre, and social critique in this text (Harootunian 2007). Harootunian draws on the concept of colliding "regimes of historicity," or structures that allow people to experience time in a particular way (Hartog 2012). If we apply this theoretical framework to literary representations of colonial Africa, the recourse to an epic regime of historicity, which attempts to shape the present by linking it to indigenous heroes of the past, can easily be thought of as locked in conflict with the colonialist temporal regime of conquest, mercantilism, and progress—as well as the European version of colonial heroism. In *Wangrin*, however, we do not have a clash of civilizations, but an entanglement of them. Regimes of historicity are knotted with each other and produced through concrete political interests and structures of power. It is the very interplay and negotiation between different regimes of historicity—in this case, traditional or epic, Islamic, and colonial—and the contestations within each one of them that constitute the thickened historical present that *Wangrin* and Bâ's memoirs portray.

Tradition and Power: A User's Guide

In *Oui mon commandant!*, Bâ describes a performance of the Bamana epic of the nineteenth-century Segu Empire that encapsulates this historical layering.[9] Segu fiercely celebrated animist practices as official until the imperial city's defeat by the jihad of Umar Tall in 1861. The performance of this narrative that Bâ witnessed, given by the griot Namissé Sissoko in 1921, begins with an account of the struggle between cultural codes that had reduced the once powerful Segu into a memory. It identifies the French presence, symbolized by the tricolor flag, as the third force that has conquered both of its predecessors, the animist Segu state and Umar's theocratic empire:

Ô Amadou fils de Hampâté! Sais-tu comment les *tondjons*, ces soldats bambaras de l'empire de Ségou . . . désignaient chacun des trois esprits du grand fétiche de la France? Ils appelaient le premier *bakagué*, le bleu, et prétendaient qu'il surveille le ciel bleu pour essayer d'empêcher Dieu d'intervenir dans les affaires des Noirs. Ils disaient que le deuxième, *gnegué*, le blanc, répand une tache blanche sur la cornée des yeux des "sujets français," pour mieux les aveugler. Quant au troisième, *torowoulen*, le rouge, pour eux il était chargé de répandre le sang des ennemis et des indisciplinés. Ce fétiche triplet de la France s'est révélé plus fort que le chapelet à cent grains, fétiche des marabouts toucouleurs, et plus efficace que les douze grands dieux du panthéon *banmana* de Ségou.[10] Oui, le fétiche français a supplanté tous les fétiches locaux et il occupe leur place. Voilà trente et un ans que cela dure, et Dieu seul sait combien de temps cela durera encore! (A. H. Bâ 1994: 29–30)

O Amadou son of Hampâté! Do you know how the *tondjons*, the Bamana soldiers of the empire of Segu . . . named each of the three spirits of the France's great fetish? They called the first *bakagué*, the blue spirit, and claimed that it watched over the blue sky in order to stop God from intervening in the Blacks' affairs. They said that the second, *gnegué*, the white spirit, spreads a white blot on the cornea of the eyes of "French subjects," the better to blind them. As for the third, *torowulen*, the red spirit, for them it was charged with spilling the blood of enemies and the undisciplined. This triple fetish of France has revealed itself to be stronger than the hundred prayer beads used by Toucouleur marabouts, and more effective than the twelve great gods of the Bamana pantheon. Yes, the French fetish has supplanted all local fetishes and taken their place. It has lasted thirty-one years now, and God only knows how long it will last yet! (my translation)

This description portrays the warring supernatural forces of distinct cultural systems at Segu in particular, and throughout the AOF more generally: ancient animist pantheons and rituals (which, it is true, had exchanged a great deal with Islam over the centuries), the reformist version of Islam specific to the nineteenth-century jihads, and the colonial state implanted by the French. The temporal dimension of the passage is especially striking, for it both historicizes the sequence of imperial periods and portrays the French colonial order as having established a present of its own that is dominant yet hybrid. It has supplanted the previous orders with itself, and yet the cultural memories of past political and cultural entities remain strong: the French occupation is interpreted through a precolonial discursive repertoire emphasizing magic objects and ritual power. The description of French power as an occult "fetish" with obscure powers—especially the allusion to the "blinding" of colonial subjects symbolized by the color white—suggests the need to remove the veil that conceals white power, to reveal to all how it works. The barely implicit message is that understanding colonial power is the first step to contesting it. The griot's emphasis on the thirty-one years that have passed since the fall of Segu to the French (in 1890) as well as his apparent desire for an end to the colonial occupation make it clear that he is expressly relating epic discourse to a very real set of political realities in the present—so much so that his boss, the local *commandant's* interpreter, threatens to report his anti-French attitude to the authorities and have him thrown in jail (A. H. Bâ 1994: 30). The idea of a Bakhtinian absolute past has no place here at all; the performance, while offering a representation of the past, is articulated in a way that produces a rather subversive picture of the present.

Wangrin offers us a vision of life in the AOF that both recalls the thick historicity of the Segu epic and contrasts with it in an important way. The Segu passage conjures a seemingly irreducible conflict between rival cultural and political norms. *Wangrin* is equally concerned with the struggle between French, Muslim, and indigenous claims to power and ways of knowing the world, but actually proposes an explicit, if temporary, solution: its characters, and most dramatically the heroic figure of Wangrin himself, must *mediate* between these norms. The question posed to Wangrin by Quinomel, chief of personnel in "Goudougaoua" (an anagram for Ouagadougou) reveals the all-importance of cultural versatility:

QUINOMEL: "Je vois dans ton dossier que tu es intelligent. Tu parles correctement le français et cinq langues africaines. On ne saurait demander mieux pour un interprète. Quelle est ta religion?"

WANGRIN: "Je n'en ai pas de bien défini," répondit Wangrin. "En tant qu'interprète, je dois ménager tout le monde. Aussi suis-je autant à mon aise dans la mosquée que dans le bois sacré des villages animistes." (A. H. Bâ 1992: 112)

QUINOMEL: "I see from your file that you are intelligent. You speak French fluently, and five African languages as well. What more can one ask of an interpreter? What is your religion?'

WANGRIN: "I don't have any special religion," answered Wangrin. "As an interpreter, it's my job to get on with everybody; I am as much at ease in a mosque as I am in the sacred groves of the animist villages." (A. H. Bâ 1999: 74)

Wangrin's enigmatic answer, an apparent celebration of syncretism and hybridity, intimates a deeper awareness of culture as a means to power—which he makes even clearer in an interview with a later boss, Arnaud de Bonneval:

> Je ne connais de religion que mon service. Plaire à mon commandant équivaut pour moi à plaire à la force supérieure d'en haut. Je "fais salame," mais je ne suis pas bigot. Je n'aime pas les chauvins, je suis pour la civilisation et particulièrement enthousiaste pour la civilisation française, mère des droits de l'homme et anti-esclavagiste! (A. H. Bâ 1992: 220)

> My duty is my only religion. To please my Commandant is to please the superior force in heaven above. I am a Muslim, but not a bigot. I dislike chauvinists; I'm in favor of civilization and I am a particularly enthusiastic admirer of French civilization, the mother of human rights and the enemy of slavery! (A. H. Bâ 1999: 154)

Wangrin refuses to define himself in an exclusive way. His suppleness is a means of accommodating the demands of outside powers and exigencies; the very enunciation of such a flexible, even sycophantic, religious identity allows Wangrin to gain his bosses' trust and exercise power in their name with minimal supervision. This gives him an obvious edge in the power play he is entering. Thus the colonial hierarchy itself joins the mosque and the sacred forest as one more domain in which Wangrin is totally at ease: he speaks its language perfectly, both literally through his perfect French and figuratively through his intuition for what to say and how to say it. His opportunistic portrayals of his own identity hint at his awareness that all of these regimes of historicity are produced by discourses of political control and domination. Moreover, his strategies of self-marketing reveal his awareness that adaptation to the historical changes sweeping across West Africa in the nineteenth and twentieth centuries would require the ability to shuttle in and out of these various cultural codes.

But even the terms of this negotiation are not taken for granted. Rather than staging competing cultural norms as locked in an essentialized combat, as we see in the passage from the Segu epic above, *Wangrin* rewrites the relationship between culture and power, while still drawing on the metaphor of the occult battle. Consider this account of the struggle between Wangrin and his enemy "Romo" (an anagram for Moro Sidibé) who is trying to punish the hero for stealing his job:[11]

Un combat entre deux sorciers ne se livre pas à la manière des lutteurs de foire, mais à coups de pratiques magiques, lancement d'effluves qui aveuglent, paralysent, rendent fou ou, parfois, tuent froidement l'adversaire. Or—et Romo le savait—Wangrin était passé maître en ces matières, à force de fréquenter et de faire travailler les plus grands dignitaires de la sorcellerie bambara, peule, dogon, marka, yarsé, samo, bobo, mossi, gourma, gourounsi, pomporon, etc. Aussi Romo n'accepta-t-il d'aller affronter Wangrin chez lui, c'est-à-dire dans son élément, avant de s'y être magiquement préparé. (A. H. Bâ 1992: 296)

A battle between two sorcerers bears no resemblance to a wrestling match in the market square; rather it is fought with occult practices, which release effluvia that bind the opponent, drive him insane—at times even kill him in cold blood! Now— and Romo knew it well—Wangrin was past master of the art, having frequented and employed the greatest exponents of Bambara, Fulbe, Dogon, Marka, Yarse, Sama, Bobo, Mossi, Gurma, Gurunsi, and Pomporon sorcery, and a few others besides. Consequently, Romo could not think of facing Wangrin in his house, on his own ground, without first undergoing some ritualistic preparation. (A. H. Bâ 1999: 210–11)

The text proceeds to describe Romo's ritual preparations in great detail. Here we do not have a struggle between cultures embodied in magic persons or objects, but rather between individuals who use a variety of culture-bound magics in the service of their interests. Wangrin is the superior sorcerer because he can conjure any of the different ritual codes at his disposition. The "etc." that finishes the litany of markers of belonging emphasizes that the list is not exhaustive and could be elaborated further. Likewise, no single element is privileged over the others; each is an instrument to be combined with others. This strategy of magical bricolage constitutes a way out of the symbolic Segovian deadlock, in which the magics of the Bamana pantheon and of the Muslim prayer beads had been crushed by that of the French tricolor flag: Wangrin is subversively heroic precisely because he is the only character who realizes that fetishes from all cultures can serve as potential tools for obtaining power. He alone can manipulate the AOF's multiplicity of coexisting cultural codes and power structures to his advantage. He juxtaposes and translates them into their underlying political interests and structures of power, which can then be evaluated, compared, and outmaneuvered.

The comparison of "fetishes"—really, of interested parties locked in a struggle for power—reveals a certain kind of anthropological relativism on the part of

Wangrin as text and of Amadou Hampâté Bâ as writer. For both colonizer and colonized, culture, including its more specific manifestations as traditionality or regimes of historicity, is constantly revealed to be the product of competing interests and mechanisms of domination, rather than a static set of beliefs and practices that simply exists in and of itself.

Bamana Religion's Mirror Image: A Weird God with a Bizarre Body

Wangrin's ability to move between cultural codes is key to his adaptability. This gift is prefigured in the setting of ritual initiation that frames the main story: the hero consecrates himself as a young adult to Gongoloma-Sooké, god of contradictions and paradoxes, "dieu bizarre," "à la fois bon et mauvais, sage et libertin," "le grand confluent des contraires" ("weird divinity," "both kindly and ill disposed, chaste and libertine," "confluence of all opposites"), who will be his main protector throughout the narrative.[12] The "weird" god underscores the ambiguity of tradition itself: rather than prescribing a set of beliefs or practices, as Bamana "religion" or *bamanaya* had been described in classic French anthropology, the god of Wangrin's initiation is presented as an amalgam of paradoxes that orients it toward fulfilling its own changing needs and desires—as well as, by extension, those of the hero whom he will protect.[13] The god's body is made up of anatomically inverted functions: he drinks from his nostrils and eats through his anus, walks with his back facing forward, his head on the ground, and his feet in the air, and with a sexual organ growing from his forehead. This topsy-turvy physiology is nevertheless made to work.

> Sa bouche n'avait pas de langue. Elle était munie de deux mâchoires édentées mais plus tranchantes qu'un rasoir neuf. Il s'en servait pour scier, couper, sculpter et excaver, selon les besoins. (A. H. Bâ 1992: 20)

> His mouth was tongueless and furnished with toothless maws—sharper, however, than a brand-new razor. These he used for sawing, cutting, sculpting, and digging, according to his needs. (A. H. Bâ 1999: 8)

Even without teeth, the divinity accomplishes whatever he needs that would require sharp tools: one way or another, he manages to perform his task. He is a god of interpretative bricolage, the reinvention and combination of concepts "according to his needs" (Lévi-Strauss 1966). The substance of this traditional deity is, in a way, inconsequential: his nose could have just as easily been razor-sharp instead of his jaws, just as his penis might as well have protruded from an arm instead of his face. Yet, regardless of how he manages to saw, cut, sculpt, and excavate, or for that matter eat or walk, he does it. His symbolic reversals of the order of the human body only serve to highlight the fact that his bodily functionality continues unimpeded. This deification of changeability reflects the fact that Wangrin will have recourse to traditional practices calling upon the god's protection to do whatever he wants, whether that be "kindly [or] ill disposed," "chaste [or] libertine." The content or intent of traditional discourse is subjugated to its use in the present: it means or justifies what its interpreter wants it to mean or justify.

There is an ethical dimension to Gongoloma-Sooké's ambiguity that extends the usability of Bamana religion even further. The spirit is described as weeping "à en tarir ses larmes" ("until his tears eventually dried up") when he hears of a birth or marriage, but laughing "à faire éclater son foie" ("till he split his sides") when he hears of death or divorce; he insults benefactors and sings the praises of enemies.[14] These contradictions suggest that he is a god of ruse, for the reader suspects that such counterintuitive behaviors must hide ulterior motives. To curse one's friends implies that the friendship was feigned, just as to praise one's enemies implies that one will get the better of them later on. On the other hand, he may also be a god of truth, willing to uncover faults and speak unpleasant realities in spite of human conventions of politeness or loyalty. Such a tension between selfish duplicity and unabashed straightforwardness is reflected in Wangrin's feats of trickery throughout the story. His strange heroism, turned in many cases away from community building and toward selfish goals, paradoxically also becomes a source of sidesplitting laughter. The text drives home the point here that traditionalizing discourse—or its objects or institutions—is capable of serving exactly opposed ends, or being used in ways exactly opposite from what we would expect.

The text's playful yet ideologically significant use of Gongoloma-Sooké is complicated by the fact that the existence of such a deity is uncertain in Bamana mythology.[15] The question of whether Bâ invented it entirely, or perhaps tweaked material he collected in order to fit his needs here, is interesting because it raises not only the issue of his authorship of *Wangrin* as text (once again), but also the possibility that the text is actually parodying, or at least stretching, Bamana mythology in a way that highlights its flexibility. Whatever the case may be, the narrative's style of cultural description here emphasizes the creativity, humor, and self-reflexivity of storytelling even in its explanation of ethnographic detail, offering a remarkable difference from, or rewriting of, classic accounts of *bamanaya* that are more intent on systematically constructing an organized scheme of beliefs and practices. We might even think of Roman Jakobson's example of an eminently dialogical Russian storyteller who tells stories "only for the sake of contradiction," that is, to contradict whatever his interlocutor has just said (Jakobson 1990: 94). Like a mirror image where everything is backward, Gongoloma-Sooké reflects its vision of *bamanaya* through *Wangrin*'s strange looking glass. For this reason, *Wangrin* can be read as a lively counterpoint both to colonial-era anthropological writing and to the "bards of Negritude": it celebrates mixing, ambiguity, and compromise instead of the classic attempts to identify a "pure" African essence.

Tricks of the Trade: Custom, Law, Panegyric

The hero's negotiation of such cultural contradictions is the major concern of *Wangrin* as narrative. One long episode (chaps. 11–15) makes the stakes of Wangrin's heroic political savvy especially visible. In hopes of making money, he inserts himself into a dispute over inheritance among local Fula nobility who fall under the jurisdiction of his post at "Yagouwahi" (Ouahigouya). Upon the death of the chief "Brildji Maduma Thiala," an old resentment between rival heirs, namely the dead man's half brother "Karibu Sawali" and son "Loli," erupts into a contest of conspiracies, with each trying to secure for himself the chief's title and wealth; Karibu feels especially snubbed because his brother's immediate family had excluded him, the natural elder, from all burial plans.[16] Wangrin, pretending to represent the colonial commandant's interest in maintaining order among indigenous elites, acts as a double agent and plays each side against the other. Wangrin causes a scandal by proposing that Karibu assert his dominance by digging up and reburying his brother—under the pretense that such are the orders of the commandant, who finds the man's death suspicious. At the same time, he assures Brildji's representatives that he will stop Karibu from performing such a shameful sacrilege. Both sides pay him to represent their interests. This episode brings out problems not only surrounding views and customs of both inheritance and exhumation, which are different in Islamic law, local traditions, and French colonialism. Each party defends the custom that protects its interests: Islamic and French law favor inheritance by the son (Loli), who has the added advantage from the colonial perspective of being a veteran of World War I, while Fula custom designates the nephew or brother as heir (Karibu); but Loli's followers point out that Islam and Fula custom abhor exhumation, while Wangrin and Karibu know that French law permits or even encourages it in cases where there is doubt surrounding the facts of a burial.[17] The characters' way of mobilizing parallel cultural systems based on their own interests creates a sort of leveling effect on the playing field. The explicit hierarchy between colonizer and colonized and the struggle for dominance between Islam and older ritual practices are simultaneously deployed and, in a way, relativized. Every cultural code can be instrumentalized or set aside in the contest for power. Wangrin is the best player in the game, the one with the most transcultural perspicacity and daring, who is "prêt à affronter textes sacrés et fournaises infernales" ("quite prepared to defy holy texts and hellfire") in order to get what he wants—in this case, to enflame both sides and solidify their dependence on him by making the idea of an exhumation seem like it might become reality.[18] The political implications of each set of symbolic grammars are carefully weighed, and yet each one serves only as an interchangeable means to an end.

However, the final compromise that settles the dispute between Loli and Karibu—giving Brildji's wealth to the former but his title to the latter—has another level of complexity. Beyond idioms of parallel cultures is the issue of honor, tied to noble status, which can be manipulated by certain actors in order to influence the behavior of others. This manipulation takes the form of flattering persons of noble status by alluding to the sense of pride and innate superiority particular to their class, or more specifically by singing their praises according to a generic pattern of traditional panegyric. Wangrin, who is of noble Bamana origin (*horon*) in Bâ's narrative,[19] agrees to forego the exhumation he has planned when the deceased man's captive, "Diofo," begs him in the name of his high traditional rank and noble blood to respect the honor of a man of equally princely rank; elegant gifts help buttress his plea.[20] Compelled by this formulaic appeal to his ego, Wangrin accedes to Diofo's request, declaring:

Wallaye! Wallaye! Diofo! Sous les coups de l'enclume et du marteau que constituent tes deux mains et sous l'effet magique de ta langue incantatrice, le plus résistant et le plus dur des métaux devient de la cire molle que tu façonnes à volonté. (A. H. Bâ 1992: 172)

Wallayi, Wallayi! O Diofo! your hands are as strokes of the hammer on an anvil and
the spell of your magical tongue reduces the most obstinate and least ductile of
metals to a supple wax which you then fashion at will. (A. H. Bâ 1999: 118)

This exclamation suggests that status-based praise has an irresistible effect on a
noble person's behavior. Praise is a specific cultural modality, with strong connections to traditional patterns of panegyric, which can again be instrumentalized
in order to achieve political outcomes. Wangrin's change of heart, which might
appear to depict vulnerability to flattery as a weakness, actually impels him to
rethink the political pros and cons of an unpopular scene of disinterment that
would be perceived as dishonorable. Moreover, praise itself, which has caused
Wangrin's change of heart, finally serves as a solution to the predicament that he
has created for himself as a double agent. Rather than desecrate Brildji's corpse, he
orchestrates a public meeting in which the family of the deceased will appease the
offended Karibu with a formal apology—complete with traditional praise, sung by
a griot and filled with examples of Karibu's heroic Fula ancestors who respected
the honor of their enemies:

Karibou! fils de Sawali le preux, petit-fils de Mawnde le vaillant pasteur qui . . .
blessait grièvement, même tuait impitoyablement ses ennemis, mais ne les déshon-
orait jamais. . . . Quand le sang d'un tel noble coule dans les veines et artères d'un
homme, dans tes artères, ô Karibou Sawali, tu ne saurais souffrir et moins encore
te complaire à voir déshonorer ton frère, alors que ton aïeul a sauvé l'honneur de
son voleur et ennemi Bila Wobogo le Mossi. (A. H. Bâ 1992: 179–80)

Karibu, son of Sawali the gallant and grandson of Mawnde, the brave shepherd
who . . . inflicted grave wounds on his enemies, and sometimes even destroyed
them ruthlessly, it cannot be said of him that he ever treated them dishonorably. . . .
Since it is the blood of so noble a knight that courses in the veins and the arteries
of his descendants, in your own arteries, O Karibu Sawali, how could you bear to,
nay, how could you delight in dishonoring your dead brother? Remember that
your ancestor restored honor to the Mossi prince Bila Wobogo, an enemy who had
robbed him! (A. H. Bâ 1999: 123)

This passage weaves heroic narrative into a didactic discourse of explicit praise and
implicit criticism, illustrating the usability of praise for political ends.

Panegyric thus becomes an interethnic idiom which, though it expresses a common set of expectations for lofty noble ideals, is deployed for concrete, politically motivated reasons that expose such ideals as dependent on the needs of the present moment. The present is, as such, the dominant temporality of praise discourse. People forget everything else in the moment when their praises are sung, becoming like "supple wax."[21] The text's relentless focus on the political and strategic machinations that precede and contextualize any traditional utterance or traditionalizing discourse, such as status-based praise, reveals that these cultural forms are tools for obtaining or exercising power, anchored in the time of present politics. The temporality of political exigency is thickened in the story by the variety of regimes of historicity at play: just as the griot's panegyric of Karibu explicitly relates his present conduct to heroic feats of the past that it poses as normative, so do Muslim and French legal systems respectively seek to enforce the historicities of West African Islamization and of the Third Republic. And yet, Bâ's *Wangrin* does not set these regimes in an irreducible clash, as the Segu epic seems to, but highlights their lapses and compromises, their use in an ongoing and ever-changing game of politically significant bricolage. For Wangrin, negotiating these regimes serves as a source of power and creativity in his scheme of deception with Brildji's family, his yielding to Diofo's praise, and his change of strategy and ultimate solution to the dispute between Brildji's heirs.

The text brings this critique of cultural forms as always relative, contingent, and connected to power to bear not only on African "traditions" or religion, based on transmission from the past, but more specifically on the French legal system as well, in spite of its pretensions to rationality and due process. *Wangrin* makes clear that French law in the colonies is always subjugated to political concerns, the most important of which is white prestige. When Wangrin machinates to conduct a cattle theft affair while getting his French superior the Count de Villermoz to take the fall for it, he knows that he risks more than the count before the French courts:

Wangrin savait également qu'une affaire dans laquelle un Européen se trouvait impliqué serait bien difficile à trancher à la colonie. Sans doute préférait-on étouffer n'importe quel crime plutôt que de condamner un Européen, à plus forte raison si ce dernier était un agent de l'autorité. Il en allait du prestige des colonisateurs, et la politique menée en ce domaine ne s'embarrassait pas de problèmes de conscience. Wangrin tira son parti de cette conjoncture pour, lui aussi, se dépouiller de tout scrupule. Se défendre par tous les moyens devint son seul objectif. . . . Et tant pis pour la morale et l'équité. (A. H. Bâ 1992: 81–82)

Besides, as Wangrin knew, any case that involved, rightly or wrongly, a European would be very hard to settle in a colony. No doubt it was preferable to ignore a crime—however serious—than to pass sentence on a European, all the more so if the latter was part of the establishment. The prestige of the colonizers was at stake, and when it came to that sort of thing policy sought to it that problems of conscience did not stand in the way. In view of that particular situation, Wangrin felt he could discard all his own scruples and behave just like his counterpart. To defend himself with every means at his disposal became his only object. . . . Too bad if, in the process, morals and justice had to fall by the wayside. (A. H. Bâ 1999: 53–54)

The fact that Wangrin is objectively guilty and Villermoz is innocent (that is, guilty at most of negligence) and a victim of Wangrin's plotting must be set aside for a moment. As an arm of the colonial apparatus, the justice system's first concern is not to right wrongs or to guarantee moral rectitude in its jurisdiction, but to maintain French control. This requires that Villermoz not be made to look guilty publically, even though evidence is stacked up against him because of Wangrin's plotting. The judicial system's general logic of treating blacks as pawns in a game of white privilege proves to be not only unjust, but outdone, since, at least in this case, the game is inverted: a black interpreter has used a French count as an unwitting pawn in his money-making ruse. While individual persons or cases may present exceptions to the legal system's logic of exploitation and racial preference, the ultimate preeminence of politics over the law in the colonies is unquestionable and insurmountable.[22] The outcome of the cattle investigation confirms this fact, for the highest judicial authority involved, the *cour d'assises* in Dakar, decides not to pronounce judgment at all, but rather to "renvoyer l'affaire dite des boeufs à l'autorité administrative pour un complément d'enquête quant aux conséquences politiques de cette affaire" ("remit the so-called 'cattle affair' to the administrative authorities so that further inquiries may be made as to the political consequences which this case may entail").[23] In other words, a lengthy trial originally referred to the judiciary by the bureau of political affairs in Bamako leads only to a cover-up by the bureau of political affairs in Dakar—which even bribes Wangrin to keep quiet afterward.

While the politicization of law is clear enough in the case of colonial French courts, it is even more so in the case of the parallel system of *tribunaux indigènes* or native courts that were set up to adjudicate affairs among Africans, the vast majority of whom were not French citizens until 1946, according to local African customs in the case of non-Muslims, or Islamic law in the case of Muslims. The codifications of native "law," written as reference books called *coutumiers* and used in native courts, were already products of the political agendas of their authors (Jézéquel 2006); even more problematically, native courts were ultimately under the authority of local colonial administrators—and their subordinates, given that most French administrators did not understand African customs deeply enough to judge cases based on them—rather than of an independent judiciary (Ginio 2006). For this reason, when Wangrin is later accused of selling alcohol illegally in "Dioussola" (Bobo Dioulasso), the narrative voice takes care to specify that

Heureusement pour lui, Wangrin fut cité devant le tribunal français. S'il avait été justiciable des tribunaux indigènes, que présidaient le commandant de cercle ou son adjoint, c'en était fait de lui. (A. H. Bâ 1992: 292)

Fortunately for him, Wangrin was summoned before the French court. If his case had been heard in the indigenous court which was presided over by the Commandant or his deputy, his goose would have been cooked. (A. H. Bâ 1999: 207)

Although Wangrin is once again taking advantage of the system, since he is guilty but ends up getting himself acquitted, what is important in the text's portrait of politicized law in the AOF is that the judicial system would have taken advantage of him if he had let it—just as, historically speaking, it doubtlessly did crush many other less shrewd, or less lucky, Africans under its unfairness.

A Transracial Looking Glass: The Double Ethnographic Gaze

Wangrin thus portrays its place and time as strongly characterized by an imperative of "eat or be eaten." The underlying structural cause of this moral mayhem is that the colonial universe of the AOF is one of competition for under-the-table favors and promises of protection from an arbitrary, authoritarian, and racist government. As we have seen, Africans and even Europeans find themselves forced to navigate this maze as best they can with whatever tools at their disposal. As such, Bâ's ethnographically thick writing does more than to turn its gaze back on the colonizer (Izzo 2015). It constantly shuttles between colonizer and colonized. Together with his memoirs, *Wangrin* elaborates a double ethnographic gaze, conjuring up a mirror image that shows the two groups as uncanny reflections of each other. In spite of the unequal power distribution between colonizer and colonized, the human beings who compose them are more alike than they are different.

Bâ's interest in detailing social hierarchies makes this concern especially recognizable in his memoirs, which are dotted with ethnographic observations and reported oral narrative from throughout his travels as a colonial bureaucrat in French Sudan and Upper Volta (today Mali and Burkina Faso). In many instances, these remarks offer historical analyses that illuminate themes in *Wangrin*. For example, the reader cannot help but see a rapprochement, on the one hand, between the meticulous descriptions of the functioning of the Toucouleur state of Masina in *Amkoullel* or the various posts and ministries of the Mossi state of Yatenga in *Oui mon commandant!*, and, on the other hand, those of the colonial bureaucracy: whether at the level of the colony (mainly Upper Volta) or the federation (the AOF), promotions and demotions, desirable and undesirable transfers, the movement of dossiers up and down the colonial ladder, and the many intrigues that these events generate or feed into constitute the bulk of the narratives of both Bâ's and Wangrin's time in the civil service.[24] Alongside these French bureaucratic hierarchies, both *Wangrin* and the memoirs describe parallel groups and subgroups of the AOF's power holders and population—church vs. state, citizen vs. subject, "White-Whites" vs. "White-Blacks" vs. "Black-Blacks," etc.—emphasizing the highly nuanced relations of domination that, at particular moments, strongly recall those of the precolonial world of African empires.[25] Both the colonial state and its precolonial predecessors described in these texts have top-down power structures with carefully delineated divisions of labor; both have capacities for military and occult power whose exercise is carefully regulated; and both are subject to disputes caused by conflicting egos. While it may seem surprising to speak of the colonial administration of having occult power, one has only to think of the image of the tricolor fetish discussed above, as well as the administrators' status as "untouchables" and "gods of the bush," not to mention the power of the Catholic Church.[26]

A consequence of this kind of political comparison is the implication that both colonial and precolonial empires have positive aspects of their political legacy, whatever their flaws or excesses. *Amkoullel* describes Amadu Lobbo's reign in Masina (1818–45) as "éclairé" or enlightened not only because it succeeded in organizing nomadic populations into a powerful state, but also because it effectively managed more mundane logistical tasks—"ce qui n'était pas une petite affaire" (which was no small feat) the author tells us—like regulating "les dates de transhumance du bétail en concertation avec les populations agricoles locales" (the dates for coordinating the movement of cattle between pastures with local agricultural populations) (A. H. Bâ 1991: 20). Similarly, even though Tidjani Tall, who reigned over Umar Tall's successor state in the same region (1864–88), was responsible for the ruthless massacre of hundreds of men, including members of Amadou Hampâté Bâ's family, in retaliation for the death of his celebrated uncle-conqueror, *Amkoullel* nevertheless reminds us that none of his subjects ever had to pay "quoi que ce soit pour sa subsistance. L'Etat leur fournissait viande et nourriture, et de grands repas étaient ouverts chaque jour aux pauvres" (anything at all for subsistence. The state provided them meat and food, and great meals were open each day to the poor) (1991: 31). Such a description contrasts noticeably with the colonial administration's impotence when it is faced with the horrific famine of 1914 (1991: 313–19). These historical details betray a certain admiration on the author's part for efficient, "enlightened" administration, even though it may be inflected with histories of violence or traces of paternalism. He echoes this love for a job well done in *Oui mon commandant!* while narrating his own work as a mail clerk in the colonial governor's office at Ouagadougou in 1924:

> [Demba Sadio] m'initia à tous les travaux bureaucratiques du cabinet, véritable coeur du grand corps qu'était un territoire colonial. . . . A l'école professionnelle de Bamako, on nous avait enseigné que le travail anoblit, et nous étions marqués par cette formation. Pour nous, il n'y avait pas d'heures fixes: tant qu'il y avait du travail, il fallait le liquider, et il n'était point besoin de nous le demander; c'était pour nous comme un point d'honneur à respecter. Le retard par simple négligence était impensable, et d'ailleurs, il faut le dire, nos chefs blancs nous donnaient l'exemple. Ni pluie ni extrême chaleur ne les empêchaient d'être à l'heure au bureau. (A. H. Bâ 1994: 230–31)

> [Demba Sadio] initiated me into all of the office's bureaucratic tasks, the true heart of the great body that a colonial territory was. . . . At the professional school in Bamako, we had been taught that work makes you noble, and we were marked by this instruction. For us, there were no fixed hours: as long as there was work

to do, we had to liquidate it, and we didn't need to be asked; it was for us a
matter of honor that needed to be respected. Lateness due to simple negligence
was unthinkable, and moreover, I must say, our white bosses set the example.
Neither rain nor extreme heat stopped them from being on time at work. (my
translation)

This passage reveals that the worth of competent management is so significant
to Bâ precisely because *in*competence and *un*enlightenment abound, among
both African rulers and colonial administrators. One has only to think of the
Dori prison disaster of 1924, in which cramped conditions result in nine deaths
by asphyxiation and disciplinary measures against several colonial employees,
both black and white, or the Fula prince Lolo—that is, "Loli" from the inheritance
dispute in *Wangrin*—whose drunkenness and eccentricity cause him to squander
his father's wealth, proving his unfitness to assume the throne that his uncle had
usurped from him.[27]

These anecdotes, which crisscross *Wangrin* and the memoirs, establish a
mirrorlike reflection effect between colonial and precolonial forms of government.
Cruelty, prejudice, and pettiness, but also dedication and attempts at reform, run
across both periods, deepening the reader's sense of the historical thickness of
life in the AOF. In spite of the profound rupture that colonialism introduced, the
constantly intersecting regimes of historicity at play still share important moments
of continuity. Good governance, abuse, and expansionism in the colonial world
all have antecedents and parallels—a sort of genealogy, or mirror images—in
African kingdoms. The time of nineteenth-century empires and heroes is once
again brought to bear on the colonial historical present.

A striking instance of this continuity is the issue of class, especially nobility,
which returns again and again throughout *Wangrin* and the memoirs as a point of
intersection between French and African structures of power. These texts reveal a
sense of mutual recognition between a number of colonial administrators who have
ties to the French aristocracy and African nobles—that is, Africans who are neither
captives nor artisans by birth, but hold the status of "freemen" (*horonw* in Bamana or
rimbe in Fulfulde). Noble origin on both continents involves a taste for honor, style,
and chivalry: in *Wangrin*, the Count de Villermoz's love for elegant horses parallels
that of Karibu Sawali; Wangrin, whose Bamana noble origins make him sensitive
to this aesthetic and moral code and who is himself described as a "chevalier" or
"gentleman," acknowledges the aristocratic count, "qui se comportait en grand

seigneur et portait un monocle" ("the fine gentleman [who] wore a monocle"), as a dignified enemy because of his "attitude de grande noblesse" or "noble nature."[28] In *Amkoullel*, during Bâ's childhood, one commandant expresses sympathy for Bâ's stepfather Tidjani Thiam, who was deposed from his chieftaincy and imprisoned in 1905, through a language of class solidarity:

> Il nous apprit qu'il se nommait de Courcelles, qu'il appartenait, en France, à un très vieux clan de chefs et que ses ancêtres, à une certaine époque qu'il appela "Révolution," avaient été, tout comme Tidjani, dépouillés de leur chefferie. Quelques membres de sa famille avaient même été exécutés et d'autres envoyés au bagne après confiscation de leurs biens. C'est dire s'il comprenait Tidjani et se sentait proche de lui! (A. H. Bâ 1991: 159)

> He told us that his name was de Courcelles, that he belonged, in France, to a very old clan of chiefs, and that his ancestors, at a certain period that he called "Revolution," had been, just like Tidjani, stripped of their chieftaincy. Some members of his family had even been executed, and others sent to prison after their property was confiscated. That should tell you whether he understood Tidjani and felt close to him! (my translation)

The style of language here is jarring with a comic effect. To refer to the nobility of the ancien régime as "clans" who were deprived of their "chieftaincies," while denotatively accurate, applies the primitivizing language of anthropology to French history. The defamiliarizing reference to "a certain period that he called 'Revolution'" furthers this ironic ethnographic self-distancing and its use to express interracial class solidarity. Interestingly, this scenario is repeated years later, in the early 1920s, when the commandant François de Coutouly declares a similar solidarity with his adult employee Amadou Hampâté in *Oui mon commandant!*:

> Tu appartiens donc à la noblesse de ton pays, comme moi-même dans le mien. Nous allons nous lier pour défendre cette institution sacrée que la Révolution française a jetée dans la poubelle. (A. H. Bâ 1994: 200)

> So, you belong to the nobility of your country, as do I in mine. We are going to join forces to defend this sacred institution that the French Revolution threw in the garbage. (my translation)

While not everyone shares such sentiments of transcultural unity, an awareness exists on each side of the colonial divide that the other side has a code of aristocracy reminiscent of its own. This cross-cultural intelligibility reflects the fascination that many colonial administrators and ethnographers had for African "upper classes," being "inclined to assimilate them into the Western aristocracy" (Jézéquel 2006: 146). Bâ seems both to channel this romanticization and to demystify it: he drives home the idea that the African code of nobility is worthy of the prestige afforded to its French counterpart; yet he also documents ambivalent attitudes toward class differences, such as that of the egalitarian Charles de Brière in *Wangrin*, who traded the *de* in his name "contre un dé à coudre," that is, the sign of his aristocratic origin in exchange for paid labor.[29] Moreover, many of the author's portraits of aristocratic Frenchmen are hardly flattering, such the administrator de Lopino, described in *Oui mon commandant!* as

> le prototype même de ces administrateurs qui, fiers de leur valeur intrinsèque ou de leur naissance, se croyaient tout permis, et dont certains écarts frôlaient l'acte d'indiscipline grave.[30]

> the very prototype of those administrators who, being proud of their intrinsic value or of their birth, thought they could do as they pleased, and whose blunders, in some cases, approached acts of grave indiscipline. (my translation)

De Lopino's abusive assertion of noble prerogatives earns him an unwanted transfer out of Upper Volta to the colony of Niger (A. H. Bâ 1994: 232–44). People like him, the Count de Villermoz, and the Fula prince Lolo are so obsessed with the outward accoutrements of their rank that they become, in the author's view, frivolous. For these men, noble status actually becomes more of a liability than an asset, as it causes them to live in a world of denial, nostalgia, and fantasy that impedes diligent, serious work. Several French administrators of noble origin are described as jumpy, nervous, and defensive of their status, as though aware of their increasing marginalization in the republican world.

Amadou Hampâté Bâ's ethnographic interest in French nobility emphasizes that it parallels its African counterpart in many ways, especially because in neither case does reality truly live up to the ideal. From an ethical point of view, this confirms the words of a griot singing Wangrin's praises:

On peut naître noble et cependant perdre sa noblesse par avarice et cupidité. La vraie noblesse est celle que l'on acquiert par sa valeur. Il en est de la noblesse comme d'un édifice. Il y a les fondations, les murs et la toiture. On hérite des fondations, mais on construit soi-même les murs et la toiture, faute de quoi l'édifice reste en ébauche et risque de retourner à l'état de terrain vague. (A. H. Bâ 1992: 122)

One may be born a nobleman, yet lose that station to avarice and greed. True nobility is contingent on values. It resembles a building which has foundations, walls, and roofing. Foundations are inherited, while walls and roofing are built by one's own effort, else the building would remain a mere outline and would risk reverting to wasteland. (A. H. Bâ 1999: 81)

Although the griot continues to proclaim that Wangrin's "edifice" is solidly built, the reader cannot help but notice the effect of dramatic irony: whether the griot knows it or not, the incompatibility of "avarice and greed" with "true nobility" pertains to the hero more than anyone. More importantly than the didactic point, however, the comparison of aristocracies allows Bâ to explore two related problems of life in the colonial world: the fact that French theories of colonialism and even nationhood are not all in harmony with each other, and the resulting fact that colonialism is not as single-minded, and certainly not as egalitarian, as some of its champions claimed it to be. "Colonialism was no one thing," writes Dipesh Chakrabarty (Ghosh and Chakrabarty 2002: 169); Alice Conklin demonstrates the point, arguing that the AOF's attempts to eradicate African aristocracies in the name of individual emancipation before World War I shifted to a more conservative co-optation of existing social hierarchies after the war (1997: 249). The colonial system appears in Bâ's writings as a machine that tries to be effective and efficient, but whose optimal functioning is hindered by disagreeing factions and individuals struggling among each other over how to operate it.

This special concern for systems of social inequality and domination turns the anthropological gaze onto the colonizers, whose contradictions and failures are exhibited in detail. It also undermines their claims to legitimacy in the colonies, as they can never quite agree among each other what the basis for this legitimacy is. Wangrin's opportunistically patriotic reference to France as "mère des droits de l'homme et anti-esclavagiste" ("the mother of human rights and the enemy of slavery") sounds even more hollow when read alongside Villermoz's spiteful frustration with "cette putain de Révolution française, mère d'une république aussi dévergondée qu'elle" ("that bitch of a French Revolution, mother of a Republic just as shameless as herself").[31] The colonial regime of historicity seems to be fractured or punctured by persistent subregimes, for the reference points of monarchy, revolution, and republic are still disputed within it. What does it mean, after all, to raise the tricolor flag over Africa when not even colonizers believe in it? We might read Bâ's prolonged explorations of tensions within the colonial bureaucracy as a kind of response to the Segu epic's portrayal of the French flag as a ritual "fetish." Both in *Wangrin* and in his memoirs, the author illustrates that the colonial hold on power simultaneously corresponds to and complicates the epic image of an occult object capable of neutralizing God (blue), blinding African eyes (white), and spilling their blood (red). The colonial government does, or tries to do, all of these things in various ways, but its power is riddled with internal inconsistencies and weaknesses. Like Wangrin's own divine protection by Gongoloma-Sooké, which lasts only as long as he keeps safe his *pierre d'alliance* or pebble symbolizing their alliance, France's control in Africa is subject to the limitations of its protective "fetish," which can be summed up as ideological violence. Abuse, resentment, conflicting agendas and collective memories, and, as we shall see, power vacuums jeopardize the colonial endeavor as it plays out on the ground. Colonialism—like the empire of Segu, and like Bamana religion—is portrayed as defined by contradiction.

The epic historicity that *L'Etrange destin de Wangrin* mobilizes through the characterization of its hero, the description of the god Gongoloma-Sooké, the incorporation of panegyric, and its framing as an oral performance is well placed to capture these paradoxes. It offers not just an alternative to the colonial regime of historicity—a thrilling narrative of an African genius thwarting his white masters and their minions—but a multitude of ways in which to explore how the regimes of historicity at work in the AOF compromise and intertwine with each other. The issues of ideology, custom, praise, status, and belonging, all of which are of crucial importance in West African heroic narrative, are explored not as components of the worldview of a neatly defined ethnic entity, as an ethnographic monograph might do, but as conjunctures where the plural cultures of the AOF meet, negotiate, and contradict themselves in a historical present. Just as colonialism is no one thing, neither are the alternatives to it, such as "African traditions," "precolonial empires," or religious belief.

The All Too Human Hero

In a sense, the most significant indictment of the colonial system in *L'Etrange destin de Wangrin* is the fact that it enables someone like Wangrin to exist. The colonial administrators' incapability of ruling on the ground in spite of their pretentions to superiority creates a power vacuum between them and their subjects, requiring recourse to intermediaries who end up corrupted by the outsized power entrusted to them. The colonial administrator Henri Labouret—a historical figure, not a character in the book—denounced this situation so precisely that he sounds like a character in the book. One can easily imagine him as yet another administrator embittered by Wangrin's swindles:

> Lorsque le milicien ne se manifeste pas, on trouve à sa place l'interprète ou le secrétaire, toujours correct, attentionné, discret, et dévoué, intermédiaire obligé entre l'administrateur, qui ne parle pas les langues du pays et les indigènes qui n'entendent pas le français. Sa tyrannie est plus intelligente, mais non moins lourde, elle est tout aussi profitable. Gardes de cercle, interprètes ou secrétaires sont presque partout les véritables chefs du pays. Ces auxiliaires, dont les méfaits ont été dénoncés en 1917 par le Gouverneur Général Van Vollenhoven dans une circulaire célèbre,[32] ont contribué pour une large part à la déposition des représentants légitimes de certaines collectivités qui auraient pu devenir de précieux collaborateurs. Ils en complotèrent souvent la perte pour prendre leur place ou y mettre une de leurs créatures. (Labouret 1931: 40)

> When it isn't the militiaman causing problems, one finds instead the interpreter or the secretary, always polite, attentive, discreet, and devoted, the necessary intermediary between the administrator, who does not speak the languages of the country, and the natives, who do not speak French. Their tyranny is more intelligent, but no less heavy, and just as profitable. Nearly everywhere, it is district guards, interpreters, or secretaries who are the real chiefs of the country. These auxiliaries, whose misdeeds were denounced in 1917 by Governor General Van Vollenhoven in a famous memo, have contributed to the ousting of legitimate representatives of certain entities who could have become precious collaborators. They have often plotted such persons' removal in order to take their place or fill it with one of their creatures. (my translation)

The fact that Labouret's colonial career unfolded in the AOF during the same period as the historical Wangrin's, combined with his allusion to concerns about interpreters at the highest levels of the administrative hierarchy, is a powerful testimony to the fact that the interpreter phenomenon was real and widespread (Lawrance, Osborn, and Roberts 2006). Having written these lines while teaching in Paris, Labouret was himself a speaker of two West African languages (Deschamps 1959: 291–92); his implication here is that French rule could be more effective if only administrators were competent enough to control their subordinates, notably through unimpeded communication and surveillance. The historian Jean Suret-Canale, commenting on Labouret's remarks, extends the critique into a denunciation of colonialism more generally:

> Pour l'administrateur qui trace ce tableau [Labouret], tout le mal vient évidemment de l'auxiliaire indigène.... En réalité, le mal vient du despotisme du "commandant," au nom duquel agissent les sous-ordres, et dont ils cherchent à tirer quelques profits personnels! (Suret-Canale 1962: 102)

> For the administrator drawing this portrait [Labouret], the whole problem is obviously the fault of the native auxiliary.... In reality, the problem is the despotism of the "commandant," in whose name the subordinates act, and from whom they seek to gain some personal profit! (my translation)

For Suret-Canale, the true problem lies in the almighty white colonial hierarchy, whose decisions are without appeal, and from whose power the interpreter draws his own. The problem is not the "tyranny" of the interpreter, but the tyranny of the system; the corrupt interpreter is but a node—and a peripheral one at that—in a vast network of exploitation.

Suret-Canale's historical analysis, which both points toward the importance of colonial interpreters like Wangrin and relativizes their corruption in the larger context of the colonial world, helps us think through the fundamental ambiguity of Wangrin as heroic model. Eileen Julien argues that *Wangrin* expresses only a hollow or impotent sort of anticolonialism: "Wangrin's defiant acts, which are so satisfying to his friends and the reader, are mere dents and scratches on the carapace of colonialism, which remains firmly in place" (1992: 66). For Pierre N'Da, Wangrin is a precursor of the neopatrimonial workings of the independent African state, whereby government employees use their access to public resources in order to acquire favor and influence from private social networks (2005). Notwithstanding all the epic dimensions of the text, and notwithstanding Bâ's repeated defense of Wangrin as a Robin Hood–type figure, this fundamental ambiguity, rooted in his opportunism and dependence on the colonial system, puts Wangrin's pure humanity at the heart of what makes him a hero.[33] Like the people around him populating the AOF, whether black, white, Christian, or Muslim, his main objective is to accumulate and wield economic, political, and symbolic capital on the colonial playing field. As such, *Wangrin*, especially when read alongside Bâ's memoirs, draws a tableau of human life in the AOF that transcends religious, racial, and colonial boundaries, including the binary of resistance and complicity. It situates the struggles for power of the colonial universe's inhabitants within the region's competing regimes of historicity. On the ground, this means that each of these collective memories is always subject to politicized interpretation by interested individuals. While the framing of this thoroughly pragmatic, cross-cultural ethnography as a kind of oral epic for modern times may strike some readers as romantic, it is, in the final analysis, anything but. In Bâ's view, neither the precolonial nor the colonial periods offer utopian answers for postcolonial Africa. The epic he sings is merely that of flawed human beings trying, and ultimately failing, to rise above the fray.

CHAPTER FIVE

Hyperprimitives, Buffoons, and Other Lies

Ironic Ethnographies from Ouologuem to Kourouma

Unlike the Africans, the French did not go to consult the seers; they went to visit the ethnologists.

—Ahmadou Kourouma, *Waiting for the Vote of the Wild Animals*

T he novels of Ivorian author Ahmadou Kourouma offer a thrilling, disorienting ride through two centuries of West African political history. The trilogy formed by *Les Soleils des indépendances* (1968), *Monnè, outrages et défis* (1990), and *En attendant le vote des bêtes sauvages* (1998)—translated respectively as *The Suns of Independence, Monnew*, and *Waiting for the Vote of the Wild Animals*—retells, in an endlessly ironic mode, the history of French West Africa from its foundation by conquest in the late nineteenth century to its impoverished, oppressive aftermath in the latter half of the twentieth. The trilogy's take on this history is both panoramic and parodic. Oral epic genres serve as a central narrative device guiding each novel's framing or storyline. Each text in the series satirizes an obstinate, backward-looking ruler who functions as a failed hero; each text privileges the roles of traditional bards in ways that suggest an explicit parallel between the novel form and oral epic narrative; and, perhaps most famously, Kourouma's language is deeply imbued with proverbs, Maninka-influenced syntax, and (sometimes ironic) praise songs: "If Kourouma mocks some content of the epic genre, he seems to be committed to its style or language."[1] The rulers ridiculously cling to the trappings of traditional heroism, including having their status recognized and their praises sung, in order to help cement their extravagant sense of their own power. Protagonist-kings insist on living in a world of denial, verging on fantasy, where precolonial authority structures remain intact. They refuse to acknowledge the marginalization irrevocably imposed on them by French colonialism (Djigui in *Monnè*) and its successor independent state (Fama in *Soleils*). The third volume, focusing on the era of single-party dictatorships, is framed as an oral hunters' epic ostensibly being performed to exalt a vicious African dictator as a hunter-hero, but actually conveying a not-so-subtle, damning criticism of his abuses (Koyaga in *En attendant*).

Cynical, antinostalgic readings are particularly entrenched in the case of *Soleils*, which takes place in the early independence era, and its prequel, *Monnè*, which unfolds in the aftermath of French conquest in the late nineteenth century. These novels are most often read as calls to a Voltairean return to reason, that is, as denunciations of their absurd protagonists' fantasies of precolonial prestige. Within this paradigm, the epic genre signifies the lost world of tradition, while the novel signifies the modern world of alienation and parody. In an emblematic study, Marion Mas writes that "le roman pervertit le modèle épique" (the novel perverts the epic model):

> Réévaluant "l'immuabilité sémantique" du régime de parole épique à la faveur des registres grotesque et ironique, le discours du roman incite à mettre en discussion les valeurs du monde de l'épopée. (2015: 313 and 315)

> Reevaluating the "semantic immutability" of the epic regime of speech in favor of grotesque and ironic registers, the novel's discourse causes the reader to question the values of the world of the epic. (my translation)

Epic's supposed "semantic immutability"—a direct reference to Bakhtin—is taken for granted in this statement and in a great deal of similar criticism. The resulting conclusion is that Kourouma's novels should be read as parody of oral tradition, especially of West African epic and its associated values of unquestioned authority and obsession with the past. However, *En attendant*'s narrative framing demands that we think about traditionality entirely outside such paradigms. This third novel is framed as a Maninka hunters' epic or *donsomana* being sung to the fictionalized tyrant Koyaga—a thinly disguised calque of Gnassingbé Eyadéma of Togo—while expressing, under cover of flattery, a denunciation of his regime. *En attendant* makes the link between oral tradition and historical reflexivity overt: ancient genres from the Mande zone can be updated to bear on the concerns of today. Its narrative setup explicitly connects oral traditions to the ability to reflect and critique recent history and structures of power. I argue that the explicit reflexivity attributed to the epic tradition in *En attendant le vote des bêtes sauvages* obliges us to rethink the issue of traditionality in Kourouma's work at large.

Indeed, the creative openness with which Kourouma reinvents epic traditions in all three of these novels is both a way of channeling oral traditions' intrinsic capacity for critical reflexivity and a product of his own authorial imagination. On the one hand, as we shall see, real hunters' songs from the Manden can reflect important historical experience, suggesting a concern that overlaps with his novelistic writing. On the other hand, Kourouma uses extreme poetic license to create his ferociously imaginative, hybrid traditionalities. A voracious reader of Africanist ethnographic writing, he regularly mixed ethnographic descriptions of distinct phenomena from the Mande cultural zone and beyond into hybridized pastiches: the *donsomana* or hunters' epic, the *korodugaw* or ritual buffoons, and the outdated colonial belief in a "paleonigritic" hypothesis, to name a few, are all recombined into unexpected formations and made to play surprising roles in his work. Even his famous use of proverbs straddles the line between quoting real sayings and making things up. That is, his texts seem to constantly be mashing up distinct traditional genres, institutions, and practices—not to mention geographies, since his novels crisscross the West African region and even the African continent—in ways that flout the serious student of anthropology. This practice of rewriting through pastiche generates a unique kind of ironic ethnography, reminiscent of Yambo Ouologuem's so-called plagiarism, by drawing from a bewildering range of source materials, including, as we shall see, questionable quoting practices. Like Ouologuem's "Shrobeniusology," Kourouma's acerbic fiction directs its parodic force toward the genre of anthropological/ethnographic writing, and especially toward its role in producing colonial stereotype. As such, Kourouma parodies not so much actual oral traditions themselves, which he sees as potential vehicles for thought, but particular representations of them as authentic, pure, static, romantic, or exotic. Above all, his work criticizes what we might call the "strawman worldview" of African obsession with a romanticized past heyday, as popularized by the Western anthropological imagination and incarnated by Djigui in *Soleils* and Fama in *Monnè*.

This chapter will study Kourouma's philosophy of traditionality through his appropriations of oral epic features in his writing. It diverges from previous studies of this subject not only in its conclusions, but in its method. We must situate Kourouma's work with regard to anthropological thought, both at the level of comparative ethnology and of ethnographic studies of Mande ritual and institutions, rather than simply importing definitions of epic from classic literary theory.[2] Using the example of *Bilali of Faransekila*, a documented epic-like hunters' song, as a point of departure, the chapter will begin by exploring the potential of this kind of oral genre to convey historical reflexivity, arguing that Kourouma's novelistic writing draws part of its critical force from it. It will then turn to Kourouma's theorization of creative traditionalities as an alternative to older binaries of primitive and scientific mentalities—the old "great divide" paradigm—that have been so influential in anthropology. It will elucidate how his historical trilogy excavates different imaginations of traditionality as a construct, ridiculing the stagnant or closed forms invented by anthropology and lived by fictional antiheroes, while calling for a new, more democratic traditionality that is neither rigid nor incompatible with progressive thought and historical change. It will conclude by comparing Kourouma's practice of ironic ethnography to that of Ouologuem, arguing that similar strategies of reading are required to access both authors' work.

Hunters' Songs: A Complex Heroic Model

En attendant le vote des bêtes sauvages frames the story of the dictator-hero Koyaga, who was trained in his youth as a master hunter, as a *donsomana*, or hunters' epic, performed by a *sèrè*, or specialized hunters' bard, named Bingo.[3] The *donsomana*, cited as an example of the corporative subset of African epics specific to a particular profession, parallels in many ways the dynastic epic genre represented by, for example, *Sunjata* (Kesteloot and Dieng 1997: 44–45). (In the Manding linguistic continuum, *donso* means "hunter" while *mana* is usually translated as "epic.") A long narrative performance, accompanied by *naamu*-sayers, instruments, and intervening songs and dances, and potentially divided over several evenings, is sung by the *sèrè* to celebrate a gathering of a local *donsoton* or hunters' association—that is, the fraternal organization within which hunters are trained, are ritually initiated, and work together.[4] The narratives celebrate legendary hunters or castigate foolish ones in their struggles in the wild: their adversaries include elephants, panthers, crocodiles, lions, and even jinns and sorcerers. These memorable combats are meant to inspire emulation by living hunters. The literary form of the *donsomana* has attracted significant scholarly attention, as have the initiatic, religious, and even political dimensions of *donsoya*, the institution of initiatic hunting spread throughout the Mande zone.[5]

In Kourouma's novel, the epic performance is staged as a series of six evening performances in which the bard Bingo, often addressing his *naamu*-sayer Tiekura, lays out Koyaga's deeds in a way that is ostensibly laudatory but transparently critical. Koyaga's feats in the bush as a young man—which include slaying a panther, buffalo, elephant, and crocodile—prepare his fearless service as a young soldier in the French colonial army, under whose auspices he distinguishes himself in Indochina, before clawing his way up the political ladder of the "Republic of the Gulf." The novel opens in a panegyric mode:

Votre nom: Koyaga! Votre totem: faucon! . . . Vous resterez avec Ramsès II et Soundiata l'un des trois plus grands chasseurs de l'humanité. Retenez le nom de Koyaga, le chasseur et président-dictateur de la République du Golfe. (Kourouma 1998: 9)

Your name: Koyaga! Your totem: the falcon! . . . Along with Ramses II and Sundyata, you will remain one of the three greatest hunters of humankind. Remember the name of Koyaga, hunter and president-dictator of the Republic of the Gulf. (Kourouma 2001: 4)

This opening sets the tone for the ironic epic that will follow. The allusions to pharaohs and to Sunjata—whose own epic, it has been suggested, may have evolved from hunting stories—situate the protagonist in a line of larger-than-life African heroes (Austen 1999b: 72). Yet while the comparison of Koyaga to a "hunter of humankind" suggests, at first glance, the image of a valiant fighter and protector, it already prefigures the degradation of the hunters' art into senseless bloodshed. Furthermore, the addition of the pejoratively charged epithet "dictator" to the title "president" hints at a call to accountability for political and human atrocities. The great African past conjured up via ancient Egypt and Mali has deteriorated into a petty, violent dictatorship.

A specific oral text, *Bilali of Faransekila,* can serve as an enlightening point of comparison to *En attendant*'s use of the *donsomana* framing. This 454-line oral hunters' song, recorded by David Conrad in Bamako in 1975, recounts the story of an African hunter who goes to Europe to fight in World War I (Conrad 1989). The song's performer, Seydou Camara of Mali, was a well-known hunters' singer. Due to his collaboration with Charles Bird and other American researchers in the 1970s, his biography and career are well documented.[6] Of blacksmith status by birth, Camara's repertoire included ritual songs, dancing songs, and epic narratives praising hunter-heroes (Bird 1974: ix). Although *Bilali* does not appear to be a widespread *donsomana* narrative, it is a composition whose style and format closely follow the *donsomana* form. The song connects the attributes of the hunter-hero to a valiant black warrior whose larger-than-life military prowess saves France from the Germans. Born an orphan, the hunter-hero Bilali establishes his valor by killing a dangerous lioness; as a young man he is conscripted to forced labor gathering rubber; known for his bravery, he is drafted to the Great War, but makes a stop on the way to put down an anti-French rebellion in Morocco; in Europe, he serves as a "one-man regiment" (line 255) who "defeat[s] the Germans for the whites and for the blacks" (line 360); upon his return to Africa, jealous relatives put a curse on him, and he dies when his boat capsizes not far from his home village. Perhaps in order to increase the dramatic tension, Seydou Camara conflates the two World Wars, referring to Charles De Gaulle and Adolf Hitler as leaders of the opposing camps of the great conflict of "fourteen-eighteen" (lines 157, 321, 353).

Bilali is a fascinating literary text that illustrates history in the process of becoming oral tradition. It can shed light on Kourouma's interest in the adaptability of the African epic form in general, and of the hunters' epic in particular. Consider the following excerpts:

> There are no last names in heaven,
> But before death a slave has no choice.
> Youth is the time to accomplish great deeds,
> A man must raise himself.
> Before he dies a slave cannot tell God what he wants to do.
> Bilali grew up unsheltered.
> No lie, Bilali had no father,
> Bilali had lost his mother.
> Strange thing,

No one sheltered Bilali. (lines 25–34)

Bilali was a slave,
A worthy slave.
A hero is welcome on troubled days.
A hero is not welcome,
A hero is welcome only on troubled days.
Bilali saved the rubber tree cutters,
The lions fell into the darkness of a musket shot. . . .
When the rubber tree cutting was over the war began,
The German war. . . .
The blacks must be called. (lines 144–64)

No lie, the wealth belongs to the white men.
The black is born with only his heart,
The black is fearless.
The black is worthy, no lie.
Bilali attacked the Germans,
The Germans surrendered to the will of the whites [i.e. the French]. . . .
Since the Germans' defeat they have respected the blacks. (lines 337–44)
(Conrad 1989: 48–56)

Three salient themes in these excerpts from *Bilali of Faransekila* illustrate why Kourouma turns to the hunters' societies and their oral literature as inspiration for his novel. First, Bilali is a low-status hero, certainly an orphan, and apparently a slave by birth (Conrad 1989: 63). This fact is important because of the *donsoton*'s emphasis on equality. In striking contrast to the rest of Mande society, inherited birth statuses have no weight within the hunters' associations: "Nul ne naît chasseur, on le devient sur la base d'un libre choix" (No one is born a hunter, one becomes it on the basis of a free choice) (Traoré 2000b: 91). The only hierarchy among the hunters is based on seniority, not on caste (Cissé 1994: 45). In other words, Bilali is a hero *even though* he has no impressive genealogy or claim to a throne. His identity as hunter compensates for his despised identities as slave and orphan. As we shall see, Kourouma, following the Malian ethnologist Y. T. Cissé, takes this egalitarianism of the Mande hunters as a model for democratic society, one that is both inspired by the heritage of tradition and purged of its structures of domination.

Second, *Bilali* illustrates the capacity of hunters' oral literature to commemorate historical experience with a critical eye. Despite the loss of historical precision that accompanies the singer's techniques of narrativization, the story of the hero's feats as a hunter and soldier is a valuable historical document because it reflects the experiences and perceptions of a great many colonial subjects from French West Africa who fought overseas as *tirailleurs* (sharpshooters) for the metropole, both in colonial conflicts and in the two World Wars (Conrad 1989). It is all the more pertinent given that both Kourouma himself and Gnassingbé Eyadéma, the author's model for Koyaga, shared in this experience by serving as *tirailleurs* in the French Indochina War. This historicity is a key feature that unites *Bilali* and Kourouma's novels. Seydou Camara fills the mythical form of the hunters' epic with allusions to African experiences of foreign wars, travel, forced labor—an important issue in *Monnè*—and leadership in shaping political affairs in both the AOF and France itself.[7] The demand for recognition and rehabilitation of the black race via Bilali's heroism reveals a critical consciousness of French hypocrisy, even though it is they that he is sent to save. All of these historical issues and their relationship to traditional narrative forms are of central interest in Kourouma's novels. The dynamism and creativity with which Kourouma infuses his representations of oral tradition in his novels are not only the result of his own authorial originality, but intrinsic traits of oral tradition that he tries to channel in his written work. As Lobna Mestaoui argues,

> dans l'Afrique moderne, l'épique n'est certes pas une matière fossilisée, sclérosée, que l'on conserve dans les musées. Plus que jamais la tradition épique fermente et bouillonne. Elle est vivante et dynamique: on la déclame.... Kourouma travaille à la jonction de ces deux univers, celui de la dictature et celui du fait héroïque épique, pour parler d'une Afrique hybride où s'interpénètrent vieux fonds archaïque et modernité, une Afrique qui, par là, s'avère capable de donner naissance aussi bien à des œuvres qu'à des êtres métissés qui portent en eux une ouverture sur la modernité sans jamais cesser de manifester un lien permanent avec les pratiques de l'héritage culturel traditionnel. (2012: 33)

> in modern Africa, epic is certainly not a fossilized, frozen matter, to be conserved in museums. More than ever the epic tradition is fermenting, ebullient. It is living and dynamic: it is performed.... Kourouma works at the junction of these two universes, the dictatorship and the heroic epic feat, to speak of a hybrid Africa where an old,

archaic stock mixes with modernity, an Africa that thereby shows itself capable of giving birth to hybrid works and beings who carry within themselves an openness to modernity without ceasing to manifest a permanent connection to practices from the traditional cultural heritage. (my translation)

While Mestaoui's recognition of the dynamism of epic is important, we must recognize that it is not only Kourouma who works at the junction of the archaic and the modern. The oral tradition from which he draws inspiration is itself already straddling that junction.

Finally, the subversive potential of oral tradition is expressed remarkably in *Bilali* through the lines, "A hero is not welcome / A hero is welcome only on troubled days" (lines 147–48). These lines, which Seydou Camara wove into many of his performances of heroic narrative, invite differing interpretations (Bird 1974: vii). For Conrad, they indicate in the context of *Bilali* that the hero was "despised" in a literal sense except in times of need—both by his own society, to some degree, because of his low status, and by the French, for whom he was still a colonized subject (1989: 64). But the lines carry a deeper significance for Charles Bird, according to whom they encapsulate

the anomalous relationship between the hero and the society. The hero is asocial, capable of unrestricted cruelty and destructiveness, whose presence is always a threat to the stability of the collectivity. He is, however, perhaps the only member associated with the group who is capable of swift and conclusive action. . . . The society is thus damned with the hero and damned without him. (1974: vii)

The particular point of the hero's capacity for "unrestricted cruelty and destructiveness" could be applied verbatim to the dictator Koyaga, whose ruthlessness is a principal concern of *En attendant le vote des bêtes sauvages*. That novel is, in one sense, a long illustration of how the "Republic of the Gulf" and its fellow dictatorships in francophone Africa are "damned" by the actions of their tyrant-heroes. And yet, even when Koyaga is deposed and an era of democracy declared, the ensuing power vacuum and social chaos lead many Gulf citizens to miss their sense of order and to pave the way for the dictator's return to power, however tenuous his hold on it might be. The public is strangely attracted to the powerful domination that he provides, even though his rule is oppressive and corrupt, because the opposition's forces are fragmented, incompetent, and just as narcissistic. The hero's destructive nature actually functions as a centripetal force against the anarchy represented by his opponents—which consist of hordes of desperate young dropouts and a completely inept National Conference. Moreover, Koyaga provides the paradoxically comforting illusion that "swift and conclusive action" can run the country although the problems facing it—neocolonialism, neoliberalism, and entrenched corruption and poverty—are rooted in historical networks of intercontinental exploitation that are far more powerful, and consequential, than he. The Republic of the Gulf is damned with or without Koyaga.

The Two-Sided Panegyric

En attendant le vote des bêtes sauvages's opening panegyric mode strongly parallels *Bilali* in both tone and content. The novel's *sèrè* Bingo, serving as narrator, recounts Koyaga's great deeds, in the second person, as a hunter and soldier in the colonial army in Indochina. Emphasizing his superhuman strength, this extended laudatory narrative begins with his father, Tchao, a master hunter from the despised community of "Paleos" or "Naked men," through his childhood in the colonial schools and military career. Through all of this, as in *Bilali*, the condescension of the French toward their African comrades is apparent: in each narrative, the hero is glorified for fighting with the French, yet both texts highlight the colonizer's hypocritical disdain. Kourouma's novel pursues this critical portrayal of the French in a more militantly anticolonial tone then Seydou Camara's song. In one digression, the novel's *donsomana* is interrupted by a long ode to Vietnamese resistance:[8]

> Ah! Tiécoura, les Vietnamiens . . . ont chassé de leurs terres tous les grands peuples
> de l'univers. Peuples grands par le nombre de leurs habitants comme les Chinois,
> peuples grands par les moyens techniques de leur armée comme les Américains,
> peuples grands par leur culture et leur histoire comme les Français. Il est à parier
> que, si l'univers entier s'alliait pour occuper le sol vietnamien, les Viets vaincraient
> et jetteraient les soldats du monde entier à la mer. . . . Inclinons-nous tous devant
> les Viets. (Kourouma 1998: 32–33)

> Ah! Tiekura, the Vietnamese . . . chased all the great peoples of the universe from
> their lands. Peoples in great numbers, such as the Chinese; peoples great by their
> technical means, like the Americans; peoples great by their culture and their history,

like the French. If the entire universe were to become allies in order to occupy Vietnamese soil, one might surmise that the Viets would be victorious and toss everybody into the sea.... Let us bow to the Viets. (Kourouma 2001:19)

Whereas *Bilali* never goes so far as to praise the Moroccans in revolt, *En attendant* attributes the kind of superhuman powers of combat and resistance that ought to be reserved for the main hero to his enemies—who are, paradoxically, oppressed by the French, just as he is. By suddenly switching gears to praise the Vietnamese guerrilla warriors who will soon demolish the reeling French army, the text both magnifies anticolonial resistance and seems to suggest that the African soldiers in Indochina would have done well to emulate their Vietnamese counterparts. This implicit comparison deflates the heroism of Koyaga, which continues to be sung on the surface, by associating it with the oppressors and their stunning, humiliating defeat at Dien Bien Phu in 1954.

Indeed, the novel's *donsomana* continues to praise Koyaga for his heroic survival skills following the destruction of his unit, as he wanders in the jungle for eight weeks. However, the text soon deploys its author's signature biting comedy: the hero also manages to save two "dondons de pouffiasses" or "fat, Moroccan whores" to whom he had been particularly attached.

Ainsi vous resterez un héros de légende de l'armée française aussi célèbre que votre père. Votre père Tchao l'est pour avoir bondi seul, sans l'ordre de son caporal, de son terrier de Verdun, et avoir enfourché dans la tranchée d'en face, avec la baïonnette, cinq guerriers allemands. Et vous le demeurerez jusqu'à la fin de l'univers pour avoir sauvé dans la jungle deux plantureuses péripatéticiennes. (Kourouma 1998: 38–39)

Thus it is that you will always be a legendary hero of the French army, as famous as your father. Your father's heroic deed was to have sprung all alone from his burrow at Verdun without any order from his corporal and, with his bayonet, to have speared five German soldiers in the facing trench. You will remain a hero to the end of the very universe for having saved two fat harlots in the jungle. (Kourouma 2001: 23)

This unflattering comparison of Koyaga to his father ridicules the hero. Whereas Tchao's exploits from World War I recall Bilali's, killing Germans as if they were pawns, the son's lasting deed is to follow his sex drive in the face of defeat. This point is all the more salient since Mande hunters are supposed to control their sexuality and avoid intercourse before any important undertaking.[9] Beneath the praise of his virility lies the suggestion that Koyaga is unfit as a hunter, and by extension as a warrior and leader.

This form of ironic praise structures the entire novel. Kourouma's invented *donsomana* recounts how Koyaga, having returned home from Indochina as a war hero, rises and falls from power as the head of the so-called Republic of the Gulf—a calque of Togo, where Kourouma lived and worked for a decade. He participates in two coups that result in the assassinations of the country's first two presidents; these closely parallel the Togolese coups of 1963 and 1967, though they are recounted in the novel with more bloodshed. The now president Koyaga goes on an initiatic voyage to meet other, equally monstrous and absurd African dictators, all of whom are given keyed names that reference real countries and their leaders: Kourouma's nemesis, Félix Houphouët-Boigny of Ivory Coast; Jean-Bédel Bokassa of Central African Republic; Mobutu Sese Seko of Zaire; Sékou Touré of Guinea; and Hassan II of Morocco. All of these real-life figures are recognizable to the attentive reader. Koyaga survives a series of attempted coups against him, while successfully mystifying the public about what really happens each time. Finally, with the eras of democratization and structural adjustment that follow the end of the Cold War, the Republic of the Gulf lurches into bloody instability as attempts to depose or assassinate the dictator alternate with attempts to keep him in power. The novel ends with Koyaga in his native village, surrounded by enemies and deprived of occult protections. Confident that he will be democratically returned to power—even if he must make the wild animals vote for him—he remembers that he must have his *donsomana* sung in order to ritually purify him of his deeds. The epic that is performed ends up being a chronicle of his cruelty and ultimately of his failure.

Endless Irony: Kourouma Between Pseudo-Ethnography and Literature

Karim Traoré, an expert on Mande hunting societies, has remarked that *En attendant le vote des bêtes sauvages* deforms certain aspects of *donsoton* ritual and the *donsomana* genre.[10] Perhaps most importantly, the purifying, ritual dimension that Kourouma attributes to the *donsomana* in order to justify why Koyaga is having it performed does not exist. While there are purifying and initiatic rituals associated with the *donsoton* involving sacrifices at the *dankun* or ritual triangle, these are in reality separate from performances of hunting epics, which serve a communal function of celebrating hunters' group identity and a didactic one of encouraging living hunters to emulate legendary heroes. Traoré ascribes a number of other inaccuracies to Kourouma's representation of hunting practices: the depiction of Tiekura, the *naamu*-sayer, as a buffoon; Koyaga's signature mutilation of his victims' corpses in reference to rituals surrounding the preparation of a dead game animal's body; and the fact that Kourouma's narrating bard is accompanied by a kora, a kind of harp that has eighteen to twenty-one strings, instead of a *nkoni* or *sinbi*, which has between four and nine and which is more contextually correct.[11]

These observations help us separate fact from fiction in our understanding of Mande hunting societies. While Kourouma is clearly inspired by real hunters' bards and their songs, as the example of *Bilali* shows, the role of authorial invention must also be accounted for in his writing. I submit that Kourouma's creative deformations of ethnographic material are themselves a deliberate literary strategy. Delving deeper into how he (mis)represents Mande traditional cultural items can help us appreciate the ultimate object of his critique: the genre of ethnographic writing itself, whose attempts at objective description and classification of peoples were historically complicit in making them colonizable subjects. This section will explore two of the representations to which Traoré objects in *En attendant*—ritual buffoons and the mutilation of corpses—before turning to Kourouma's interest in the so-called paleonigritic hypothesis, a colonial diffusionist theory that tried to account for isolated pockets of peoples seen as more primitive or archaic than their neighbors, including Koyaga's own ethnic group of "Paleos" or "Naked people." These examples will show that the author need not be read as ignorant or contemptuous of traditional culture, but as unleashing his parodic force on ethnographic attempts to represent it as a fixed, stable, or static object in writing.

En attendant describes the supposed ritual force of the *donsomana* as follows:

Je dirai le récit purificatoire de votre vie de maître chasseur et de dictateur. Le récit purificatoire est appelé en malinké un *donsomana*. C'est une geste. Il est dit par un sora accompagné par un répondeur *cordoua*. Un cordoua est un initié en phase purificatoire, en phase cathartique. Tiécoura est un cordoua et comme tout cordoua il fait le bouffon, le pitre, le fou. Il se permet tout et il n'y a rien qu'on ne lui pardonne pas. (Kourouma 1998: 10)

I will recite the purificatory narrative of your life as master hunter and dictator. The purificatory narrative is called, in Maninka, a *donsomana*. That is an epic. It is recited by a *sèrè* accompanied by a responder or *koroduwa*. A *koroduwa* is an initiate in the purificatory stage, the cathartic stage. Tiekura is a *koroduwa*, and like all *koroduwa*, he plays the buffoon, the clown, the jester. He does anything he wants, and nothing he does goes unpardoned. (Kourouma 2001: 3)

Traoré is, to my knowledge, the only scholarly reader of this novel to have questioned its equation of the roles of epic responder or *naamu*-sayer and that of buffoon. In an article that may have served as one of Kourouma's sources for this conflation, another Malian anthropologist, Pascal Baba Couloubaly, had proposed that the epic performer "takes as his witness a villager who is well known for his buffoonery and/ or for the liveliness of his wit" (1993: 53). In a long footnote rebutting this claim, Traoré writes that "Nous nous ne partageons absolument pas le point de vue de Couloubaly qui considère le *naamunamine* comme un bouffon" (I absolutely do not share Couloubaly's point of view that makes the *naamu*-sayer into a buffoon) (2000b: 168 n. 57). Kourouma goes even farther than Couloubaly, specifying that the *naamu*-sayer is, in his novel, a *koroduwa* or *koroduga*, that is, a member of a fraternity of traditional clowns associated, especially in the past, with the *kore* initiation society and having defined roles in various collective rituals, but today observed mostly in the context of festivals and entertainment for the public, particularly in Bamana-speaking areas (Carbonnel 2015: 40–53). Although identity as a *koroduga* can be inherited, its associations recruit members from all social classes, and even compare their institutional identity to that of the *donsoton*: "Nous sommes comme les chasseurs" (We are like the hunters) (quoted in Carbonnel 2015: 30).

Kourouma's literary transformation of this social fact needs to be examined. The *koroduga* clowns make an art out of outrageous behavior:

L'identification des bouffons rituels repose tout d'abord sur un type de comportement à la fois ludique et subversif. Les bouffons se bâfrent au lieu de manger, font fuir les femmes en exposant un phallus en bois, ils pètent en public ou sur "la tête de Dieu," ils se servent en premier dans les plats, refusent de partager, se moquent de la religion, tiennent tête aux autorités, affirment l'immortalité, détournent les objets, interagissent tout le temps avec tous. Ils présentent des comportements subversifs faisant fi des hiérarchies et des règles de bienséance, mêlés à une esthétique joviale et enthousiaste, faite de danses et de plaisanteries. (Carbonnel 2015: 16)

The identification of ritual clowns depends above all on a type of behavior that is both ludic and subversive. The clowns gorge themselves rather than eat, chase away women by exposing a wooden phallus, fart in public or on "the head of God," serve themselves first in communal dishes, refuse to share, mock religion, talk back to authority, declare their belief in immortality, distort things, interact constantly with everyone. They perform subversive behaviors in defiance of social hierarchies and rules of decorum, mixed with a jovial and enthusiastic aesthetic, made of dances and jokes. (my translation)

This account of the subversiveness of the *koroduga*'s art sheds light on its role in *En attendant*. For the professional ethnographer, conflating the antics of a clown with the seriousness of the role of *naamu*-sayer—an essential role in the production of an epic text in the Mande zone—may seem inappropriate or downright wrong. But it offers Kourouma the ability to incorporate a certain carnivalesque dimension into his invented epic. The *koroduga*'s ability to flout social taboos, to insult, to speak vulgarly, and even to blaspheme, represents a license that the novel claims for itself, over and above the adaptability and reflexivity of the *donsomana* genre that is its first inspiration. These aspects may not be part of the epic tradition itself, but they are part of the larger set of traditional practices that persist in the Mande zone, opening the door to a vision of reimagined, reinvented traditionality that combines aspects from particular practices and genres into a hybridized, creative, bitingly critical whole.

For example, it is Tiekura, the character who serves as both *naamu*-sayer and *koroduga*, who criticizes Koyaga most openly:

> Koyaga, vous avez des défauts, de gros défauts. Vous fûtes, vous êtes autoritaire comme un fauve, menteur comme un écho, brutal comme une foudre, assassin comme un lycaon, émasculateur comme un castreur, démagogue comme un griot, prévaricateur comme un toto, libidineux comme deux canards. Vous êtes . . . Vous êtes . . . Vous avez encore d'autres défauts qu'à vouloir présenter en entier, à aligner en toute hâte, on se déchirerait sans nul doute les commissures des lèvres. Enumère le répondeur cordoua en multipliant des lazzis—qui arrachent un sourire bon enfant à celui qu'ils paraissent injurier. (Kourouma 1998: 315)

> Koyaga, you have faults, great faults. You were, and you still are, authoritarian like a wild animal, as mendacious as an echo, as brutal as the lightning, as bloodthirsty as a lycaon, as much of an emasculator as the castrating priest, as much of a demagogue as a griot, as prevaricating as a louse, as libidinous as two ducks. You

are . . . You are . . . You have so many other faults that to try to present them all, to lay them out one by one, even in great haste, would doubtless split my lips. So recites the responder *koroduwa* as he indulges in other gibes, bringing a smile to the lips of the person they appear to insult. (Kourouma 2001: 214)

This litany of insults does more than lay bare the truth about Koyaga's cruelty and unfitness as a leader. It is defined by an aesthetic of comic excess derived directly from the art of the *koroduga*. Tiekura fires shots not only at the dictator's brutality, but at his excesses in every domain, including in speech and in sex. The comparison "demagogue as a griot" stands out for indicting griotic speech as potentially complicit in his authoritarianism. Tiekura is comically unable to even finish his insults, suggesting that to truly say everything would leave him too parched to speak. The French word "lazzis" captures the clownish spirit of this nevertheless serious criticism by evoking not just a mocking joke or "gibe," but also a specifically theatrical sense denoting buffoonish actions in stage comedy. The fact that this series of extravagant condemnations elicits a childish smile from Koyaga brings home the overarching message: he is not just unfit, but over the top—frighteningly ridiculous.

En attendant's seemingly odd combination of two different performance traditions thus constitutes a kind of pastiche that is worth thinking about. The text slips between "realistic" modes of cultural borrowing, such as the theme from the epic tradition that a master hunter can become a famous warrior, and "fantastic" ones, products of his own imagination, such as the notion that an epic performance involves buffoonery or serves a purifying function. The disturbing manner in which Koyaga mutilates the corpses of his victims offers another illustration of this slippage. When he and his accomplices assassinate Fricassa Santos, the text veers into a fantastic mode again, recalling the sexual dimensions of Tiekura's accusations:

Ils déboutonnent le Président, l'émasculent, enfoncent le sexe ensanglanté entre les dents. C'est l'émasculation rituelle. Toute vie humaine porte une force immanente. Une force immanente qui venge le mort en s'attaquant à son tueur. Le tueur peut neutraliser la force immanente en émasculant la victime. (Kourouma 1998: 100–101)

They unbutton the president's trousers, emasculate him, and stuff the bloody penis into his mouth. This is the ritual emasculation. Every human life holds an imminent force, a force that avenges a murder by attacking the killer. The killer must neutralize that imminent force by emasculating the victim. (Kourouma 2001: 66–67)

This appalling mutilation is repeated several times in killing scenes throughout the novel. In this instance, as soon as the ghastly act is complete, the narration moves into a pseudo-ethnographic register, explaining it in descriptive terms as a "ritual." Traoré points out that there is a ritual hunting practice that involves cutting off an animal's tail, not its genitals, and certainly not putting them into its mouth, in order to neutralize a dead animal's *nyama* or "immanent force":

Fondamentalement, le *donsoya*, la pratique de la chasse, relève de l'animisme: on croit que tous les êtres portent en eux un principe vital appelé ɲama. . . . Le chasseur qui tue un animal sauvage, libère le ɲama de ce dernier. Il doit procéder à des rites particuliers pour tenter de maîtriser les forces ainsi libérées; elles pourraient agir négativement sur lui. . . . L'hippotrague . . . est dit habité par l'une des formes de ɲama les plus dangereuses qui soient. Dès qu'un chasseur abat un hippotrague, il procède immédiatement au rituel d'exorcisation et tranche la queue de l'animal. On appelle cette cérémonie ɲamabɔ, "l'extirpation du ɲama." (Traoré 2000b: 204)

Fundamentally, the *donsoya*, or practice of hunting, is part of animism: it is believed that all beings carry within them a life principle called *nyama*. . . . A hunter who kills a wild animal liberates its *nyama*. He must proceed to particular rites in order to attempt to master the forces just unleashed; they might act negatively upon him. . . . The roan antelope . . . is said to be inhabited by one of the most dangerous forms of *nyama* that exist. As soon as a hunter kills one of these antelopes, he immediately proceeds to the exorcism ritual and cuts off the animal's tail. This ceremony is called *nyamabo*, "*nyama*-extirpation." (my translation)

The practice of cutting off an animal's tail in order to neutralize its *nyama* is confirmed by Cissé (1994: 115–17, 225). Kourouma reinvents the *nyama*-extirpation rite in a way that emphasizes Koyaga's corruption and depravity. The rite is no longer performed in the service of feeding or protecting the community, but of a twisted sadomasochism. The substitution of the human penis for an animal's tail and the entirely made-up detail of placing it in the victim's mouth recall Koyaga's unbridled sexuality, a transgression that, for a good hunter, requires atonement. Yet his sexuality is more than just excessive: it is perverse and narcissistic, exulting in the bloody emasculation of victims, and even in the suggestion of necrophilic sex acts, to confirm the killer's masculinity. One source of this grotesque detail in Kourouma's imagination may have been the polysemy of the French word *queue*: in a first sense, it signifies the tale of an animal, but by extension, it can refer colloquially to a man's penis.

Kourouma's gruesome transformation of the hunters' tail-cutting ritual straddles the line between ethnographic detail and perverse fantasy. However, what is important is not so much the fact that these scenes might give an inaccurate picture of Mande hunting practices, but the fact that they contribute to the underlying critique of Koyaga's unfitness as a hunter and tragic absurdity as leader. By indexing violent battles for power over the signification of the human body, they produce an "aesthetics of vulgarity," which Achille Mbembe sees as typical of postcolonial dictatorships (2001a). Moreover, they refuse any straightforward relationship between literature and ethnography—or, to put it slightly more provocatively, any submission of literature to ethnography. Rather than allowing the reader to assume that the novel is a transparent reflection of any particular West African culture, they invite her or him into a multilayered narrative universe in which irony is always operating at some level.

As a final example, Kourouma explicitly connects his disfiguration of ethnography to an anticolonial critique by exaggerating stereotypes of primitiveness for parodic effect. The dictator-hero Koyaga comes from a community of "Naked people" or "savages among savages" who resisted the European conquest for a long time thanks to their isolation in the mountains (Kourouma 2001: 5). Kourouma frames his description of this group as a parody of how ethnographic writing overdetermined the notion of primitiveness:

> [Les Européens] se trouvent face aux hommes nus. Des hommes totalement nus. Sans organisation sociale. Sans chef. Chaque chef de famille vit dans son fortin et l'autorité du chef ne va pas au-delà de la portée de sa flèche. Des sauvages parmi les sauvages avec lesquels on ne trouve pas de langage de politesse ou violence pour communiquer. . . . Les conquérants font appel aux ethnologues. Les ethnologues les appellent les hommes nus. Ils les appellent les paléonigritiques—le mot est trop long, contentons-nous de l'abréviation "paléos."
>
> Les ethnologues recommandent aux militaires de contourner les montagnes et de poursuivre leurs conquêtes victorieuses et sanguinaires dans les savanes parmi les Nègres habillés, les Nègres organisés, hiérarchisés. (Kourouma 1998: 12)

[The Europeans] find themselves face-to-face with the Naked people. People who are completely naked. No social organization. No chief. Each head of the family lives in his fortified village, and the chief's authority carries no farther than the range of his arrows. These are savages among savages with whom one can neither use polite language nor violence for purposes of communication. . . . The conquerors call in the ethnologists. The ethnologists give a name to the Naked people. They call them the Paleonigritic people—and, since the word is too long, let's be content with calling them by the abbreviation, the "Paleos."

The ethnologists recommend that the soldiers go around the mountains and pursue their victorious and bloody conquests among the costumed, organized, and hierarchized Black peoples and the savannas. (Kourouma 2001: 5)

This passage makes express reference to the place of ethnology as discipline, and of ethnography as writing, in inventing ethnic identifications and in facilitating colonial conquest. The short, choppy rhythm of its sentences emphasizes that the Naked people are conceived in terms of lack: lack of clothes, lack of political or social organization, lack of contact. These lacks are, in turn, dependent on the kind of binaries typical of classic Africanist anthropology: state vs. stateless, mountains vs. plains, archaic vs. evolved, etc. The shortness of this description gives way to an equally rapid series of events, underlining the reductionism of colonial logic as depending on its need to make fast, convenient decisions: the military calls up the ethnologists, who in turn invent an ethnic category and offer a recommendation of what to do. The notion of "savages among savages" places the Naked people at the bottom of an evolutionist typology according to which the heirs of the ancient West African empires are more civilized. Even the neologism "Paleonigritic," which by its etymology evokes a prehistoric version of blackness or "savages among savages," must be shortened to "Paleos" because of the need for a quick and easily digestible system of classification.

Kourouma's use of this term warrants attention. It alludes to the paleonigritic theory of the mid-twentieth century, according to which isolated communities living in hills or mountains across a huge zone stretching from Senegal to eastern or southern Africa had resisted conquest by others, maintaining an archaic civilization with some traits in common, including near-nudity (Baumann and Westermann 1957: 65–69). Some anthropological scholarship, both during and after the colonial era, classified the Kabre people of northern Togo, which produced the real-life Gnassingbé Eyadéma, as an example of a paleonigritic people.[12] Just as the novel's protagonist Koyaga mirrors the historical Eyadéma, the so-called Paleos or Naked people mirror the Kabre. The novel's narration of tensions between Paleos and the southern inhabitants of the Republic of the Gulf closely follows the historical tensions between Togo's Kabre from the north and Ewe from the south, which, for example, caused Eyadéma to be initially rejected from the Togolese army because of his ethnicity (Piot 1999: 44–45), just as the young Koyaga is rejected from the army of the Republic of the Gulf. The Kabre's fortunes changed upon Eyadéma's seizure of power: though they constituted a minority in the country, the dictator and his entourage favored this ethnic group as their kinsmen in the attribution of power and resources. Kourouma's use of the term "Paleo" clearly channels colonial-era ethnography by highlighting its fixation with primitiveness—a discourse that has survived in contemporary Togo, since the Kabre are still stereotyped as "ancient" or "traditional" by foreigners and as "inferior" by some southerners (Piot 1999: 28, 41, 44).

Although Kourouma himself expressed a certain credence in the paleonigritic theory, this strategy of writing it into his novel while avoiding the term "Kabre" emphasizes the inventedness of ethnic categories as a cog in the machine of colonial governance.[13] He deploys hyperprimitivizing descriptions of the Kabre as a strategy of parodic hyperbole that exaggerates colonial stereotypes in order to expose their origins as self-contradictory fictions (Kabanda 2010: 259). This analysis is confirmed when we turn to *En attendant*'s predecessor novel, *Monnè, outrages et défis*, which applies a similarly hyperprimitivizing description to the Maninka. This is striking not only because it is Kourouma's own ethnic group, but because the Maninka *are* hierarchized, wear clothes, and have a long history of empire building and contact with outsiders:

> Depuis des siècles, les gens de Soba et leurs rois vivaient dans un monde clos à l'abri de toute idée et croyance nouvelles. Protégés par des montagnes, ils avaient réussi, tant bien que mal, à préserver leur indépendance. C'était une société arrêtée. Les sorciers, les marabouts, les griots, les sages, tous les intellectuels croyaient que le monde était définitivement achevé et ils le disaient. C'était une société castée et esclavagiste dans laquelle chacun avait, de la naissance à la mort son rang, sa place, son occupation, et tout le monde était content de son sort; on se jalousait peu. La religion était un syncrétisme du fétichisme malinké et de l'islam. Elle donnait des explications satisfaisantes à toutes les graves questions que les habitants pouvaient se poser et les gens n'allaient pas au-delà de ce que les marabouts, les sorciers, les

devins et les féticheurs affirmaient: la communauté entière croyait à ses mensonges. Certes, ce n'était pas le bonheur pour tout le monde, mais cela semblait transparent pour chacun, donc logique. . . . C'était beaucoup. (Kourouma 1990: 21)

For centuries the people of Soba and their kings had lived in a closed world, sheltered from new ideas and beliefs. Protected by a range of mountains, they had succeeded for better or for worse in conserving their independence. It was a fixed and immovable society. All the intellectuals, the sorcerers, marabouts, griots, and wise men believed in the absolute permanence of this world, and that's the way they told it. It was a society of caste and slavery, in which each person from birth to death had his rank, position, occupation; everyone was satisfied with his fate, there was very little jealousy. The religion was a syncretism of Malinke fetishism and Islam. It gave satisfactory explanations for everything serious that people can wonder about, so they didn't try to go beyond the affirmations of marabouts, sorcerers, soothsayers, and fetishers: the whole community believed in their lies. Of course they were not all happy, but since everything seemed perfectly clear to them, it made sense. . . . And that was enough. (Kourouma 1993: 10)

Again in a mode that parrots colonial ethnography's fast generalizations, this passage shows that the trope of hyperprimitivism was applied not just to African peoples thought to be at the bottom of the evolutionary scale, but to any African people at all who needed to be expediently categorized. Instead of proving primitivism through a lack of clothes, hierarchy, or state, which would be impossible for the Maninka, the emphasis is put on their "closed world," where each person's place in the social hierarchy is predetermined and never challenged. Above all, this passage emphasizes the fixity of belief systems. Deference to wise men and to a syncretic practice of Islam, which itself ought to be a fertile ground for exploring the history of challenges to belief systems via contact with outsiders, is never questioned because it is "satisfactory," "perfectly clear," and *logique*—literally, logical.

This passage drops stereotypes about precolonial African beliefs so deftly that one might almost be tempted to read Kourouma as being taken in by them. Isidore Okpewho complained that anthropological worldview analyses portrayed Africans as "slaves to ritual" (1979: 1–2). Could Kourouma be one of Okpewho's targets? No: the above passage's relentless insistence on closure comes across as written self-consciously and hyperbolically. There is an excess of closure that makes one suspicious: the world is "closed," "fixed," "immovable," absolutely permanent, and satisfactory. The presence of a surprising word, "lies," finally belies the stereotype explicitly. It immediately unveils the so-far implicit ironic register in the narrating voice, thereby preventing the reader from taking the passage at face value. Who is lying, and why? Traoré has investigated what he calls Kourouma's "aesthetics of lying," focusing on this novel's recurring expressions of stereotypes of Africans as liars and idlers as a strategy for undermining them (1999). This aesthetics of lying—that is, a relentless use of irony—needs to be extended as a critique of ethnology and ethnographic writing, for it is in no small part from this discipline and genre, and their proliferation of "closed" worldviews, that such negative stereotypes are derived.

In particular, Kourouma's portrayal of the Paleos and the kingdom of Soba evokes the so-called rationality debates that asked, with an attempt at academic rigor, whether and how "traditional African societies" can be said to think (Wilson 1970). In a well-known essay first published in 1967, Robin Horton, an anthropologist, wrote that

> in traditional cultures there is no developed awareness of alternatives to the established body of theoretical tenets; whereas in scientifically oriented cultures, such awareness is highly developed. It is this difference we refer to when we say that traditional cultures are "closed" and scientifically oriented cultures "open." (1993a: 222)

According to this statement, a traditional worldview is essentially a philosophy that knows no alternatives to itself. Reacting fifteen years later to the largely negative critical response to this paper, Horton would acknowledge some of the shortcomings of this understanding (1993b). He recognized the reductionism of aligning the open/closed dichotomy with the tradition/modernity divide.[14] In one important critique of Horton, Jack Goody tried to replace the opposition between closed tradition and open modernity with that of closed orality and open writing, suggesting that modes of thought born from orality are more closed because they cannot generate the more open "critical tradition" enabled by writing (Goody 1977: 43). Regardless of where these authors, following Lévi-Strauss (1966), place the great divide—between closed and open, oral and writing, or hot and cold—they all argue for it. Since then, a great deal of scholarship attempted to redefine tradition in a way that cuts across or abolishes the divide: tradition should not be understood as a series of tenets making up a worldview different from a post-Enlightenment Western norm, but as a genre of speech or performance that is both dependent on and constitutive of context. Horton's reductionism exemplifies the stereotypes of primitivism, particularly of nonthought, that were once so influential in Africanist social sciences and that have continued to permeate the popular imagination to this day.

I argue that we ought to read Kourouma as parodying the extreme "Otherism" that subtends the work of Horton, Goody, and even the venerable Lévi-Strauss, whose work is still classic. This strain of anthropology's never-ending search for Western modernity's truly different Other finds fictional incarnations in Kourouma's hyperprimitive characters and heroes. And yet, one might object that some of these characters really are backward-looking, nostalgic, or otherwise stubbornly walled off from the modern world: Don't they represent a parody of real African behaviors rather than of Western anthropology? Doesn't Horton's worldview theory illuminate how these characters should be read, namely, as representatives of archaic worldviews? No: these characters are hyperbolic, and therefore ironic, rather than realistic. It is true that Fama and Djigui, respectively the protagonists of *Les Soleils des indépendances* and *Monnè, outrages et défis*, do seem to exemplify Horton's equation of tradition with closure. Not only are they forever obsessed with a precolonial past that no longer exists, but they always fail or refuse to recognize alternatives to their invincible belief in their invincible legitimacy. Any acceptance of historical change is anathema to Fama, whose thoughts are always trained on the Horodougou, his idealized lost homeland:

> La colonisation, les commandants, les réquisitions, les épidémies, les sécheresses, les Indépendances, le parti unique et la révolution sont exactement des enfants de la même couche, des étrangers au Horodougou, des sortes de malédictions inventées par le diable. (Kourouma 1970: 132)

> Colonization, district commissioners, requisitions, epidemics, drought, Independence, the single party and the revolution are all bred of the same dam, all foreign to Horodugu, a kind of curse brought upon them by the devil. (Kourouma 1981: 91)

This litany, which rejects the consequences of historical change as the scandalous inventions of foreigners and demons, echoes Djigui's quixotic rejection of reality in *Monnè* when he tries to declare by fiat that colonialism never happened at all: "ni la colonisation, ni les travaux forcés, ni le train, ni les années, ni notre vieillesse n'avaient existé" ("neither the colonization nor the forced labor nor the train nor the years nor our agedness had existed").[15] Both of these examples of men living in denial match up well with Horton's rather extreme vision of the traditional concept of time:

> One might well describe the Western Sudanic cultures as obsessed with the annulment of time to a degree unparalleled in Africa as a whole.... This widespread attempt to annul the passage of time seems closely linked to features of traditional thought which I have already reviewed.... The new and the strange, in so far as they fail to fit into the established system of classification and theory, are intimations of chaos to be avoided as far as possible. Advancing time, with its inevitable element of non-repetitive change, is the vehicle *par excellence* of the new and the strange. Hence its effects must be annulled at all costs. (Horton 1993a: 247–48)

Horton's use of forceful vocabulary—"annul," "obsessed," "unparalleled," "at all costs"—suggests an extreme level of past-worship that corresponds to the most absurd excesses of characters like Djigui and Fama.

Kourouma takes this kind of ethnological hyperbole and turns it into literary irony. He transposes the hyperbolic formulations of colonial and professional ethnologists into the complex historical settings of real colonial and postcolonial West Africa in order to expose them as dead ends. This strategy simultaneously ridicules the absurdity of excessively Othering anthropological schemes and elicits empathy for the tragicomedy of the region's political history. After all, Fama's and Djigui's absurdity as protagonists is never in doubt. To suggest that these characters' behaviors are in any way representative of traditional or African worldviews is like suggesting that Don Quixote's assault on windmills represents a typical Spanish or European worldview. (What would Horton have to say about the civilizational implications of Marcel Proust's *In Search of Lost Time*?) Kourouma's extreme Othering of Djigui and Fama, of Soba and the Paleos, is rooted not in these depictions' supposed plausibility, but in an ironic recycling of stereotypes taken from colonial and professional ethnographic writing. All of these figures should be read as *reductiones ad absurdum* of the kind of civilizational stereotype in which Kourouma was immersed throughout his decades as a reader of such writing.

As a result, Kourouma's writing refuses to respect ethnographic detail in any transparent way at all. His literature is an endlessly ironic tirade for which the Western anthropological imagination is a primary working material. For this writer, any straightforward attempt to represent what African cultural practices "mean"—purifying transgressions, neutralizing *nyama*, annulling time, etc.—is in need of reinvention. Even the documentation of folklore is subject to authorial creativity. Nothing illustrates this better than the unclear status of Kourouma's proverbs, which pepper all his novels. He claimed in an interview that they were all authentic, that is, taken from the known repertoire of Maninka proverbs:

> Dans le *donsomana*, les gens disent un ou deux proverbes. Moi j'en ai fait un procédé systématique et j'ai beaucoup exploité les livres de proverbes africains. Les proverbes que vous trouvez dans le roman sont tous authentiques. (Kourouma in Chemla 1999: 29)

> In the *donsomana*, people say one or two proverbs. I have made it into a systematic technique and have drawn heavily from books of African proverbs. The proverbs that you find in the novel are all authentic. (my translation)

However, the critic Jean Derive offers a different explanation:

> Il me souvient avoir un jour eu une conversation privée avec Kourouma sur les nombreux proverbes qui émaillent tous ses romans. Ayant moi-même recueilli de la tradition orale dans la zone mandingue, je connaissais une bonne partie d'entre eux mais il y en avait un certain nombre d'autres que je n'avais jamais rencontrés. Quand je lui demandais de m'en donner la version originale en malinké, Kourouma me confessa avec un sourire qu'il avait inventé plusieurs d'entre eux, directement en français. . . . Kourouma en truffait le texte de ses romans en mélangeant de vrais adages du répertoire avec des trouvailles de son cru tellement bien construites sur le modèle canonique, tellement bien adaptées dans la fiction à l'usage qui était fait dans la réalité, qu'il était presque impossible de faire le départ entre proverbes réels et proverbes créés. (Derive in Mestaoui 2012: 12–13)

> I remember having a private conversation one day with Kourouma about the many proverbs that embellish his novels. Having collected oral traditions myself in the Manding zone, I knew a good number of them but there were certain others that I had never encountered. When I asked him to give me the original version of these in Maninka, Kourouma confessed to me with a smile that he had invented many of them directly in French. . . . Kourouma filled the text of his novels by mixing real sayings from the repertoire with discoveries of his own creation that were

so well constructed on the canonical model, so well adapted in his fiction to the usage of proverbs in reality, that it was almost impossible to distinguish between real proverbs and created ones. (my translation)

Read together, these two accounts of how Kourouma saw his practice of writing folklore are jarring in their contradiction. As Derive emphasizes, Kourouma's invention of proverbs is so skillful and careful that it is extremely difficult to tell which are invented and which are collected or quoted. That in itself implies a faithfulness to the style and models of oral tradition on Kourouma's part that may suffice to justify his proverbs' claim to authenticity. However, if creativity and invention have a place within an "authentic" practice of writing folklore, then they must also be an intrinsic element in Kourouma's vision of traditionality itself. Traditions are, in such a view, subject to change, to reinvention, and to creative reimaginings.

As this interest in proverbs, praise-songs, and the *donsomana* genre demonstrates, Kourouma's novels do not abandon the category of "tradition" altogether as yet another Western fantasy. Since ideologies of closure represent dead ends in the face of colonialism and the global capitalist economy, the central imperative of his work becomes to explore what alternatives to them are available. Given the experience of the Paleos, who are forced to betray their customs of sacred nudity in order to integrate into clothed society, or of Fama and Djigui, who both succumb to indifferent, brave new worlds, betrayed by their unshakeable attachment to the ways of the past, it might seem that Kourouma's novels serve primarily as a call for his compatriots to abandon their Hortonesque traditional worldviews altogether. But, I ask, what tools do these novels offer to help us theorize a more creative approach to traditionality?

Imaginary and Imaginative Traditionalities

We have already seen one answer to this question in Kourouma's slippages between realistic and fantastic uses of ethnographic detail. His imaginative fusion of the roles of *naamu*-sayer and *koroduga*, his deformation of the *nyama*-extirpation rite, and his half-invented proverbs represent authorial intrusions into ethnographic-style description that lend additional layers of creativity to the *donsomana* genre. This artistic license recalls Okpewho's impassioned defense of the "basic play interest of the artist" (1979: 1–2), except that the artist includes both the oral performer of epic and the creative writer. In spite of such inauthenticities creeping into Kourouma's accounts of Mande oral genres and traditional practices, his writing remains grounded in the domain of "the traditional," however creatively reimagined this category may be, as a way to think through the historical evolution of African political crises. In fact, this strategy of representing traditions as always somehow inauthentic and open to authorial creativity constitutes an aesthetic philosophy that helps Kourouma's slippery, often confusing texts make sense. Hortonesque depictions, and Kourouma's caricatures, of primitive or traditional worldviews contrast markedly with this love of creativity and openness. *Monnè*'s Djigui, chastened by his failures and disillusioned by old age, articulates this attitude quite explicitly. He tells his son Bema at the end of the novel that

> on peut planter un fruitier sans ramasser les gousses, ramasser les gousses sans les ouvrir, les ouvrir sans les consommer. Le monde est toujours plus nombreux et plus large qu'on ne le croit. Allah peut plus que ce que tu connais; trop de choses que nous ne soupçonnons pas sont vraies; tout ce que nous pouvons concevoir est du domaine du possible. Personne ne connaît le monde en totalité; il ne faut jurer de rien. (Kourouma 1990: 264)

> we can plant a fruit tree without gathering the pods, gather the pods without opening them, open them without partaking of them. The world is always bigger and more numerous than we think. Allah can do more than you know; anything we conceive of lies in the realm of the possible. No one knows the world in its totality. We must not swear to anything. (Kourouma 1993: 239)

The image of the tree, instead of signifying rootedness or a totalizing ideology, signifies the "realm of the possible," a series of experiences of the world that can always be deepened by more experience. No matter how much we know, there is more to know. The variety of the world and the volatility of the future underscore the incompleteness of human knowledge and call for a philosophy that is always aware of its own limits—of what Horton would call "alternatives" to itself. This statement emphasizes the openness of the future. More explicitly, this passage points to the constant adaptation and readjustment of one's beliefs, whether these are traditionally transmitted or not, in order to account for new and previously unsuspected data. Ironically, even though it is Djigui who pronounces these words, his inability to adjust his own beliefs to reality at various points in the novel is precisely what makes both him and his counterpart Fama in *Soleils* pathetic imitations of epic heroes.

This openness is applied to the specific domain of the traditional by Djigui's griot, Djeliba:

> L'infini qui est au ciel a changé de paroles; le Mandingue ne sera plus la terre des preux. Je suis un griot, donc homme de la parole. Chaque fois que les mots changent de sens et les choses de symboles, je retourne à la terre qui m'a vu naître pour tout recommencer: réapprendre l'histoire et les nouveaux noms des hommes, des animaux et des choses. . . . Je m'en vais pour réapprendre les nouvelles appellations de l'héroïsme et celles des grands clans du Mandingue. Comment se nomment maintenant les Touré, les Koné, les Kourouma, . . . maintenant que leur terre mandingue est vaincue et possédée par des infidèles d'incirconcis, fils d'incirconcis et de non incisées? (Kourouma 1990: 42–43)

> Infinity which is in the heavens above has changed words; the Mandingo [Manden] will no longer be the land of the valiant. I am a griot, that is, a man of the word. Each time there is a change in the meanings of words and the symbols for things, I return to the land where I was born to begin all over again, relearn history and the new names for men, for animals, and for things. . . . I am going off to relearn the new appellations of heroism and of the great clans of the Mandingo. How are they named now, the Toure, Kone, Kourouma. . . . Now that their Mandingo is vanquished and possessed by uncircumcised infidels, sons of the uncircumcised and the unexcised. (Kourouma 1993: 29–30)

It is significant that this project of renaming the world in light of the profound changes that have taken place belongs to a griot, a specialist of traditional speech. Even though he declares that the time of "the valiant" has given way to the shame of colonialism, the notion of heroism will not be forgotten—only perhaps recounted in a different way. Djeliba does not claim that he is permanently unable to understand or to comment on the new, strange events that are unfolding. Rather, he intends to go back to his ancestral home—the site par excellence for the transmission of traditions, and presumably where he learned his craft—in order to relearn his craft.

As it turns out, Djeliba stays at Djigui's court, but remains committed to inventing a new song for the new times. Rather than singing epics that praise the royal Keita clan—to which both Sunjata and Djigui belong—he composes "sur sa cora un nouvel air" ("a new song on his kora") that is specially adapted to the times of *monnè*, of dishonorable subjugation to the French:

Le soleil rougit, ombre par ombre la nuit triomphe
Les fromagers se déverdissent avec l'harmattan
Se reverdissent avec l'hivernage.
Arrête de soupirer, de désespérer, Prince.
Rien ne se présente aussi nombreux et multicolore que la vie....
Djéliba une fois encore a repris son air qui, aussitôt, a été appelé le chant des monnew. (Kourouma 1990: 49)

The sun reddens, shadow for the triumphant night
The silk-cotton trees yellow with the harmattan
Turn green again with the rains
Do not sigh, do not despair, Prince
Nothing is as numerous and multicolor as life....
Djeliba took up his song again; it was immediately named the chant of the monnew.
(Kourouma 1993: 36)

This song takes up the multifaceted Manding word *tele* or *tile* that gives *Les Soleils des indépendances* its title, the image of the sun or day signifying an era. But instead of placing the sun at its zenith, which in oral epic connotes a heroic time in which the hero defines his age, the sun is at its setting. The heroless nighttime of colonial domination begins. But even then there is room for hope: the seasonal rhythm of fading and returning green leaves reminds the listener that the passage of time brings new life—and, no doubt, another day when the sun will be at its highest again. Even though heroism seems gone from this new era of shame, the fact that the griot's performance still has the power to name the times with the word *monnè* ("dishonor") signifies the relevance of his traditional function in spite of profound historical change. If anything, profound change *requires* the griot to find a name for it: Djeliba describes his mission as one of learning the "new names for men, for animals, and for things" (Kourouma 1993: 29). Moreover, the naming of the era as one of *monnè* actually reinscribes the memory of heroism into the representation of the times of colonialism. According to the griot's song, the new era is not an end, but a transition, a night between two days. The line that "Nothing is as numerous and multicolor as life" celebrates this diversity of experience in time, reminding the listener that the unpredictability of the future is actually a reason for hope.

A certain optimism located in the adaptability of oral tradition offers itself to readers not just of *Monnè*, but of the whole trilogy. We have seen at some length how creative reformations of tradition serve the critical functions of *En attendant*. But the notion of an "opened" or creative traditionality can also be applied to *Soleils*, Kourouma's first and most famous novel, and arguably the most cynical of the three. There, the quixotic hero Fama, "dernier et légitime descendant des princes Doumbouya du Horodougou" ("the last legitimate descendent of the Dumbuya princes of Horodugu"), dies an absurd and seemingly hopeless death after an endless series of humiliations at the hands of the postcolonial state.[16] Having failed throughout the novel to have his kingly legitimacy recognized by society, including by the praise-singers who ought to have been proudly singing his royal epic, he is fired upon while crossing an international border whose legitimacy he refuses to recognize, and attacked by a sacred crocodile who he thought would "never dare attack the last descendent of the Dumbuya" (Kourouma 1981: 133). This tragicomic end is too easily read as the apocalyptic extinction of a precolonial dynasty, that is, the inevitable fate of someone whose closed worldview could not adapt. Is such a reading justified? One clue can be found in *Soleils*'s closing words, which conspicuously echo its opening, in which Fama had attended a funeral:

> Un Malinké était mort. Suivront les jours jusqu'au septième jour et les funérailles du septième jour, puis se succéderont les semaines et rrivera le quarantième jour et frapperont les funérailles du quarantième jour et ... (Kourouma 1970: 196)

> A Malinke had died. Day would follow day until the seventh day and the seventh-day funeral rites, then after a few weeks would come the fortieth day and the fortieth-day funeral rites, and ... (Kourouma 1981: 136)

The ellipsis at the end of this closing passage invites the reader to wonder what will come next. Will the novel's plot simply repeat itself in a vicious circle—the cyclical stagnation of primitivism and tradition—until there is no one left to mourn? Or is there some possibility for a different kind of action, a new heroism for new times that does not appear in the novel itself? I think that *Monnè* and *En attendant* should be read as proposed answers to this question, especially given that *Monnè*'s publication in 1990 was a long-anticipated literary event, following the hugely successful *Soleils* by over twenty years. Even then, the answer is ambiguous. Djigui and Koyaga are heroes who are as doomed as Fama. And yet, the latter two novels make explicit the theme of reimagining traditionalities for new times. All three protagonists may be failed heroes, but there is enough space within oral heroic genres, especially as reinvented by Kourouma, to criticize their failings and to call for new, better, perhaps still unborn heroes to take their place.

The main task, then, for the reader of Kourouma is to figure out how to make sense of his creativity. Within his narrative universe, we can never take a given representation of Maninka (or any other African) worldview at face value. Nor can we assume that a given ethnographic description or detail is true or false. Rather, the imperative that Kourouma places on his reader is to examine how each voice layered into his novels—the voices of antiheroes, dictators, bards, *koroduga naamu*-sayers, marabouts, interpreters, digressing subplots, real or invented oral texts and ethnographic data, as well as the endlessly ironic narrative voice that colors all of these—reflects on each other voice through highly context-specific strategies. To what extent, for example, does the authoritative voice of an epic-singing bard end up being complicit in legitimizing authoritarian ideologies? Or, by contrast, to what extent does it call out abuses of power and celebrate the need for change? In a parallel way, which of these functions does a real or invented ethnographic description serve?

From this perspective, the motivation behind Kourouma's interest in Mande hunting societies in *En attendant* becomes clear. Just as Mohamed Saidou N'Daou interprets the *Sunjata* epic as a model for the democratic governance of African nations (2007), Ahmadou Kourouma sees the hunting association or *donsoton* as a model for an egalitarian, democratic, participatory form of self-government. Every narrative is ideological, but the ideology that Kourouma infuses into the *donsoton* is clearly more salutary and constructive than the monstrous absolutism of the dictator:

> Le donso-ton est en fait une franc-maçonnerie, une religion. . . .
>
> La confrérie a été fondée pour résister à l'oppression des gouvernants et combattre l'esclavage. Elle prêche l'égalité, la fraternité entre tous les hommes de toute race, toute origine sociale, de toutes les castes, de toutes croyance et fonction. Elle reste depuis cinquante siècles le lieu de ralliement de tous ceux qui, sous tous régimes, disent deux fois non: non à l'oppression, non au renoncement devant l'adversité. (Kourouma 1998: 312)

The *donsoton* is, in fact, a freemasonry, a religion. . . .

The brotherhood was established to resist oppression by rulers and to combat slavery. It preached equality and fraternity among all men of every race, social origin, caste, belief, and duty. For fifty centuries it had remained the way to rally all those who, under all regimes, said no two times: no to oppression and no to renunciation in the face of adversity. (Kourouma 2001: 211–12)

The hunting association is, for Kourouma, exemplary in its egalitarianism. Unlike other Mande cultural settings, social status has no significance at all within the *donsoton*: the only hierarchy that exists among its members is one of seniority based on order of initiation. Kourouma's interpretation of this egalitarianism as a manifestation of resistance to oppression, captured in the repeated word "no," recalls the memory of the emphatic "Samorian 'no'" as the ideal of anticolonial resistance in *Monnè*.[17] Paradoxically, the French words *égalité* and *fraternité* allude noticeably to the motto of the French Republic, a surprising declaration of universality in the context of a precolonial African ritual practice inflected with anticolonial overtones. This allusion is not by chance: a few pages later, the novel associates the *donsoton* with liberty and revolution: "Toutes les révolutions, toutes les luttes pour la liberté dans le monde Bambara, malinké, sénoufo des peuples de la savane ont été initiées par les chasseurs" ("All the revolutions, the struggles for freedom in the world of the Bambara, Mandingo, and Senufo peoples of the savanna were initiated by the hunters").[18] Thus, the triad of *liberté, égalité, fraternité* is complete within the world of the *donsoton*. The anthropological fact of the hunting society is, in the world of this novel, inseparable from its interpretation by Kourouma as an African predecessor of French-style revolution and democratic shared governance, as opposed to the abusive authoritarian regimes of colonialism and dictatorship. The representation of this institution and its associated traditions is indistinguishable from their value as ideological alternative.

Admittedly, this is all extremely idealistic. Real hunter identity in West Africa is rich and ambiguous, and associated to no small degree with potential or actual violence. One anthropologist who underwent initiation into a hunters' society in Burkina Faso found that "rivalry, jealousy, and hatred" were a significant dynamic among the hunters (Ferrarini 2016: 89). It is significant that Kourouma's description of the *donsoton* is drawn almost verbatim from the work of Y. T. Cissé, the Malian anthropologist and collaborator of Wa Kamissoko, whose view of the *donsoton* has also been accused of excessive romanticism.[19] In a monograph on Maninka hunting associations, Cissé recounts the mythic origin story

> d'une confrérie de type maçonnique prêchant la liberté pour chacun, l'égalité, la fraternité et l'entente entre tous les hommes, et ceci quelles que soient leur race, leur origine sociale, leurs croyances, ou la fonction qu'ils exercent.... Ainsi naquit la *donso tòn*, "société des chasseurs," qui, depuis, resta le lieu de ralliement de tous ceux qui disent non à l'oppression, non au renoncement devant l'adversité, et qui n'entendent obéir qu'à des autorités qui émanent de leur confrérie ou qui ont son approbation. (1994: 25–26)

> of a masonic-type fraternity preaching liberty for everyone, equality and fraternity and harmony among all men, regardless of their race, social origin, beliefs, or position. . . . Thus was born the *donsoton*, the "society of hunters," which, since then, has remained the rallying place for all those who say no to oppression, no to renunciation in the face of adversity, and who intend to obey only those authorities from within their fraternity or who have its approval. (my translation)

The resemblance between the passages from Kourouma and Cissé is striking; the former clearly borrowed from the latter. Cissé's wording conspicuously incorporates the complete triad of *liberté, égalité, fraternité* into its interpretation of the *donsoton's* significance. Each text includes a comparison to Freemasonry (a European esoteric initiation society proposed as comparable to the *donsoton*), very similar insistences on the equality of all members, and allusions to resistance, rallying, and adversity that are phrased in similar language. Even the double "no" of protest against oppression is here. Kourouma's recycling of Cissé's language reframes the ideological nature of the *donsoton* in a way that links it to the intrinsically ideological nature of anthropology as well. Just as Kourouma parodies the "paleonigritic" as an invention of colonial ethnography located in the need to dominate and control, so is Cissé's idealized interpretation of the *donsoton* marshaled in order to self-consciously construct a countermythology of cooperation and mutual aid that refuses the authoritarianism of colonialism and its grotesque imitator, the postcolonial dictator. By referring to Cissé, an expert on the *donsoton*, and reproducing his voice, Kourouma implicates anthropology in his own ideological project of imagining a more egalitarian Africa, even as he critiques this discipline once again as always implicated in an ideological project of some kind.

Significantly, this is not the only passage in *En attendant* that Kourouma borrows from Cissé. A long section of the novel's part 5 recounts, in some detail, rituals associated with *donsoton* membership and initiation. Much of this section is recycled, with slight changes in wording that nevertheless make the borrowing transparent, from various passages in Cissé (1994), which offer detailed ethnographic descriptions, transcriptions, and translations of the same rituals. While it would be too tedious to examine every correspondence between novelist and ethnographer line by line, let it suffice to advise the reader to compare Kourouma's description of the *dyandyon* (hymn of heroism reserved for master hunters) and other songs, as well as the *dankun-son* ceremony ("sacrifices and offerings at the ritual crossroad"), to Cissé's.[20]

Without meaning to accuse Ahmadou Kourouma of plagiarism, it is worth remembering how much trouble such cannibalistic practices of quotation caused for that other inveterate parodist of ethnography, namely, Yambo Ouologuem. Ouologuem, whose novel *Le Devoir de violence* came out in Paris in 1968, the same year as *Les Soleils des indépendances* did in Montreal, famously reused words, sentences, and bits of text from a dizzying array of sources, resulting in a lawsuit from Graham Greene and the *Devoir* being banned from French publishers for decades. The parallels between the two novelists—one of whom has been wrongfully vilified by France's literary institutions, and the other of whom has been elevated by them to near-"universal" prestige after an initial rebuff, are significant.[21] Both ridicule the role of ethnographic/ethnological writing in generating colonial stereotypes of African cultures: Delafosse and Frobenius in Ouologuem's case; the paleonigritic myth and other ideologies of closure in Kourouma's. Both rely heavily on acerbic humor, irony, and authorial license to denounce these stereotypes; and both engage in practices of unmarked quoting in order to make their works into ironic pastiches that slide elusively between pseudo-ethnography, quasi-epics, and novels. In Kourouma's case, the use of Cissé is celebratory, rather than parodic. One can feel how deeply the novelist was influenced by this ethnographer's belief in the *donsoton* as a precolonial African iteration of *liberté-égalité-fraternité*. The fact that Cissé's ideologically slanted ethnography fits so well into Kourouma's novelistic vision exposes the subjectivity of ethnography: Can ethnography ever have a truly scientific voice, or is it always at risk of devolving into literature (Debaene 2014)? With all of this said, it is not just the recycling of several passages from Cissé that is at stake in Kourouma's pseudo-ethnographic literature, but also his fusion of real and invented proverbs and anthropological descriptions. All of this should be seen as part of the same subversive style of ironic pastiche. I submit that Kourouma's evident "creative borrowing" from Cissé in the service of creating a multilayered text ought to further exonerate Ouologuem, who, as has been shown, borrowed from not just one or two published works, but a plethora of them. Ironic pastiche is an intrinsic piece of both writers' takedown of the myth of ethnographic certainty.

Of Heroes and History

Kourouma's practice of fiction takes on a multifaceted set of tasks. It excavates hegemonic discourses and dominant myths—nationalist, colonialist, ethnographic, nostalgic—in order to draw attention to their inventedness, their fictionality. While the closed discursive regime of imposed, unquestionable truth belongs to dictators, single-party rule, and the fictional hyperprimitives and diehard nostalgics imagined by anthropology, a sense of adaptability and openness to the Other is imagined as the defining characteristic of the democratic hunters' association and its narrative form, the *donsomana* or epic. The reader is invited to make sense of these conflicting narratives by participating in Kourouma's vision of the traditional democracy, a fiction that privileges tolerance and creativity and that can perhaps serve as a new, more salutary kind of communal guiding myth than the "unwelcome hero." In this sense, the most significant parallel between the *Bilali* song, with which I began, and Kourouma's novels may not be their dependence on heroes as such, but their use of the hero as a device through which to refract representations of collective experience and historical change.

CHAPTER SIX

Defiant Women, Noble Slaves, and Gays, or, The Problem with Wolof Virtue

Furthermore, what is authorized if we identify the goal of feminism as producing stable subjects who can 'resist' tradition? Do we not risk trying to accomplish, in criticism, what colonial education purportedly set out to do?

—Tobias Warner, "How Mariama Bâ Became World Literature"

Aminata Sow Fall has a place among the most prolific and successful living Senegalese women writers. Yet many readers have struggled on just how to read her as a *woman* writer. Is she a feminist—or not? Because of her novels' apparently stark opposition between so-called authentic African tradition and alienating Europhile modernity, wherein "good" women are frequently aligned with the former and "bad" ones with the latter, Sow Fall has provoked a series of readings that try to make sense of her (anti)feminism.[1] Her second novel, *L'Appel des arènes* (The Call of the Arena) (1982), exemplifies the trouble that feminist readers have had with her characters. The central conflict there is between a young boy, Nalla, who is attracted to the world of traditional Senegalese wrestling, shrouded in ritual and folklore, and his mother, Diattou, whose French education and resulting superiority complex make her try to keep him out of that world, which she finds backward and barbaric. Diattou represents an archetype of the alienated modern woman that runs throughout several more of Sow Fall's novels—notably Yama in *Le Revenant* (The Ghost) (1976) and Tacko in *Le Jujubier du patriarche* (The Patriarch's Tree) (1993). Meanwhile, *L'Appel*'s world of traditional wrestling, which strongly resembles a utopian, authentically African antidote to the ills and corruption of postcolonial Senegalese society, is reserved for men: it consists above all of the heroes of the sport themselves, but also of their coaches and apprentices. Women can play supporting roles, like spectator or praise-singer, but it is certainly out of the question for them to participate in the athletics or the prerequisite initiation. In contrast to Diattou, the only woman who comes across positively in this novel is her mother, Mame Fari, an archetype of the sensible traditional elder, who teaches Nalla folktales and lets him savor the carefree joys of childhood, while disapproving of "les nouvelles manières de sa fille qu'elle accusait intérieurement d'avoir renié ses origines" (the new manners of her daughter whom she inwardly accused of having denied her origins) (Sow Fall 2012: 75). Curiously, Mame Fari is something of a masculine, or at least androgynous, figure herself: she is "tout à la fois mère, père, frère et compagnon de jeux" (at the same time mother, father, brother, and playmate) for Nalla (2012: 22). Her attachment to *cosaan* or traditional culture and her love of physical play prefigure Nalla's brotherly, homosocial relationships with the wrestlers, while at the same time replacing his emotionally distant mother with an affectionate maternal presence.

At any rate, in trying to determine whether Sow Fall writes in a masculine or feminine voice, Nicki Hitchcott traces a certain evolution through the author's work: "Whilst Sow Fall's early novels"—such as *L'Appel des arènes*—"often revealed a 'masculinist' and sometimes anti-feminist ideology, the more recent texts suggest a move towards a more 'feminine' and indeed feminist point of view" (2000: 109). Hitchcott attributes Sow Fall's feminist turn in large part to the novel that I study in detail in this chapter, namely *Le Jujubier du patriarche*. In this short but incredibly complex text, Naarou, a Senegalese girl of mixed noble and slave descent, appropriates her adopted noble family's epic as her own, both singing it like a griot and making scandalously explicit her place in the family tree—thereby seeming to tarnish it, in the eyes of some. As such, Naarou is one of the most empowered female characters in Sow Fall's novels, and fascinating for this study because of her layered relationship to the category of tradition. Unlike Mame Fari, or more submissive women characters who populate Sow Fall's novels, Naarou does not just transmit traditional knowledge, but reframes it, while challenging the power structures around it, for her own purposes. This relationship is at the same time respectful, audacious, creative, oppositional, and, most importantly, mediated by differing social interpretations of caste, order, class, and gender. That is, disagreements over status—who has the right to do or say what, and when—paint the portrait of a family whose members are divided by individual interests and by social hierarchies in flux. To summarize *Jujubier*'s core conflict in a way that reflects its stunning combination of simplicity and complexity: Does a financially successful half-slave have the right to sing her bankrupt noble foster-family's epic like a griot, and have her own lineage recognized in it, as though she were one of them, a noble in her own right? What is at stake in such a move? The answer, as we shall find, is that it depends on whom we ask. By working through this entangled set of issues, I will elucidate an important aspect of Aminata Sow Fall's critique of so-called traditional values: namely, their multifaceted relationship with changing structures of power. In doing so, I hope to offer a new contribution to the understanding of this important writer's vision of a more inclusive Wolof society.

Wolof Moral Philosophy Revisited

One of Sow Fall's best-known readers, Médoune Guèye, has made sense of the diversity of her work by offering an interpretive approach focused on a specifically Wolof ethics. He suggests that her novels exemplify the point-by-point account of Wolof moral philosophy elaborated by Assane Sylla in *La Philosophie morale des Wolof* (Wolof Moral Philosophy). For Guèye, the heart of both Sylla's and Sow Fall's work is the Wolof proverb "Nit, nit ay garabam" ("Humankind is its own remedy") (Guèye 2005: 53–54). He sees both the novelist's and the philosopher's writings as being preoccupied with the restoration of dehumanized society:

> Selon Sylla, les penseurs wolof n'ont pas exposé leurs idées dans des ouvrages, mais l'œuvre d'Aminata Sow Fall, par son adaptation de l'esthétique du récit traditionnel oral, rassemble les éléments de cette pensée wolof et lui confère une existence scripturaire. . . . *Le Revenant* constitue donc une œuvre révélatrice de la pensée wolof par excellence. (2005: 54–55)

> According to Sylla, Wolof thinkers did not expose their ideas in books, but Aminata Sow Fall's novel, by its adaptation of the aesthetics of oral traditional narrative, gathers the elements of this Wolof thought and confers a written existence upon it.

... *Le Revenant* thus constitutes a work that reveals Wolof thought par excellence. (my translation)

Although this comment is embedded in a discussion of *Le Revenant*, the alignment of Sow Fall with Sylla applies to the whole of her work, as Guèye says earlier (2005: 21–22). But who, asks Ivy Mills, is the *nit* in "Nit, nit ay garabam" (2011: 126)? Mills carefully excavates *Le Revenant* to ask what vision of the Wolof human (*nit*) it offers (2011: 132–51). Is the Wolof human a gendered subject, a classed subject, a subject dependent on the division between nobility and caste, a subject produced by discourses of honor and shame? Mills demonstrates that the ideal Wolof human, as imagined by Sylla and Guèye, is a highly prescriptive construct. Actual human subjects operating within this normative code of behaviors have a much messier relationship with it than either Sylla or Guèye acknowledges. In Mills's view, each of these categories—gender, class, caste, and honor—overlap and interact in contradictory ways to produce conflicting understandings of the Wolof human that are in competition with each other in Senegalese society today, and in *Le Revenant* in particular. That is, the Wolof human is unstable, caught between a series of older and newer versions of these discursive structures.

Inspired by Mills's work, I would like to rethink the relationship between *Le Jujubier du patriarche* and so-called Wolof moral philosophy. Like its predecessor, this novel analyzes the instability of a fundamental imperative on which Wolof moral philosophy is based. In order to demonstrate this instability, let us recall the four basic precepts of Wolof moral philosophy, as articulated by Sylla:

1. Etre maître de soi, pour pouvoir conserver, dans la joie comme dans l'adversité, les qualités du *gor* (homme de bien).
2. Faire preuve en toute circonstance de ces qualités du *gor*. . . .
3. Se maintenir, au sein des différents milieux sociaux (famille, groupe d'âge, milieu professionnel etc.), au même niveau de respectabilité de ses *nawle* [égaux], donc s'efforcer de réussir comme eux, d'assumer les mêmes droits et devoirs et ne point accepter de démériter par rapport à eux.
4. Eviter à tout prix le déshonneur qui équivaut à une déchéance irréparable. (Sylla 1978: 166)

1. To be one's own master, in order to conserve, in both joy and adversity, the qualities of a *gor* (a good man).

2. To demonstrate in all circumstances the qualities of a *gor*. . . .
3. To maintain oneself, within different social circles (family, age group, professional environment, etc.), at the same level of respectability as one's *nawle* [equals], therefore, to make every effort to succeed as they do, to assume the same rights and responsibilities as them, and not to accept any demerit in comparison to them.
4. To avoid dishonor at all costs, since this constitutes an irreparable disgrace. (my translation)

In point 3 of this statement, it is imperative to maintain one's respectability in the eyes of one's *nawle* or peers—that is, persons of equal status, most obviously in terms of caste or age group, but also in terms of gender and, increasingly, wealth. A key concern of all of Aminata Sow Fall's writing, including the so-called masculinist or antifeminist novels, is to account for how the principle of *nawle* has transformed, for lack of better terms, from a traditional to a modern iteration: how Senegalese society has moved from defining respectability in terms of the status into which one was born, to defining respectability by engaging in ostentatious displays of one's wealth before one's peers. *Le Jujubier du patriarche* focuses more on the "traditional" side of this concern than its predecessor, *Le Revenant*—which had told the story of a man who fakes his own death, then appears as a ghost at his funeral in order to take revenge on his wealth-obsessed sister. *Jujubier*, on the other hand, rather than concentrating its energy on criticizing society's love of spending money to keep up appearances, seizes on the moments of instability of the traditional hierarchy of statuses itself, the power structure defined by birth. For the sake of clarity, I offer in the next section a very brief discussion of classic Wolof social status, as described by A. B. Diop, before exploring the novel's systematic problematization of it.

Wolof Social Hierarchy

Wolof social statuses are defined by A. B. Diop as a system of castes and orders, which are represented in figure 7. As figure 7 shows, nobles are at the top of the social hierarchy, endogamous professional groups or castes are in the middle, and slaves at the bottom. The institution of slavery was legally abolished in Senegal by the colonial administration in the early twentieth century. Nevertheless, slave status is still hereditary, and a slave family can still hold a kind of client relationship to the

FIGURE 7. Wolof Social Hierarchy

	CASTES		ORDERS
Nobles (Wolof: *géer* or *garmi*)			Free persons (*gor* or *jàmbur*)
'Casted' persons: Endogamous groups based on professional activity (*ñeeño*)			
Artisans (*jëf-lekk*): blacksmiths, weavers, woodworkers, etc.	Griots (*sab-lekk* or *géwel*)	Marginal group of griots (*ñoole*)	
			"Slaves" (*jaam*)

See A. B. Diop (1981: 33–35 and 115–16). This diagram does not retain all the nuances of Diop's categorizations. He recognizes four Wolof castes, all of which are shown here, though some of them have subcastes. But he enumerates five orders under the Wolof monarchical states (sixteenth to nineteenth centuries), based on the difference between chiefs (*buur*), notables (*jàmbur*), the general populace (*baadoolo*), slaves of chiefs (*jaami buur*), and slaves of the general populace (*jaami baadoolo*). Note that the meaning of *jàmbur* shifted over time to encompass not only notables, but all free persons or nonslaves. However, the only aspect of order that is relevant for my analysis here is the distinction that Diop recognizes as fundamental, namely slave vs. free.

noble family that is supposed to protect it. This is the relationship between Naarou and her adopted family. As Sow Fall says,

> Jusqu'à présent dans nos sociétés, à Dakar comme dans tout le Sénégal et ailleurs peut-être, on peut reconnaître les descendants des anciens esclaves, mais souvent aujourd'hui ce sont des gens qui sont considérés comme des parents. On ne dira jamais, sauf quelqu'un qui manque de tact: "Celui-là c'est le fils de l'esclave de mon arrière-grand-père." On dira: "Il est mon cousin." (in Schiavone 1994: 89)

> Even now in our societies, whether in Dakar, the rest of Senegal, or perhaps elsewhere, one can recognize the descendants of the slaves of old, but such people are often considered today as relatives. Unless someone lacks tact, one would never say, "That is the son of my great-grandfather's slave." One would say: "He is my cousin." (my translation)

In *Jujubier*, Naarou's slave origins are known to everyone, but when Tacko tries to use them against her to exclude her from equality with the rest of the family, she breaks a taboo because she is disrupting social harmony. The word "slave" thus represents a present but repressed status, a part of Wolof social harmony only as long as it remains unspoken. Rather than putting the word "slave" in quotation marks every time it appears in this chapter, I trust the reader's judgment to infer that in the postcolonial era, it refers not to any form of actual enslavement, but to the inheritance of inferior social status based on the enslavement of one's ancestors. On the other hand, when it appears in epic discourse, including *Jujubier*'s invented epic, it does in fact imply captivity, whether inherited or imposed as a consequence of war.

This differentiation of status is embedded in any possible understanding of Wolof moral philosophy because the principle of keeping up with one's *nawle* implies, in itself, a differentiation of statuses. That is to say, a major part of the Wolof value system, as Sylla sees it, is to accept one's own rank and to behave according to it. Sylla says as much in his own definition:

> *nawle*: pour chaque personne, l'ensemble des individus qui ont même rang social et partagent même niveau de conscience morale que lui. . . . Jusqu'à nos jours, il est très difficile à un homme appartenant à la caste des ñeeño, si riche soit-il, d'obtenir la main d'une femme de la classe des *géer*. A un tel prétendant, on répond invariablement: allez épouser votre *nawle* (une femme de votre rang). (1978: 87)

> *nawle*: for each person, the set of individuals who have the same social rank and share the same level of moral consciousness as him or her. . . . Even today, it is very difficult for a man of ñeeño caste, however rich he may be, to obtain the hand of a woman of *géer* class. To such a suitor, one responds invariably: go marry your *nawle* (a woman of your rank). (my translation)

In many situations, most importantly marriage, high- and low-status persons are maintained separate from each other. Indeed, the very existence of high and low statuses depends on the exclusion of the low from the high. Additionally, one must note in Sylla's formulation the porousness between social status and "conscience morale": to be someone's *nawle* is not just to figure into the same category as her, but to share the same level of moral conscience. That is, according to him, persons of higher status have a sharper, more acute sense of "morals," of what is acceptable as honorable behavior, precisely because they have more to lose in case of dishonor. This concords with A. B. Diop's description of the reputation of slaves as having an

> absence de sens de l'honneur, indignité, malhonnêteté, indécence. Cette infériorité s'appuyait sur une idéologie biologique de discrimination et de reproduction de

l'ordre social servile. . . . Les esclaves étaient considérés comme des êtres de nature inférieure dont l'impureté de sang (*derat ju gàkk*) se transmettait par hérédité. (1981: 161)

absence of any sense of honor, lack of dignity, dishonesty, indecency. This inferiority was based on a biological ideology of discrimination and reproduction of the servile social order. . . . Slaves were considered as inferior beings whose impure blood was transmitted hereditarily. (my translation)

And yet, in spite of this passing allusion to the conflation of social status with moral conscience, Sylla never addresses the fact that the principles of honor that his book elucidates in such detail really apply above all to a certain kind of Wolof subject—namely, a high-status one, whose honor is predicated upon the exclusion of lower-class subjects from equality. As Mills argues,

In Sylla's account of the Wolof human, however, the entanglement of Wolof phi-losophy with the caste system and the order of slavery is obfuscated. If the human is produced by his indoctrination into an ethics of honor, and the lower castes and slaves are, in *géer* supremacist discourse, always-already dishonored in relation to the *géer/gor*, then the normative human of whom Sylla speaks must be free and non-casted. One could argue that the lower castes can possess caste-specific forms of honor, and that they see themselves as playing a fundamental and honorable role in the reproduction of the social order. . . . In spite of these caste- and status-specific forms of honor, it is the honor of the *géer/gor* that is privileged and normalized in most iterations of the Wolof human, and this honorable subject always has its foil. (2011: 147–48)

For Mills, there are different, caste- and order-specific codes of honor, although these are not necessarily intelligible as "honor" in the *géer*-centric sense.[2] Sylla's Wolof moral philosophy passes a specifically noble form of honor as universal. Mills goes farther, also pointing out the genderedness of honor and its obfuscation: "Gender is another covert but necessary property of the Wolof human. Nonconformity with the normative performance of gender and gendered honor would thus exclude the subject from the Wolof human" (2011: 149). If we take Sylla's vision of the Wolof human as a highly normative construct rather than a universally applicable declaration of values for the whole Wolof community, then it becomes possible to see how cloudy things get when we try to apply his principles to nonnormative Wolof humans—people whose ambiguous identities straddle the well-defined boundaries of caste, order, gender, and class. For these people, it is contestable to identify what it means to "know one's place," for it is unclear who their *nawle* are.

I locate *Le Jujubier du patriarche* squarely within this project of destabilizing Wolof moral norms. By depicting a series of characters who transgress the categories that they are supposed to fit in, *Jujubier* challenges the very possibility of authentic noble identity based on the exclusion of low-status subjects and, I would add, of a normative masculinist identity based on the exclusion of the feminine or queer. But far from dismissing the concept of the moral as such, by criticizing these processes of exclusion as being impossible contradictions at the heart of so-called traditional values, the novel calls for a more inclusive, egalitarian vision of Senegalese community that effaces the hierarchy of statuses implied by the Wolof principle of *nawle*. As such, I am reading *Le Jujubier du patriarche* to some extent both with and against the grain of Wolof moral philosophy. The text invites us to rethink the ethics of the Wolof human outside oppositions of *gor* or *géer* vs. *jaam* and male vs. female.

From Family Tree to Labyrinth

Jujubier weaves its critique of traditional structures of power within a critical reinvention of oral epic. In spite of its brevity, the text has a very complex plot that alternates between two imbricated stories: a novel proper, which recounts the story of a middle-class family in late twentieth-century Dakar, and an epic, the oral traditional narrative recounting the feats of this family's heroic ancestors, which is constantly alluded to throughout the text. Thus the reader's attention is constantly shifting between Dakar today and the ancient time of legendary West African heroes. The modern family in Dakar is, for the most part, of noble lineage. Naarou, the protagonist, is the exception, being of mixed noble and slave ancestry, a fact that generates most of the novel's drama. Figure 8 demonstrates this genealogical complexity. It is divided into epic characters on top and novel characters on the bottom. Horizontally, it is divided by caste and order distinctions—griot, noble, and slave—in order to represent the relationships between the multitude of characters. Naarou, at the bottom right, as well as her brother and mother, straddles the line between the categories of slave and noble.

The relationship of the modern family to its epic ancestors is the key stake of the text. At the beginning of the novel, Naarou's adopted noble parents, Yelli and Tacko, have lost a great deal of material wealth, and Yelli in particular takes a nostalgic refuge in the heritage of his family's heroic past in order to forget his material downfall and the wretchedness of the present. His wife Tacko mocks him:

> Monsieur pense qu'il est encore au Moyen Âge; il veut être impeccable parce qu'il est le descendant de Yellimané le héros du Natangué. Yelli, reviens sur terre. Tu n'es ni Sarebibi l'Almamy, ni Yellimané son fils, ni Gueladio le chasseur que courtisaient les fauves, encore moins Dioumana qui pouvait se payer le luxe d'aller dormir dans le ventre d'une baleine tout simplement parce que son Almamy d'époux refusait de l'aimer jusqu'à la folie. . . . Ecoute: Tu es, Yelli. Tu vis la fin du vingtième siècle avec ses dures réalités. (Sow Fall 1993: 16)

> Monsieur thinks he is still in the Middle Ages; he thinks he is perfect because he is descended from Yellimané the hero of Natangué. Yelli, come back down to earth. You are not the Almami Sarebibi, nor Yellimané his son, nor Gueladio the hunter who courted the wild beasts, nor still are you Dioumana, who could afford the luxury of sleeping in the belly of a sea monster just because her Almami husband refused to love her to the brink of insanity. . . . Listen to me: You are Yelli. You are living the end of the twentieth century with its tough realities. (my translation)

Like Ahmadou Kourouma's heroes Djigui and Fama, Yelli is caught in a world of rosy-eyed, nostalgic gallantry but fails, at least in his wife's eyes, to measure up to the champions of yore. Each of the heroes Tacko mentions here has his or her story developed in the epic portion of the text. As the family tree diagram shows, Naarou is a second cousin of Yelli's wife Tacko, and she was entrusted to them as a baby. Naarou is the descendant of a scandalous marriage between a noble grandfather, Waly, and his slave Sadaga. The conflict in the novel is over who "owns" the family epic. That is, who is a legitimate heir to the cultural patrimony that the sung narrative represents: only those who are of exclusively noble birth, and for whom the performance of the epic is supposed to serve as a way of singing their praises? Does Naarou have the right to have the epic sung to her by a griot or, for that matter, to sing it herself? Naarou is exposed from a young age to her adopted family's oral epic through the griot Naani. She comes to know it, to memorize it, and to appropriate it as her own:

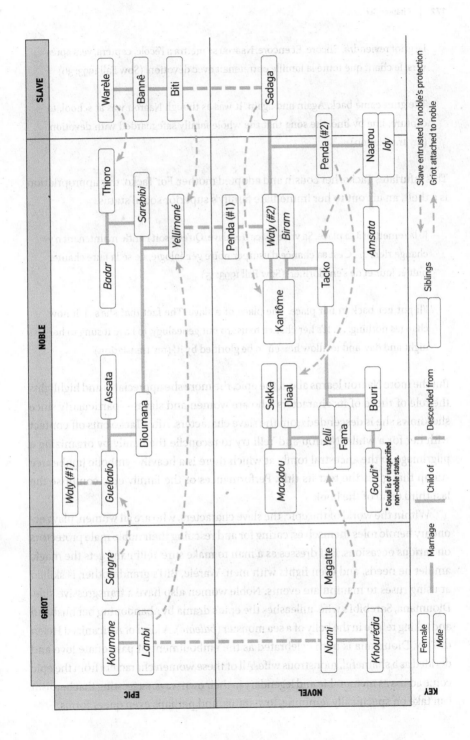

Le griot reviendra. Encore. Et encore. Naarou se mettra à l'école, captera, vers après vers, le chant que toute la famille entretenait avec dévotion. (Sow Fall 1993: 36)

The griot came back. Again and again. It was as though Naarou was at school, to capture, line by line, the song that the whole family safeguarded with devotion. (my translation)

This infuriates Tacko, her cousin and adopted mother. For Tacko, this appropriation is a theft, an affront to her immediate family's superior social status.

Je la remettrai à sa place. Sa vraie place d'esclave. Qu'elle soit nantie maintenant n'y change rien. . . . C'est sa chance d'usurper notre généalogie, de se la faire chanter nuit et jour et de s'en glorifier! (Sow Fall 1993: 15)

I'll put her back in her place. The place of a slave. The fact that she's rich now changes nothing. . . . It's her chance to usurp our genealogy, to have it sung to her night and day, and to allow herself to be glorified by it! (my translation)

But the more Naarou learns about the epic, the more she appreciates and highlights the role of those of its characters who are women and slaves—particularly since she knows she is descended from the slave characters. After Tacko cuts off contact with her for a while, Naarou and Yelli try to reconcile the family by organizing a pilgrimage to the ancestral tomb, at which there is a heavily symbolic jujube tree stump that gives the text its title. Performances of the family epic comprise the last third or so of the book.

Within the world of the epic, the slave characters, who are all women, play secondary heroic roles themselves, caring for and rescuing their noble male protectors on various occasions. Biti dresses as a man to make sure Yellimané gets the magic amulet he needs, and even fights with men. Warèle, Biti's grandmother, is skilled at using ruses to manipulate events. Noble women also have a transgressive side. Dioumana, Sarebibi's wife, unleashes the epic's drama by abandoning her husband and taking refuge in the belly of a sea monster (*baleine*). A kind of Africanized Helen of Troy, Dioumana is both celebrated as the embodiment of passionate love and derided as a shameful, monstrous wife. All of these women characters from the epic come across as memorable and legendary in their own ways, suggesting that heroism can take on specifically feminine, low-status, and perhaps even queer forms.

It is worth noting that this epic plotline was entirely made up by Aminata Sow Fall. The heroes and characters do not correspond to any particular oral traditional narrative that exists in reality. Gueladio is a name borrowed from the Fulfulde-speaking context of the Futa Toro, along the Senegal River, where the hero Samba Gelajo Jegi is well known as a hero of the Deniyanke dynasty. But the character Gueladio of Sow Fall's creation and the Samba Gelajo Jegi of the Futa Toro kingdom have little in common (see Belcher 1994: 76–77). Moreover, the novel refers repeatedly to its invented epic as the "épopée du Foudjallon" (epic of Foudjallon), apparently in reference to a completely different precolonial kingdom of the Fulfulde language family, that of Futa Jallon in what is today Guinea. But, as Sow Fall says, she uses these names simply to

embrouiller les pistes et c'est pourquoi je parle même du Foudjallon. Je ne connais même pas tellement bien le Fouta-Toro, mais des Poulars m'ont dit qu'ils s'y retrouvaient parfaitement. . . . Lorsque j'ai écrit cette épopée, la grande peur que j'avais c'était de produire une chose bâtarde; qui n'aurait pas le ton, la tonalité, le mouvement d'une épopée authentique. Bien qu'elle ne soit pas authentique, parce que je l'ai inventée, même si j'ai emprunté le ton de l'époque, j'avais peur vraiment de passer à côté. Alors une satisfaction est venue du fait que des gens qui ont passé leur vie à étudier les épopées, comme Lilyan Kesteloot par exemple, pour la citer, sont venus me dire: "Mais est-ce que c'est vraiment une épopée que tu as inventée ou est-ce que tu l'as cherchée quelque part?" Et là j'étais rassurée. (in Schiavone 1994: 94–95)

hide my tracks and that's why I even talk about the Foudjallon. I don't even know the Futa Toro that well, but some Pulars have told me that they felt right at home in it. . . . When I wrote this epic, my biggest fear was to produce something bastardized; which would have neither the tone, the tonality, nor the movement of an authentic epic. Even though it isn't authentic, because I invented it, although I borrowed the tone of the time, I was afraid I would miss the mark. So it was some satisfaction that people who have spent their lives studying epics, like Lilyan Kesteloot for example, to cite her, came to me saying: "But is this really an epic you invented or did you find it somewhere?" So that reassured me. (my translation)

This quote reveals with insistence both that the author invented this epic narrative and that she made a serious effort to make it seem real. Moreover, her statement makes explicit a certain transethnic dimension to the invented narrative, as it seems to draw from both Wolof and Fula material, and the Fula material is from different places. Certainly, many Fula communities share ideologies of caste, order, and gender that are similar to so-called Wolof moral philosophy.[3] Even so, reading *Jujubier* through a specifically Wolof lens is justified by the simple fact that outside of a few character and place names, Wolof cultural context and language are omnipresent in the novel, as they are throughout Sow Fall's oeuvre.

Defiant Women, Noble Slaves

Within *Jujubier*'s invented epic, the characters of Biti, Warèle, and Dioumana deserve special attention due to their ambiguous status. As the family tree diagram shows, Biti and Warèle are slaves, ancestors from whom Naarou is descended. Dioumana is noble, but her flight from both her husband Sarebibi and her father Gueladio sparks the main action of the epic, namely her son Yellimané's pursuit of the sea monster in whose belly she hides. All three of these characters cross limits imposed on their conduct by their place in the social hierarchy, their gender, or both. All three are heroicized in the family epic to greater or lesser degrees. This valorization of exceptional behavior by individuals who defy expectations regarding their place in society runs into *Jujubier*'s novel proper, the twentieth-century family in modern Dakar, whose members try to find in these epic characters a source for inspiration in the postcolonial age.

One description of Warèle, the elder slave, provides a point of reference against which to define this recurring theme of female transgression. At first glance, Warèle seems to incarnate an idealized servile behavior rooted in submission:

> Pas une fois, au cours de sa longue vie, Warèle n'avait programmé une action en faveur de sa personne. Son existence s'était diluée dans la quête perpétuelle du bien-être et de la réussite de ses maîtres. (Sow Fall 1993: 23)

> Not once, throughout her long life, had Warèle undertaken an action in her own interest. Her existence had been effaced in a perpetual quest for the well-being and success of her masters. (my translation)

Self-effacement in service of the master, or "honor-in-submission," makes a model slave, at least from the master's point of view (Mills 2011: 148 n. 311). Bassirou Dieng's study of the depiction of slaves in Wolof oral epic partially confirms the paradigm of honor-in-submission, arguing that "fidélité" (faithfulness) is the key value of the slave in epic (2008: 210). However, he goes further, suggesting in the same breath that "le dévouement au maître est une vertu héroïque" (devotion to the master is a heroic virtue). Dieng's analysis of the heroic slave motif in the context of Kajoorian epic narrative actually allows for the slave—and, for that matter, the griot—to become a kind of double of the noble hero, even though the noble hero must always be at the center of epic:

> A partir du XVIIIe s., dans un Kajoor féodal, les captifs composent la force armée. Moteur de la guerre et de l'appareil politique, ils finiront, avec le personnage de Demba Waar, à se substituer au héros *garmi* [noble] dans la quête du pouvoir. . . . . La représentation épique réduit encore à ce niveau les inégalités sociales par l'esthétisation morale. (Dieng 2008: 87–88)

> From the eighteenth century on, in the feudal kingdom of Kajoor, captives made up the armed forces. As the motor of war and the political apparatus, they ended up, through the figure of Demba Waar, replacing the *garmi* [noble] hero in the quest for power. . . . Once again, the epic representation here reduces social inequalities through moral aestheticization. (my translation)

This elevation in status has mixed significance for the slaves in *Jujubier*. For Dieng, the loyal support of the royal captive—that is, slave to the crown—in battle can actually elevate him to the rank of a quasi-noble or almost-hero, a substitute for the actual noble hero. He refers here to Demba Waar, a captive (male) warrior who, according to the epic Dieng collected, advised Lat-Dior in the latter's campaigns against the French the end of the nineteenth century. Dieng's analysis is focused on a specific historical phenomenon, that of the royal captives (*jaami buur*) who were made into powerful Wolof state armies beginning in the late seventeenth and eighteenth centuries, in conjunction with the rise of the Atlantic slave trade, and of which Demba Waar is an example (Dieng 1993a: 187 n. 173). This very particular, historically fraught case is quite different from the slave characters in *Jujubier*, who are women and clearly not meant to be understood as deriving their heroism from their ability to run armies or conduct slave raids for trade. In spite of these differences, Dieng's theorization of the "almost-noble" epic slave can serve as a useful point of comparison. The very possibility for slaves and griots to attain a noble-like status within epic discourse creates a certain contradiction at the heart of the Wolof caste and order structure. On the one hand, as we have seen through Mills and Diop, *géer*-supremacist discourse frames lower-status subjects as always-already dishonored. On the other, Dieng argues that epic's procedure of "moral aestheticization" can actually reduce the inequality on which the caste and order system is based—at least in the exceptional circumstances generated by epic, where extraordinary virtue is expected. Aesthetically, a slave or a griot can be as noble as a noble is supposed to be by birth, even if, from the *géer*-centric point of view, they remain always-already impure.

But what does it mean to be a heroic, or almost-noble, slave, for Aminata Sow Fall? Does it mean to attain heroic virtue through the ideal of honor-in-submission? Or does it mean to share the hero's struggle and join his quest for power? The slaves in *Jujubier*'s invented epic fall somewhere between these poles. Biti, Warèle's granddaughter, is described by a griot singing the epic as "l'amazone à l'allure de guêpe et au cœur de lion" (the Amazon with the speed of a wasp and the heart of a lion) (Sow Fall 1993: 29). Here, Amazons and lions, evoked by a twentieth-century griot in a praise line, suggest an aura of virile nobility and bravery in battle usually reserved for a male hero, not domestic servitude or feminine submission. Biti's virtue is her masculine fearlessness. When we learn her story, it becomes clear why: she is responsible for making sure that Yellimané receives a necessary amulet, a magic copper ball without which he cannot defeat Taarou the sea monster in pursuit of his mother Dioumana. He must throw the ball in the fire at the celebration ceremony for his age group's circumcision, an exclusively male coming-of-age ritual event. Biti dresses as a newly circumcised boy in order to slip him the magic charm. On her way out of the chaotic crowd, she gets drawn into a wrestling bout with another boy:

> Atmosphère enivrante. Dans la mêlée, on saisissait au hasard un adversaire que l'on tentait de terrasser, comme à la lutte, pour démontrer son adresse et sa combativité. C'est ainsi qu'un adolescent avait provoqué Biti par un croche-pied qui ne la déséquilibra pas. S'en suivit un corps-à-corps difficile que dénouèrent l'intelligence et l'expérience de Biti; . . . celle-ci bondit, saisit le garçon par la taille et le déposa sur l'humus en une fraction de seconde. Dans sa chute, le jeune homme avait touché le sein de Biti. En se relevant, il avait crié avec une puissance féroce: "C'est une femme! C'est une femme!" (Sow Fall 1993: 135)

> Heady atmosphere. In the melee, people were grabbing adversaries at random in an attempt to bring them down, like in wrestling, to demonstrate their skill and

combativeness. One adolescent provoked Biti by trying to trip her up, but she did not lose her balance. A difficult hand-to-hand struggle followed, in which Biti's intelligence and experience prevailed; . . . she leapt, grabbed the boy by the waist and dropped him on the humus in a fraction of a second. As he fell, the young man felt Biti's breast. Pulling himself up, he cried with a fierce intensity: "She's a woman! She's a woman!" (my translation)

Within seconds of being unmasked, Biti is killed by a poisoned arrow because "c'était la loi" (that was the law) (1993: 135). She must be punished for violating the taboo of the space reserved for boys becoming men. This scene is fascinating for a number of reasons. It immediately recalls the androgynous women warriors discussed elsewhere in this study: One-Breasted Denba and the cross-dressing women of Nder. But it also harkens back to the masculinist world of wrestling and initiation celebrated in Sow Fall's earlier novel *L'Appel des arènes*. Whereas no woman in *L'Appel* dares to approach the wrestling arena as a combatant or the sacred forest as an initiate, Biti is heroic precisely because she is unafraid to insert herself into a similarly manly domain. Like Dieng's warrior slaves, she is extraordinary because of her valor: the main hero of *Jujubier*'s invented epic, Yellimané, to whose service she is bound, remembers her after her death as "une heroïne tombée au champ de bataille" (a heroine fallen on the battlefield) (Sow Fall 1993: 136). As such, she goes well beyond the role of the docile slave. It is true that she is determined to get Yellimané his copper ball in the nick of time because of the duty imposed by her family's bondage to his; she is still a slave. This sense of duty accounts for her disguising herself as a circumcised boy, for it helps her achieve her task. But her second transgressive act, actually wrestling with a boy in the crowd, is not strictly necessary for the accomplishment of her task. By that point, she has already delivered the copper ball and is on her way out. Presumably, she could have dodged the boy's provocation or feigned defeat in order to make good her escape. She accepts his challenge not out of loyalty to her master or commitment to the task at hand, but because she is proud, and she can.

Thus, Biti fits uneasily within the paradigm of honor-in-submission that is used to describe her grandmother Warèle. She is a loyal and faithful servant, but she also has an excess of defiant energy that seems to spill over those constraints. Yet even Warèle, the self-effacing ideal slave, has a wily side that seems like something other than submissiveness. From the beginning, years before the circumcision-wrestling episode, Warèle had successfully stolen the magic copper ball for safekeeping until Yellimané's coming-of-age, even though her master had expressly refused to take it. In order to obtain the charm by trickery, Warèle feigns injury to Gueladio's messengers, slips them a sleeping potion when they try to help her, and rifles through their clothes until she finds the copper ball, all in defiance of her master's orders (Sow Fall 1993: 128). The success of the future hero Yellimané, still a child in this early episode, is Warèle's motivation, so she can still be seen as loyal; but she cannot be seen as obedient per se.

Later on in this invented epic, Sarebibi remembers Warèle accompanying his mother Thioro when they were young women:

> Quand ses souvenirs lui renvoyaient l'image de sa mère, elle entraînait inéluctable-ment celle de Warèle, l'esclave choisie parmi tant d'autres pour tenir compagnie à Thioro lorsque l'heure vint, pour cette dernière, de quitter son Baol natal afin de rejoindre l'Almamy [Badar] son époux. Deux silhouettes: celle de la mère, grande, altière, sachant être volontaire quand les circonstances l'exigeaient; celle de Warèle, vive, attentive et du caractère, quel caractère! Deux silhouettes mais la même détermination à assurer la protection du jeune Sarebibi. (Sow Fall 1993: 154)

> When his memories conjured up the image of his mother, it ineluctably summoned with it that of Warèle, the slave chosen from so many others to accompany Thioro when the hour came for the latter to leave her native Baol in order to join the Almami [Badar] her husband. Two silhouettes: his mother, tall, proud, capable of being strong-willed when circumstances demanded it; and Warèle, lively, attentive, and with character, such character! Two silhouettes, but with the same determina-tion to protect the young Sarebibi. (my translation)

Warèle acts as a double to her owner Thioro—so much so that when Sarebibi thinks of his own mother, his mind "ineluctably" wanders to Warèle as well. Both are "silhouettes," almost indistinguishable in his memory, and sharing equally in the determination to protect him in his youth. While the reader might expect the princess Thioro's stately bearing to contrast with a humble or homely slave, the two women are more similar than not: just as Thioro is "strong-willed" when she needs to be, Warèle is "lively" and full of "character, such character!" Neither woman is presented as meekly awaiting someone else's orders. On the contrary, in yet another episode, Warèle helps Thioro fake illness so that the latter can see her son, again the young Sarebibi, who is made to spend his days in training with other boys in his age group (Sow Fall 1993: 155–57). When we think of this behavior alongside Warèle's trickery in stealing the copper ball, and Biti's trickery in infiltrating the circumcised boys, we see a pattern of slave behavior that is audacious, proud, cunning, and unfazed by gender barriers. While Warèle is not heroicized as explicitly as Biti, her close relationship with Thioro, like two silhouettes that are always seen together, recalls Bassirou Dieng's description of the epic slave who serves as double to the noble he or she serves.

Finally, the case of Dioumana, the mysteriously beautiful wife who flees her husband and father—the Almami Sarebibi and Gueladio, respectively—and dies at the end of *Jujubier*'s epic, recalls the motif of the femme fatale, whose ambiguity David Conrad has analyzed in the context of Mande epic (1999: 192–94). She is simultaneously irresistible and treacherous, a source of destruction and creativity. A great beauty with a certain seductive power over her husband, and filling the role of mother-to-the-hero for Yellimané, it is her flight that causes her husband and her father to chase after her, leading to years of conflict between their clans. The ensuing war takes on overtones of a civilizational clash between Islam, represented by the Almami, and the non-Muslim hunting societies represented by Gueladio: "Guerre longue et ravageuse entre le clan du Livre et celui des chasseurs magiciens" (Long and destructive war between the clan of the Book and that of the hunter magicians) (Sow Fall 1993: 130). For this reason, Dioumana's mother Assata

> n'avait pas longtemps survécu à "la grande honte," selon ses propres dires, d'avoir mis au monde une fille terrible, un monstre terrible au point de déserter—pour des broutilles—l'alcôve d'un Almamy et d'aller se jeter dans la gueule d'une baleine; terrible au point de provoquer toutes ces tueries sauvages et de semer la haine entre des communautés qui auraient pu vivre éternellement en paix. (1993: 142)

> did not long survive "the great shame," as she called it, of having brought into the world a terrible daughter, a monster so terrible as to desert—over nonsense—an Almami's bedchamber and to throw herself into the maws of a sea monster; so terrible as to provoke all of these savage killings and to sow hatred between these communities that could have lived in peace forever. (my translation)

This maternal condemnation by Assata expresses the feelings of many toward Dioumana. A "monster" for being selfish, she is seen as responsible for the impossibility of peace within the community. This attitude takes up the negative side of the femme fatale motif: according to Conrad, Mande griots may express sentiments along the lines of "If you see men fighting, it is women who make us fight" (1999: 193).

Yet, against this maternal and communal condemnation, and even within the framework of the femme fatale, *Jujubier* emphasizes that Dioumana's flight should be understood as an excessive—heroic?—adherence to precepts of noble conduct, idealized to the point of superseding any social relations she might be bound to respect. Similar Wolof sayings are used to explain both why she had fled and why she dies at the end of the narrative, impaled by a spear intended for Sarebibi. Compare the following two passages, the first of which represents Dioumana's voice within the epic, and the second of which represents the voice of the song's narrator:

1. Adieu mère-ô, pardon mon père

   Adieu Assata

   Mère de l'enfant unique

   Tu m'as appris *gacce-ngaalaama*

   Fondre comme noix de karité . . .

   Plutôt que de porter la honte à califourchon. . . .

   Toute honte bue, toute honte bue,

   Je prends le chemin du retour

   A l'ancêtre du premier jour. (Sow Fall 1993: 185)

   Farewell mother-o, pardon me father

   Farewell Assata

   Mother of an only child,

   You taught me *No-to-shame*,

   To melt like shea butter . . .

   Rather than to be straddled by shame. . . .

   All shame endured, all shame endured,

   I set out to return

   To the ancestor of the first day. (my translation)

2. Le chant:

   Subhaanama Dioumana

   L'antilope du Foudjallon.

   Bañ gacce nangu dee. (1993: 162)

The song:

Admirable Dioumana,

Antelope of Foudjallon.

Refuse shame, accept death. (my translation)

Both passages suggest that the motivation for Dioumana's flight is not monstrous selfishness, but an escape from shame, a word that appears in both passages: *gacce* in Wolof, *honte* in French. The expression "porter la honte à califourchon" (to be straddled by shame) is especially evocative, conjuring up a beast of burden bending under the weight of a heavy rider. These passages show that shame is perceived differently by different people; unlike a supposedly monolithic code of Wolof morality, it is subject to contestation. Whereas for Dioumana's mother, and for Sarebibi, Dioumana's abandonment of her marriage and family is the "great shame," for Dioumana herself, her disappearance is the remedy to a great shame imposed on her by her marriage. But in what way was her marriage shameful? The text never quite says, though it implies that her husband Sarebibi had refused to continue having sexual relations with her, in spite of his overwhelming desire, in the interest of ascetic self-mastery.[4] Dioumana interprets this treatment as a form of repudiation, even though no formal repudiation ever happens. Rather than divorcing her husband and returning to her father's home, she takes refuge in the belly of a sea monster, where she can be free from all masculine domination. The characters' obsession with avoiding dishonor at all costs—which is, as we will recall, the fourth of Sylla's precepts of Wolof moral philosophy—is taken to hyperbolic levels in the case of Dioumana, helping set the epic tone that Sow Fall is aiming for in her invented tale. Whether or not we read Dioumana's behavior as heroic, or as some kind of feminist rebuke of patriarchy, it certainly constitutes a transgression of the norms of wifely submission in the name of noble pride. The common thread of transgression links all three female epic characters—Dioumana, Biti, and Warèle—to the topsy-turvy world of twentieth-century Dakar, where relations between high and low status, caste and wealth, and belonging and exclusion are constantly being blurred, inverted, and renegotiated.

An Inclusive Epic

Turning back to Dakar, the setting of the novel proper, Naarou is determined to follow the model of these epic women, transgressing social boundaries in her own world while deliberately effacing boundaries in her account of theirs. As she declares:

> Je vais revendiquer ma part de l'épopée.... Je n'ai jamais pensé à une cloison entre Warèle, Biti, Sarebibi, Dioumana et les autres, mais comme Mère [Tacko] me traite d'esclave, je revendique Warèle et Biti, je revendique leur part d'héroïsme.... Qui dit qu'elles n'étaient pas de sang royal comme ces millions d'êtres dont le destin a basculé le temps d'un éclair parce que des aventuriers les ont arrachés à leur famille, à leur terre, à leur histoire, ou parce qu'ils ont perdu un combat. (Sow Fall 1993: 88–89)

> I am going to claim my share of the epic.... I have never thought of a barrier between Warèle, Biti, Sarebibi, Dioumana, and the others, but since Mother [Tacko] calls me a slave, I claim Warèle and Biti, I claim their share of heroism.... Who says that they were not of royal blood like those millions of souls whose fate was reversed in the blink of an eye because raiders tore them from their family, their land, their history, or because they lost a battle. (my translation)

The verb *revendiquer*, to claim or demand, signals an expression of ownership in a moment of the protagonist's coming-into-consciousness. Naarou denies that there is a barrier between the slave and noble characters, but faced with Tacko's exclusion of her, Naarou declares that she will recognize the slave characters as having a share in the epic's celebration of heroism. Thus, in the same breath, Naarou both effaces the slave/noble distinction and valorizes the heritage of slaves *as* slaves: she claims her slave ancestors Warèle and Biti, as though naming them in a genealogy. This is a transgressive move: slave genealogies are never sung in epic. And yet, Naarou has paradoxically framed her *revendication* of slave heritage in a way that still makes sense to a *géer*-centric audience. Her reference to "sang royal" or noble blood that may flow in the veins of slave ancestors suggests not that all humans are born radically equal, but that low-status persons may in fact have noble origins of some sort. After all, the truth of "who begot whom" is lost to the mists of time. Sow Fall's democratization of Wolof tradition does not seek to abolish the hierarchy of statuses directly, but to convince even the reader attached to so-called Wolof moral philosophy that the values and public esteem enshrined in such codes ought truly to belong to everyone based on the benefit of the doubt. *Jujubier* does not criticize the existence of noble privilege as such, but its foundation on the exclusion of impure inferiors. Aristocrats, in her view, conveniently forget that blood lineages are more mixed than they would like to remember.

This *revendication* is not merely a private affair that Naarou formulates in her heart. It causes scandal by reminding everyone publically that she is related by blood to Tacko's noble family. Naarou's biological mother, Penda, had downplayed the animosity between Tacko's family and theirs, in hopes of not stirring up the pot too much:

> A quoi bon raconter à Naarou que cette parenté avec Tacko était un sujet tabou depuis l'unanimité automatique contre Sadaga. (Sow Fall 1993: 94)

> What good would it have done to tell Naarou that this kinship with Tacko had been a taboo subject since everyone had automatically, unanimously turned against Sadaga. (my translation)

The fact that their blood relation is a taboo subject is key, for only by it remaining a taboo subject can the delicate peace between the two lines of the family, one noble and one mixed noble and slave, be preserved. This necessity for discretion to maintain social harmony corresponds to another traditional Wolof moral value, that of *sutura*, which, in a crucial moment of the novel that has been neglected by critics, Naarou may be said to violate. Sylla defines *sutura* as

> ce qui cache aux yeux du public les faiblesses et les défauts de quelqu'un pour ne laisser paraître que ce qui le rend respectable. . . . Il est donc souhaitable que l'on sache taire les tares des autres, ce qui est d'ailleurs un important facteur de paix sociale. Un proverbe déclare: *fu jàmm yendu, waaya fa xam lu mu waxul*, là où la paix règne, se trouve quelqu'un qui a su taire ce qu'il sait. Autrement dit, la paix ne règnerait nulle part si l'on se permettait de dire ce que l'on sait des autres. (1978: 89)

> that which hides from public sight someone's weaknesses and faults in order only to show what makes him or her respectable. . . . It is therefore desirable to know how to keep the flaws of others unspoken, which is in any case an important factor of social peace. A proverb declares: *fu jàmm yendu, waaya fa xam lu mu waxul,*

wherever peace reigns, someone has managed to keep quiet what he knows. In other words, peace would not reign anywhere if we allowed ourselves to say what we know about others. (my translation)

Rather than preserve the peace with her cousin and adoptive mother Tacko by maintaining a discreet silence about the slave side of the family, Naarou deliberately composes a verse that acknowledges this slave genealogy at a funeral attended by many people:

O Waly le dieu des fauves
Tu te reposais dans l'antre du lion
En attendant que le maître de céans
T'apportât la proie convoitée.
Le sang ne mentira pas
Waly fils de Penda Sar
Kor Kantôme kor Sadaga
Penda Waly Penda eyôô
Je te salue Tacko Biram Penda. (Sow Fall 1993: 97)

O Waly, god of wild beasts
You rested in the lion's den
Waiting for its master
To bring you its coveted prey.
Blood will not lie,
Waly son of Penda Sar
Kor Kantôme kor Sadaga
Penda Waly Penda eyôô,
I salute you, Tacko Biram Penda. (my translation)

In these last lines, Naarou reminds everyone publically of her own kinship with Tacko. As the family tree shows, "Waly, god of wild beasts" is the first ancestor, from whom the hero Gueladio is descended. Naarou then segues into honoring his modern homonym, Waly her biological grandfather, who was married to both Kantôme, Tacko's mother, but also to Sadaga, his slave; a footnote reminds us that the word *kor* means "beloved of." The modern Waly's mother and daughter were both named Penda; therefore the expressions "Penda Waly Penda" (Penda daughter of Waly son of Penda) and "Tacko Biram Penda" (Tacko daughter of Biram son of Penda) explicitly reference the connectedness of both lineages, one of which maintains its nobility untainted, and the other of which includes slave blood. In other words, everyone is connected. Whether she likes it or not, Tacko has slaves in her family, and thanks to Naarou's performance in a public setting, now anyone who may have forgotten that fact is reminded of it. As the text says:

> Quelques instants plus tard, un seul sujet de conversation agitait toutes les lèvres: la lutte épique entre Sadaga la mère de Penda et Kantôme la mère de Tacko, l'audace de Sadaga et la jalousie morbide de Kantôme. (Sow Fall 1993: 97)

> A few seconds later, a single topic of conversation excited everyone's lips: the epic battle between Sadaga mother of Penda and Kantôme mother of Tacko, Sadaga's audacity and Kantôme's morbid jealousy. (my translation)

Indeed, this performance generates a great deal of drama in the family. Interestingly, the use of the expression "la lutte épique" to refer to the rivalry between Sadaga and Kantôme—both of whom belong to the world of the novel proper—suggests a parallel or overlap between the worlds of epic and novel. Sadaga's struggle for recognition, and Naarou's after her, echo the struggles of the epic's women characters, of slaves effacing the boundaries that exclude them from nobility. Tacko, furious, seeing herself as having been publically dishonored, cuts all ties with Naarou until the very end of the novel.

This episode raises important questions. Who in this conflict is right according to Wolof moral philosophy? Who is or is not violating traditional Wolof values? On the one hand, the text makes it clear that by rejecting the relationship of mutual obligation that has united their lineages for years, Tacko has violated the value of *wollëre*, a word that the author translates as "le devoir de sauvegarder les liens, le sens de la fidélité" (the duty to conserve relationships, the sense of faithfulness."[5] Most critics have followed this line of reasoning, reading Tacko as an archetypal alienated woman.[6] But I would like to suggest that Tacko's behavior actually illustrates the principle of respectability in front of one's *nawle* or peers, in this case her fellow persons of noble status, as well as the imperative to avoid dishonor at all costs—both of which are pillars of Wolof moral philosophy, according to Sylla. Therefore, for Tacko, Naarou's performance is shameful to the family because it violates the pact of *sutura* or discretion by making private information public.

Tacko feels she has been shamed—made equal to a slave wife—whereas Naarou does not feel she has shamed anyone, but only asserted her rightful prerogative as a member of the family.

The salience of *sutura* as a point of contestation is made clear by Naarou's ambiguous attitude toward it. Before her scandalous performance, she thinks a great deal about how to "donner la réplique convenable à Tacko en ménageant les formes. Ne pas tomber dans l'irrespect" (give an acceptable reply to Tacko while keeping up appearances. Without falling into disrespect) (Sow Fall 1993: 95). But after the performance, when her biological mother Penda begs her to reconcile with Tacko, Naarou refuses:

> "Je le ferais bien si je pouvais, mais je ne peux pas, c'est plus fort que moi." . . . Naarou éclata d'un rire que Penda trouva déplacé, à la limite impertinent. (1993: 105)

> "I would if I could, but I cannot; it is stronger than I." . . . Naarou burst into laughter in a way that Penda found inappropriate, even impertinent. (my translation)

Whereas before the performance she had thought carefully about how to assert her claim to family belonging "while keeping up appearances," that is, while respecting the limits of *sutura*, once the damage is done she feels that it is more important to stand her ground than to maintain peace in the family. Naarou's action poses a challenge to all the values we have discussed so far: *wollëre*, *sutura*, *nawle*, and avoiding dishonor. She pursues a line of action that her adopted mother finds scandalous and that leads directly to the rupture of their relationship. She claims that her *nawle* or peers are not dependent on caste or order, whereas for Tacko they most certainly are. She finds her own honor in asserting her right to belonging in the family, regardless of the scandal or dishonor the rest of the family feels that such an assertion casts upon them. In a way that recalls the differing interpretations of Dioumana's relationship to shame that we saw above, Wolof moral philosophy is again subject to contestation. The traditional values themselves seem at odds with each other, and different characters resolve those conflicts for themselves according to their own vested interests.

But while the main object of the text's criticism might seem to be the inequality of the Senegalese caste and order system, it goes even farther in its criticism of genealogical thinking. Beyond the questions of *wollëre* and *sutura*, *Jujubier* emphasizes that genealogy itself is malleable and subject to interpretation. In spite of what people believe or say their ancestry to be, the truth of one's ancestry is often unknown or unprovable, and the discourse of genealogy in the present is therefore subject to infinite manipulation. As Naarou says in the quote analyzed above, people who were known as slaves may in fact have had noble lineages after being "arrachés à leur famille, à leur terre, à leur histoire, ou parce qu'ils ont perdu un combat" (torn from their family, their land, their history, or because they lost a battle) (Sow Fall 1993: 89). But the phenomenon works the other way as well. When Yelli and Naarou advertise their pilgrimage to the patriarch's tomb on the radio, they are aware of the common practice of inventing noble ancestors for oneself:

> Quelques semaines plus tard, une machine infaillible fut mise en branle. Pourquoi ne pas emprunter une voie bien rôdée par tant de gens qui, de plus en plus fréquemment, exhumaient une sainteté, un héros ou une tête couronnée parmi leurs proches parents jusqu'alors inconnus! De nouveaux monuments s'érigeaient et on les célébrait en grande pompe. Des généalogies inédites étaient mises à jour, tout le monde était content et chacun pouvait reconnaître les "grandes naissances."
>
> L'objectif de Naarou et de Yelli n'était pas du même genre, bien sûr, mais il fallait user de moyens efficaces. Un communiqué de presse parut dans le journal, par lequel les descendants de l'Almamy Sarebibi conviaient toute la communauté sans distinction de sexe, d'ethnie ou de religion, au pèlerinage à Babyselli pour honorer la mémoire du saint homme.... Magatte la griotte investit la radio publique pour expliquer la genèse de l'épopée du Foudjallon en débitant des énormités qui ne choquèrent que deux personnes: Yelli et Naarou. Les autres ne retinrent que la longue liste des personnalités citées qui, *ndekete yoo*, étaient des descendants de l'Almamy-empereur. Yelli, contre toute attente, eut droit à la visite d'hommes et de femmes nantis qui lui remirent leur contribution, en espèces ou en nature, à l'occasion du pèlerinage qui les honorait tous.
>
> Petit à petit, Tacko y crut. (1993: 116–18)

> A few weeks later, an infallible machine was set in motion. Why not follow a path already taken by so many people who, with increasing frequency, exhumed a saint, a hero, or a crowned head from among previously unknown close relatives! New monuments were built and celebrated with great pomp. Genealogies never heard before were updated, everyone was happy, and everyone could recognize "great births."
>
> Naarou and Yelli's objective was not of this kind, of course, but they had to

use effective means. A press release appeared in the newspaper in which the descendants of Almami Sarebibi summoned the whole community regardless of sex, ethnicity, or religion to a pilgrimage to Babyselli honoring the memory of the holy man. . . . Magatte the griot woman invaded the public radio to explain the origins of the epic of Foudjallon while gushing with exaggerations that shocked only two people: Yelli and Naarou. Everyone else only remembered the long list of personalities she cited, who, *what a surprise!*, were descendants of the Alma-mi-emperor. Yelli, to the surprise of all, was treated to visits from wealthy men and women who offered him their contribution, in cash or in goods, on the occasion of this pilgrimage that would honor them all.

Little by little, Tacko believed. (my translation)

The text is careful not to question Naarou and Yelli's integrity, suggesting that their objectives are not the same as unscrupulous social climbers who "exhume" or "update"—that is, invent—a previously unknown family connection to a saint, hero, or king, in hopes of profiting from it materially or symbolically. Nonetheless, Naarou and Yelli need to get the word out about their event so that it can represent a dignified homage to their family's heritage; therefore, they do not act to prevent the use of tactics of self-marketing and exaggeration that are typical of less well-intentioned opportunists. They enlist the help of Magatte, a typically opportunistic female griot who is referred to as the "griotte des temps nouveaux" or griot of modern times, a worshipper of the god of money who had deserted her patron Yelli when he lost his material wealth (1993: 79). When Magatte goes on the radio to call all of Sarebibi's descendants to participate in the pilgrimage, she exaggerates who actually belongs to the family in an attempt to get more people to show up. No one rebukes her for doing this. Regardless of their personal integrity, Naarou and Yelli must lower themselves to the point of using, or at least not preventing, the same publicity tricks as imposters and sycophants, a fact that risks making their motivation of true familial fidelity indistinguishable on the outside from base self-promotion. Nevertheless, the pilgrimage benefits from its all-inclusiveness: everyone is welcome regardless not only of their age, sex, or religion, but also regardless of the authenticity, or lack thereof, of their kinship connection to the family. The malleability of genealogy and the opportunism of Magatte, the griot of modern times, are actually celebrated in this passage. The public brouhaha around this expansive family pilgrimage is the only thing that helps Tacko come around, and become open to reconciliation with Naarou: "Little by little, Tacko believed." The idea of belief suggests that the whole pilgrimage is a fiction, or a partial fiction, but in any case, a healthy one, because it brings everyone together through a belief—a faith, a trust—that everyone belongs together.

As such, the text does not only criticize the inventedness of genealogy. It actually embraces this inventedness as part and parcel of how people understand, or ought to understand, kinship. The pilgrimage to the patriarch's tomb errs on the side of bringing people into the flock rather than keeping them out; it is an inclusive venture rather than an exclusive one. This fact is all the more evident in the striking inclusiveness of the party of pilgrims once the event is under way:

> Parmi eux, Amath [le libraire] et les retraités, et Lobé le *goor jigéen*, la crème politique, religieuse et coutumière, des hommes et des femmes d'affaires. Tous parés de leurs plus beaux atours, en blanc. Tous. Et aussi des gens humbles. (Sow Fall 1993: 118)

> Among them, Amath [the bookseller] and the retirees, and Lobé the *góor-jigéen*; political, religious, and customary elites, businessmen and -women. All in white, garbed in their best attire. Every one of them. And also people of humble means. (my translation)

The pilgrims represent not just a collection of family members and acquaintances, but a cross-section of Senegalese society—rich and poor, old and young, men and women, traditional and modern, presumably Muslim and non-Muslim, all dressed in white robes that efface their differences. Perhaps most attention-grabbing of all in this list is the explicit and visible participation of Lobé the *góor-jigéen*, the homosexual or cross-dressing man, a category made abject by the homophobic moral panic that has pervaded Senegalese discourse in recent years (Mills 2011: 119). Even this person with nonconforming sexuality is brought into the family fold, suggesting that queer identities can have, and indeed have had, a recognized place in Senegalese social life.[7] One might cautiously venture that the presence of Lobé the *góor-jigéen* authorizes, however distantly, a queer reading of Biti, the cross-dressing woman slave who fights men in the epic to get Yellimané the magic amulet he needs. Without claiming that Aminata Sow Fall's writing necessarily has a pro-LGBT agenda in the sense intended by contemporary regimes of universal human rights, it is worth noticing that homosexual sex, queer identities, and practices of cross-dressing have all historically been collapsed under the Wolof term *góor-jigéen* (Niang 2010: 117 and 120). Therefore, if we see an overlap between the theme of the androgynous or cross-dressing woman warrior, which runs throughout real oral West African epic, and the homosexual or cross-dressing man who is included in the pilgrimage, this overlap can only serve to reinforce my argument that nonconforming gender behaviors are incorporated into this novel's vision of Senegalese community. The community envisaged here is informed by oral tradition but stripped of its exclusive hierarchies of class, caste, order, and gender.

Oral Performance and Women's Agency

Let us return for a moment to the argument that *Le Jujubier du patriarche* represents a feminine or feminist spin on its masculinist predecessors. "Here," writes Nicki Hitchcott, "for the first time, in Sow Fall's writings, a silenced woman voices her own identity" (2000: 108). Yet the masculinist intertext of this novel is not just the author's previous novels, but the epic genre itself. For Hitchcott, "The privileging of African oral elements is relatively rare in Sub-Saharan African women's writing in French and tends to be associated with literature written by men" (2000: 109). Eileen Julien had previously made the same point a bit more forcefully:

> I should like to advance another hypothesis: women writers, by and large, may not be drawn to the epic, initiation story, or fable in their traditional acceptations. There may be little surprise in the absence of an epic tendency among women writers. This hierarchic form is tied to nationalist agendas and military might, which have been and continue to be, for the most part, provinces of patriarchy. (1992: 27)

The case study of *Jujubier* that I have conducted here hardly serves as a blanket contradiction to these observations. Indeed, it is curious that one of the few West African women writers to deal in depth with epic material is the very one who has most often been called "masculine," traditionalist, and "retrograde."[8] Even *Jujubier*, with its emphasis on strong, transgressive female characters in both its epic and novel sections, seems for some critics to be built upon a patriarchal edifice. For Florence Martin,

> L'épopée noble devient alors pré-texte au futur texte de Naarou: au sein du vieux chant patriarcal aristocratique, elle cherche les noms de ses aïeules afin de récupérer

son histoire à elle, enfouie sous celle, "magistrale" à tous égards, de la dynastie des Almamy. . . . Il ne s'agit pas de vol à la Cixous, mais plutôt de rattrapage, de la récupération, à partir du pré-texte indigent de l'épopée des Almamy, de son texte clanique à elle. (2000: 300)

The noble epic becomes, then, a pre-text to Naarou's future text: within the old aristocratic patriarchal song, she searches for the names of her women ancestors in order to retrieve her own history, buried beneath that of the Almamis' dynasty, which is in every way a "master" history. . . . This is not a Cixous-style theft, but rather a recovery, a retrieval, of her own clanic text, from the indigent pre-text of the Almamis' epic. (my translation)

This emphasis on reading women's roles into an "indigent," masculinist, master discourse has its own value, according to Martin, but the most significantly feminist aspect of the text is Naarou's expression of her own voice. By having the courage to stand up to the forces that attempt to silence her, Naarou's voice becomes a resistance to the silence imposed upon African women.

The ambiguity of *Jujubier*'s relationship to larger structures of gendered power reflects current directions in oral tradition studies. An increasing amount of attention has been paid to women's interventions in a variety of oral genres in Senegalese contexts and beyond. In Wolof, research on poems of praise or satire (*taasu*) by Lisa McNee, on wedding insult songs (*xaxaar*) by Judith Irvine, and on *xaxaar* and other women's songs by Marame Gueye have significantly problematized the idea that written francophone literature by women fills any kind of void or "silence" at all.[9] Indeed, as research on songs from Senegal and elsewhere on the continent has shown, African women play extremely active roles in a variety of understudied oral literary genres that possess significant room for self-expression and social criticism.[10] Meanwhile, since the 1990s, a certain strain of scholarship has devoted itself specifically to the question of whether women can be said to perform epics in West Africa.[11] The results of that research, though still contested, suggest that women often serve roles as intervening singers rather than narrators in the performance of a classic epic like *Sunjata*.[12] While this contribution deserves to be valorized in itself, there is some evidence that the exclusion of women from narrating political epics may be softening in various places throughout West Africa, and some scholars have argued that specific women's genres should be included in the scholarly understanding of epic.[13] Aïssata Sidikou has gone farthest in defending the notion of a West African women's epic, documenting the career of a Nigerien griotte named Fati Diado Sékou, who, like Naarou, had plans (at the time of Sidikou's writing) for future performances and compositions that would highlight women's roles in well-known epic narratives about male heroes—in spite of the opposition and criticism of certain male and even fellow female performers (Sidikou 2001: 111–29).

This research helps us read *Jujubier* in a larger West African context. While a West African epic "about women and by women" may still be largely a genre of the future, some precedents for it have been established: by oral performers and researchers, as the case of Fati Diado Sékou and Aïssata Sidikou suggests, and in creative writing, as Aminata Sow Fall's novel demonstrates (Sidikou 2001: 118). If *Jujubier* does represent a real woman writer's—and a fictional woman performer's—intervention in a masculinist genre, it has been preceded and followed by a number of real women performers working in genres whose importance is only just beginning to be understood by academics. And yet, the question of what it means for Aminata Sow Fall to write as a woman is, at the end of the day, limiting. If anything, the partial or total dismissal of her as insufficiently feminist—and the concurrent canonization of Mariama Bâ, a Senegalese writer of more or less the same generation, as antitraditional and antipatriarchal—say more about the expectations of Western critics than they do about these writers' incredibly layered and nuanced texts (Warner 2016). For Sow Fall, gender is but one more pillar in the overarching structure of social norms subtending so-called traditional values, whether we consider these to be the social function of epic or the points elaborated in Sylla's Wolof moral philosophy. Sow Fall's contribution is to reveal that, in spite of Sylla's obfuscation of the fact, these norms, values, and traditions are dependent on socially regulated hierarchies of caste, order, gender, and, increasingly, economic class, which are subject to renegotiation and reimagination. For her, the traditional power structure must be transformed into egalitarian terms if it is to serve the needs of the future; and a first step can be taken by reimagining oral tradition itself.

Through Lat-Dior's Looking Glass

You know, vampires have no reflections in a mirror? There's this idea that monsters don't have reflections in a mirror. And what I've always thought isn't that monsters don't have reflections in a mirror. It's that if you want to make a human being into a monster, deny them, at the cultural level, any reflection of themselves. And growing up, I felt like a monster in some ways. I didn't see myself reflected at all. I was like, "Yo, is something wrong with me? That the whole society seems to think that people like me don't exist?" And part of what inspired me, was this deep desire that before I died, I would make a couple of mirrors. That I would make some mirrors so that kids like me might see themselves reflected back and might not feel so monstrous for it.

—Junot Díaz, speaking to students at Bergen Community College in 2009

This book has studied critically minded mobilizations of West African epic in literary writing. On the one hand, the idea of an African epic provided a paradigm from the colonial period onward that has made the continent legible in comparison to Europe. Much comparative literary theory, especially studies of the novel, has imagined epic as the novel's Other: the former represents a lost world of wholeness and presence, whereas the latter represents the alienation of the now. While this theoretical approach, which has been easily transposed into studies of African literature, allows for the novel to mimic features of orality, tradition, and epic, it always presumes a teleology according to which the novel bears a more panoramic perspective, a more critical and ironic stance within which traces of orality are the sign of a modern novel's Africanness. On the other hand, independently of this commentary, oral heroic narratives in the West African context continue to exist as living, evolving traditions, which constantly update themselves in order to remain pertinent in changing times. I have argued that the novel is neither a replacement nor a successor to forms of traditional oral narrative, but rather overlaps with them by sharing their function of critical reflexivity, that is, the ability of individual texts and performances to reflect critically on the social world and on their own status as objects in the world.

The work of D. T. Niane, Laye Camara, Cheikh Aliou Ndao, Yambo Ouologuem, Amadou Hampâté Bâ, Ahmadou Kourouma, and Aminata Sow Fall illustrates this vision of traditionality as a dynamic concept that has continued to be relevant through colonial and postcolonial contexts. Much of their work resists and criticizes the metanarrative of nostalgia for dying, pristine ways of life, a trope dear to colonial ethnography as well as to the field of African literary studies that succeeded it. These writers' multifaceted deployment of traditional epic forms in their writing makes room for questioning the authority of tradition itself and to opening it up to outside influences. Their uses of epic tradition emphasize its capacity for adaptation, innovation, and even reinvention.

This conclusion offers a case study that will bring this trajectory to what I hope is a thought-provoking endpoint. A contemporary writer, Boubacar Boris Diop of Senegal, embeds oral traditions from a specifically Wolof context in his writing in a remarkably multidimensional way, simultaneously monumentalizing them as landmarks of cultural heritage, questioning their authenticity, and framing them as utterances in an ongoing dialogue that has no teleological end. In a way reminiscent of Dominican-American writer Junot Díaz's brilliantly worded sense of mission, quoted above, oral traditions serve as part of a larger role of cultural reconstruction, namely the creation of a thoughtful mirror for the postcolonial African subject. Reflected in the spectacle of images around it, the postcolonial subject can, in the end, choose what image of itself to see: either a false, dehumanizing stereotype projected by neocolonial power structures and the Western media; or a corrective, affirming collage that is pieced together after a careful search for the fragments of identity. In either case, the mirror depends to a large extent on the seeing subject and surrounding discursive structures. It cannot offer a perfect reflection corresponding to some stable notion of truth.

In order to elucidate this game of mirrors, I will examine Diop's use of traditions and epic in the bilingual Wolof/French-language novel *Doomi Golo* (Children of the Monkey) (2003 and 2009) through the lens of the literary postmodern. This once fashionable category, which is notoriously hard to define across all the domains to which it has been applied, nevertheless offers a powerful critique of modernity and its attendant metanarratives explored in the introduction to this book. By moving from the traditional to the postmodern while skipping the seemingly necessary step of the modern, I hope to underscore how contingent all of these categories are, insofar as any one of them is understood as exclusive of the others. Most importantly, I hope to drive home the point that oral traditional discourse is pertinent even in the highly skeptical and disenchanted realm of extremely contemporary world literature. *Doomi Golo*, which exemplifies the traits of postmodern narrative at many levels, draws a good deal of its skepticism—its subversiveness of norms and metanarratives of truth—from Wolof traditional sources. The proverbs of the sage Kocc Barma (pronounced "coach") and the epic of the Senegalese national hero Lat-Dior are not treated as sacred, authoritative texts to be revered, but as part of an ongoing social conversation whose rules can change over time—that is, as mirrors that reflect what we choose to see in them. This theorization springs from the depiction of Kocc Barma in the traditions themselves: the maxims of this key figure in Wolof tales are not eternal truths, but language games. As such, *Doomi Golo* is not just a "modern" novel that subverts "traditional values" or subjects them to nostalgia; rather, its postmodern language games inherit and replay some of the same rules as traditional discourse itself. Still, rather than merely performing an exercise in linguistic play, this reading opens an important commentary on the ability of the African subject to construct a sense of self amid the chaos of the postcolonial age.

Tradition and the Postmodern

The foundational account of the postmodern is that of Jean-François Lyotard, who famously summarized it as an "incredulity towards metanarratives" (1984: xxiv). In particular, his incredulity is directed toward the metanarrative of scientific truth that "the most highly developed" societies attempted to institutionalize as final

(1984: xxiii). Lyotard's critique is based on the dissemination of language games in society, of which scientific discourse is merely one; lacking any stable authority, these games are subject to renegotiation by agonistic players, especially through popular speech and literature (1984: 10 and 40). This account is by no means the only one possible: various postmoderns have been conceptualized in disciplines ranging from architecture to political theory (Appiah 1992: 143). Despite this diversity of thought, there is a consensus that in literature, the postmodern refers to narratives that question the truth of who is speaking or what is being said. Techniques of indeterminacy, whether in the sequencing of represented events or in the focalization of a narrative's diegetic levels, generally signal a rupture from both classic realist conventions (e.g., Honoré de Balzac, Charles Dickens) and so-called high modernism (e.g., fin-de-siècle avant-gardes, Marcel Proust, James Joyce), although the latter point is subject to debate (Kafalenos 1992). Such techniques of narrative indeterminacy are exemplified in the work of Italo Calvino and Alain Robbe-Grillet.

As this genealogy shows, the postmodern, like epic, is originally a category of European critical thought. Scholars were hesitant to apply the notion outside of Europe's borders until relatively recently. Kwame Anthony Appiah, who wittily referred to the postmodern as the "metanarrative of the end of metanarratives" (1992: 140), nevertheless saw a certain parallelism between this Euro-American category and its mirror image, the Third World's postcolonial. The dilemma of the postcolonial intellectual, unable to choose definitively between Western education and his or her native heritage, and disappointed by the failed promises of the nation-state, generated fragmented narratives about the fragmentation of identity. Such narratives of fragmentation are, in large part, what academics refer to under the label of "postcolonial literature." Nevertheless, for Appiah, the postmodern and the postcolonial have historically shared a tendency to ignore the everyday experience of African life. If the former was fundamentally Western, then the latter, emblematized for Appiah in the genre of the novel, and more specifically in Yambo Ouologuem's *Devoir de violence*, was a profoundly Westernized creature that remained at constant risk of turning Africans into "Otherness-machines" for inevitably Western readers:

This is especially true when postcolonial meets postmodern, for what the postmodern reader seems to demand of its Africa is all too close to what modernism—as documented in William Rubin's Primitivism exhibit of 1985—demanded of it. The role that Africa, like the rest of the Third World, plays for Euro-American postmodernism—like its better-documented significance for modernist art—must be distinguished from the role postmodernism might play in the Third World. What that might be it is, I think, too early to tell. (1992: 157)

This indictment of the African novel, with Ouologuem's highly intellectual cynicism squarely in the crosshairs, seems to question whether African writers can speak to African audiences, and to doubt that postmodern narrative techniques can carry their message. On the one hand, this skepticism might seem warranted: Ousmane Sembène's famous turn to realist cinema as a "night school for the masses" conducted in African languages sought to address precisely Appiah's concern, namely the need to speak to everyday Africans on their own turf, rather than through intellectual mumbo jumbo, as far back as the early 1960s. On the other hand, the example of Sembène is ambiguous: though profoundly uninterested in any avant-garde, he never abandoned literature entirely for the pursuit of cinema; that is, he never stopped writing novels in French, even as he made movies in African languages. Why? While it is certain that cultural production in any medium has its pitfalls, it is worth remembering that African writers—including Ouologuem—have struggled for decades to find a voice capable of reaching beyond Western and Westernized audiences, and that this search has taken shape through many experimentations with form, both within and outside the generic limits of the novel. Contemporary examples—specifically, as I will argue here, that of Boubacar Boris Diop—offer us the possibility to reevaluate the work that novelistic writing is capable of performing on the African continent, including the work of the literary postmodern.

A group of Ivorian scholars has traced the African literary postmodern through writers like Henri Lopes, Tahar Ben Jelloun, and Alain Mabanckou, via a recurring motif of ironic distance from the social realism of Sembène's generation (Coulibaly et al. 2011). The editors object to the summary exclusion of Africa from the debate over postmodernism, including Lyotard's narrow focus on so-called "advanced and postindustrial societies" (Coulibaly et al. 2011: 7–10). Narrative indeterminacy and hyperintertextuality are key factors in their application of the term "postmodern" to specific African literary works. Although these questions may seem pedantic—should we treat work X as modern or postmodern? postmodern or postcolonial?—there is an important analytical benefit to be gained from dwelling on the skepticism toward metanarratives of truth that is embedded in some African narratives. In particular, this reflection can help us rethink the place of oral tradition in the contemporary world by breaking it out of the "jail of difference" where the category of the modern has locked it up (C. Miller 1990: 24). And in any case, there is no need to establish a rigid boundary between modern and postmodern: as Lyotard himself writes, the postmodern

is undoubtedly a part of the modern.... In an amazing acceleration, the generations precipitate themselves. A work can become modern only if it is first postmodern. Postmodernism thus understood is not modernism at its end but in the nascent state, and this state is constant. (1984: 79)

Referring here to fin-de-siècle European painting, Lyotard describes how each microgeneration challenged the preceding one, creating ephemeral postmodern-isms that coalesced over the long run into what we generally think of as modern painting. The point, then, is not to make tedious distinctions about what label to use when. The African literary postmodern can easily, and indeed ought to, be counted among the contradictions of Afromodernity studied in the introduction. It should be conceptualized alongside those aspects of urban Senegalese cultural production that constitute "une entreprise de désorganisation qui est aussi une aventure de réorganisation et de recomposition de plusieurs héritages historiques" (an enterprise of disorganization that is also an adventure of reorganizing and recomposing several historic heritages) (M. Diouf 2002: 262).

Roger Tro Dého's work is especially illuminating in this regard, since it offers a first examination of the possibility of a postmodern literary practice rooted in African oral traditions (2011). Two basic assertions ground his argument. First, novels like those of Jean-Marie Adiaffi and Ahmadou Kourouma follow certain relevant traits of the traditional folktale: this oral genre has vague chronological sequencing, an easy ability to shuttle between realist and fantastic registers, and a quilt-like quality that incorporates "patches" of other tales into itself (Tro Dého 2011: 148–69). To this effect, Tro Dého quotes Adiaffi:

Pour ma part, je garde de la tradition orale les traits esthétiques de nature à innover, à réinventer un nouveau langage. Il y a des moments où la tradition est plus révolutionnaire que la modernité déjà radotante. (Adiaffi 2000: 5, quoted in Tro Dého 2011: 146)

For my part, I keep from oral tradition aesthetic traits that can innovate or reinvent a new language. There are moments when tradition is more rev-olutionary than modernity's babbling. (my translation)

Second, such novels have a polyphonic style of narration where each first-person narrator has his or her own version of truth. This polyphony is complemented by a patchwork and often mixed-up intertextuality within which oral traditional elements play a role, but not the central role. The focus of the novel is to de-essentialize traditional material and to distance itself from it, not to elevate it as an essential sign of African identity (2011: 168–79).

This analysis leads us to two possible propositions that are never explicitly distinguished in Tro Dého's work: that a postmodern aesthetics subverts the metanarrative of tradition; or a postmodern aesthetics can draw some of its subversiveness toward the metanarrative of truth, associated with colonial modernity, from traditional discourse. Given my overarching focus on tradition as construct rather than essence, and as speech genre in flux rather than stable system of values, this concluding essay will argue for the second proposition through the specific example of Boubacar Boris Diop's novel *Doomi Golo*. In doing so, it aims to build on Tro Dého's insight while exploring a new terrain for the African literary postmodern via the connection to oral tradition and epic studies.

Doomi Golo in context

While Boubacar Boris Diop became well known on the world literary scene for his work on the Rwandan genocide, his reputation is growing for his scholarly and literary commitment to the Wolof language.[1] *Doomi Golo* represented the beginning of this ongoing adventure. Originally publishing the novel in Wolof in 2003, Diop published a noticeably different adaptation of *Doomi Golo* in French, titled *Les petits de la guenon*, in 2009. Both the Wolof and French titles literally mean "Children of the Monkey." In the French reworking, some passages are deleted or reordered, details are added, and an occasional name or setting is changed. In spite of these differences, a paratextual note in *Les petits de la guenon* states that it is the "version française de *Doomi Golo*" (French version of *Doomi Golo*) and that "la traduction en a été librement assurée par l'auteur lui-même" (the translation was freely undertaken by the author himself), thereby raising interesting questions around self-translation and the relationship of europhone writing to efforts to promote literature in African languages. The Wolof *Doomi Golo* was made into a downloadable audio format (E-Book Africa, 2013), which was also broadcast in parts on Senegalese radio, in hopes of reaching the large potential audience that understands Wolof orally but does not read it. An English print version, *Doomi Golo:*

The Hidden Notebooks, appeared in 2016. The introduction states that this English version "is a direct translation of *Les petits* into English" (Wülfing-Leckie in B. B. Diop 2016: vii); nevertheless, the back cover declares that we are holding in our hands "the first novel to be translated from Wolof to English."

Full of digressions, dream sequences, passages of uncertain ontological status, and intertwining subplots whose characters form uncanny mirror images of each other, this postmodern novel consists of a series of notebooks written by an elderly grandfather in Senegal, Nguirane, chronicling life in Dakar to his absent émigré grandson, Badou. Upon Nguirane's death, the narration is taken over by the local madman, Ali Kaboye, who doubles as a kind of supernatural spirit who can cross space and time. The novel is thus divided between two narrators(—or is it?[2]): Nguirane's six notebooks, each with its own assigned title and number, comprise part 1, while a long, unbroken section attributed to Ali Kaboye makes up part 2. Scholarly readers of *Doomi Golo* have focused on its linguistic militancy as a text written in the Wolof language, or on the differences between the Wolof and French versions.[3] The author himself gives some credence to a militant antifrancophone reading, explaining that his turn to Wolof and rejection of French was a result of his disgust for the role of the Francophonie in perpetrating the Rwandan genocide. However, Diop has also told critics of his linguistic choice that he never intended his turn away from French to be permanent or absolute; rather, "nos langues devraient avoir leur chance" (our languages should have their chance) (Diop in Zanganeh 2010).

Diop's engagement with oral tradition has been discussed far less. Many Wolof oral traditions are interspersed throughout the novel: the intellectual jousts between Kocc Barma and the *dammel* Daaw Demba,[4] remembered in the historical traditions of the precolonial kingdom of Kajoor; the legend of the "Tuesday of Nder," in which women from the kingdom of Walo heroically commit suicide in order to avoid capture; the battle of Guy Njulli, where a royal father and son faced each other as enemy combatants for the throne of the kingdom of Saalum; Lat-Dior, the last great *dammel* of Kajoor, remembered as a resister to the French encroachment, famous for sabotaging the Dakar–St. Louis railroad, and canonized by Senghor as a national hero of Senegal; the apparently related legend of the vengeful Kagne, who haunts the forest between Dakar and Thies, threatening to derail the train that dared intrude on his lands; and the half-legend of Ali Kaboye, a mysterious urban figure still remembered by older generations in Medina, a working-class neighborhood of Dakar on which the novel's fictional neighborhood of Niarela is based.[5] These legends are documented to greater or lesser degrees, some richly; the last two are the least well-documented, being the subject of relatively recent urban myths.[6]

To fully plumb Diop's usages and transformations of all of this oral material would, unfortunately, require significantly more space than a single chapter. Here, I will limit myself to discussing two central issues: the "gaming proverbs" of Kocc Barma as a figure for the African postmodern; and the reinvented epic hero of Lat-Dior as a salutary but nonessentialist model for black African identity. I will base my analysis on both the Wolof and French versions of the novel. Because of the complexity of citing *Doomi Golo* in several languages—the Wolof original, the significantly different French adaptation, and the published English translation of the French—and in hopes of making my analysis accessible to anglophone readers, I will offer quotations in the following format:

Wolof original (B. B. Diop 2003)	direct English rendering of the Wolof (my translation)
French adaptation (B. B. Diop 2009)	published English translation of the French (B. B. Diop 2016)

Occasionally, something I want to cite is from only the Wolof or the French; in these cases, only one of the two versions will be quoted. After analyzing Boubacar Boris Diop's dynamic traditional aesthetic through a series of close readings in these three languages, I will turn to the significance of the author's postmodern writing project as a reflection on the problem of constructing and caring for an African self.

Gaming Proverbs: The Example of Kocc Barma

A prime illustration of Diop's dynamic traditional aesthetic is Kocc Barma, a character in Senegalese oral literature who is credited as a hero—not as a warrior-hero, but as a hero of the mind. Kocc is a sage to whom many Wolof proverbs are attributed. The well-known Guinean historian Djibril Tamsir Niane argued that Kocc Barma was a real person who lived in the late sixteenth and early seventeenth centuries in the precolonial kingdom of Kajoor; in Diop's novel, he belongs to the early seventeenth century, specifically to the year 1619.[7] Whether or not Kocc really existed, he is a major figure in Wolof traditional knowledge. In the oral narratives about him, he regularly bests an intellectual adversary, often the arbitrary and despotic *dammel* Daaw Demba, who keeps him around as a source of advice. Both Kocc Barma and Daaw Demba, as mentioned above, are recurring characters in *Doomi Golo*. In Diop's vision, Kocc himself is not as rigid or conservative as people tend to imagine (see Repinecz 2015). Reimagining the severe sage whom no one can contradict, Diop reads Kocc's utterances as a kind of language game, as the product of someone "qui ne prenait personne au sérieux et surtout pas lui-même" ("who never took anyone seriously—himself included").[8]

Such an interpretation turns out not to be entirely made up by Boubacar Boris Diop: it is represented in the oral tradition itself. In the narratives about Kocc collected by Mamoussé Diagne from the performer Koli Mbaye, the sage is always engaged in a battle of wits not only with the king Daaw Demba, but with his own family. In one scene, Kocc plays a game of *yoote* (similar to checkers) with his eldest son, where each time a player makes a move in the game, the move is accompanied by a proverb, or half-proverb, to which a witty repartee in the spirit of contradiction must be given:

Kocc ni ko: "Dalal!"—Doom ji ni ko: "Baay, dalal yaw!"

Kocc said to him: "Play!" His son said to him: "Father, you play!"

—Kocc ni cëpp, moom baay bi, ni ko: "Lu bees rafet!"

Kocc made his move, and said to his son: "What is new is beautiful!"

—Doom ja ni cëpp, tontu ko ak beneen kàddu, ni ko: "Ba mu des bàmmeel!" (Xam nga ni bàmmeel de, bees taxul mu rafet.)

The son made a play, and answered with another expression: "Except a tomb!" (You know, the fact that a tomb is fresh does not make it pleasant to see.)

—Kocc neeti cëpp, ni ko: "Neex ngont!"

Kocc played again, saying to his son: "It is good to travel in the afternoon!"

—Doom ja ni cëpp, ni ko: "Xam fooy fanaanee ko gën!" . . .

The son made his play, saying: "It is better to know where you will spend the night!" . . .

—Kocc ni ko: "Sempil, dàq nga!" (in Diagne 2014: 228–30)

Kocc answered: "Pick up your pieces, you win!" (my translation)

The game played by Kocc and his son illustrates that the traditional philosopher's wisdom is not located in eternal truths, but in the art of conversation and, specifically, in the art of formulating and placing proverbs in such a way as to illustrate one's own brilliance in a given context. Here, Kocc's son wins because he has mastered the game well enough to let no word from his father go unanswered.

This game of proverbs recalls, quite strikingly, Lyotard's interpretation of what Ludwig Wittgenstein called "language games":

> What he means by this term is that each of the various categories of utterance can be defined in terms of rules specifying their properties and the uses to which they can be put—in exactly the same way as the game of chess is defined by a set of rules determining the properties of each of the pieces, in other words, the proper way to move them.... Every utterance should be thought of as a "move" in a game. This last observation brings us to the first principle underlying our method as a whole: to speak is to fight, in the sense of playing, and speech acts fall within the domain of a general agonistics. (1984: 10)

Lyotard sees the postmodern language game as agonistic, meaning that each utterance provokes a responding and somewhat competing utterance according to established rules of a particular speech genre. Although a particular language game or genre might include structures of authority or legitimacy that authorize some utterances in the mouths of only certain speakers, such as an epic performance from the mouth of a reputed griot, a larger schema of generally agonistic utterances is at work anyway. This is especially easy to envisage in the above scene of battling proverbs: the only use of the proverb-like formula for Kocc and his son is to be contradicted, that is, for each one to be met by its match. Kocc doesn't play to "win," but for the pleasure of the game.

This description suggests that so-called traditional wisdom requires more than one strategy of interpretation. Kocc's proverbs have a kind of ironic quality because they possess multiple possible meanings. They are always context-dependent; they cannot be taken as infallible truths, in spite of how Kocc is sometimes canonized in the Wolof imaginary, particularly in the tale of the "four truths."[9] Diop's revisionist portrayal of the philosopher as a "tortueux et agaçant dialectician" ("devious and sarcastic dialectician") is, in fact, not all that revisionist, as the scene of the *yoote* match suggests: oral tales already cast him in that light.[10] As though imitating Kocc's son's way of "speaking back" to his father's half-proverbs, *Doomi Golo* serves as a long response to Kocc's so-called truths. For example, rather than giving the last word to the famous Koccian proverb, taken from the tale of the four truths, that "Mag mat naa bàyyi cim réew" (Elders are worth keeping in the nation) (B. B. Diop 2003: 32), the novel puts itself in the position of Kocc's son, finding counterpoints to this accepted wisdom. In doing so, it seeks to reframe "tradition" not as a Weberian structure of power, but as a language game situated in the superstructure of an ongoing conversation. Indeed, its reformulation of the following proverb honoring elders could very easily be imagined in the mouth of Kocc's son: society does not only need to listen to its elders, but to its youth, including its girls.

Gone mat naa bàyyi cim réew. (B. B. Diop 2003: 10 and 32)	Children are worth keeping in the nation. (my translation)
Malheur au peuple qui ne sait plus écouter ses petites filles. (B. B. Diop 2009: 9 and 37)	Shame on the nation that doesn't listen to its little girls. (B. B. Diop 2016: 1 and 18)

This act of "talking back" to accepted wisdom serves as a philosophical foundation for *Doomi Golo* as a whole. The reformulated proverb replacing "old men" with "little girls" is used as the epigraph to the novel's first section, narrated by Nguirane Faye. The second and final section, narrated by Ali Kaboye, bears an epigraph that reformulates the same proverb yet again:

Dof mat naa bàyyi cim réew. (B. B. Diop 2003: 286)	Crazy people are worth keeping in the nation. (my translation)
Malheur au peuple qui ne sait plus écouter sa part de folie. (B. B. Diop 2009: 323)	Shame on the nation that is deaf to its own madness. (B. B. Diop 2016: 195)

Here, madness becomes a sign of daring to speak truth to power: the epigraph refers to the local neighborhood's eccentric wanderer, Ali Kaboye, who gains respect as a kind of prophet and is even compared to Patrice Lumumba because he is unafraid to give voice to uncomfortable realities that irritate the authorities.[11] Again, a marginalized social group is brought to the fore and given the prestige reserved by Kocc's proverb to elders. The marginalized figure of the madman bears a noticeably close resemblance to the "deviant and sarcastic" figure of Kocc himself.

This reflection on the nature of traditionality as contradictory and malleable through the example of Kocc Barma serves to reinscribe his sayings in an explicitly dialogical context. Rather than a one-way transmission of messages from the past to the present, the authority of the proverb is relativized as an utterance in an ongoing conversation—that is, an utterance that can be repeated, echoed, modified, or replied to. The image of the ongoing conversation is, in this analysis, the best way to understand traditional discourse itself.

Of Monkeys and Mirrors I: Self-Loathing and Postcolonial Alienation

In spite of its critique of traditions as always somehow made up or inauthentic, Diop's "remix" of traditional Wolof discourse nevertheless serves as an important alternative to the continuing social ill of internalized racism and black self-hatred. Unlike Mbarka Dia, an emblem of female resistance and agency in the "Tuesday of Nder" substory, the character of Yacine Ndiaye in *Doomi Golo*'s main frame story seems to incarnate the opposite role: she is a self-hating black woman, an obsessive francophile who appears to emblematize alienation. The frame story recounts how Yacine moves in with Nguirane in Dakar after repatriating the body of his son Assane, with whom she had been married; both their marriage and Assane's death come as a surprise to the family, with whom he had cut contact after moving to Europe. Badou, the absent grandson to whom Nguirane's notebooks are addressed, is the son of Assane and his previous wife Bigué Samb, whom he had abandoned in Senegal when he left for Europe; Bigué, wounded at the discovery of a rival in her time of mourning, plots revenge on the intruder Yacine, while feigning friendship. Yacine's rudeness and condescending attitude only make it easier for her Senegalese family and neighbors to turn against her. She ignores, rather crudely, Senegalese norms of hospitality, politeness, and respect for elders. Her preference for all things white, her resulting aloofness toward her in-laws and neighbors, and the ill manners of her two children Mbissine and Mbissane make her a pariah in the neighborhood. In a climactic, magical realist turn, Yacine, with the help of a marabout's occult magic and under the influence of Bigué Samb's machinations, transforms into the white woman of her dreams: a certain Marie-Gabrielle von Bolkowsky, brunette and beautiful. But her arrogance seals her fate. Her French passport mysteriously disappears, and Yacine/Marie-Gabrielle is forced to flee back to France, abandoning her two children, who, for their part, have apparently turned into monkeys. Monkeys are, of course, the very symbols of mimicry, as captured in the French word *singer* (to imitate). In this context, the meaning of the novel's Wolof title becomes clear. The expression "doomi golo" is itself a reference to a proverb: "Doomu golo, golo rekk lay doon" (A monkey's offspring is nothing but a monkey). This saying classically refers to the idea that a child will grow up to behave according to its upbringing, and specifically according to the education it received from its mother. Thus Yacine Ndiaye's children are terribly behaved throughout the novel because, at one level, she has not taught them properly to respect others. The link between her (and her children's) monkey-ness and imitation becomes legible here: they are like monkeys because of their excessive attachment to what Diop has elsewhere called a "désir de francité" or desire for Frenchness (B. B. Diop 2012). A refusal of this kind of alienation and its effects led directly to Diop's choice to write a Wolof novel.

Or so it seems. The above reading of Yacine suggests that her arrogance is principally the result of a single underlying trait, namely, a fetishization of whiteness. Nevertheless, we must not neglect her character's fundamental ambiguity: she is not merely an archetype of the alienated black woman, but also a victim of prejudice, including on the part of her extended family in Dakar, who quickly judge, exclude, and abuse her. The ambiguity of Yacine Ndiaye fits in well with that of the novel in general, where labyrinthine language games mean that nothing is quite what it seems. That is to say, if Yacine Ndiaye is to serve as a cautionary tale whose moral is "know thyself," "black is beautiful," or "return to the roots," she also demonstrates that the causes of postcolonial alienation run very deep and cannot only be attributed to the problem of mimicry, a classic theme of postcolonial theory. To illustrate this ambiguity, I will conduct a close reading of several scenes of metamorphosis in *Doomi Golo*: first where Yacine appears to become a white woman, then when her children appear to become monkeys. These crucial sequences are full of narrative indeterminacy. It is never irrefutably clear whether the text is actually operating in a magical realist register, which would invite the reader to conclude that Yacine or Mbissine and Mbissane have indeed changed form, or whether the narrative mode is, rather, recounting a hallucinatory delirium in which their grip on reality has slipped, under pressure from both internal and external factors. This indeterminacy complements the ambiguity of traditional discourse. The novel uses this ambiguity, as well as that of Lat-Dior, explored in the next section, to outline constructive uses of Wolof traditionality as a healthy alternative to Yacine Ndiaye's postcolonial self-loathing, yet refuses any facile or essentialist opposition between the two.

The key to these shape-shifting comparisons is the figure of the mirror, which uncannily reflects both objective and subjective realities (Ngom 2014). In particular, the marabout presiding over Yacine's metamorphosis, named Sinkoun Tiguidé Camara, orders her to look several times into the mirror as her transformation into Marie-Gabrielle is taking place. In a figurative sense, she has always seen a split image of herself in her reflection: her real, hated, black body clashes with her fantasies of whiteness and Europeanness. This split image is reflected quite literally in the mirror:

Janoo naak seetu bi lu yàgg, gisu ci ku dul boppam. Mu gis ni xeesal bi yàqe kanam gi, daldi gën a tiit. Céy, su ko Sinkun Kamara mënoon a defal li mu ko ñaan! Ndaw bànneex bu réy! Ñuulaay bi dafa rekk doy. Ku ragalul wax dëgg, xam ne moos lu ñuul mënul a baax. Der boo xam ne bala moo jag nga top ciy fóot ni yëre bu tilim, yendoo fete, fanaanee fete! (B. B. Diop 2003: 315–16)	She faced the mirror for a long moment, seeing nothing there but herself. She saw how skin-bleaching products had damaged her face; then she became more afraid. Oh, if only Sinkoun Camara could do for her what she asked of him! What bliss! She had had enough of being black. Anyone unafraid of the truth knows for sure that black cannot be good. Skin that, before it can look right, you have to wash like dirty clothes, scrubbing all day, scrubbing all night! (my translation)
Elle vit dans le grand miroir son visage affreusement brûlé par le *xeesal*. Plusieurs années auparavant, elle avait essayé, faute de mieux, de rendre sa peau au moins un peu plus claire. Un vrai désastre, au final. Mon Dieu, comme le monde serait merveilleux si chacun pouvait choisir la couleur de sa peau! Ah! Si Sinkoun Tiguidé pouvait exaucer son voeu! Elle ne voulait plus être noire.... Il y a une couleur pour la crasse et jusqu'à la fin des temps ce sera la couleur noire (B. B. Diop 2009: 385)	In the big mirror, she saw her face, dreadfully burned by the *xeesal*. Several years ago, she had tried to lighten her skin at least slightly, since that was all she could do. It ended up being a real disaster. My God, wouldn't the world be a wonderful place if everybody could choose the color of their skin! Ah! If only Sinkoun Tiguidé could grant her wish! She did not want to be black anymore.... Filth always has one and the same color, and until the end of time, that will be black. (B. B. Diop 2016: 233)

The *xeesal*, or skin-whitening product, reveals the splitness of Yacine's self-image at two levels. On the one hand, the mirror conveys a reflection of her skin as it is: black, but burned by soaps and creams containing bleaching agents, as directly referenced in Wolof through the image of scrubbing skin like laundry. More importantly, this marred physical appearance is only an effect of the passage's main focus, namely Yacine's desire to be white. Blackness is, for her, not just a concentration of melanin, but a sign carrying exclusively negative meanings, one that must be replaced by the desirable meanings of whiteness. To look into the mirror is not just to pick up light waves being bounced back into the ocular apparatus, but to conjure in one's own mind a series of images of the self that are shaped by prejudice and desire—that is, imaginings of oneself as one fears and wants to be seen by others.

The mirror image thus has a double function: it reflects both a physical reality and a socially constructed sense of self. These functions are nevertheless blurred. In addition to herself, Yacine continues to see other eerie figures appear in the mirror. While questioning her own perception and sanity, she sees not one but two other women enter the room; Camara does not acknowledge their presence; they seem to morph into each other, then into a beautiful blonde standing behind her; finally they appear to become one with Yacine herself. Throughout, they remain uncannily, simultaneously, Other. The text stubbornly refuses any straightforward interpretation of this narrative sequence:

YAASIN: "Ana ndaw si fi taxawoon léegi?"
. . .

KAMARA: "Yaay moom, mooy yow."

YAASIN: "Ba léegi sa wax dese naa leer ci man, góor gi."

KAMARA: "Dama ne, bul ma tanqal Mari-Gabriyelaa Won Bolkowski! Xam nga ne moos kooku fi dugg sànq du kenn ku dul yow! Daa weex nga ñuul rekk, waaye benn ngeen. Xoolal seetu bi bu baax, laa wax!"
. . .

YACINE: "Where is the lady who was here just now?" . . .

CAMARA: "You are she, she is you."

YACINE: "Your words are still unclear to me, sir."

CAMARA: "I say, don't annoy me, Marie-Gabrielle von Bolkowsky! You certainly know that the person who just came in here was none other than yourself! The only difference is that she is white and you are black, yet you are the same person. Look hard into the mirror, I tell you!" . . .

Mu gëmm, xippi, gissaat jeegu
Tubaab bi mu taxaw ci ginnaawam.
Yaasin yëkkati loxo càmmooñam,
xool ko lu yàgg, daldi gis ni mu
weexe. (B. B. Diop 2003: 317–18)

She closed her eyes, opened them,
and saw once again the young
white lady standing behind her.
Yacine lifted her left hand, looked
at it for a long moment, then saw
how white it was. (my translation)

YACINE: "Où est passé la dame que j'ai vue
tout à l'heure?" . . .

CAMARA: "Tu es elle. Elle est toi."

YACINE: "Je ne sais toujours pas ce que tu
veux dire, Camara."

CAMARA: "Tu me fatigues, Marie-Gabrielle
von Bolkowsky. Qui peut-elle être,
sinon toi-même? Tu es noire, elle
est blanche, mais vous êtes bien
une seule et même personne. Je
te l'ordonne une dernière fois:
regarde-toi bien dans le miroir." . . .

YACINE: "Where is she, the lady I have just
seen?" . . .

CAMARA: "You are she, she is you."

YACINE: "I still don't know what you are
trying to say, Camara."

CAMARA: "You are beginning to
irritate me, Marie-Gabrielle von
Bolkowsky. Who can she be, if
not you yourself? You are black,
she is white, but you are one and
the same person. I order you one
last time to look at yourself in the
mirror." . . .

Elle ferma les yeux puis les rouvrit
aussitôt. La femme réapparut derrière
elle à travers le miroir. Yacine Ndiaye
remua discrètement la main gauche
puis la souleva. L'autre en fit autant.
Elle comprit alors que la femme
blanche debout derrière elle dans le
miroir était elle-même. (B. B. Diop
2009: 387–88)

She closed her eyes and opened
them again immediately. When she
did look into the mirror, the woman
reappeared behind her. Yacine Ndiaye
slightly moved her left hand, then
lifted it up. The other one did the
same. Now she had understood that
the white woman standing behind
her in the mirror was herself. (B. B.
Diop 2016: 234–35)

The white lady in the reflection disappears and reappears. Whenever she is visible, she appears as a distinct and separate person from Yacine. In both language versions, Camara calls Yacine by her new, European-sounding name, assures her that she and her white reflection are "the same person," but also reminds her of their difference: "You are black, she is white." These multiple violations of the law of noncontradiction suggest that Yacine's metamorphosis into Marie-Gabrielle is merely a figment of her imagination, the result of cruel mental manipulation by the marabout and Bigué Samb. This reading becomes even more plausible when we consider that Camara behaves entirely like a charlatan. As the above quote illustrates, he never acknowledges the mysterious white figures in the mirror until she does first, only building on what Yacine has said she sees. Then he orders her to have sex with him as part of the magic ritual—a classic trick of the archetypal fraudulent marabout in West African literature. Whether the metamorphosis is real within the narrative world or not, he is a lying opportunist willing to prey on people's superstitions in order to extort money and sex. Indeed, his resemblance to that archetype gives credence to the notion that the transformation is all in Yacine's mind, under his influence. The moment of epiphany, when Yacine "realizes" that she has transformed into a white person, is framed slightly differently in each language, but even that does not change the moment's fundamental ambiguity. In Wolof, she looks directly at her own left hand and "saw how white it was" ("gis ni mu weexe"); in French, she follows the identical movements of her white double's hand and then "understood" (*comprit*) that her own hand and the white hand in the mirror are the same hand. What is meant by "seeing" and "understanding," when both modes of perception are filtered by what is seen in the mirror, and what is seen in the mirror may simply be a function of what one wants or is made to see there under social pressure? The text, so far, leaves room for interpreting the metamorphosis as entirely imaginary.

Later, the same ambiguity of a possible but uncertain transformation is repeated in the case of Yacine's children, Mbissine and Mbissane, who *may* have turned into monkeys after her flight from Dakar. Note how different the French and Wolof versions are:

Mbisin ak Mbisaan, mag ji, ñoo génn xeet tey!	Mbissine and Mbissane, the elder sibling, have totally gone ape [lit. *left the species*] these days!
Log ay baat yu masul a tëmb ci sa meewu ndey, di leen sàqami ndànk, ñuy seey ci sa làmmiñ, saf suukar, di la jox bànneex bu kenn xamul nu mu tollu.	You stuff your cheeks with words that never floated in your mother's milk; you chew them slowly, let them melt on your tongue and turn sweet to

Walla kàddu yooyu tancaloo ci sa put ba far la fotloo.

Maam ne la:

NGIRAAN: "Neel Penda Saar ca Ngawle!"

Nga lànk, mu jaral la gaañ sa bopp ba waccu deret di la ci fekk. Nga xëm, ñu ximmali la, ngay xataraayu, di yuuxu:

MBISIN-MBISSAAN: *"Je dis merde à la vieille Penda Saar, moi! C'est où ça d'ailleurs, votre putain de merde de Ngawuule, là?"*

Céy lii! (B. B. Diop 2003: 323)

the taste, giving you a pleasure that no one can fathom.[12]

But those words stick in your throats as if you were choking on fish bones.

Grandfather tells you:

NGUIRANE: "Say *Penda Saar in Ngawle!*"

You refuse, and it makes you hurt yourself, vomiting blood on yourself. You faint, we wake you, you resist, shouting:

MBISSINE AND MBISSANE, IN FRENCH: *"To hell with your old Penda Sarr! Where is it anyway, your stupid goddam Ngawle?"*

Sheesh! (my translation)

Depuis que leur mère, devenue complètement folle, prétend s'appeler Marie-Gabrielle von Bolkowsky, les deux enfants de Yacine Ndiaye ne sont plus les mêmes. Personne ne peut les approcher, car ils s'enfuient aussitôt avec des cris de terreur et montent se cacher dans les arbres. De là-haut ils essaient de nous dire des choses, mais nous n'entendons que des sons grêles et confus. On dirait que les mots, trop nombreux ou mal rangés au fond de leurs gorges étroites, s'en échappent en désordre. Parfois cela se termine mal. Quand ils veulent parler, les deux petits s'étranglent, font des grimaces et vomissent un peu de sang. (B. B. Diop 2009: 397)

Since their mother, who has now completely lost her marbles, started claiming that her name is Marie-Gabrielle von Bolkowsky, Yacine Ndiaye's two children are no longer the same. If anybody goes near them, they immediately run away screaming and terrified, and then they start clambering up into the trees to hide themselves. Then they try to talk to us from up there, but all we can hear is shrill, confused sounds. Maybe their words get stuck at the bottom of their narrow throat, maybe they're all topsy-turvy and when they come out, they're totally muddled up. That might end badly. Trying to speak makes the two little ones choke, then they start grimacing and they vomit a bit of blood. (B. B. Diop 2016: 241)

Both versions of the passage clearly compare the two children to little monkeys without using the explicit word *golo* in Wolof or *singe* in French. In both versions, they fail to speak intelligibly; in the Wolof, they stuff their cheeks with garbled sounds in a way that recalls monkeys storing food in cheek pouches; in the French, they climb trees and hide in branches. Perhaps the most charged expression is the Wolof *génn xeet*: *génn* simply means "to go out," but *xeet* has a range of meanings, including "maternal lineage," "race," "ethnic group," or even "species." In normal speech, *génn xeet* can simply mean something like "to marry below the family's rank," but in the thematic context of the novel, it carries multiple valences at once. The children, like their mother, have left their mother's family, that is, the black race; therefore they have also, in some sense, left the human race. Their self-abasement as alienated francophiles has, somehow, turned them into monkeys. The racial and linguistic dimensions of this abjection are made more explicit in Wolof than in French, since the original text specifies that the gibberish noises that the children produce are due to their inability, indeed their refusal, to speak Wolof because of a belief in the superiority of French. It is the Wolof language that makes them choke on their words and vomit blood. When Nguirane tells them to speak the name of Penda Sarr while they are choking on their own hate, it is in allusion to a legendary heroine of the Futa Toro region of northern Senegal who is invoked for people choking on fish bones.[13] Their reaction is to curse in French and to refuse to participate in the traditional discursive matrix. Even though this detail is eliminated in the French adaptation, both versions of the text refuse to spell out for the reader whether the children's monkey-ness is literal or metaphorical. The French even throws further confusion on the status of their mother, stating that she has gone mad and that she *claims* (*prétend*) to be named Marie-Gabrielle, suggesting that Yacine is delirious in her belief that she is white.

What is important in these scenes is not so much the question of whether the transformations are literal or not, as frustrating as it is for the reader to decipher them. I submit that Diopian metamorphosis is another agonistic language game, with any number of twists, turns, and contradictions as we wander in the labyrinth of his writing. The text persistently blurs the lines between literal and figurative referentiality. Regardless of this smoke-and-mirrors effect, the figure of the monkey remains constantly legible as the novel's central critique of mimicry and alienation.

What, then, is the solution to alienation, given all of its complex aspects and factors? An interesting moment of compassion appears in the scene where Nguirane confronts Bigué Samb over her malicious manipulation of Yacine Ndiaye. But this passage is present only in French, not in the Wolof original:

Nguirane Faye murmure quelques versets du Coran et tout en traçant des signes sur le sable s'adresse à Bigué Samb....

NGUIRANE: "Voici ce que j'ai à te dire: ces enfants ne t'ont fait aucun mal."

BIGUÉ: "Quels enfants, Nguirane? Les deux petits de cette guenon?" ...

NGUIRANE: "Ce sont aussi tes enfants, Bigué. Prends bien soin d'eux. Fais-en des êtres humains."

BIGUÉ: "Je t'ai entendu, Nguirane."

NGUIRANE: "Oui. Personne ne peut être à la fois un enfant et un singe." (B. B. Diop 2009: 412–13)

Nguirane Faye is murmuring verses from the Koran and tracing signs in the sand. He turns to Bigué Samb....

NGUIRANE: "Here is what I have to say: these children haven't done you any harm."

BIGUÉ: "Which children, Nguirane? Do you mean the two little offspring of this monkey?" ...

NGUIRANE: "They are your children, too, Bigué. Look after them well. Turn them into human beings."

BIGUÉ: "I have heard you, Nguirane," she says.

NGUIRANE: "Yes. Nobody can be a child and a monkey at the same time." (B. B. Diop 2016: 250–51)

Here, Bigué's identification of Yacine/Marie-Gabrielle as a monkey (*guenon*) is clearly meant as an insult: nothing in any of the transformation scenes suggested she had literally turned into an animal. This (for once clear) use of metaphor again casts into doubt the literalness of other passages where she is said to "be" a white person, as well as the literalness of the references to her children as monkeys in this passage. But more importantly, this exchange is remarkable because it explicitly calls the reader not just to judgment, but to compassion for the postcolonial alienated subject. While Yacine Ndiaye has done her fair share of harm to herself and others, and taught her children to reproduce her hateful behavior, the passage suggests that the community must find a way to make a future for such people, as imperfect as they are. Revenge and ridicule must give way to empathy in order for human beings to be fully human. The "children of the monkey" who give the novel its title are not just the characters Mbissine and Mbissane, but all postcolonial subjects afflicted with an inferiority complex toward the former colonizer or the West. The remedy to internalized racism is not vengeance, but greater understanding of the historical and affective pain that is at its root. As the famous Wolof proverbs states, *Nit, nit mooy garabam*: "Man is the remedy of man."

Of Monkeys and Mirrors II: "Lat-Dior Remix" and Discourses of Resistance

The association between monkeys and mimicry runs deep in the text. Monkeys reappear in several subplots and dream sequences that all seem to carry uncanny doubles of Yacine Ndiaye and her children. All of these examples could be explored at greater length. However, I would like to close this book by zooming in on one of *Doomi Golo*'s last variations on the theme of monkeys and mirrors, a strange flashback involving two gorillas, a giant mirror, and anticolonial epic heroes. This episode is complex enough to necessitate an extended analysis on its own, one that will bring the trajectory of this book full circle by harkening back to the reflection on alternative modernities and traditionalities with which I began the introduction.

During Ali Kaboye's narration, toward the end of *Doomi Golo*, the main plot veers off into one of many digressions and substories: a flashback to the year 1940, during the colonial period, when the narrator Ali says he was ten years old in the village of Ndimboye.[14] The French-built Dakar–St. Louis railroad is being sabotaged each night, presumably by bandits, specifically in the region of the forest of Kagne, which lies between Dakar and Thies. Two (fictional) French administrators—André Castorel, then Robert Langlade—are successively charged with the mission of stopping the sabotage. Castorel uses mere threats of brute force, but subverted by his own interpreter, he fails to catch or stop the saboteurs and, in a fit of madness, shoots himself. His successor, Langlade, is savvier. Rather than resorting to threats, he quietly observes the villagers' habits and ventures alone into the forest at night to lie in wait for the culprits. Discovering that the saboteurs are, in fact, two gorillas—doubles of the frame narrative's characters Mbissine and Mbissane—he defeats them through wit, installing a giant mirror in the forest that he knows will trick them into killing each other. The plan works. Convinced that their own reflections are enemies trying to conquer their territory, the two gorillas, drunk on palm wine, foolishly attack the mirror, wound themselves with broken glass, then turn against each other, battling to the death. Langlade takes the gorillas' heads to his superior and is never heard from again.[15]

This haunting substory brings together all of the threads that I have highlighted in this chapter. The rich symbolism of monkeys and mirrors is as present as ever. Just as Yacine Ndiaye is dehumanized by the hatred she feels for her own reflection, the gorillas only fall prey to Langlade's ruse when they see themselves in the mirror. They are obsessed with the defense of their territory against illusory invaders—and therefore, distracted and forgetful of the real invaders' ruses. This episode seems to represent another allegorical variation on the theme of racial self-hatred, while also harkening back to the theme of resistance during the colonial period: one frequent explanation for the nineteenth-century Senegambian kingdoms' inability to ward off the French intrusion is their own infighting.[16] The core of the gorilla story's plot, the sabotaging of the railroad to subvert colonial rule, references two important Wolof traditions about anticolonial resistance. First, there is Lat-Dior, one of the last *dammels* of Kajoor, who passed into the epic of that kingdom as a hero for the feat of having repeatedly sabotaged the same Dakar–St. Louis railroad before finally falling at the hands of the French at the Battle of Dékheulé on October 26, 1886. Among the most famous elements of the story of his resistance are Lat-Dior's declaration that *Gan du tabax!* ("A guest does not build!") and his oath that his beloved steed Malaw would never see the railway completed. Senghor erected Lat-Dior as a national hero, a symbol of Negritude and of the Parti socialiste sénégalais, inserting him into a broader twentieth-century panoply of anticolonial heroes.[17] The epic of this illustrious national hero parallels, and indeed may well be conflated with, a second legend, that of a jealous landowner named Kagne—for whom the forest is said to be named—who, though far less known than Lat-Dior, is also supposed to have sabotaged the same railroad in order to prevent the French from encroaching upon his lands.[18]

To conclude this final chapter, I will explore the novel's reframing of these two traditional stories as alternative "mirrors" for the postcolonial subject. Together, these related historical legends illustrate the novel's interest in displacing traditional narratives while sounding them for alternative meanings and models for identity. While continuing to celebrate the theme of resistance against colonial rule, they also refuse the paternalist, nationalist, racial-essentialist interpretation of Lat-Dior favored by Negritude. Rather than keeping Lat-Dior on this static pedestal, the novel tries to tell the creative, fragmented, compromised stories of how his legacy inspires—or fails to inspire—other people over time. This strategy of spinning a "Lat-Dior remix" seeks to free the hero's memory from the mummification it has undergone and to erect it as an alternative mirror for the postcolonial subject.

As a first example, the Wolof and French versions of *Doomi Golo* introduce the gorilla substory very differently. The Wolof original frames the act of sabotage that is about to be recounted through a comparison to Lat-Dior, while the corresponding French passage frames it through a comparison to Kagne. Because these passages are totally different in content, I will take each language's version one at a time:

Ku xamul fu Àllu Kaañ nekk it, dégg nga turam. . . . Gis nga, Badu, jamono dina ñëw, aw askan ni:

"Sunu réew mi de, ba mu sosook tey, bés bi ci ëpp solo, bés sàngam la ndax bés boobu la lépp sotti."

Kuy faral di déglu woyu géwél yi dinga xam li may bëgg a wax foofu.

Tey jii, koo laaj, mu ne la 26 ci weeru oktoobar, ca atum 1886, bés bi Lat Joor desee Déqële, ca la Kajoor màbb, tas, Xonq-Nopp yi féex, sog a xam ni buumu njaam gi ñu nu takke dëgër na dëgër gu, caaxaan du ko fecci.

Fàttaliku Déqële, lu nu war la. Waaw.

Waaye man Aali Këbóoy, bu doon sama sago de, waa réew mi dinañu bàyyi xel ci beneen bés. Ci sama gis-gis, bés boobu kenn fullaalul, moo ëpp fopp solo xare Déqële. (B. B. Diop 2003: 286–87)

Anyone who does not know where the Forest of Kagne is has heard its name. . . . You see, Badou, the time will come when the country will say:

"From the foundation of our nation until today, the most important day was such-and-such, because that is when everything was accomplished."

Anyone in the habit of listening to griots' songs will know what I mean by that.

Today, anyone you ask will tell you that October 26, 1886, the day when Lat-Dior lay dead at Dékheulé, is when Kajoor collapsed, fell apart, when the whites rejoiced, when we first realized that as tightly as they had bound us with the bonds of slavery, it would take more than a joke to loosen them.

It is our duty to remember Dékheulé, yes.

But if it were up to me, Ali Kaboye, our compatriots would set their minds on another day. As I see it, no one takes this day seriously, but it is by far more important than the Battle of Dékheulé. (my translation)

Although this excerpt recognizes the importance of Lat-Dior in national and in Wolof memory, it refuses to join the long list of griots and writers celebrating him as the incarnation of the anticolonial resistance or the Senegalese nation. Lat-Dior has two meanings here. He represents a dramatic, inspirational moment in the history of anticolonial resistance in Senegal; but his universal recognition as such has caused his heroism to become frozen in people's minds, the symbol of a nationalist, patriarchal state shepherded by Senghor, to the exclusion of other possible modes of resistance. The strange narrator Ali Kaboye will explore such alternative modes of resistance not by memorializing Lat-Dior once again, but by composing a collage or remix of stories of train sabotage by fantastic but marginal figures. It is these shards of memory and creativity that will fill his stories of "another day . . . far more important than the Battle of Dékheulé." They will update, while celebrating in their own way, the thrilling example of the Wolof anticolonial hero.

The French adaptation of the same passage already illustrates this point. It does not even mention Lat-Dior. It refers instead to the legend of Kagne, though the attentive reader cannot help but notice the multiple parallels with the wonderful legacy of the *dammel*:

Même si tu n'y as jamais mis les pieds, tu as sûrement entendu parler de la Forêt de Kagne. Sur la route nationale entre Dakar et Thiès, le voyageur . . . peut-être se souviendra-t-il vaguement de ce bandit d'honneur—il s'appelait justement Kagne—qui y faisait régner sa propre loi, dure mais juste, à l'époque des Toubabs. . . . Des bruits si contradictoires continuent à courir au sujet de Kagne qu'il est bien difficile, plus de soixante ans après, de décider s'il fut un justicier et un patriote ou un vulgaire coupeur de route. Mais pour nous qui avons grandi à l'ombre de ce rebelle, la fascination, résumé par deux mots—Àllu Kaañ—reste intacte aujourd'hui encore. Toute mon enfance a été bercée par les péripéties de sa lutte solitaire et implacable contre le pouvoir colonial. .	Even if you have never set foot there you must surely have heard about the Forest of Kagne. A traveler on the highway from Dakar to Thiès . . . may even have a few vague memories of a local Robin Hood who simply called himself Kagne, and who during the era of the *Toubabs* imposed his own rules there—harsh but just. . . . People's views about Kagne are so contradictory that now, sixty years later, it's very hard to decide whether he really "took from the rich and gave to the poor" [lit. *whether he was a dealer of justice and a patriot*] or whether he was just an ordinary highwayman. But for those of us who grew up in the shadow of this rebel, our fascination—encapsulated in the words Àllu Kaañ [the Forest of Kagne]—remains alive to this day.

..Aujourd'hui, je vais plutôt te raconter	The ups and downs of his hard, lonely
ce qui est arrivé, vers 1940, à un miroir.	battle against the colonial powers form
(B. B. Diop 2009: 351)	an integral part of my childhood. . . .
	Right now, though, I want to tell you
	what happened to a mirror in 1940 or
	thereabouts. (B. B. Diop 2016: 212)

Leaving aside the English translator's added references to Robin Hood, it is striking how this passage is so different yet so similar to its Wolof original. The replacement of Lat-Dior with his less famous, more elusive counterpart parallels the Wolof version's suspicion of national heroes and official histories. Instead of kings, griots, and the shadow of Senghor, we now have a truly popular legend that circulates only locally about a hero who may well be a "vulgar" highwayman. This removes the connotations of aristocratic- or *géer*-supremacist discourse, canonization, and nationalism associated with Lat-Dior, yet the theme of disrupting the railroad to subvert the French remains intact. Moreover, reading both versions of the passage together actually invites the reader to further question the legacy of Lat-Dior. As is the case with anticolonial and national heroes from many contexts, historians have questioned the received memory of this figure as a martyr of resistance, pointing out that the man who really lived collaborated at times with the French intruders.[19] If we read the French version of the passage while mentally substituting "Lat-Dior" for "Kagne," the core message still holds. Just as contradictory rumors and opinions make Kagne's legacy depend on the eye of the beholder, so do they for Lat-Dior.

The inspiration that *Doomi Golo* gleans from Lat-Dior, then, whether he is named explicitly or masked in the ambivalent figure of Kagne, does not flow from his status as national hero or martyr to the French. Rather, it stems from the creative rearticulations of his story that constantly resuscitate his memory over time. Indeed, the feats of Lat-Dior and of Kagne may well be folkloric rearticulations of each other. The importance of Lat-Dior's memory as an evolving creative inspiration is made clear in both language versions of the novel in a scene of translation gone awry. As the commander Castorel is menacing the villagers of Ndimboye to let the railroad be built, his Wolof interpreter, Baye Sèye, starts out unambiguously enough, faithfully exhorting his compatriots not to obstruct the march of progress. But his translation is soon derailed, so to speak, veering into a subversive double-entendre conveyed by allusions to the epic of Lat-Dior, which had had no place in Castorel's speech:

"Am na ku fi doon jaay njàmbaar de, di rab-rablu, naan Maalaw du gis raay bi! Ana mu tey? Song nanu ko Déqële, duma ko. Nun Tubaab yi nag, doole lanu am ba mu doy! Ku nu bëgg a jommal, dangay sonnal sa bopp. Deretu Maalaw màndil na suufu Kajoor, def ab déeg ca Déqële, nga nuur ca, faf lab. Kenn waxatul say wax. Dunu la rey Déqële, ngay dekki Àllu Kaañ! . . . Yéen waa Kajoor Kumandaŋ Kastorel moo leen di laaj: ndax jàmbaar dëgg dina làqatu di buddiy raay saxaar, di sànni sëminoo yi ay xeer? Nu ngeen tudde loolu? Réy làmmiñ moom def na ko, waaye fit dara la ci amul! Mbër dëgg, su la sa moroomu mbër daanee, dangay ngembuwaat, . . . ngeen sëggaat, léewtoo. Doo xaar ba guddi nga taxaw ci sàkketu këram di ko saaga, te su ubbee buntam wutsi la nga daw!" (B. B. Diop 2003: 294–95)

"There used to be someone who would boast of his own heroism, while hiding like a ghost, saying Malaw would never see the rails! Where is he now? We attacked him at Dékheulé and beat him there. We whites have all the strength! Anyone trying to embarrass us will only waste his own efforts. The earth of Kajoor is drunk with the blood of Malaw; it left a pool there in which you sank and drowned. No one is saying what you once said. We cannot kill you at Dékheulé only for you to return to the Forest of Kagne! No, good people. . . . People of Kajoor, Commandant Castorel is asking you: would a real hero pull out a train's rails and throw rocks at railroad workers? What would you call that? Bigmouth did it, but there is no courage there! When a champion wrestler gets knocked down by his fellow champion, he fixes his loincloth, meets him where his drum is planted in the arena, . . . they lean back in, and prepare to strike. You don't wait until nighttime to stand at the fence of someone's house, insulting him, only to run away when he opens the door to face you!" (my translation)

"Vous devez le savoir, déclare-t-il, celui qui ne pense qu'à détruire finit toujours par être détruit lui-même. Où est-il donc, ce Damel qui disait que jamais son pur-sang Malaw ne verrait de ses yeux le rail posé par les Blancs? La terre de Dékheulé est rouge du sang

"You need to know," he declared, "that he who thinks of nothing but destruction will always end up being destroyed himself. Where is he now, your Damel who said that Malaw, his thoroughbred, would never see the railway built by the whites with

de Malaw et tu es mort, oublié de tous, mon pauvre ami. N'essaie pas de me faire croire que, réduit en poussière à Dékheulé, tu peux réapparaitre sur la cime des arbres de Kagne. Puisque tu as si peur de la mort, tiens-toi tranquille dans ton tombeau au lieu de saboter le travail de nos braves cheminots!" (B. B. Diop 2009: 360)

his own eyes? In Dékheulé, Malaw's blood tinged the earth red, while you are dead and forgotten by all, my poor friend. Don't waste your time trying to convince me that you can reappear on the treetops of Kagne after having been reduced to dust in Dékheulé. Since you are so afraid of death, it's best if you stay quietly in your grave instead of sabotaging the work of our loyal railway workers!" (B. B. Diop 2016: 218)

This appeal begs to be taken at the second degree. The hero's magnificent feats of defiance pierce through the obfuscation of Baye Sèye's mocking rhetoric. Under the guise of dissuasion, the speech has the ironic effect of seeming to incite colonial subjects, or the reader, to follow the *dammel*'s example. In both versions of the passage, the speaker addresses a "you" that vacillates between the villagers before him and the spirit of Lat-Dior himself: a statement such as "No one is saying what you once said" ("Kenn waxatul say wax"), addressed to Lat-Dior, is ostensibly intended to insult his memory by conveying the futility of his efforts, but it sounds so close to a praise line that it all but invites the hero to inspire the peasant masses to speak in a voice of resistance. In the Wolof version, what is supposedly contemptible about Lat-Dior is the discrepancy between his boastfulness and his sneakiness, as though cutting up a railway at night were an act of cowardice that distinguishes a "bigmouth" ("réy làmmiñ") from a "real hero" ("jàmbaar dëgg"). But this already shaky claim leads Baye Sèye's argument away from its starting point: the analogy of wrestlers meeting each other in the arena seems to advocate open rebellion against the French presence, not resignation to it. Furthermore, his listeners would surely know that the epic tradition portrays Lat-Dior as anything but a coward. Far from being afraid of death ("tu as si peur de la mort"), he met the French head-on at the battlefield of Dékheulé and was only killed because of the treachery of his own royal captive, Demba Waar.[20]

Similarly, Baye Sèye's mockery of the horse Malaw, whose "blood tinged the earth red," is immediately dismissable, because according to the epic tradition, Malaw died honorably, *before* the French could force him to lay eyes on the abomination of the railway. Lat-Dior's oath was not violated. Both hero and horse may have been killed, but they were spared the worse fate of humiliation. The incoherencies in his speech lead us to conclude that either Baye Sèye intends all along to twist the meaning of Castorel's words, deceptively calling upon the fallen hero Lat-Dior to incite the villagers to keep resisting, or that he has every intention of conveying his master's meaning, but, as though co-opted by the spirit of Lat-Dior, his own translation runs away from him when he tries to buttress Castorel's threats with examples from a Wolof cultural framework.

Either way, the result of the interpreter's speech is just as ambiguous as the speech itself. In both language versions, the village chief of Ndimboye steps up to promise assistance in finding and punishing the guilty parties. But when Baye Sèye transmits this message, the paranoid Castorel immediately becomes furious, shoves Baye Sèye to the ground, and accuses the chief of lying and hypocrisy. Even without having understood the substance of the interpreter's speech—or perhaps, precisely because it is opaque to him—Castorel is suspicious of the potential for treachery in language and intuits that he is being made a fool of. Confirming his intuition, once his back is turned, the sabotage continues. The reader is left to wonder if Baye Sèye's devious speech inspired the village chief to give a devious answer. After all, it may be true that the saboteurs turn out to be gorillas, not villagers, but what prevents the villagers from discovering the culprits, as the chief promises, and as the Frenchman Langlade eventually does? Nothing means what it seems to mean on the surface in this game of mirror-effects in language.

And yet, for all this linguistic and cultural instability, the text insists that forgetfulness of stories like that of Lat-Dior is at the heart of colonial—and, by extension, postcolonial—alienation. The figure of Castorel takes on a larger-than-life role, serving as metonymy for the centuries-long process of colonial brainwashing, like an epic villain in his own right who has replaced and effaced the memory of indigenous heroes like Lat-Dior among the villagers of Ndimboye. As a result, the Wolof text also hammers home the idea that the fawning leaders of Ndimboye are not living up to their birth rank: it is not just anyone, but the "best-born" ("ñi gën juddu"), that is, the *géer* or nobles whose honor depends upon the exclusion of innately dishonored casted subjects and slaves, who have abased themselves by becoming sycophants. The Wolof text addresses a reproach at the nobility that is lost in French:

Du kenn ci réew mi ku sañ ne: There is no one in the country who
"Sama baay Dammel lawoon."   dares to say:

Mbaa:
"Man mii, néégu Gééj laa bokk." (B.
B. Diop 2003: 292)

"My father was a *dammel*.
Or:
"I belong to the house of Geej."[21]
(my translation)

Bref, au bout de la route de Castorel
naquit pour nous le temps de l'absolu
présent. Le passé de Ndimboye, déri-
soire ou glorieux, avait sombré dans le
néant. (B. B. Diop 2009: 358)

In brief, the end point of Castorel's path
coincided with the birth of the absolute present for us. Ndimboye's past,
whether it was glorious or insignificant,
has dissolved into thin air. (B. B. Diop
2016: 216)

In essence, the Wolof text is accusing the nobles of having abandoned the values of pride, courage, and preference of death to shame that the discourse of *géer* supremacy is supposed to engender. The passage imputes the apparent failure of a resistance movement inspired by Lat-Dior to a failure of the caste system and its expectations that noble birth should produce honorable behavior on pain of shame. According to this critique, the nobles' forgetfulness of their hereditary obligations, including the memory of Lat-Dior as role model for their rank, allowed the French to dishonor them. The French adaptation, for its part, retains the theme of forgetfulness due to colonial brainwashing, but elides the allusion to hereditary birth statuses. Instead, it adds some potent language of its own: the notion of an "absolute present," the loss of the memory of the past, is the mental time structure that is at the heart of colonial and postcolonial alienation. Reminiscent of Bakhtin's equation of the epic heritage with an "absolute past" (2002), this absolute present, or state of perpetual forgetting, causes the mentally colonized African, emblematized by the nobles of Ndimboye and Yacine Ndiaye, to be so dazzled by the white conqueror as to forget their own indigenous legacies of heroism and resistance. As the example of Lat-Dior demonstrates, the oral epic genre is a key piece of these legacies.

The foolish gorillas who kill each other after seeing their reflections in the mirror are the final, climactic incarnation of absolute presentism.

Nekk nañu fa lu yàgg sax, di jam seetu
bi. Mujje gi, ku nekk ci ñoom ñaar di
gaañ boppam. . . . Dàngin yi dem ba

They remained there a long moment,
hurling projectiles at the mirror. Finally,
each one of them started inflicting

seen takkandeer ak seen jëmm maasa-
loo. Ñaari ponkal yi fàtte seetu bi, nag
daldi songante.

Xeex bu yàgg sax, te metti, Badu!
Benn dàngin gi ne kàttit dagg
baatu moroom mi, ba noppi tiim ko,
saw ci kow néewam. Waaye ba mu
demee ba defe ne xeex bi jeex na, la
gisaat beneen dàngin ci biir seetu bi.
...Xeex bi neeti kurr. Dàngin giy jamat
boppam ba yaram wépp dagg. . . .

Mu jékki-jékki bàyyeeku, àgg suff,
ne yàcc. . . . Xetu sàngara geek xetu
deret ji ubale Állu Kaañ. (B. B. Diop
2003: 303–4)

wounds on himself. . . . The gorillas kept
at it until their reflections and bodies
seemed to be one and the same. The
two brutes forgot the mirror, attacking
each other all the more.

A long and agonizing fight, Badou!
With a single stroke one gorilla slit
his companion's throat, then stood over
him and pissed on his corpse. But when
he thought that the fight was over, he
saw another gorilla in the mirror. . . .
The fight broke out again. The gorilla
kept throwing things at himself until
his whole body was cut up. . . .

Suddenly, he collapsed and hit
the ground, lifeless. . . . The smell of
alcohol and blood pervaded the Forest
of Kagne. (my translation)

En proie à une fureur sauvage, ils
s'acharnèrent tant contre le miroir qu'ils
furent eux-mêmes bientôt couverts de
sang de la tête aux pieds. . . . Puis vint le
moment où, incapables de distinguer
entre leurs corps et ceux des intrus, les
deux gorilles se dressèrent l'un contre
l'autre. . . . Arrachant d'un seul coup la
tête de son adversaire, [le second go-
rille] poussa un sinistre cri de victoire
et, sous nos regards stupéfaits, se mit à
pisser, avec des mouvements de reins
obscènes, sur le corps inerte.

Il n'eut pas le temps de savourer
soon triomphe, car un autre gorille se
dressa aussitôt face à lui dans le miroir,
une barre de fer à la main. Il se précipita

Gripped by an uncontrollable rage, they
kept attacking the mirror until they
were covered in blood all over. . . . Then
came the moment when—incapable of
distinguishing between their own bodies and those of the intruders—the two
gorillas turned on each other. The second one . . . tore off his opponent's head
without flinching, uttered a sinister cry
of victory and then proceeded—with us
as his stupefied onlookers—to piss on
the inert body with obscene gyrations
of his loins.

There was no time for him to enjoy
his triumph though, because another
gorilla, brandishing an iron bar, immediately appeared in the mirror in front

vers l'audacieux et le combat reprit, encore plus sauvage et cruel que celui qu'il venait de remporter. En quelques minutes, le gorille se lacéra tout le buste, les cuisses et une partie du visage . . . avant de se laisser lourdement tomber à terre. . . . Autour de leurs corps rouges et noirs, l'air empestait le sang, le vin de palme et l'urine. (B. B. Diop 2009: 370–71)

of him. He pounced on the impertinent fellow and the fight resumed, more savage and ferocious than the one he had just won. Within a few minutes, the gorilla had gravely lacerated his chest, his thighs and part of his face . . . before slumping heavily to the ground. . . . Their bodies, streaked with red and black, exuded a smell of blood, palm wine and urine. (B. B. Diop 2016: 224)

Forgetfulness is the gorillas' key error. The Wolof says explicitly that they attacked each other because they "forgot the mirror" ("fàtte seetu bi"), and both versions make clear that they are incapable of distinguishing between themselves and their reflections. Their orgiastic self-abandonment to bodily instincts and pleasures—drinking themselves silly, urinating to mark victory, gyrating obscenely—signify that they inhabit the space of absolute present. They even recall the orgies of killing narrated in *Murambi*, Diop's novel of the Rwandan genocide (2000). The gorillas represent the potential for extreme animalization of human beings, the abject degeneration of resistance. Even though their previous acts of sabotaging the French railroad look, on the surface, like the heroic feats of Lat-Dior, they were merely the result of a primal urge to defend territory. Resistance requires thought, clear vision, and self-knowledge, including knowledge of the past. The gorillas, having none of these, yet remaining uncannily close to humans, serve as a cautionary tale.[22] Their inability or refusal to conceptualize their actions like reflexive beings leads directly to their downfall.

What, then, is the antidote to forgetfulness? For *Doomi Golo* as a whole, it is not necessarily to enthrone Lat-Dior as an iconic hero, as Senghor did, but to remember the past in all of its complexity, whether "glorious or insignificant," abject or heroic, ambiguous or clear; to let it speak to the present; to shuttle between Yesterday and Today by destroying the partitions between "absolute present" and "absolute past." It is to look into a mirror and, rather than myopically fixating on the essentialist illusions of black abjection or its opposite, Negritude, to invoke, with Frantz Fanon, the famous prayer: "Ô mon corps, fais de moi toujours un homme qui interroge!" ("O my body, make of me always a man who questions!").[23]

This imperative to *xam sa bopp* or "know thyself" through an ongoing critical reflection on identity is incumbent on everyone, not just nobles (B. B. Diop 2003: 120, 199). The Wolof text quickly moves away from its own *géer*-centric interpretation of the legacy of Lat-Dior, suggesting that democratically inspired resistance may have replaced the dishonored and irrelevant nobility:

Am na nag ay bañkat yu fi jógoon ciy jamono ni loolu fàww mu dakk, ñu gar ci seen bakkan. Sa maam Ngiraan Fay bokkoon na ci jàmbaar yi fi taxawoon, yëkkati seen baat ci kow, ni: Moom sa réew! (B. B. Diop 2003: 292)

But there were resistors from here who, at such times, put their whole lives into making them end. Your grandfather Nguirane Faye was one of those heroes who stood up and raised their voices, crying: Independence! (my translation)

[Nguirane Faye] au moins a payé de sa personne pour que cesse la tyrannie d'André Castorel. Ton grand-père a fait partie de ceux qui exigèrent la liberté aux cris de "*Moom sa réew!*" (B. B. Diop 2009: 358)

[Nguirane Faye], at least, was personally involved in bringing about the end of André Castorel's tyranny. Your grandfather was one of the people who demanded liberty by clamoring, "*Moom sa réew* ['Independence']!" (B. B. Diop 2016: 216)

Immediately after having castigated the nobility for forgetting its duty, the Wolof text equates nonspecifically noble "resistors" (*bañkat*) with "heroes" (*jàmbaar*) during the independence era. Heroism, then, can take the democratic forms of attending rallies, mobilizing voters, and pressuring politicians, not just the ancient codes of honor tied to heredity. This democratization of heroism suggests that anyone can participate in the legacy of Lat-Dior by resisting the structures of colonization, personified in Castorel, that persist long after independence:

Ci sama gis-gis de, yëf yi dafa xaw a tane rekk. Baay Séy, dunguru bu ñakk faayda baa ngi fi ba tey, di def ay yëfi goloom, di sibooru Kastorel, di ko toppandoo. (B. B. Diop 2003: 292)

As I see it, things are only slightly better now [than under colonialism]. Baye Sèye, that spineless bootlicker, is still here today, doing his monkeyish tricks, fawning to Castorel, following him around. (my translation)

Et, à en croire ceux qui savent, tout ce cirque ça avait été pour rien car André Castorel, que l'on ne peut plus dire ni noir ni blanc, continue à montrer en coulisse le chemin à suivre. (B. B. Diop 2009: 358)	And, according to those in a position to know, this whole circus was in vain, because André Castorel, who is no longer either totally black or totally white, continues to prescribe the path we must follow from behind the scenes. (B. B. Diop 2016: 217)

The phenomena of mimicry and self-loathing cannot be reduced to an eternal battle of white and black. While the racial dimension of postcolonial mimicry is still important due to its continuing influence on the imagination, as demonstrated by Baye Sèye and Yacine Ndiaye, people of any color can occupy the positions of colonizer and colonized, mimicker and mimicked. Whereas Baye Sèye is merely another monkeyish copycat in the Wolof, he is absorbed completely into the raceless spirit of Castorel in the French, suggesting that through mimicry colonized and colonizer can become one. The spirit of Castorel can haunt, and the spirit of Langlade can delude, anyone. In contrast, the heroic memory of Lat-Dior, though subject to interrogation and constant readaptation to new circumstances, can rehumanize citizens by inspiring them to thoughtfully resist oppressors of any color.

The Postmodern Challenge

The postmodern challenge of *Doomi Golo* is not quite to make mirrors where there are none, as this chapter's epigraph from Junot Díaz might suggest. *Doomi Golo* assumes there are mirrors everywhere; the question is what we make ourselves see in them. The novel's labyrinthine structure represents the onslaught of language games among whose contradictory messages the subject must construct its own reflection and sense of meaning. What will the postcolonial subject see when it looks in the mirrors offered to it by society: an introspective, questioning self-image based on an informed dialogue between traditions of the past and changes of the present; or a vampiric caricature, flattened as absolute past or animalized as absolute present, the vestige of centuries of colonial delusion?

The dialogue between present and past is the common thread that unites all of the written reinventions of West African oral epic that I have brought together in this book. By seizing on traditional narratives' capacity for creativity, innovation, and subversion of norms, including in oral settings, the region's francophone writers have sought to make them continually pertinent in a wider range of times and places. In this sense, the African postmodern can be seen alongside all the other literary strategies studied here as continuing the work of oral tradition. They harness its potential for critical reflexivity and translate it into a medium that can travel farther on the continent and in the globalized world. The challenge posed to colonially imposed modernity by these texts constitutes a major trend within broader efforts to decolonize the mind.

NOTES

INTRODUCTION: ALTERNATIVE TRADITIONALITIES

1. See Gaonkar (2001: 18); Banégas and Warnier (2001); Diouf and Fredericks (2013 and 2014); Mbembe (2002).

2. On Afromodernity as diasporic consciousness, see Gilroy (1993) and Hanchard (2001). Frederick Cooper has countered that all this modernity talk only serves to flatten history and to limit the possibilities for new insight or fresh lines of inquiry (2005: 133–49). Yet it is incontestable that a desire for inclusion in global circuits of wealth and for increased symbolic capital on the world stage is real, and that many people designate this desire for upward mobility as a desire for modernity.

3. See Ferguson (2006 and 2009); Hilgers (2012 and 2013).

4. Aïda Souka is the fictional protagonist of Mansa Sora Wade's 1992 film of the same name, about the art of seduction of Senegalese women. Coumba Gawlo is a Senegalese singer.

5. Louis Faidherbe was a nineteenth-century French general who headed much of the effort to establish the French colony of Senegal. Lat-Dior was involved in many struggles and negotiations with him over the years. The epic tradition remembers Faidherbe as the white titan whom Lat-Dior and other Senegalese heroes resisted.

6. See Dieng (1993a: 374–440); Diagne (2014: 21–65).

7. See Roberts and Roberts (2000a: 288) and 2003; Roberts et al. (2005: 190–91);

Leduc-Gueye (2016: 7).

8. See Hobsbawm and Ranger (1983); Dimitrijevic (2004); Ranger (1993); Briggs (1996); Clifford (2004).

9. See Bauman and Briggs (2003); Briggs and Naithani (2012).

10. At the Battle of Guilé, on June 6, 1886, Albouri Ndiaye of the kingdom of Jolof rebuffed an attempted invasion by Samba Lawbé Fall, the last sovereign of the neighboring kingdom of Kajoor. For published documentation of an epic performance of the Battle of Guilé, see Diagne (2014: 67–119). See also Amadou Duguay-Clédor's historical account *La Bataille de Guîlé* (1985).

11. See Moretti (1996); Dimock (2006, 2013a, and 2013b); Fusillo (2006).

12. See Finnegan (1970: 108). In 2012, Finnegan added a preface to the 2nd edition of *Oral Literature in Africa* recognizing the controversy the book had caused and acknowledging that "Epic now has its place in the corpus of recognized African literature" (xxxi–xxxii).

13. See Jansen and Maier (2004: 7–10). Jansen's contribution in the same volume suggested that the "epic of Samori" might not exist at all (Jansen 2004). David Conrad objected in a response (Conrad 2008). In spite of this debate, a publically accessible, academically rigorous transcription/translation of a complete *Samori* performance has long been in existence. It was prepared by Laye Camara in his doctoral thesis (1971). Elara Bertho argues that the known texts on *Samori* are disparate enough that they form an "épopée en devenir" (epic in process) rather than a unified cycle (2016a).

14. For studies of "the epic" worldwide that include African material, see Madelénat (1986) and Derive (2002). For attempts to establish specific criteria that would define African epic, see Okpewho (1979); Johnson (1980 and 2003); Seydou (1982 and 1988); Boyer (1982); Kesteloot and Dieng (1997); and Belcher (1999a). A useful summary of these definitions can be found in Barber (2007: 48–58). Regarding expanded disciplinary approaches, see Boyer's studies on tradition as a cognitive structure (1984 and 1990), and the studies of music in Knight (1973); Okpewho (1979); Seydou (1998); Durán and Furniss (1999); and Charry (2000). Finally, in addition to the argument over the epic status of *Samori*, see also scholarly disagreements over the narratives of *Sara* and *Askia Mohammed* (Jansen and Maier 2004; Conrad 2008; Janson 2004; Sidikou 2001; Okpewho 1996: 122; Hale 1996).

15. For theories on the existence of one or more "epic belts" in Africa, see Johnson (1980: 321–22); Kesteloot and Dieng (1997: 15).

16. Surveys of African epic include Kesteloot and Dieng (1997); Johnson et al. (1997); Belcher (1999a).

17. Tal Tamari estimates the number of West African peoples having castes at fifteen or more

(1991: 221; 1995: 61). She suggests that the "vocationally specialized groups that would rapidly develop into endogamous bard and blacksmith groups first appeared among the Manding [Mali Empire] in the thirteenth century, as a result of the Sosso/Malinke war," which is the subject of the *Sunjata* epic. "Such an early date for Manding caste origins raises the possibility (though of course it does not prove) that even Wolof and Soninke castes ultimately developed from Manding ones" (1991: 235).

18. Madelénat classifies epics as having subject matter that is either mostly historical—that is, based on real-life figures and events—or mostly mythological (1986). Derive follows this general distinction, noting that West African epics tend to be of the mostly historical variety, with the exception of what Kesteloot and Dieng call "corporative" epics, that is, narratives specifically related to activities such as hunting or fishing, and which may or may not refer to historical events (Derive 2002: 82; Kesteloot and Dieng 1997: 39–50). Belcher's anthology draws a parallel between the zones that are peripheral to the Mande heartland along the Guinea/Mali border—Senegambia to the west and farther down the Niger River to the east—noting the "importance of relatively recent history" in epics from these two regions (1999a: 164); whereas he groups Central African narratives separately, "sharing as they do a similar style of performance, a focus on the actions of a mythical or ancestral hero, and a lack of reference to recent political history" (1999a: 27).

19. See Clifford (1988); Bauman and Briggs (1990); Okpewho (1992); Tedlock and Mannheim (1995); Debaene (2014).

20. On the consequences of literacy, see Goody and Watt (1975). In a more recent text, Goody baselessly claims that oral forms of fiction and epic narrative only exist in Africa thanks to the influence of written Islamic culture (2006: 15–16). He bases this conjecture on the authority of Finnegan (1970) while ignoring the decades of disagreeing scholarship that that particular source provoked. It is sufficient to recall the numerous studies on the shift from pre-Islamic to Islamic themes in West African heroic narrative and folktales to dismiss Goody's argument in the case of epic, and to seriously question it in the case of fiction (Dieng 1993b; Dieng et al. 2004; Dieng and Kesteloot 2015).

CHAPTER 1. THE HALF-BLACK ILIAD: AFRICAN EPIC AND THE RACIALIZATION OF COMPARATIVE LITERATURE

1. Finnegan's original argument had disqualified texts published as "epics" because "these works turn out to be in prose, not verse" (1970: 108). The prose/verse distinction, while itself a culture-bound criterion, was addressed directly by Johnson, who argued that performances of the *Sunjata* epic are indeed poetic because they contain lines

determined by musical accompaniment, rather than the more familiar European concept of meter (2003: 7–8).

2. See Conrad (1984: 37); Kelly (1984); Bulman (2004).

3. For discussions of commentators who denied the possibility of an African epic in the colonial era, see Ben-Amos (1983 and 1999); Biebuyck and Mongo-Mboussa (2004). The most important ones were Hector Munro Chadwick, Nora Chadwick, and Cecil Maurice Bowra.

4. Diffusionist theories suggest that civilization flows from more advanced peoples to less advanced ones. The Hamitic myth is an example. Evolutionist theories try to demonstrate the natural (but unequally paced) progression of human civilizations from primitive to civilized, with intermediate stages such as the barbarian or, more relevantly for this study, the heroic age. See Johnson (1982) and Biebuyck and Mongo-Mboussa (2004).

5. See for example Conrad (1984), Austen (1999b), Belcher (1994; 1999a: 94–95 and 193–212), Bulman (1997 and 1999), and Masonen (2000).

6. See Delafosse (1912, 3:125–43), Amselle (1990: 72), and Triaud (1998: 218–19) for discussions of this evolution.

7. Delafosse calculates that this supposed Judeo-Syrian migration, whose arrival in North Africa predated the Arab conquest, is what the *Tarikh es-Sudan* was referring to, and that it ruled Ghana from the fourth to eighth centuries CE (1912, 2:23–25; see also 1:198–220). In doing so, he dismisses the medieval Arab historians Ibn Khaldūn's and Al-Idrisi's reports of the first dynasty of Ghana being Arab, descended from Ali the companion of Muhammed, because for Delafosse this dynasty must have preceded the time of Muhammed (Delafosse 1912, 2:24; Levtzion and Hopkins 1981: 320 and 109).

8. Louis Tauxier traces the belief in Jewish Fulbe origins through several French and English authors going back to the end of the eighteenth century (1937: 44–45).

9. *Contes indigènes* was republished in a single volume in 1972 by Robert Cornevin as *Contes populaires d'Afrique occidentale*, together with a set of previously unpublished manuscripts originally intended to be a fourth tome. These extra materials were given to Cornevin, who was himself a colonial historian and enthusiastic reader of Equilbecq, by the latter's daughter in 1966 (Cornevin in Equilbecq 1972: 15). I use page numbers from Cornevin's reprint.

10. The 1914 manuscript of *Samba Guélâdio* was given in 1966 by Equilbecq's daughter to Cornevin, who edited it and had it published in 1974 (Cornevin in Equilbecq 1974: 7). Cornevin, for his part, after his career in the colonial administration, wrote a number of histories of Africa and commentaries on the continent's literature, all of which are generally procolonial. He implausibly takes credit for coining the notion of a "living

African epic" and praises Equilbecq as having had unprecedented insight into oral literature (Cornevin 1976: 58–61 and 93–98). It is noteworthy that Mongo Béti, an important Cameroonian writer, denounced Cornevin's work in an article memorably titled, "Contre M. Robert Cornevin et tous les pharisiens de l'Afrique de Papa" (Against Mr. Robert Cornevin and All the Pharisees of Papa's Africa) (Béti 1978).

11. See Belcher (1999a: 80). Korongo has been identified as Kieba Kuyate, a Maninka griot "whom Frobenius encountered (possibly at Kankan [present-day Guinea]) sometime between 1907 and 1912" (Bulman 1999: 236). See also Bulman (1997: 84).

12. I am counting these writings as four different articles (1907a, 1907b, 1907c, and 1907d), although the boundaries between them are unclear because of Lanrezac's habit of publishing serially, as was a common practice in colonial journals. Some of these writings were republished separately as an "Essai sur le folk-lore au Soudan," an offprint of *La Revue Indigène*, in 1908.

13. See C. Monteil (1905: 3; 1968: 2–3 and 54–55; 1953: 366).

14. These traditions are recorded in Arabic-language manuscripts. See, for example, Mohammed Bello's account of "The Origin of the Fulbe," a translated excerpt from his longer work *Infāq al-maysūr fī tārīkh bilād al-takrūr*, written between 1806 and 1809 (Bello in Palmer 1931). Bello was the second ruler of the Sokoto caliphate, which was established and led by a Fula ruling class under his father Usman dan Fodio in what is today northern Nigeria. According to Bello's narrative, to the west of the Bambara "come the Taurud [cf. Torodo, sg. of Torobe], as also the kingdom of Futa. The latter is of great extent, and was inhabited by the Taurud and the Sarakolli [cf. Sarakole or Soninke] from Fars [Persia]. The Taurud are said to be of Jewish origin: others say they were Christians; others again that they were the Bambarra mentioned above as being Sudanese. Formerly the Taurud lived in the neighbourhood of the two rivers, Nile and Firat [Euphrates], but moved here and settled in the neighbourhood of the Jews, who lived in the region of the island [cf. *al-jazira*]" (in Palmer 1931: 19). H. R. Palmer, Bello's translator—and the British governor of Gambia—interprets "the island" as referring to Masina in eastern Mali (1931: 19 n. 4). A virtually identical document, apparently a copy of Bello's text, is found in the annex to Scottish explorer Hugh Clapperton's journal of his second visit to Sokoto, first published in 1829 (Clapperton 1966). This annex is a translation of Arabic papers in Clapperton's possession at the time of his death near Sokoto in 1827. However, Abraham Salamé, the nineteenth-century translator of Clapperton's papers, thinks that the "Nile" should be understood as the Tigris, since *Al-Jazira* ("the island") is a term referring to the land between that river and the Euphrates (in Clapperton 1966: 337). Finally, see Delafosse's own compilation and translation of two Arabic manuscripts from the Futa

Toro, written in the first decade of the twentieth century, by one Sirê-Abbas Sôh, an
apparently famous genealogist who committed his own knowledge of traditional history
to writing. According to Sôh, the first king of Futa was "Dya'ukka" or "Dya'ogo," who
"provenait, dit-on, des Coptes d'Egypte; ses ancêtres habitaient dans une localité du nord
de la Syrie appelé *'Ukka*" (came, it is said, from among the Copts of Egypt; his ancestors
lived in a place of northern Syria called 'Ukka) (Sôh 1913: 15). Fleeing Arab invasions,
Dya'ukka went first to the land of Tor, which Delafosse insists was in Sinai, then to the
Futa Toro, where he reigned for 130 years (1913: 15–18). Putting aside the philological
difficulties, both Bello's and Sôh's accounts, written down at a distance of two thousand
miles and a hundred years, attribute Fula origins to an ancient eastern ancestry. Part
of their similarity may be due to the Torobe lineage that is sometimes, but not always,
attributed to Usman dan Fodio (see Willis 1978: 195 n. 2).

15. Monénembo (2004: 13–14). Monénembo derives this origin story, both in its cosmological
content and in its wording, from Amadou Hampâté Bâ (see A. H. Bâ 1966a and 1985).
Compare it with this tongue-in-check moment in Bâ's own discussion of Fula origins: "Si
vous me demandiez de vous situer par longitude et latitude les pays des Peuls et de vous
en décrire l'aspect, vous me mettriez dans un gros embarras. Pourquoi? Parce qu'une
bonne genèse débute par: 'Au commencement il y eut ceci, il y eut cela . . .' et la narration
situe le lieu où la création fut opérée. Et le lieu devient l'habitat, le terroir de la créature.
Hélas! on ne pourrait en dire autant pour la création des Peuls. Pour eux la formule serait
toute autre. Elle pourrait être ceci: 'Il y eut des Blancs. Il y eut des Noires. Et les Blancs
virent que les Noires étaient belles. Et les Blancs dirent que les Noires étaient bonnes.' Et
de là, les Peuls furent procréés" (If you asked me to indicate the latitude and longitude
of the Fulbe's homeland and to describe it for you, you would put me in a great difficulty.
Why? Because a good creation story starts with: 'In the beginning there was this, there
was that . . .' and goes on to describe the place where the creation happened. And that
place becomes the habitat, the home of the creature. Alas! No such thing can be said
for the creation of the Fulbe. For them the formula would have to be different. It might
go like this: 'There were white men. There were black women. And the whites saw that
the blacks were beautiful. And the whites said that the blacks were good. And from that
union came the Fulbe) (Bâ 1966a: 26).

16. See O. Kane (2004: 87 and 25); Conrad (1983).

17. Hall (2011: 103). On Uqba, conqueror of the Maghreb, see Mohammed Bello's early
nineteenth-century account of "The Origins of the Fulbe," already referenced above. It
asserts that Uqba married into the Torobe lineage, which was already of a mysterious
eastern origin from before the time of the Hijra: the children of "Okba" and the daughter

of the "Taurud Chief . . . married and begat the Fulani" (Bello in Palmer 1931: 20). Fula traditions about Uqba are recounted in other sources as well, often but not always with close ties to Bello's Sokoto caliphate: see the Arabic manuscripts from Sokoto belonging to Hugh Clapperton, also referenced above (Clapperton 1966: 338); the traditions reported by C. Vicars Boyle in Adamawa (eastern Nigeria), which had been part of the caliphate (1910: 73); and the Arabic documents collected by Paul Guebhard in Futa Jallon (today central Guinea) (1909: 105–7). Several of these documented traditions were sources for Delafosse (1912, 1:213 n. 1). On Ali, companion of the Prophet, see Ly's transcription of the *Samba Gelajo Jegi* epic, performed by the bard Pahel of the Futa Toro. It attributes the Torobe lineage to Arab ancestors descended from Ali (Ly 1991: 37, lines 392–404).

18. See Delafosse (1913: 19); Niane (1960: 14); Conrad (1985: 35–39); Cissé and Kamissoko (2000: 26); O. Kane (2004: 515 n. 40).

19. See *Sahih Bukahri*, book 46; book 57, hadiths 97–99; and Koran 90:13.

20. Sôh (1913: 21). Both Sôh's chronicles and Ly's version of the *Samba* epic, the latter performed by the bard Pahel, make Koli Tengela, founder of the Deniyanke dynasty and ancestor of Samba Gelajo, the son of Sunjata (Sôh 1913: 21; Ly 1991: 21–29). Pahel goes so far as to insist that "Samba appartient à l'ethnie Malinké, / ce sont des Malinké, / dont le patronyme est Kéita, chez nous" (Samba belongs to the Maninka ethnicity / they are Maninka / whose patronym, among us, is Keita) (Ly 1991: 21, lines 47–49).

21. Austen (1999a: 2); citing Saul Bellow in Atlas (1988: 31).

CHAPTER 2. THE SUNS OF INDEPENDENCE: ANTICOLONIAL HEROISMS AND THEIR LIMITS

1. N'Daou claims that Niane's *Soundjata, ou l'épopée mandingue* was "first published in sequences in *Horoya*" (N'Daou 2007: 172). However, this newspaper did not exist until April 1961, whereas the original *Présence africaine* edition of *Soundjata* is dated 1960. The serial publication of *Soundjata* in *Horoya* began in issue 2, dated April 22, 1961, and appears to have stopped by July (see issue 34, dated July 13), with less than half of Niane's text appearing in the newspaper's pages. This odd interruption may be related to Niane's fall from grace with Sékou Touré: Niane was imprisoned later in the year for his involvement in a teachers' strike that was in full swing in September and October, but that had been preceded by governmental plans for education "reform" as early as June and July. Thus, while the *Soundjata* book appears to have preceded the serial publication in *Horoya*, and the serial publication itself was incomplete, the PDG clearly co-opted

the epic for its own political ambitions, at least as long as Niane was on good terms with party leadership. This confirms yet nuances N'Daou's assertion that the earliest Guinean readership read Niane's *Soundjata* as a symbol of Sékou Touré's anticolonial heroism.

2. L. Camara (1971, 1:15; 1978: 36; 1980: 33).

3. N'Daou (2007: 149, 169 n. 121, 172–73).

4. Lieutenant Emile Hourst, in an account of his mission to map the Niger River in 1895–96, comments that "Samori, Malinké lui-même, prétend à l'heure actuelle qu'il est Soundiata revenu sur terre" (Samori, himself Maninka, claims at this very moment that he is Sunjata returned to earth) (1898: 52).

5. The fragments of a *Samori* narrative published by Conrad in Johnson et al. (1997: 68–79) also emphasize this theme. They seek to justify why the hero "brutally conquers each of the towns that gave him trouble" by explaining them as a result of previous humiliations at the villagers' hands (71).

6. Senghor credits Sadji as a practitioner of Negritude within Senegal, far from where it was theorized in Paris: "Abdoulaye Sadji appartient, comme Birago Diop, au groupe des jeunes gens qui, dans les années 1930, lança le mouvement de la *Négritude*. . . . Il fut l'un des premiers jeunes Sénégalais, entre les deux guerres mondiales, à combattre la thèse de l'assimilation et la fausse élite des 'évolués'" (Abdoulaye Sadji belongs, like Birago Diop, to the group of young men who, in the 1930s, launched the Negritude movement. . . . He was one of the first young Senegalese, between the two world wars, to fight the idea of assimilation and the false elite of the "évolués") (*Le Soleil*, Feb. 19, 1982; quoted in A. B. Sadji 1997: 58.)

7. A. Sadji (1936: 119). *Ce que dit la musique africaine* was later republished as a children's book (A. Sadji 1985).

8. L. Camara (1978: 16–17; 1980: 19–20). Isidore Okpewho's nearly contemporaneous landmark study and defense of African epic reiterates the argument that oral performance should be understood aesthetically rather than merely ethnographically (1979: 1–2).

9. On Albouri, see the episode of the Battle of Guilé performed by Ousseynou Mbéguéré, transcribed in Diagne (2014: 67–119). However, note that Cheikh Aliou Ndao's play does not focus on that battle, which took place in 1886, but rather on Albouri's exile, which began in 1890 (Charles 1971: 375). On Guy Njulli, which refers to events in 1861–62 (Klein 1968: 74–75), see Demba Lamine Diouf's performance, transcribed in Dieng (1993a: 168–91).

10. See Julien (1992: 42); Austen (1999b: 84); Nyela (2006: 149).

11. Ouologuem (1968: 11; 2008: 7).

12. Appiah (1999: 58); Mouralis (1987: 86).

13. Chaulet-Achour (1999: 94); C. Miller (1985: 231); Hale (1999: 167).

14. Ouologuem (1968: 14; 2008: 10); Hall (2011).

15. See 1 Kings 10:1–13; 2 Chronicles 9:1–12.

16. See Mills (2011: 123–28) for a thorough discussion of the racialization of Wolof caste ideology.

CHAPTER 3. AGAINST BAKHTIN: AFRICAN MISADVENTURES OF "EPIC AND NOVEL"

1. For West Africanist studies that rely on Bakhtin's paradigm of epic and novel, see Koné (1985: 136); Julien (1992: 46–47, 52–53); Gorman (2003: 18–21); Bisanswa (2007: 82–84); and Mas (2015: 310). Even though Julien provides a long refutation of Mohamadou Kane's argument that the written novel complexifies the relatively simple schemes of the oral narrative (see M. Kane 1982), she still resorts to Bakhtin's binary of epic and novel in her analysis of Amadou Hampâté Bâ's *L'Etrange destin de Wangrin*. Regarding the birth of the novel, see Lukács (1971) and Watt (1957). Lukács sees in the novel an alienated consciousness that replaces the holism of epic. He equates the age of epic with one of childlike wholeness (1971: chaps. 1–3). Watt sees the novel's emphasis on individual experience as replacing the more collectivist, universalist orientation of "literary traditionalism," including epic (1957: 13).

2. Moretti (1996); Dimock (2006, 2013a, 2013b).

3. Fabian (1983); Tedlock and Mannheim (1995).

4. See, for example, discussions of dialogism in Bakhtin (1984: 182–85); Bakhtin (1986: 67–76); and Vološinov (1973: 38–41).

5. A. Sadji (1936: 121); L. Camara (1971, 1:212–13 and 266); Seydou (2010: 117–23 and 256–57); Seye (2003: 15).

6. Conrad (1999: 201); see also Conrad (2004: 52–73).

7. Seydou (2010: 138–39 and 254–55, 162–65 and 208–11); Dieng et al. (2004: 60–63).

8. Dieng et al. (2004: 82–83); Seydou (2010: 272–75).

9. Dieng et al. (2004: 82–83); Seydou (2010: 272–75).

10. See, for example, Amselle in Amselle et al. (1979: 383); C. Monteil (1968: 54).

11. In the introduction to one of his collections of *Sunjata* songs, Diabaté acknowledges this political malleability of the traditional heritage: "Nous les jeli, les maîtres de la parole sans maître, nous avons alors considéré le patrimoine du Mali comme un bien mobilier, cela de père en fils. Oui, souvent nous avons joué pour l'occupant les hymnes consacrés à Sun Jata, à Samory, à El Hadj Omar" (We griots, masters of the word bound to no master,

have been treating the patrimony of Mali as a transferable property for generations. Yes, we have often played for the occupier hymns dedicated to Sunjata, Samori, and Umar) (1970: 16). Toward the end of his life in 1988, Massa Makan Diabaté expressed great disappointment with what he saw as the degradation of traditional class values, seeing griots of his day as cheap entertainers, and politicians claiming noble origin as impostors (Keïta 1988: 59–60). This led him to declare in a 1984 interview that Mali needs modern statesmen who are willing to break with heroic models of the past (Thiers-Thiam 2005: 130).

12. C. Miller (1990: 99), McGuire (1999: 253–57).

13. L. S. Senghor's personal griotte was Yandé Codou; Abdoulaye Wade's official griot was Ablaye Mbaye Pexh.

14. Apter (2007: 33). For Roth, "Praise formulae can be seen as occupying a continuum between the utterance of an individual clan name and a complete epic recitation" (2008: 76). For a discussion of how panegyric or "praise-poems" are embedded in epic, see Johnson (2003: 7–10). Okpewho also reflects on the interrelatedness of panegyric, epic, and criticism of a ruler (1979: 70; 1999: 147–51). Austen argues that the *Sunjata* epic as we know it today took shape in past centuries as panegyric combined with narrative motifs from Mande folktales and hunters' stories (1999b: 70–72). Andrew Apter discusses the complex uses of panegyric at length (2007: 32–49), drawing on the work of John Comaroff on the Southern Bantu (1975: 144–49) and of Ruth Finnegan in Sierra Leone (1970: 142).

15. Farias suggests, regarding Mande historical discourse, that the increasing degrees of secrecy surrounding the most esoteric layers of traditional knowledge provide "a necessary screen, behind which required rethinkings of tradition can be initiated and given restricted circulation, and behind which they can mature and become established among the *cognoscenti*, before being released to wider circles" (1993: 31). Apter applies this argument in detail to the case of Yoruba ritual genres that are reserved to priestesses, and more generally to what Mudimbe calls African gnosis or secret knowledge: for Apter, practices of gnosis do not necessarily have fixed content, but can have their meanings shaped and reinterpreted by authorized arbiters according to the needs of the moment (Apter 2007: 50–63 and 97–129; Mudimbe 1988). For analyses of the social and class transformations that Malian performers of oral tradition have undergone in the wake of colonization and independence, see Keïta (1988), Mamadou Diawara (1996), Schulz (1997 and 2001), McGuire (1999), and Roth (2008).

16. A third SCOA conference was held in Niamey, Niger, in 1977, but Kamissoko did not live to participate in it. Nevertheless the participants continued to discuss his work and

legacy.

17. Farias (1993: 15, 22–23, 28–29); Cissé and Kamissoko (2000: 16).

18. Concerning the figure of the anthropologist, I am thinking in particular of Marcel Griaule's careful orchestrations of his own ethnographic authority. Often comparing himself to an "examining magistrate" or *juge d'instruction* who must sift through witnesses' testimonies and "documents," Griaule saw himself as finding truth and coherency among the chaotic fragments supplied by his informants (Clifford 1988: 74–75, 85). Their perspectives were limited, but his was panoramic.

CHAPTER 4. THROUGH WANGRIN'S LOOKING GLASS: POLITICS OF THE MIRROR IN THE AOF

1. Bâ did write poetry in Fulfulde, his native language, the vast majority of which is unpublished. See Heckmann in A. H. Bâ (1994: 479–80 and 504 n. 128).

2. A. H. Bâ (1966b); see also Sow (1970) and Devey (1993: 183–92).

3. Konaté discusses the provenance and proverb-like quality of this sentence, which Bâ expressed in different variations on different occasions, yet which has come to be generally remembered in this form I quote here. According to Konaté, Bâ first used the formula in a speech before the executive board of UNESCO in 1962: "Apprenez que dans mon pays, chaque fois qu'un vieillard meurt c'est une bibliothèque qui a brûlé" (Know that in my country, every time an old man dies, it's a library burning) (in Konaté 2005: 58). However, an even earlier variant appears in a speech that Bâ delivered to UNESCO's Programme Commission in December 1960: "Pour moi, je considère la mort de chacun de ces traditionalistes comme l'incendie d'un fonds culturel non exploité" (For my part, I see the death of each one of these traditionalists as the destruction by fire of an unexploited cultural wealth) (A. H. Bâ 1960: 16 min., 43 sec.).

4. "Wangrin" is a pseudonym for a real person who went by the names Samako Gnembélé (or Niembélé) and Samba Traoré, and whose life trajectory corresponds more or less with that recounted in Amadou Hampâté Bâ's literary narrative (Austen 2007: 150; A. H. Bâ 1994: 394–95). Fourchard interviewed people in the 1990s in Bobo Dioulasso who remembered the real Wangrin's rise and fall from power (2003).

5. Jean-Francis Ekoungoun (2014: 8–11) gives a thorough overview of the state of Bâ's archives, which are divided between the Fondation Amadou Hampâté Bâ (FAHBA) in Abidjan and the Institut mémoires de l'édition contemporaine (IMEC) in Normandy. The archives at IMEC are off limits to the public pending resolution of a lawsuit from the writer's family seeking to have them returned to Abidjan. Meanwhile, the FAHBA

is functioning with extremely limited means, including a limited ability to protect and inventory the large number of fragile documents and books that it holds on its premises. As of this writing, the future of Bâ's archives remains uncertain.

6. See A. H. Bâ's foreword and 1986 afterword in *Wangrin* (1992: 7–9, 359–66; 1999: xvii–xix, 257–60). See also Austen's historical scrutiny of the text (2007 and 2015). In an annex to *Oui mon commandant!*, Hélène Heckmann, Bâ's wife and literary executor until her own death in 2001, recounts that he wrote *Wangrin* in Paris in 1971–72, after the historical Wangrin had already died. Bâ would burst into laughter as he wrote in the evenings, saying that "ce n'était pas son écriture qu'il entendait, mais la voix de Wangrin en train de lui raconter son histoire, et qu'il avait l'impression de se retrouver chez lui, à Bobo Dioulasso, tandis que le griot Diêli Maadi jouait doucement de sa guitare" (it wasn't his own writing that he heard, but the voice of Wangrin telling his story, and that he felt himself transported to Wangrin's home in Bobo Dioulasso, while the griot Diêli Maadi softly played his guitar) (Heckmann in A. H. Bâ 1994: 480).

7. Austen (2015: 45); see also Austen (2007).

8. Koné (1985); Wynchank (1991); Julien (1992); Gorman (2003); Austen (2007: 154–55).

9. For complete documented versions of this epic, see Kesteloot (1993b) and Conrad (1990).

10. Muslim prayer beads are represented as a "fetish" symbolizing the power of Islam. Islam was imposed on Segu by Umar Tall's conquest of the city in 1861.

11. Bâ reveals that "Romo" is code for Moro Sidibé (1994: 97–98). See historical research on this person in Fourchard (2003: 18–19) and Austen (2007).

12. A. H. Bâ (1992: 20–21; 1999: 8).

13. Tauxier (1927); Dieterlen (1951).

14. A. H. Bâ (1992: 21; 1999: 8).

15. Amadou Hampâté Bâ may have invented this figure entirely, or based it on a "rearrangement" of allusions to traditional material. All scholarly references to Gongoloma-Sooké that I have found can be traced back to Bâ's authority, but not independently verified (see, for example, Dumestre 2011: 379). David Conrad thinks that Gongoloma-Sooké's reversed physiology may be derived from the Bamana and Maninka spirit *wòkilò* (personal communication, September 2, 2018; see also Conrad 1990: 67, n. 544).

16. That is, Djibril Mamadou Ala-Atchi, Boukari Salihou, and Lolo, respectively (A. H. Bâ 1994: 88–96).

17. At least, this is how Islamic law is interpreted in the episode. Islamic law permits exhumation in certain circumstances, though Karibu's ultimate motives of vengeance and seizure of power would hardly meet its criteria.

18. A. H. Bâ (1992: 176; 1999: 121).

19. Ralph Austen suggests that the historical Wangrin may have been a captive who took the surname of a noble family (2007: 152), but his analysis does not address the fact that the literary Wangrin is specifically praised as a born noble, not as having a captive background: Diofo addresses him as "le noble fils de nobles chefs" who has "sucé un noble lait" ("the noble son of noble chiefs," "suckled on noble milk") (A. H. Bâ 1992: 167; 1999: 114).

20. That is, Goffo (A. H. Bâ 1994: 88).

21. See, for example, Manthia Diawara's description of this phenomenon in a Mande context: "Suddenly, a griot woman rose and burst into her own 'Duga' song. She . . . turned to me and called me a hero like my great-great-grandfather, Daman Guile Diawara. It was breathtaking. . . . Toumani [Diabate]'s music had created an atmosphere of heroism that had taken away my self-control. . . . The money that Sly and I gave to the griot woman acknowledged the incomparable supremacy of that moment of return. The only thing that counts is that moment; it makes people forget all the pain and humiliation they went through in exile" (1997: 25, 28).

22. *Wangrin* and Bâ's memoirs provide several examples of colonial judges and officials who are admirable for their sense of fairness. However, these individual cases do not undo the systemic injustice of the colonial world. See, for example, the Martinican magistrate assigned to the cattle affair, whose "droiture en tant que juge fut totale" ("manner of judging was unquestionably upright") (1992: 85, 1999: 56); the inspector Robert Arnaud, whose "sens aigu de la justice [s']appliquait indifféremment aux Blancs et aux Noirs" (acute sense of justice was applied indifferently to whites and blacks) (1994: 218); and Edouard Hesling, governor of Upper Volta, who declares that "le plus grand prestige de la France . . . est de commettre ni injustice ni abus de pouvoir" (the greatest glory of France is to commit neither injustice nor abuse of power) (1994: 243).

23. A. H. Bâ (1992: 95; 1999: 63).

24. A. H. Bâ (1991: 32–34; 1994: 100–102, 162–64).

25. A. H. Bâ (1994: 228–30; 1992: 25, 203; 1999: 11, 141).

26. A. H. Bâ (1994: 220–21; 1992: 9–10; 1999: xviii).

27. A. H. Bâ (1994: 212–26, 96); Pondopoulo (2010: 242–47).

28. A. H. Bâ (1992: 63, 172–74, 218; 1999: 39, 118–20, 152).

29. A. H. Bâ (1992: 75; 1999: 48).

30. A. H. Bâ (1994: 232). It appears that Bâ misspelled this administrator's name, which shows up in AOF documents of the time as "A. de Loppinot." See, for example, the article "Souvenirs d'Aguibou" (De Loppinot 1919), which discusses the reign of Aguibou

Tall, Umar's son who was installed as "king" of Masina by the French after the fall of Bandiagara, and who was responsible for the deposition and imprisonment of Bâ's stepfather Tidjani Thiam.

31. A. H. Bâ (1992: 220, 62; 1999: 154, 39).

32. See Van Vollenhoven (1917).

33. Already in *Wangrin*, Bâ describes the hero as "enclin à la charité" ("inclined towards helping the poor"), and as seeing the colonizers as "exploiteurs de la masse paysanne" ("exploiters of the peasant masses") (1992: 229; 1999: 160).

CHAPTER 5. HYPERPRIMITIVES, BUFFOONS, AND OTHER LIES: IRONIC ETHNOGRAPHIES FROM OUOLOGUEM TO KOUROUMA

1. Traoré (2000a: 1361). Kourouma's linguistic experimentation, specifically his relexification of Maninka expressions into French to create a hybrid literary language, is the single most commented on aspect of his work. The landmark study of this issue is Gassama (1995). Zabus helpfully contextualizes it with regard to other African writers' "indigenization" of European languages (2007: 143–47).

2. For examples of this kind of criticism, see Borgomano (1998 and 2000); Bisanswa (2007); Yapo (2008); Kyoore (2010); Rochat (2011); and Mas (2015).

3. The word used in Kourouma's original French text to name Bingo's profession is *sora* (1998: 9); this is rendered in Coates's English translation as *sèrè* (2001: 4). Traoré, who prefers the latter word in his own scholarship, notes that hunters' bards can be designated by either term, or by the more problematic *donsojeli* (1999: 172; 2000b: 155–65). By its etymology, *donsojeli* literally means "hunters' griot"; while there are important similarities between hunters' bards (*sèrè*) and the caste of griots (*jeli*), such as the patron-client relationship between praiser and praised, the status of griot can only be inherited by birth, whereas the vocation to become a hunters' bard can be chosen by a man of any caste or status. The latter represents a hereditary belonging, and therefore an inherited profession, while the former does not (Conrad 1989: 46 n. 9).

4. Traoré (2000b: 165–76). In an epic performance, the "*naamu*-sayer, or responding person, is a secondary performer whose job it is to reply and to encourage the main performer with short, interjected comments. The most common interjection is *naamu*, for which there is no very accurate translation, though it is what people also say when they hear their name called, and it can be rendered as 'yes' or 'I hear you'" (Conrad 2004: xviii; see also Johnson 2003: 69 n. 15). Often apprentices, *naamu*-sayers are crucial in both dynastic and hunters' epics: "It is extremely rare to hear a performance of any epic

without a namu-sayer, and many bards will simply not perform without one" (Bird 1974: xiii; see also Traoré 2000b: 167).

5. For documented *donsomana* texts, see Bird (1974); Cashion (1984); Cissé (1994); and Thoyer (1995 and 1999). See also analyses in Traoré (1999 and 2000b). A great deal of anthropological scholarship has examined the changing activities and forms of the *donsoya* itself in various countries, including hunters' roles as quasi-police and even, in Ivory Coast, perpetrators of war atrocities in the context of state collapse; see Hellweg (2011 and 2012) and Kedzierska-Manzon (2014).

6. Seydou Camara had a close working relationship with Charles Bird, who introduced him to other scholars. His son Sékou Camara, also a performer of oral tradition, worked with a number of American researchers as well (Conrad 2002: vi). As such, his biography is well documented in the scholarly literature (Bird 1974; Cashion 1984; Conrad 1989; Traoré 2000b: 179–80). Born in 1917, Seydou Camara served in the French colonial army and only began learning his art during an illness as an adult, winning his first competition in 1953. According to Traoré, he gained such a national reputation as a hunters' singer that he began to negotiate fees from the *donsoton* who would invite him, contravening the sense of solidarity expected of him. For this reason, he was banned from performing at hunters' meetings and depended on urban performances and American academics to make his living. He died in 1981.

7. Seydou Camara's son Sékou, discussing the text with David Conrad, suggested that the invented hero Bilali was inspired at least partially by Blaise Diagne, the Senegalese deputy to the French National Assembly who negotiated certain reforms in the colonies in exchange for African participation in World War I (Conrad 1989: 43–44 and 61 n. 45).

8. On intervening praise-songs in real *donsomana*, see Traoré (2000b: 171).

9. Cissé (1994: 88); Traoré (2000b: 94).

10. These remarks are from an unpublished paper, titled "Kourouma and the Hunters, Kourouma's Hunters," given at the Modern Language Association national conference in 2014 (Traoré 2014). I was one of the author's copanelists. As noted in the main text, many of Traoré's observations from this paper echo statements that appear in his published scholarship.

11. Cissé (1994: 109–58); Traoré (2000b: 163–64, 174–75); Traoré (2014).

12. See Froelich (1964 and 1968); Frobenius (1968); and Cornevin (1969). Mercier analyzes and challenges the primitivist ethnography of a neighboring people with paleonigritic characteristics, namely the Somba of what is today northern Benin (1968).

13. Kourouma stated in an interview that "Les hommes nus étaient en Afrique un peuple important, s'étendant du Sénégal jusqu'au Soudan actuel" (The naked men were an

important people in Africa, and could be found from Senegal to what is today Sudan) (Le Renard and Toulabor 1999: 178). The paleonigritic theory has lost currency today. Bayart, following earlier sources, nevertheless marshals it as an example of stateless societies being capable of political innovation (1993: 17). In contrast, Piot's book-length study of the Kabre in northern Togo problematizes that group's reputation for primitiveness yet makes no mention of its supposed belonging to a larger paleonigritic category (1999).

14. Nonetheless, Horton's 1982 reformulation was not radically different from that of 1967. He was still invested in establishing a great divide between tradition and modernity; each side of the divide was still characterized by a distinct concept of time and theorization of knowledge (1993a: 220–42).

15. Kourouma (1990: 181; 1993: 162).

16. Kourouma (1970: 11; 1981: 4).

17. Kourouma (1990: 275; 1993: 249).

18. Kourouma (1998: 315; 2003: 214).

19. Traoré has long criticized Cissé's depiction of the *donsoton* as overromanticizing its democratic potential and noticed Kourouma's reliance on it in *En attendant* (2000b: 95–96; 2014). However, to my knowledge, he has not pointed out the near-verbatim correspondence between a number of passages in *En attendant* and Cissé (1994), as I have here.

20. Kourouma (1998: 313–14, 317–18); Kourouma (2001: 212–13, 215–16); Cissé (1994: 109–10, 126–27, and 148–53).

21. The plagiarism scandal had a devastating effect on Ouologuem's writing career (see Wise 1999). Kourouma, for his part, famously had *Les Soleils des indépendances* published by the University of Montreal in 1968 after failing to find a Parisian house that would accept it. Soon after, Seuil bought the rights to *Soleils* and has been its exclusive French publisher since 1970. It is now an undisputed classic. On the question of Kourouma's "universality," see Voisin (2015) and Repinecz (2017).

CHAPTER 6. DEFIANT WOMEN, NOBLE SLAVES, AND GAYS, OR, THE PROBLEM WITH WOLOF VIRTUE

1. See Borgomano (1989: 90), Cazenave (1991: 59), Stringer (1996: 104–5), Guèye (1998: 313–18 and 2005: 18–21), Hitchcott (2000: 89–112), Martin (2000), Kesteloot (2001: 288), and Mills (2011: 132–47).

2. Researchers have often discussed how nobles' condescending discourse on casted subjects (ñeeño in Wolof, *nyamakalaw* in Manding) and slaves as inferior stands in

contradiction with the importance of the latter groups' functions in their societies and what they have to say about their own honor. In a Wolof context, see Dieng's discussion of the ambiguous roles of ñeeño in general and of griots in particular (2008: 29 and 34). In distinct but related contexts, see Conrad and Frank's general discussion of the issue in the Mande cultures, and Mamadou Diawara's thorough study of the specific oral traditions transmitted by casted groups (*nyaxamalo*), women, and slaves in what was once the Soninke kingdom of Jaara (Conrad and Frank 1995: 1–2; Mamadou Diawara 1990). Indeed, to demonstrate the notion of a "servile" honor opposed to the noble denigration of slaves, Diawara gives the example of a duo of women slave artists who "célèbrent la 'noblesse' de la servitude, réduisant la notion de 'noblesse' à son contenu moral, d'où le paradoxal éloge de leur état" (celebrate the "nobility" of servitude, reducing the notion of "nobility" to its moral content and thereby enabling a paradoxical praise of their status) (1990: 139).

3. See Christiane Seydou's discussion of the *pulaaku* or idealized Fula code of conduct (2010: 9–13). See also Boubacar Barry's descriptions of social hierarchies and associated norms in Futa Toro and Futa Jallon (1998: 89–91, 99–101).

4. Upon being reunited with Dioumana, Sarebibi feels "un courant voluptueux travers[ant] ses veines" (a voluptuous current flooding his veins) (Sow Fall 1993: 147). He believes this attraction to be satanic, returning instead to his "résolution d'aller le plus loin possible dans la maîtrise de mes instincts" (resolution to seek absolute mastery of my instincts) (151).

5. Sow Fall (1993: 67 n. 1). Nevertheless, the word *wollëre* has different shades of meaning. For Sylla, it depends mostly on friendship rather than kinship, as it does for Sow Fall: a "*wolëré*" is an "ami auquel on est lié par une longue et profonde relation d'assistance mutuelle. Deux personnes sont *woléré* l'une de l'autre si elles ont connu ensemble un long passé d'amitié, d'entraide, d'échange de *tarànga*, de solidarité entretenue jusque dans des situations difficiles" (friend to whom one is bound by a long and deep relationship of mutual assistance. Two people are each other's *wollëre* if they have shared together a long past of friendship, reciprocity, exchanges of hospitality, and solidarity through difficult situations) (1978: 89). Jean-Léopold Diouf's dictionary offers a still more simplified definition that one hears frequently in everyday urban life: "relation; quelqu'un avec qui on a de bonnes relations" (relation; someone with whom one has good relations) (2003: 370).

6. Hitchcott (2000: 105–6); Guèye (2005: 126–30).

7. Cheikh Niang (2010) describes the settings within which *góor-jigéen* have been accepted as members of the social world of women in Senegal. Their existence and activities were

documented as early as the nineteenth century. For a variety of reasons, since the 1960s, they have become victims of increasing exclusion and homophobic violence.

8. Borgomano (1989: 90); Kesteloot (2001: 288).
9. See Irvine (1993); Gueye (2004, 2010a, 2010b, 2014); and McNee (2000).
10. See Mamadou Diawara (1990: 119–43); Hale (1994 and 1998: 217–43); Sidikou (2001); Sidikou and Hale (2012); and Hale and Sidikou (2014).
11. Hale argues that the scholarly understanding of African epic should be adjusted to include women's contributions to performances of it (1998: 227–33). See also Durán (1995).
12. Marloes Janson challenges the idea that women are excluded from narrating the *Sunjata*, giving two examples from the Gambia of senior Mandinka griottes who narrated part of that epic to her. She further sees the lack of attention to women's roles in epic as a product of male researchers' bias (2004: 81–87).
13. Some research has reported instances of women singing long epics, such as the genre of *saabi* in Niger (Durán 1995; Sidikou 2001: 131–67). Several researchers have argued that a text called the "Song of Sara"—performed by the *jelimuso* or griotte Siramori Diabaté, whose career has been well documented (Jansen 1996; Camara and Jansen 2014)—should be considered as epic in spite of its short length (Bird in Johnson et al. 1997: 114–23; Hale 1998: 230). Janson disagrees (2004: 82).

CONCLUSION: THROUGH LAT-DIOR'S LOOKING GLASS

1. See the novel *Murambi: Le Livre des ossements* (2000), translated into English as *Murambi: The Book of Bones* (2006), but also the first several essays in B. B. Diop (2007 and 2014).
2. According to Wülfing-Leckie, "The true nature of Part Two is never revealed, but if it is indeed the seventh *Notebook* or *The Book of Secrets*, Ali Kaboye has to be understood as a figment of Nguirane Faye's imagination. This, in turn, makes the latter the one and only narrative voice in *Doomi Golo*" (in B. B. Diop 2016: xxii).
3. Wane (2004); O. Ngom (2012); Goldblatt (2014). The call to read and write in African languages was most famously articulated by Ngũgĩ wa Thiong'o of Kenya (1986).
4. *Dammel* was the title of the kings of Kajoor.
5. My Wolof teacher, Paap Sow, first informed me that Ali Kaboye was a real person who had passed into the local urban mythology of Medina (personal communication, August 14, 2013). Boubacar Boris Diop confirmed this in an email, in English, which I quote below. He was hesitant to use the words "oral tradition" in as wide a sense as I, under the

influence of American folkloristics, regularly do: "As for Ali Kaboye's character, Paap Sow is right. During my childhood he was a kind of urban legend, especially in Medina, where I was born, and in surrounding areas like Gueule-Tapée. I remember he was a very tall man with a bare head and a powerful voice. He was always speaking alone without even seeming to realize that people were hearing what he was saying. Apparently he didn't care at all. He couldn't go to cinema, of course, but he liked very much all these American movies about the Far West, that we called 'western' or 'cowboys/bandits' movies. By the way, Gary Cooper was the typical figure of the cowboy. Ali used to call himself 'Ali the Cow Boy' (meaning the brave guy) and by alteration it became 'Ali Kaboye.' But if you go today to Medina, only old people, people of my generation will remember him. But, there a risk of misunderstanding if you say he was 'a figure of oral tradition' since people may think he was a kind of 'griot.' No, he wasn't, even if in my novel he talks like a griot. I made some important changes and I think it is important to make a clear distinction between the real Ali and who he became in my story. He is half real, half imaginary" (personal email from Diop to me, slightly edited for typographic errors, January 21, 2014).

6. On Kocc Barma and Daaw Demba, see transcriptions of Wolof traditions in Dieng (1993a: 62–79); Kesteloot and Mbodj (2006: 165–177); and Diagne (2014). On the Tuesday of Nder, see Seye (2003: 152–56); Serbin (2004: 158–63); and the theatricalized version in Bèye (1990). On Guy Njulli, see the transcription of Wolof tradition in Dieng (1993a: 168–82); see also the theatricalized version in Ndao (1983 and 2002). On Lat-Dior, see transcriptions of Wolof traditions in Dieng (1993a: 183–91 and 374–440); and Diagne (2014: 21–65). See also the theatricalized version in T. Bâ (1987). On Kagne, see A. Sadji (1958: 193–94).

7. B. B. Diop (2009: 346). See issues 2 and 3 of the Senegalese review *Demb ak Tey* (Yesterday and Today) (1975 and 1976), directed by Djibril Tamsir Niane, which are devoted specifically to oral traditions surrounding Kocc Barma. Niane argues that Kocc's historical existence is certain. Mamadou Diouf also seems to consider Kocc Barma as a real historical figure, writing in passing that Daaw Demba was deposed as *dammel* in 1647 thanks to his machinations (1990: 61). Given the disagreeing traditional stories about how Kocc's conflicts with Daaw Demba turned out, this statement seems subject to debate.

8. B. B. Diop (2009: 37; 2016: 18).

9. For documentation of this tale, see Kesteloot and Mbodj (2006: 165–77) and Diagne (2014: 234–37). See also a more extended analysis in Repinecz (2015).

10. B. B. Diop (2009: 37; 2016: 18).

11. B. B. Diop (2003: 271–77; 2009: 330–34; 2016: 199–202).

12. The Wolof text refers to Mbissine and Mbissane in the second person singular from this point on in the passage ("sa"), even though it referred to them in the third person plural in the preceding sentence ("ñoo"). This stylistic choice could be interpreted in two ways. First, the narrator Ali Kaboye could be addressing the children as a unit, collapsing them into a singular addressee. Or, the shift to second person could be an unusual application of the generic "you," typically used in Wolof in subordinate clauses, especially in proverbs, to replace a nonspecific third-person antecedent. Creissels has studied this construction in Mandinka, though he notes that it is typical of other West African languages, including Wolof (2013: 54). If the switch to second person here is a use of the generic you, it is unusual because the antecedent, Mbissine and Mbissane, is specific in this case. Reading the singular "you" here as generic would suggest that the novel, via the current narrator Ali Kaboye, is addressing not only the children, but a nonspecific, virtual addressee, such as the Wolof-language reader, warning him or her of the dangers of internalized racism.

13. Penda Sarr is a legendary figure revered in the Pular-speaking region of the Futa Toro, especially in the village of Ngawle (Sow 1982: 291–98; Lorin 2015: 40–52). She is said to be the daughter of the village's founder, and to have accompanied Umar Tall's jihad in the nineteenth century. She is revered as a kind of patron of the village and of fishers, endowed with various miraculous capacities. Although she is essentially a heroine of Pular historical tradition, Lorin notes that she has a "translocal" reputation outside of the Futa Toro due to her many travels, and that she is said to be a "master of the waters" not only along the river, but also along the Wolof-dominated Atlantic coast (2015: 46). This may be why *Doomi Golo* associates the Pular adage invoking Penda Sarr for people choking on fish bones with the Wolof language in the above passage. Within the world of the novel, Penda, who is only alluded to in this brief passage in Wolof and entirely eliminated in French, may also be read as an echo of Mbarka Dia, the heroine of the "Tuesday of Nder." According to Marie Lorin, she is a "féministe malgré elle," or feminist in spite of herself: "Penda est une femme forte qui a refusé de se laisser soumettre. C'est en cela que son exemple est remarquable. Dans l'historiographie largement dominée par les hommes qui est en cours au Foûta, il est absolument remarquable que le récit de la vie d'une telle femme remettant en cause l'ordre établi ait pu accéder à une telle postérité" (Penda is a strong woman who refused to submit. For this reason, her example is remarkable. In the commonly accepted historiography of the Futa, which is heavily dominated by men, it is absolutely remarkable that the story of a woman questioning the established order could reach such a wide posterity) (2015: 47).

14. B. B. Diop (2003: 288; 2009: 351–52; 2016: 213).

15. B. B. Diop (2003: 286–305; 2009: 351–72; 2016: 212–25).

16. Internal struggles for power made nineteenth-century Senegambian kingdoms more vulnerable to the French expansion (M. Diouf 1990; Barry 1998). Cheikh Aliou Ndao's plays *L'Exil d'Albouri* (1969) and *Gouye Ndiouli* (1983), the latter of which was also published in a Wolof version (2002), thematize internal vulnerability as tragedy in the cases of Jolof and Saalum, respectively; Alioune Badara Bèye's *Nder en flammes* (1990) treats the same theme inversely, by suggesting that the alliance between Futa Toro and Walo against Trarza and the French prefigured the Senegalese nation.

17. See M. Diouf (1990: 282–85); Thioub (2002: 134–35, 144–46); and Thierno Bâ's play *Lat-Dior, ou le chemin de l'honneur* (1987).

18. The legend of Kagne is documented in Abdoulaye Sadji's novel *Maïmouna* (1958: 193–94).

19. Mamadou Diouf describes Lat-Dior's position toward the French, which included both support to their campaigns and open insurrection at various times, as one of "opportunisme politique" or political opportunism (1990: 252). See also V. Monteil (1963: 92–96).

20. The battle of Dékheulé, including Demba Waar's betrayal and the deaths of Lat-Dior and Malaw, is recounted in a documented epic performance by Ousseynou Mbéguéré (in Diagne 2014: 61–65).

21. The house of Geej was the matrilineal royal line (*meen*) that dominated the throne of Kajoor throughout much of the eighteenth and nineteenth centuries, and to which Lat-Dior himself belonged (M. Diouf 1990: 61, 76, 210).

22. For a fascinating discussion of instances of blurred identities between humans and apes, see Herzfeld and Van Schuylenbergh (2011).

23. Fanon (1952: 188; 2008: 206).

REFERENCES

Abdoul, Mohamadou. 2005. "Urban Development and Urban Informalities: Pikine, Senegal." In *Urban Africa: Changing Contours of Survival in the City*, edited by Abdoumaliq Simone and Abdelghani Abouhani, 235–60. Chicago: University of Chicago Press.

Adiaffi, Jean-Marie. 2000. *Les Naufragés de l'intelligence*. Abidjan: CEDA.

Afriques Créatives et al. 2012. *Rapport Final: Atelier régional de partage des résultats de recherche du projet de recherche "Participation politique des jeunes femmes d'Afrique de l'Ouest francophone: Formes, enjeux, politiques."* Dakar.

Amselle, Jean-Loup. 1990. *Logiques métisses: Anthropologie de l'identité en Afrique et ailleurs.* Paris: Payot.

Amselle, Jean-Loup, Zumana Dunbya, Amadu Kuyate, and Mohamed Tabure. 1979. "Littérature orale et idéologie: La Geste des Jakite Sabashi du Ganan (Wasolon, Mali)." *Cahiers d'Études Africaines* 19 (73/76): 381–433.

Appadurai, Arjun. 1996. *Modernity at Large: Cultural Dimensions of Globalization*. Minneapolis: University of Minnesota Press.

Appiah, Kwame Anthony. 1992. *In My Father's House: Africa in the Philosophy of Culture.* Oxford: Oxford University Press.

———. 1999. "Yambo Ouologuem and the Meaning of Postcoloniality." In *Yambo Ouologuem: Postcolonial Writer, Islamic Militant*, edited by Christopher Wise, 55–63.

Boulder, CO: Lynne Rienner.

Apter, Andrew H. 2007. *Beyond Words: Discourse and Critical Agency in Africa.* Chicago: University of Chicago Press.

Arnaud, Robert. 1912. *L'Islam et la politique musulmane française.* Paris: Comité de l'Afrique Française.

Atlas, James. 1988. "Chicago's Grumpy Guru: Best-Selling Professor Allen Bloom." *New York Times Magazine.* January 3.

Austen, Ralph, ed. 1999a. *In Search of Sunjata: The Mande Oral Epic as History, Literature and Performance.* Bloomington: Indiana University Press.

———. 1999b. "The Historical Transformation of Genres: Sunjata as Panegyric, Folktale, Epic, and Novel." In *In Search of Sunjata: The Mande Oral Epic as History, Literature and Performance,* edited by Ralph Austen, 69–87. Bloomington: Indiana University Press.

———. 2007. "Who Was Wangrin and Why Does It Matter? Colonial History 'from the Middle' and Its Self-Representation." *Mande Studies* 9: 149–64.

———. 2015. "Finding the Historical Wangrin or the Banality of Virtue." *Journal of West African History* 1 (1): 37–58.

Bâ, Amadou Hampâté. 1960. *Discours de Hamadou Hampâté Ba à la Commission Afrique de l'UNESCO.* Audio recording. http://www.ina.fr/audio/PHD86073514.

———. 1966a. "Les Foulbé du Mali et leur culture." *Abbia: Cameroon Cultural Review* 14–15: 23–54.

———. 1966b. "Pour un retour fécond aux sources de l'art nègre." In *Premier festival mondial des arts nègres: Dakar, 1–24 avril 1966.* Paris: World Festival of Negro Arts.

———. 1972. *Aspects de la civilisation africaine.* Paris: Présence africaine.

———. 1981. "The Living Tradition." In *UNESCO General History of Africa,* vol. 1: *Methodology and African Prehistory,* edited by Joseph Ki-Zerbo, 166–203. Berkeley: University of California Press.

———. 1985. *Njeddo Dewal: Mère de la calamité; Conte initiatique peul.* Abidjan: Les Nouvelles Éditions africaines.

———. 1991. *Amkoullel, l'enfant peul.* Arles: Actes Sud.

———. 1992. *L'Etrange destin de Wangrin, ou les roueries d'un interprète africain.* Paris: Editions 10/18.

———. 1994. *Oui mon commandant!* Arles: Actes Sud.

———. 1999. *The Fortunes of Wangrin.* Translated by Aina Pavolini Taylor. Bloomington: Indiana University Press.

Bâ, Thierno. 1987. *Lat-Dior, ou le chemin de l'honneur: Drame historique en huit tableaux.* Dakar: Nouvelles Editions Africaines.

Bagayogo, Shaka. 1987. "L'Etat au Mali: Représentation, autonomie, et mode de fonctionnement." In *L'Etat contemporain en Afrique*, edited by Emmanuel Terray, 91–122. Paris: L'Harmattan.

Bakhtin, Mikhail. 1984. *Problems of Dostoevsky's Poetics*. Translated by Caryl Emerson. Minneapolis: University of Minnesota Press.

———. 1986. *Speech Genres and Other Late Essays*. Edited by Michael Holquist and Caryl Emerson. Translated by Vern McGee. Austin: University of Texas Press.

———. 2002. "Epic and Novel." In *The Dialogic Imagination*, edited by Michael Holquist, translated by Caryl Emerson and Michael Holquist, 3–40. Austin: University of Texas Press.

Banégas, Richard, and Jean-Pierre Warnier. 2001. "Nouvelles figures de la réussite et du pouvoir." *Politique africaine* 82: 5–23.

Barber, Karin. 2007. *The Anthropology of Texts, Persons and Publics: Oral and Written Culture in Africa and Beyond*. Cambridge: Cambridge University Press.

Barber, Karin, and P. F. de Moraes Farias, eds. 1989. *Discourse and Its Disguises: The Interpretation of African Oral Texts*. Birmingham: Centre of West African Studies, University of Birmingham.

Barkan, Sandra. 1985. "*Le Devoir de violence*: A Non-History." In *Interdisciplinary Dimensions of African Literature*, edited by Kofi Anyidoho et al., 101–12. Washington, DC: Three Continents Press.

Barnes, Teresa. 2011. "Soccer Nation/Corporation." *Journal of Sport & Social Issues* 35 (1): 101–6.

Barry, Boubacar. 1998. *Senegambia and the Atlantic Slave Trade*. Translated by Ayi Kwei Armah. Cambridge: Cambridge University Press.

Bauman, Richard. 1992. "Contextualization, Tradition, and the Dialogue of Genres: Icelandic Legends of the Kraftaskáld." In *Rethinking Context: Language as an Interactive Phenomenon*, edited by Alessandro Duranti and Charles Goodwin, 125–45. Cambridge: Cambridge University Press.

Bauman, Richard, and Charles Briggs. 1990. "Poetics and Performance as Critical Perspectives on Language and Social Life." *Annual Review of Anthropology* 19: 59–88.

———. 2003. *Voices of Modernity: Language Ideologies and the Politics of Inequality*. Cambridge: Cambridge University Press.

Baumann, Hermann, and Diedrich Westermann. 1957. *Les Peuples et civilisations de l'Afrique. Suivi de Les Langues et l'éducation*. Translated by Lilias Homberger. Paris: Payot.

Bayart, Jean-François. 1993. *The State in Africa: The Politics of the Belly*. London: Longman.

Beebee, Thomas O. 1994. *The Ideology of Genre: A Comparative Study of Generic Instability*. Philadelphia: Pennsylvania State University Press.

Belcher, Stephen. 1994. "Constructing a Hero: Samba Gueladio Djegui." *Research in African Literatures* 25 (1): 75–92.

———. 1999a. *Epic Traditions of Africa*. Bloomington: Indiana University Press.

———. 1999b. "Sinimogo, 'Man for Tomorrow': Sunjata on the Fringes of the Mande World." In *In Search of Sunjata: The Mande Oral Epic as History, Literature and Performance*, edited by Ralph Austen, 89–110. Bloomington: Indiana University Press.

Ben-Amos, Dan. 1983. "Introduction." In "Epic and Panegyric Poetry in Africa," special issue, *Research in African Literatures* 14 (3): 277–82.

———. 1999. "Oral Epics from Africa: Vibrant Voices from a Vast Continent (Review)." *Comparative Literature Studies* 36 (3): 259–64.

Bertho, Elara. 2015. "Médias, propagande, nationalismes. La filiation symbolique dans les chants de propagande: Robert Mugabe et Mbuya Nehanda, Ahmed Sékou Touré et Samory Touré." *Cahiers de littérature orale* 77–78: 171–93.

———. 2016a. "Existe-t-il une épopée de la résistance à la colonisation? De quelques 'épopées en devenir' africaines." *Le Recueil ouvert*. http://ouvroir-litt-arts.univ-grenoble-alpes.fr/revues/projet-epopee/182-du-recit-de-l-heroique-resistance-a-l-epopee-nehanda-samori-sarraounia.

———. 2016b. "Filmer la résistance à la colonisation." *Cahiers d'études africaines* 224 (4): 875–90.

Béti, Mongo. 1978. "Contre M. Robert Cornevin et tous les pharisiens de l'Afrique de Papa." *Peuples Noirs, Peuples Africains* 4: 77–96.

Bèye, Alioune Badara. 1990. *Nder en flammes: Théâtre*. Dakar: Nouvelle editions africaines du Sénégal.

Biebuyck, Brunhilde, and Boniface Mongo-Mboussa. 2004. "Introduction." In "Griot réel, griot rêvé," special issue, *Africultures* 61: 5–12.

Biebuyck, Daniel. 1976. "The African Heroic Epic." *Journal of the Folklore Institute* 13 (1): 5–36.

Bird, Charles, ed. 1974. *The Songs of Seydou Camara*. Bloomington: African Studies Center, Indiana University.

———. 1999. "The Production and Reproduction of Sunjata." In *In Search of Sunjata: The Mande Oral Epic as History, Literature and Performance*, edited by Ralph Austen, 275–95. Bloomington: Indiana University Press.

Bisanswa, Justin. 2007. "The Adventures of the Epic and Novel in Ahmadou Kourouma's Writings." *Research in African Literatures* 38 (2): 81–94.

Borgomano, Madeleine. 1989. *Voix et visages de femmes dans les livres écrits par des femmes en Afrique francophone*. Abidjan: CEDA.

———. 1998. *Ahmadou Kourouma: Le Guerrier griot*. Paris: L'Harmattan.

————. 2000. *Des hommes ou des bêtes: Lecture de "En attendant le vote des bêtes sauvages" d'Ahmadou Kourouma*. Paris: L'Harmattan.

Boyer, Pascal. 1982. "Récit épique et tradition." *L'Homme* 22 (2): 5–32.

————. 1984. "La Tradition comme genre énonciatif." *Poétique* 58: 233–51.

————. 1990. *Tradition as Truth and Communication: A Cognitive Description of Traditional Discourse*. Cambridge: Cambridge University Press.

Boyle, C. Vicars. 1910. "Historical Notes on the Yola Fulanis." *Journal of the Royal African Society* 10 (37): 73–92.

Briggs, Charles. 1996. "The Politics of Discursive Authority in Research on the 'Invention of Tradition.'" *Cultural Anthropology* 11 (4): 435–69.

Briggs, Charles, and Sadhana Naithani. 2012. "The Coloniality of Folklore: Towards a Multi-Genealogical Practice of Folkloristics." *Studies in History* 28 (2): 231–70.

Bulman, Stephen. 1997. "A Checklist of Published Versions of the Sunjata Epic." *History in Africa* 24: 71–94.

————. 1999. "Sunjata as Written Literature: The Role of the Literary Mediator in the Dissemination of the Sunjata Epic." In *In Search of Sunjata: The Mande Oral Epic as History, Literature and Performance*, edited by Ralph Austen, 231–51. Bloomington: Indiana University Press.

————. 2004. "A School for Epic? The 'Ecole William Ponty' and the Evolution of the Sunjata Epic, 1913–c.1960." In *Epic Adventures: Heroic Narrative in the Oral Performance Traditions of Four Continents*, edited by Jan Jansen and Henk Maier, 34–45. Münster: Lit Verlag.

Busch, Annett, and Max Annas. 2008. *Ousmane Sembène: Interviews*. Jackson: University Press of Mississippi.

Calmettes, Joël, dir. 2003. *A Mi-Mots*. TV Broadcast. April 4. Arte.

Camara, Brahima, and Jan Jansen. 2014. "A Heroic Performance by Siramori Diabate in Mali." In *Women's Songs from West Africa*, edited by Thomas A. Hale and Aïssata G. Sidikou, 136–50. Bloomington: Indiana University Press.

Camara, Laye. 1971. "Le Haut Niger vu à travers la tradition orale: Kuma Lafoloo Kuma, Kuma Koroo, Kuma Korootoola, Kuma." PhD diss., Université Cheikh Anta Diop de Dakar.

————. 1978. *Le Maître de la Parole: Kouma Lafôlô Kouma*. Paris: Plon.

————. 1980. *The Guardian of the Word: Kouma Lafôlô Kouma*. Translated by James Kirkup. London: Fontana.

Camara, Sana. 2002. "Birago Diop's Poetic Contribution to the Ideology of Negritude." Translated by R. H. Mitsch. *Research in African Literatures* 33 (4): 101–23.

Carbonnel, Laure. 2015. "Les Kòròdugaw du Mali: Comportements et Groupements Bouffons." PhD diss., Université Paris Nanterre.

Cashion, Gerald Anthony. 1984. "Hunters of the Mande: A Behavioral Code and Worldview Derived from the Study of Their Folklore." PhD diss., Indiana University, Bloomington.

Cazenave, Odile. 1991. "Gender, Age, and Reeducation: A Changing Emphasis in Recent African Novels in French, as Exemplified in *L'Appel des arènes* by Aminata Sow Fall." *Africa Today* 38 (3): 54–62.

Charles, Eunice A. 1971. "Ouali N'Dao: The Exile of Alboury N'Diaye." *African Historical Studies* 4 (2): 373–82.

Charry, Eric. 2000. *Mande Music: Traditional and Modern Music of the Maninka and Mandinka of Western Africa.* Chicago: University of Chicago Press.

Chaulet-Achour, Christiane. 1999. "Writing as Exploratory Surgery: Yambo Ouologuem's *Bound to Violence.*" Translated by Ann George. In *Yambo Ouologuem: Postcolonial Writer, Islamic Militant,* edited by Christopher Wise, 89–107. Boulder, CO: Lynne Rienner.

Chemla, Yves. 1999. *"En attendant le vote des bêtes sauvages* ou le donsomana: Entretien avec Ahmadou Kourouma." *Notre Librairie* 136: 26–29.

Cissé, Youssouf Tata. 1994. *La confrérie des chasseurs malinké et bambara: Mythes, rites et récits initiatiques.* Ivry: Editions Nouvelles du Sud.

Cissé, Youssouf Tata, and Wa Kamissoko. 2000. *La grande geste du Mali.* 2nd ed. Paris: Karthala.

Clapperton, Hugh. 1966. *Journal of a Second Expedition into the Interior of Africa.* London: F. Cass.

Clifford, James. 1988. *The Predicament of Culture: Twentieth-Century Ethnography, Literature, and Art.* Cambridge, MA: Harvard University Press.

———. 2004. "Traditional Futures." In *Questions of Tradition,* edited by Mark Phillips and Gordon Schochet, 152–68. Toronto: University of Toronto Press.

Comaroff, Jean, and John Comaroff. 2004. "Notes on Afromodernity and the Neo World Order: An Afterword." In *Producing African Futures: Ritual and Reproduction in a Neoliberal Age,* edited by Brad Weiss, 349–43. Leiden: Brill.

Comaroff, John. 1975. "Talking Politics: Oratory and Authority in a Tswana Chiefdom." In *Political Language and Oratory in Traditional Society,* edited by Maurice Bloch, 141–61. London: Academic Press.

Condé, Maryse. 1984. *Ségou: Roman.* 2 vols. Paris: R. Laffont.

———. 1988. *Segu.* Translated by Barbara Bray. New York: Ballantine.

Conklin, Alice. 1997. *A Mission to Civilize: The Republican Idea of Empire in France and West Africa, 1895–1930.* Stanford: Stanford University Press.

Conrad, David. 1983. "Maurice Delafosse and the Pre-Sunjata Trône du Mandé." *Bulletin of the School of Oriental and African Studies* 46 (2): 335–37.

———. 1984. "Oral Sources on Links between Great States: Sumanguru, Servile Lineage, the Jariso, and Kaniaga." *History in Africa* 11: 35–55.

———. 1985. "Islam in the Oral Traditions of Mali: Bilali and Surakata." *Journal of African History* 26 (1): 33–49.

———. 1989. "'Bilali of Faransekila': A West African Hunter and World War I Hero According to a World War II Veteran and Hunters' Singer of Mali." *History in Africa* 16: 41–70.

———. 1990. *A State of Intrigue: The Epic of Bamana Segu According to Tayiru Banbera.* Oxford: Oxford University Press.

———. 1999. "Mooning Armies and Mothering Heroes: Female Power in Mande Epic Tradition." In *In Search of Sunjata: The Mande Oral Epic as History, Literature and Performance*, edited by Ralph Austen, 189–229. Bloomington: Indiana University Press.

———. 2002. *Somono Bala of the Upper Niger: River People, Charismatic Bards, and Mischievous Music in a West African Culture.* Leiden: Brill.

———, ed. 2004. *Sunjata: A West African Epic of the Mande Peoples.* Indianapolis: Hackett.

———. 2008. "Almami Samori in Academic Imagination: Constructing Epic Adventures to Realize Ambitions and Dreams." *Mande Studies* 10: 175–214.

———. 2010. "Bold Research during Troubled Times in Guinea: The Story of the Djibril Tamsir Niane Tape Archive." *History in Africa* 37: 355–78.

Conrad, David, and Barbara Frank, eds. 1995. *Status and Identity in West Africa: Nyamakalaw of Mande.* Bloomington: Indiana University Press.

Cooper, Frederick. 2005. *Colonialism in Question: Theory, Knowledge, History.* Berkeley: University of California Press.

Cornevin, Robert. 1969. *Histoire du Togo.* 3rd ed. Paris: Berger-Levrault.

———. 1976. *Littératures d'Afrique noire de langue française.* Paris: Presses universitaires de France.

Coulibaly, Adama, et al., eds. 2011. *Le Postmodernisme dans le roman africain: Formes, enjeux et perspectives.* Paris: L'Harmattan.

Couloubaly, Pascal Baba. 1993. "The Narrative Genre among the Bamana of Mali." Translated by Richard Bjornson. *Research in African Literatures* 24 (2): 47–60.

Creissels, Denis. 2013. "The Generic Use of the Second Person Pronoun in Mandinka." In *Languages Across Boundaries: Studies in Memory of Anna Siewierska*, edited by Dik Bakker and Martin Haspelmath, 53–67. Berlin: Walter de Gruyter.

De Loppinot, A. 1919. "Souvenirs d'Agibou." *Bulletin du Comité d'études historiques et scientifiques de l'Afrique Occidentale Française* 2 (1): 24–61.

Debaene, Vincent. 2014. *Far Afield: French Anthropology between Science and Literature.* Translated by Justin Izzo. Chicago: University of Chicago Press.

Delafosse, Maurice. 1912. *Haut-Sénégal-Niger*. 3 vols. Paris: Emile Larose.

———. 1913. *Traditions historiques et légendaires du Soudan occidental traduites d'un manuscrit arabe inédit*. Paris: Comité de l'Afrique Française.

Derive, Jean, ed. 2002. *L'épopée: Unité et diversité d'un genre*. Paris: Karthala.

Deschamps, Hubert. 1959. "Nécrologie: Henri Labouret." *Journal des Africanistes* 29 (2): 291–92.

Devey, Muriel. 1993. *Hampaté Bâ: L'Homme de la tradition*. Abidjan: LivreSud.

Dia, Mamadou. 1985. *Memoires d'un militant du Tiers-Monde*. Paris: Publisud.

Diabaté, Massa Makan. 1970. *Janjon et autres chants populaires du Mali*. Paris: Présence africaine.

Diagne, Mamoussé. 2005. *Critique de la raison orale: Les Pratiques discursives en Afrique noire*. Paris: Karthala.

———. 2014. *Le Preux et le sage: L'Epopée du Kayor et autres textes wolof*. Paris: Editions Orizons.

Diawara, Mamadou. 1990. *La Graine de la parole: Dimension sociale et politique des traditions orales du royaume de Jaara (Mali) du XVème au milieu du XIXème siècle*. Stuttgart: F. Steiner.

———. 1996. "Le Griot mande à l'heure de la globalisation." *Cahiers d'études africaines* 36 (144): 591–612.

Diawara, Manthia. 1992. "Canonizing Soundiata in Mande Literature: Toward a Sociology of Narrative Elements." *Social Text* 31/32: 154–68.

———. 1997. "The Song of the Griot." *Transition* 74: 16–30.

Dieng, Bassirou. 1993a. *L'Epopée du Kajoor*. Paris: Agence de coopération culturelle et technique; Dakar: Centre africain d'animation et d'échanges culturels.

———. 1993b. "Narrative Genres and Intertextual Phenomena in the Sahelian Region (Myths, Epics, and Novels)." Translated by Kwaku A. Gyasi. *Research in African Literatures* 24 (2): 33–45.

———. 2008. *Société wolof et discours du pouvoir: Analyse des récits épiques du Kajoor*. Dakar: Presses universitaires de Dakar.

Dieng, Bassirou, and Lilyan Kesteloot. 2015. *Contes et mythes wolof: Du tieddo au talibé*. 3rd ed. Paris: L'Harmattan.

Dieng, Bassirou, et al. 2004. *L'épopée de Boubou Ardo: L'islamisation des traditions de l'Ouest africain*. Amiens: Presses du Centre d'études médiévales, Université de Picardie–Jules Vernes.

Dieterlen, Germaine. 1951. *Essai sur la religion bambara*. Paris: Presses universitaires de France.

Dimitrijevic, Dejan, ed. 2004. *Fabrication de traditions, invention de modernité*. Paris: Maison des sciences de l'homme.

Dimock, Wai Chee. 2006. "Genre as World System: Epic and Novel on Four Continents." *Narrative* 14 (1): 85–101.

———. 2013a. "Low Epic." *Critical Inquiry* 39 (3): 614–31.

———. 2013b. "Recycling the Epic: Gilgamesh on Three Continents." *English Language Notes* 51 (1): 19–33.

Diop, Abdoulaye Bara. 1981. *La Sociéte wolof: Tradition et changement. Les Systèmes d'inégalité et de domination*. Paris: Karthala.

Diop, Birago. 1961. *Les Contes d'Amadou-Koumba*. Paris: Présence africaine.

———. 1966. *Tales of Amadou Koumba*. Translated by Dorothy Blair. London: Oxford University Press.

Diop, Boubacar Boris. 2000. *Murambi: Le Livre des ossements*. Paris: Stock.

———. 2003. *Doomi Golo*. Dakar: Papyrus.

———. 2006. *Murambi: The Book of Bones*. Translated by Fiona Mc Laughlin. Bloomington: Indiana University Press.

———. 2007. *L'Afrique au-delà du miroir*. Paris: P. Rey.

———. 2009. *Les petits de la guenon: Roman*. Paris: P. Rey.

———. 2012. "Arab Spring: A View from Sub-Saharan Africa." Video-recorded presentation. Stanford Forum on African Studies. October 27. https://vimeo.com/52752879.

———. 2013. *Doomi Golo*. Dakar: E-Book Africa.

———. 2014. *Africa beyond the Mirror*. Translated by Vera Wülfing-Leckie and Caroline Fache. Banbury, UK: Ayebia Clarke.

———. 2016. *Doomi Golo: The Hidden Notebooks*. East Lansing: Michigan State University Press.

Diop, Cheikh Anta. 1959. *L'Unité culturelle de l'Afrique noire*. Paris: Présence africaine.

———. 1979. *Nations nègres et culture*. 3rd ed. Paris: Présence africaine.

Diouf, Jean Léopold. 2003. *Dictionnaire wolof–français et français–wolof*. Paris: Karthala.

Diouf, Mamadou. 1990. *Le Kajoor au XIXe siècle: Pouvoir ceddo et conquête coloniale*. Paris: Karthala.

———. 1991. "L'Invention de la littérature orale: Les Epopées de l'espace soudano-sahélien." *Etudes littéraires* 24 (2): 29–39.

———. 2002. "Des cultures urbaines entre traditions et modernité." In *Le Sénégal contemporain*, edited by Momar Coumba Diop, 261–88. Paris: Karthala.

———. 2013. "Les jeunes dakarois, la scène urbaine et le temps du monde à la fin du XXe siècle." In *Les arts de la citoyenneté au Sénégal: Espaces contestés et civilités urbaines*, edited by Mamadou Diouf and Rosalind Fredericks, 47–91. Paris: Karthala.

Diouf, Mamadou, and Rosalind Fredericks. 2013. *Les arts de la citoyenneté au Sénégal: Espaces contestés et civilités urbaines.* Paris: Karthala.

———, eds. 2014. *The Arts of Citizenship in African Cities: Infrastructures and Spaces of Belonging.* New York: Palgrave Macmillan.

Dirks, Nicholas. 1990. "History as a Sign of the Modern." *Public Culture* 2 (2): 25–32.

DiVanna, Isabel. 2011. "Politicizing National Literature: The Scholarly Debate around La Chanson de Roland in the Nineteenth Century." *Historical Research* 84 (223): 109–34.

Donohue, Brian. 2009. "Pulitzer Prize-Winning Author Junot Diaz Tells Students His Story." NJ.com. October 21. http://www.nj.com/ledgerlive/index.ssf/2009/10/junot_diazs_new_jersey.html.

Duboc, Albert. 1947. *Samory le sanglant.* Paris: SFELT.

Dugger, Celia W. 2010. "South Africa Pushes to Make the Cup Its Own." *New York Times,* May 23. http://www.nytimes.com/2010/05/24/sports/soccer/24safrica.html.

Duguay-Clédor, Amadou. 1985. *La Bataille de Guîlé.* Paris: Agence de Coopération Culturelle et Technique.

Dumestre, Gérard. 2011. *Dictionnaire bambara-français: Suivi d'un index abrégé français-bambara.* Paris: Karthala.

Durán, Lucy. 1995. "Jelimusow: The Superwomen of Malian Music." In *Power, Marginality and African Oral Literature,* edited by Graham Furniss and Elizabeth Gunner, 197–207. Cambridge: Cambridge University Press.

Durán, Lucy, and Graham Furniss. 1999. "Introduction." In *Sunjata,* by Bamba Suso and Banna Kanute, edited by Gordon Innes and Bakari Sidibe, vii–xxix. London: Penguin.

Ekoungoun, Jean-Francis. 2014. "Archives Amadou Hampâté Bâ: Vers une politique de conservation cohérente." *Continents Manuscrits* 1: 1–18.

Equilbecq, François-Victor. 1913–16. *Essai sur la littérature merveilleuse des Noirs, suivi de Contes Indigènes de l'Ouest-Africain français.* 3 vols. Paris: Ernest Leroux.

———. 1972. *Contes populaires d'Afrique occidentale.* Edited by Robert Cornevin. Paris: Maisonneuve et Larose.

———. 1974. *La Légende de Samba Guélâdio Diêgui, Prince du Foûta.* Edited by Robert Cornevin. Dakar: Nouvelles Editions Africaines.

Fabian, Johannes. 1983. *Time and the Other: How Anthropology Makes Its Object.* New York: Columbia University Press.

———. 1991. *Time and the Work of Anthropology: Critical Essays, 1971–1991.* Chur: Harwood Academic Publishers.

Fanon, Frantz. 1952. *Peau noire, masques blancs.* Paris: Seuil.

———. 1991. *Les Damnés de la terre.* Paris: Gallimard.

———. 2005. *The Wretched of the Earth.* Translated by Richard Philcox. New York: Grove Press.

————. 2008. *Black Skin, White Masks*. Translated by Richard Philcox. London: Pluto Press.

Farias, P. F. de Moraes. 1993. "The Oral Traditionist as Critic and Intellectual Producer: An Example from Contemporary Mali." In *African Historiography: Essays in Honour of Jacob Ade Ajayi*, edited by Toyin Falola, 14–38. Essex: Longman.

Ferguson, James. 2006. *Global Shadows: Africa in the Neoliberal World Order*. Durham, NC: Duke University Press.

————. 2009. "The Uses of Neoliberalism." *Antipode* 41: 166–84.

Ferrarini, Lorenzo. 2016. "The Dankun Network: The Donso Hunters of Burkina Faso between Ecological Change and New Associations." *Journal of Contemporary African Studies* 34 (1): 80–96.

Finnegan, Ruth. 1970. *Oral Literature in Africa*. London: Clarendon Press.

————. 2012. *Oral Literature in Africa*. 2nd ed. Cambridge: Open Book Publishers.

Fourchard, Laurent. 2003. "Propriétaires et commerçants à Ouagadougou et à Bobo-Dioulasso, fin 19ème siècle–1960." *Journal of African History* 44 (3): 433–61.

Frobenius, Leo. 1911. *Auf dem Wege nach Atlantis*. Berlin: Vita, Deutches Verlaghaus.

————. 1912. *Und Afrika sprach . . . bericht über den Verlauf der Dritten Reise-Periode der D.I.A.F.E. in den Jahren 1910 bis 1912*. Berlin: Vita.

————. 1921–28. *Atlantis*. 12 vols. Jena: E. Diederichs.

————. 1924. *Der Kopf als Schicksal*. Munich: K. Wolff.

————. 1968. *The Voice of Africa: Being an Account of the Travels of the German Inner African Exploration Expedition in the Years 1910–1912*. 2 vols. New York: B. Blom.

Froelich, Jean-Claude. 1964. "Les Problèmes posés par les refoulés montagnards de culture paléonigritique." *Cahiers d'Études Africaines* 4 (15): 383–99.

————. 1968. *Les Montagnards paléonigritiques*. Paris: O.R.S.T.O.M., Berger-Levrault.

Fusillo, Massimo. 2006. "Epic, Novel." In *The Novel*, vol. 2: *Forms and Themes*, edited by Franco Moretti, 32–63. Princeton, NJ: Princeton University Press.

Gaonkar, Dilip Parameshwar, ed. 2001. *Alternative Modernities*. Durham, NC: Duke University Press.

Gassama, Makhily. 1995. *La langue d'Ahmadou Kourouma, ou le français sous le soleil d'Afrique*. Paris: Karthala.

Geschiere, Peter. 1997. *The Modernity of Witchcraft: Politics and the Occult in Postcolonial Africa*. Translated by Janet Roitman and Peter Geschiere. Charlottesville: University of Virginia Press.

Ghosh, Amitav, and Dipesh Chakrabarty. 2002. "A Correspondence on Provincializing Europe." *Radical History Review* 83 (1): 146–72.

Gilroy, Paul. 1993. *The Black Atlantic: Modernity and Double Consciousness*. London: Verso.

Ginio, Ruth. 2006. "Negotiating Legal Authority in French West Africa: The Colonial Administration and African Assessors, 1903–1918." In *Intermediaries, Interpreters, and Clerks: African Employees in the Making of Colonial Africa*, edited by Benjamin N. Lawrance, Emily Lynn Osborn, and Richard L. Roberts, 115–38. Madison: University of Wisconsin Press.

Goldblatt, Cullen. 2014. "Lëndëmtu: Réflexions sur *Doomi Golo* et *Les Petits de la guenon*." In *Des mondes et des langues: L'Ecriture de Boubacar Boris Diop*, edited by Nasrin Qader and Souleymane Bachir Diagne, 61–83. Paris: Présence africaine.

———— [Clea]. 2015. "Places of Complicity in Narratives of Historical Violence: Thiaroye (Dakar) and District Six (Cape Town)." PhD diss., University of California, Berkeley.

Gontovnik, Monica. 2010. "Tracking Transnational Shakira on Her Way to Conquer the World." *Zona Próxima* 13: 142–55.

Goody, Jack. 1977. *The Domestication of the Savage Mind*. Cambridge: Cambridge University Press.

———. 2006. "From Oral to Written: An Anthropological Breakthrough in Storytelling." In *The Novel*, vol. 1: *History, Geography, and Culture*, edited by Franco Moretti, 3–36. Princeton, NJ: Princeton University Press.

Goody, Jack, and Ian Watt. 1975. "The Consequences of Literacy." In *Literacy in Traditional Societies*, edited by Jack Goody, 27–68. Cambridge: Cambridge University Press.

Gorman, Susan. 2003. "Generic Ideologies: The Intersection of Empire, the Epic, and the Novel in French West African and Latin Literatures." PhD diss., University of Michigan.

Guebhard, Paul. 1909. "Les Peulh du Fouta Diallon." *Revue des études ethnographiques et sociologiques* 2: 85–108.

Gueye, Marame. 2004. "Wolof Wedding Songs: Women Negotiating Voice and Space through Verbal Art." PhD diss., State University of New York, Binghamton.

———. 2010a. "The Battle of the Words: Oratory as Women's Tool of Resistance to the Challenges of Polygamy in Contemporary Wolof Society." In *African Women Writing Resistance: An Anthology of Contemporary Voices*, edited by Jennifer Browdy de Hernandez, 149–66. Women in Africa and the Diaspora. Madison: University of Wisconsin Press.

———. 2010b. "Woyyi Céet: Senegalese Women's Oral Discourses on Marriage and Womanhood." *Research in African Literatures* 41 (4): 65–86.

———. 2014. "Wolof Women Break the Taboo of Sex through Songs." In *Women's Songs from West Africa*, edited by Thomas A. Hale and Aïssata G. Sidikou, 9–33. Bloomington: Indiana University Press.

Guèye, Médoune. 1998. "La Question du féminisme chez Mariama Bâ et Aminata Sow Fall." *French Review* 72 (2): 308–19.

———. 2005. *Aminata Sow Fall: Oralité et société dans l'œuvre romanesque.* Paris: L'Harmattan.

Hale, Thomas. 1990. *Scribe, Griot, and Novelist: Narrative Interpreters of the Songhay Empire.* Gainesville: University of Florida Press.

———. 1994. "Griottes: Female Voices from West Africa." *Research in African Literatures* 25 (3): 71–91.

———. 1996. "Misrepresenting and Misreading 'The Epic of Askia Mohammed.'" *Research in African Literatures* 27 (3): 128–35.

———. 1998. *Griots and Griottes: Masters of Words and Music.* Bloomington: Indiana University Press.

———. 1999. "Rewriting the Songhay Past in Yambo Ouologuem's *Le Devoir de Violence.*" In *Yambo Ouologuem: Postcolonial Writer, Islamic Militant,* edited by Christopher Wise, 155–74. Boulder, CO: Lynne Rienner.

Hale, Thomas A., and Aïssata G. Sidikou, eds. 2014. *Women's Songs from West Africa.* Bloomington: Indiana University Press.

Hall, Bruce. 2011. *A History of Race in Muslim West Africa, 1600–1960.* Cambridge: Cambridge University Press.

Hanchard, Michael. 2001. "Afro-Modernity: Temporality, Politics, and the African Diaspora." In *Alternative Modernities,* edited by Dilip Parameshwar Gaonkar, 272–98. Durham, NC: Duke University Press.

Handler, Richard, and Jocelyn Linnekin. 1984. "Tradition, Genuine or Spurious." *Journal of American Folklore* 97 (385): 273–90.

Hardy, Georges. 1921. *Les Eléments de l'histoire coloniale.* Paris: La Renaissance du livre.

———. 1929. *Ergaste ou la vie coloniale.* Paris: Larose.

Harootunian, Harry. 2007. "Remembering the Historical Present." *Critical Inquiry* 33 (3): 471–94.

Hartog, François. 2012. *Régimes d'historicité: Présentisme et expérience du temps.* Paris: Points.

Havard, Jean-François. 2013. "L'Etat, la nation et la laïcité au Sénégal." In *L'Afrique des laïcités: Etat, religion et pouvoirs au sud du Sahara,* edited by Gilles Holder and Moussa Sow, 171–81. Paris: Institut de Recherche et de Développement.

Hellweg, Joseph. 2011. *Hunting the Ethical State: The Benkadi Movement of Côte d'Ivoire.* Chicago: University of Chicago Press.

———. 2012. "La chasse à l'instabilité: Les dozos, l'état et la tentation de l'extralégalité en Côte d'Ivoire." *Migrations Société* 144: 163–82.

Herzfeld, Chris, and Patricia Van Schuylenbergh. 2011. "Singes humanisés, humains singés: Dérive des identités à la lumière des représentations occidentales." *Social Science Information* 50 (2): 251–74.

Hilgers, Mathieu. 2012. "The Historicity of the Neoliberal State." *Social Anthropology* 20 (1): 80–94.

———. 2013. "Embodying Neoliberalism: Thoughts and Responses to Critics." *Social Anthropology* 21 (1): 75–89.

Hiribarren, Vincent. 2017. "Borno (Bornu, Kanem-Borno, Kanem-Bornu)." In *African Kingdoms: An Encyclopedia of Empires and Civilizations*, edited by Saheed Aderinto, 37–40. Santa Barbara, California: ABC-CLIO.

Hitchcott, Nicki. 2000. *Women Writers in Francophone Africa*. Oxford: Berg.

Hobsbawm, Eric, and Terence Ranger, eds. 1983. *The Invention of Tradition*. Cambridge: Cambridge University Press.

Horton, Robin. 1993a. "African Traditional Thought and Western Science" [1967]. In *Patterns of Thought in Africa and the West: Essays on Magic, Religion, and Science*, 197–258. Cambridge: Cambridge University Press.

———. 1993b. "Tradition and Modernity Revisited" [1982]. In *Patterns of Thought in Africa and the West: Essays on Magic, Religion, and Science*, 301–46. Cambridge: Cambridge University Press.

Houmfa, Mohamadou. 2010. "Shakira Used Cameroonian Pop Song for World Cup Anthem … Without Asking." France 24. May 13. http://observers.france24.com/en/20100513-shakira-used-cameroon-pop-song-world-cup-anthem-without-asking.

Hountondji, Paulin. 1996. *African Philosophy: Myth and Reality*. Translated by Henry Evans and Jonathan Rée. 2nd ed. Bloomington: Indiana University Press.

Hourst, Émile-Auguste-Léon. 1898. *Sur le Niger et au pays des Tuaregs: La Mission Hourst*. Paris: Plon.

Ibn Khaldūn. 1958. *The Muqaddimah: An Introduction to History*. Translated by Franz Rosenthal. New York: Pantheon Books.

Innes, Gordon. 1973. "Stability and Change in Griots' Narrations." *African Language Studies* 14: 105–18.

———. 1993. "Obligations to the Word: Ritual Speech, Performance, and Responsibility: Verbal Abuse in a Wolof Village." In *Responsibility and Evidence in Oral Discourse*, edited by Jane H. Hill and Judith T. Irvine, 105–34. Cambridge: Cambridge University Press.

Izzo, Justin. 2015. "The Anthropology of Transcultural Storytelling: *Oui Mon Commandant!* and Amadou Hampâté Bâ's Ethnographic Didacticism." *Research in African Literatures* 46 (1): 1–18.

Jahn, Janheinz. 1974. *Leo Frobenius, the Demonic Child*. Austin: University of Texas at Austin, African and Afro-American Studies and Research Center.

Jakobson, Roman. 1990. *On Language*. Edited by Linda R. Waugh and Monique

Monville-Burston. Cambridge, MA: Harvard University Press.

Jansen, Jan. 1996. "'Elle connaît tout le Mande': A Tribute to the Griotte Siramori Diabate." *Research in African Literatures* 27 (4): 180–97.

———. 2001. *Epopée, Histoire, Société: Le Cas de Soundjata; Mali et Guinée.* Paris: Karthala.

———. 2004. "The Adventures of the 'Epic of Samori' in 20th-Century Mande Tradition." In *Epic Adventures: Heroic Narrative in the Oral Performance Traditions of Four Continents,* edited by Jan Jansen and Henk Maier, 71–80. Münster: Lit Verlag.

Jansen, Jan, and Henk Maier, eds. 2004. *Epic Adventures: Heroic Narrative in the Oral Performance Traditions of Four Continents.* Münster: Lit Verlag.

Janson, Marloes. 2004. "The Narration of the Sunjata Epic as a Gendered Activity." In *Epic Adventures: Heroic Narrative in the Oral Performance Traditions of Four Continents,* edited by Jan Jansen and Henk Maier, 81–88. Münster: Lit Verlag.

Jayyusi, Lena, ed. 1996. *The Adventures of Sayf Ben Dhi Yazan: An Arab Folk Epic.* Bloomington: Indiana University Press.

Jézéquel, Jean-Hervé. 2006. "Collecting Customary Law': Educated Africans, Ethnographic Writings, and Colonial Justice in French West Africa." In *Intermediaries, Interpreters, and Clerks: African Employees in the Making of Colonial Africa,* edited by Benjamin N. Lawrance, Emily Lynn Osborn, and Richard L. Roberts, 139–58. Madison: University of Wisconsin Press.

Johnson, John. 1980. "Yes, Virginia, There Is an Epic in Africa." *Research in African Literatures* 11 (3): 308–26.

———. 1982. "On the Heroic Age and Other Primitive Theses." In *Folklorica: Festschrift for Felix J. Oinas,* 121–38. Bloomington: Indiana University Press.

———. 1999. "The Dichotomy of Power and Authority in Mande Society and in the Epic of Sunjata." In *In Search of Sunjata: The Mande Oral Epic as History, Literature and Performance,* edited by Ralph Austen, 9–23. Bloomington: Indiana University Press.

———. 2003. *Son-Jara, the Mande Epic: Mandekan/English Edition with Notes and Commentary.* 3rd ed. Bloomington: Indiana University Press.

Johnson, John, et al., eds. 1997. *Oral Epics from Africa: Vibrant Voices from a Vast Continent.* Bloomington: Indiana University Press.

Julien, Charles André. 1946. *Les techniciens de la colonisation (XIXe-XXe siècles).* Paris: Presses Universitaires de France.

Julien, Eileen. 1992. *African Novels and the Question of Orality.* Bloomington: Indiana University Press.

———. 2006. "The Extroverted African Novel." In *The Novel,* vol. 1: *History, Geography, and Culture,* edited by Franco Moretti, 667–96. Princeton, NJ: Princeton University Press.

Kabanda, Théophiste. 2010. "Théâtralité et formes parodiques dans *En attendant le vote des bêtes sauvages d'Ahmadou Kourouma*." In *L'imaginaire d'Ahmadou Kourouma: Contours et enjeux d'une esthétique*, edited by Jean Ouédraogo, 245–67. Paris: Karthala.

Kafalenos, Emma. 1992. "Toward a Typology of Indeterminacy in Postmodern Narrative." *Comparative Literature* 44 (4): 380–408.

Kane, Mohamadou. 1982. *Roman africain et traditions*. Dakar: Nouvelles Editions Africaines.

Kane, Moustapha, and David Robinson, eds. 1984. *The Islamic Regime of Fuuta Tooro: An Anthology of Oral Tradition Transcribed in Pulaar and Translated into English*. East Lansing: African Studies Center, Michigan State University.

Kane, Oumar. 2004. *La Première hégémonie peule: Le Fuuta Tooro de Koli Tengella à Almaami Abdul*. Paris: Karthala.

Kedzierska-Manzon, Agnieszka. 2014. *Chasseurs mandingues: Violence, pouvoir et religion en Afrique de l'Ouest*. Paris: Karthala.

Keïta, Chérif. 1988. "Jaliya in the Modern World." *Ufahamu* 17 (1): 57–67.

———. 1995. *Massa Makan Diabaté: Un griot mandingue à la rencontre de l'écriture*. Paris: L'Harmattan.

Kelly, Gail P. 1984. "The Presentation of Indigenous Society in the Schools of French West Africa and Indochina, 1918 to 1938." *Comparative Studies in Society and History* 26 (3): 523–42.

Kesteloot, Lilyan. 1993a. "Introduction." In "Oral Literature," special issue, *Research in African Literatures* 24 (2): 7–11.

———, ed. 1993b. *L'Epopée bambara de Ségou*. 2 vols. Paris: L'Harmattan.

———. 2001. *Histoire de la littérature négro-africaine*. Paris: Karthala.

Kesteloot, Lilyan, and Bassirou Dieng, eds. 1997. *Les Épopées d'Afrique noire*. Paris: Karthala.

Kesteloot, Lilyan, and Chérif Mbodj. 2006. *Contes et mythes wolof*. Dakar: IFAN and Enda Tiers-Monde.

Klein, Martin A. 1968. *Islam and Imperialism in Senegal: Sine-Saloum, 1847–1914*. Edinburgh: Edinburgh University Press.

Knight, Roderick. 1973. "Mandinka Jeliya." PhD diss. University of California, Los Angeles.

Konaté, Yacouba. 2005. "Le Syndrome Amadou Hampâté Bâ ou comment naissent les proverbes." In *Amadou Hampâté Bâ, homme de science et de sagesse: Mélanges pour le centième anniversaire de la naissance d'Hampâté Bâ*, edited by Ahmadou Touré and Ntji Idriss Mariko, 49–68. Paris: Karthala.

Koné, Amadou. 1985. *Du récit oral au roman: Étude sur les avatars de la tradition héroïque dans le roman africain*. Abidjan: Ceda.

———. 2004. "Entre hommage et abâtardissement: La Tradition subvertie." *Notre Librairie* 155–56: 49–53.

Kourouma, Ahmadou. 1970. *Les Soleils des indépendances*. Paris: Seuil.

———. 1981. *The Suns of Independence*. Translated by Adrian Adams. London: Heinemann.

———. 1990. *Monnè, outrages et défis: Roman*. Paris: Seuil.

———. 1993. *Monnew: A Novel*. Translated by Nidra Poller. San Francisco: Mercury House.

———. 1998. *En attendant le vote des bêtes sauvages*. Paris: Seuil.

———. 2001. *Waiting for the Vote of the Wild Animals*. Translated by Carrol Coates. Charlottesville: University of Virginia Press.

Kyoore, Pascal Kyiiripuo. 2010. "L'humour satirique dans *En attendant le vote des bêtes sauvages* d'Ahmadou Kourouma." In *L'imaginaire d'Ahmadou Kourouma: Contours et enjeux d'une esthétique*, edited by Jean Ouédraogo, 225–44. Paris: Karthala.

Labouret, Henri. 1931. *À la recherche d'une politique indigène dans l'Ouest africain*. Paris: Comité de l'Afrique française.

Lam, Aboubacry Moussa. 1993. *De l'origine égyptienne des Peuls*. Paris: Présence africaine; Gif-sur-Yvette: Khepera.

Lanrezac, Henri. 1907a. "Au Soudan: La Légende historique." *La Revue Indigène* 16–19: 292–97, 380–86, 420–30.

———. 1907b. "La Légende soudanaise." *La Revue Indigène* 13: 163–73.

———. 1907c. "Légende et chants de guerre soudanais." *La Revue Indigène* 14: 210–15.

———. 1907d. "Légendes soudanaises." *Bulletin de la Société de Géographie Commerciale de Paris* 29 (10): 607–19.

———. 1908. "Essai sur le folk-lore au Soudan." Offprint. *La Revue Indigène*.

Lawrance, Benjamin N., Emily Lynn Osborn, and Richard L. Roberts, eds. 2006. *Intermediaries, Interpreters, and Clerks: African Employees in the Making of Colonial Africa*. Madison: University of Wisconsin Press.

Le Chatelier, Alfred. 1899. *L'Islam dans l'Afrique occidentale*. Paris: G. Steinheil.

Le Renard, Thibault, and Comi Toulabor. 1999. "Entretien avec Ahmadou Kourouma." *Politique africaine* 75: 178–83.

Leduc-Gueye, Christine. 2016. "Du Set Setal au Festigraff: L'Evolution murale de la ville de Dakar." *Cahiers de Narratologie: Analyse et théorie narratives* 30.

Lévi-Strauss, Claude. *The Savage Mind*. London: Weidenfeld & Nicolson.

Levtzion, Nehemia. 1971. "The Early States of the Western Sudan to 1500." In *History of West Africa*, edited by J. F. Ade Ajayi and Michael Crowder, 120–57. London: Longman.

Levtzion, Nehemia, and J. F. P. Hopkins, eds. 1981. *Corpus of Early Arabic Sources for West African History*. Cambridge: Cambridge University Press.

Lord, Albert Bates. 1960. *The Singer of Tales*. Cambridge, MA: Harvard University Press.

Lorin, Marie. 2015. "La Poésie orale peule des pêcheurs de la vallée du fleuve Sénégal (Pékâne):

Approche géopoétique." PhD diss., University of Paris-Sorbonne.

Lukács, György. 1971. *The Theory of the Novel: A Historico-Philosophical Essay on the Forms of Great Epic Literature*. Translated by Anna Bostock. Cambridge, MA: M.I.T. Press.

Ly, Amadou. 1991. *L'Epopée de Samba Guéladiégui*. Ivry: Editions nouvelles du sud.

Lyotard, Jean-François. 1984. *The Postmodern Condition: A Report on Knowledge*. Minneapolis: University of Minnesota Press.

Mackey, Robert. 2010. "Shakira Remixes African Hit for World Cup." *The Lede* (blog), *New York Times*. May 24. http://thelede.blogs.nytimes.com/2010/05/24/shakira-remixes-african-hit-for-world-cup/.

Madelénat, Daniel. 1986. *L'Epopée*. Paris: Presses universitaires de France.

Mariko, Ntji Idriss. 2005. "Amadou Hampâté Bâ: Défense et illustration de la tradition." In *Amadou Hampâté Bâ, homme de science et de sagesse: Mélanges pour le centième anniversaire de la naissance d'Hampâté Bâ*, edited by Ahmadou Touré and Ntji Idriss Mariko, 19–26. Paris: Karthala.

Martin, Florence. 2000. "Échos et grains de voix dans *Le Jujubier du Patriarche* d'Aminata Sow Fall." *French Review* 74 (2): 296–307.

Mas, Marion. 2015. "Epique et Travestissement burlesque dans *Les Soleils des indépendances*: Valeurs politiques de la bâtardise." In *Ahmadou Kourouma: Entre poétique romanesque et littérature politique*, edited by Patrick Voisin, 309–25. Paris: Classiques Garnier.

Masonen, Pekka. 2000. *The Negroland Revisited: Discovery and Invention of the Sudanese Middle Ages*. Helsinki: Finnish Academy of Science and Letters.

Mateso, Emmanuel Locha. 1986. *La Littérature africaine et sa critique*. Paris: A.C.C.T. and Karthala.

Mbembe, Achille. 2001a. *On the Postcolony*. Berkeley: University of California Press.

———. 2001b. "Ways of Seeing: Beyond the New Nativism. Introduction." *African Studies Review* 44 (2): 1–14.

———. 2002. "African Modes of Self-Writing." Translated by Steven Rendall. *Public Culture* 14 (1): 239–73.

McGuire, James. 1999. "Butchering Heroism? Sunjata and the Negotiation of Postcolonial Mande Identity in Diabaté's Le Boucher de Kouta." In *In Search of Sunjata: The Mande Oral Epic as History, Literature and Performance*, edited by Ralph Austen, 253–73. Bloomington: Indiana University Press.

McNee, Lisa. 2000. *Selfish Gifts: Senegalese Women's Autobiographical Discourses*. Albany: State University of New York Press.

Meillassoux, Claude, and Abdoulaye Sylla. 1978. "L'Interprétation légendaire de l'histoire de Jonkoloni (Mali)." In *Fonti Orali: Antropologia e Storia*, 347–92. Milan: Franco Angeli Editore.

Mercier, Paul. 1968. *Tradition, changement, histoire: Les Somba du Dahomey septentrional.* Paris: Éditions Anthropos.

Mestaoui, Lobna. 2012. *Tradition orale et esthétique romanesque, aux sources de l'imaginaire de Kourouma.* Paris: L'Harmattan.

Miller, Christopher. 1985. *Blank Darkness: Africanist Discourse in French.* Chicago: University of Chicago Press.

———. 1990. *Theories of Africans: Francophone Literature and Anthropology in Africa.* Chicago: University of Chicago Press.

———. 1999. "Trait d'Union: Injunction and Dismemberment in Yambo Ouologuem's *Le Devoir de Violence.*" In *Yambo Ouologuem: Postcolonial Writer, Islamic Militant,* edited by Christopher Wise, 109–19. Boulder, CO: Lynne Rienner.

Miller, Joseph. 1999. "History and Africa/Africa and History." *American Historical Review* 104 (1): 1–32.

Mills, Ivy. 2011. "Sutura: Gendered Honor, Social Death, and the Politics of Exposure in Senegalese Literature and Popular Culture." PhD diss., University of California, Berkeley.

Monénembo, Tierno. 2004. *Peuls.* Paris: Seuil.

Monteil, Charles. 1905. *Contes soudanais.* Paris: E. Leroux.

———. 1953. "La Légende du Ouagadou et l'origine des Soninké." In *Mélanges ethnologiques,* 359–408. Dakar: IFAN.

———. 1968. *Les Empires du Mali: Etude d'histoire et de sociologie soudanaises.* Paris: Maisonneuve et Larose.

Monteil, Vincent. 1963. "Lat Dior, Damel du Kayor, et l'islamisation des Wolofs." *Archives de sociologie des religions* 16 (1): 77–104.

Moretti, Franco. 1996. *Modern Epic: The World-System from Goethe to García Márquez.* London: Verso.

Mouralis, Bernard. 1987. "Un carrefour d'écritures: *Le Devoir de violence* de Yambo Ouologuem." In *Recherches et travaux: Littératures africaines d'écriture française,* 75–92. Grenoble: Université de Grenoble, U.F.R. de Lettres.

Mudimbe, V. Y. 1988. *The Invention of Africa: Gnosis, Philosophy, and the Order of Knowledge.* Bloomington: Indiana University Press.

Nagler, Michael. 1974. *Spontaneity and Tradition: A Study in the Oral Art of Homer.* Berkeley: University of California Press.

Nandwa, Jane, and Austin Bukenya. 1983. *African Oral Literature for Schools.* London: Longman.

N'Da, Pierre. 2005. "*L'Etrange destin de Wangrin,* un étrange roman." In *Amadou Hampâté Bâ, homme de science et de sagesse: Mélanges pour le centième anniversaire de la naissance d'Hampâté Bâ*, edited by Ahmadou Touré and Ntji Idriss Mariko, 191–208. Paris: Karthala.

Ndao, Cheikh Aliou. 1983. *Du sang pour un trône, ou Gouye Ndiouli un dimanche*. Paris: L'Harmattan.

———. 1985. *L'Exil d'Albouri; La Décision; Le Fils de l'Almamy; La Case de l'homme*. Dakar: Nouvelles Editions Africaines.

———. 2002. *Guy Njulli*. Dakar: Ministère de la culture et de la communication.

N'Daou, Mohamed Saidou. 2007. "Djibril Tamsir Niane and David Conrad: Collaborative Re-Imagining of the Mande Past Across the Atlantic." In *Mande Mansa: Essays in Honor of David C. Conrad*, edited by Stephen Belcher and Jan Jansen, 144–73. Münster: Lit Verlag.

———. 2008. "Almamy Samori Touré: Politics of Memories in Post-Colonial Guinea (1968–Present)." *Mande Studies* 10: 149–73.

Ngom, Ousmane. 2012. "Militantisme Linguistique et Initiation Littéraire dans Doomi Golo—Roman Wolof de Bubakar Bóris Jóob." *Repères-Dorif* 2. http://www.dorif.it/ezine/ezine_articles.php?art_id=34.

———. 2014. "Métaphores obsédantes du seetu et reflets identitaires dans *Doomi Golo* et *L'Afrique au-delà du miroir* de Boubacar Boris Diop." *Groupe d'études linguistiques et littéraires, Université Gaston Berger de Saint-Louis* (blog). July 6. http://gellugb.over-blog.com/2014/07/metaphores-obsedantes-du-seetu-et-reflets-identitaires-dans-doomi-golo-et-l-afrique-au-dela-du-miroir-de-boubacar-boris-diop-par-ous.

Ngũgĩ wa Thiong'o. 1986. *Decolonising the Mind: The Politics of Language in African Literature*. London: Heinemann.

Niane, Djibril Tamsir. 1960. *Soundjata, ou l'épopée mandingue*. Paris: Présence africaine.

———. 1965. *Sundiata: An Epic of Old Mali*. London: Longman.

———. 1975. *Le Soudan occidental au temps des grands empires: XIe–XVIe siecle*. Paris: Présence africaine.

———, ed. 1975–76. *Demb ak Tey: Cahiers du mythe* 2 and 3.

———. 2009. *Sikasso, ou la dernière citadelle, suivi de Chaka*. Edited by Ray Autra. Abidjan: NEI/CEDA; Conakry: SAEC.

Niang, Cheikh. 2010. "Understanding Sex between Men in Senegal." In *Routledge Handbook of Sexuality, Health and Rights*, edited by Peter Aggleton and Richard Parker, 116–24. London: Routledge.

Nora, Pierre, ed. 1996. *Realms of Memory: Rethinking the French Past*. Translated by Arthur Goldhammer. 3 vols. New York: Columbia University Press.

Norris, Harry. 1972. *Saharan Myth and Saga*. Oxford: Clarendon Press.

Nyela, Désiré. 2006. "Subversion épique, verve romanesque dans *Le devoir de violence* de Yambo Ouologuem." *Revue de l'Université de Moncton* 37 (1): 147–61.

Okpewho, Isidore. 1979. *The Epic in Africa: Toward a Poetics of the Oral Performance.* New York: Columbia University Press.

———. 1992. *African Oral Literature: Backgrounds, Character, and Continuity.* Bloomington: Indiana University Press.

———. 1996. "How Not to Treat African Folklore." *Research in African Literatures* 27 (3): 119–28.

Ouologuem, Yambo. 1968. *Le Devoir de violence.* Paris: Seuil.

———. 1971. *Bound to Violence.* Translated by Ralph Manheim. New York: Harcourt Brace Jovanovich.

———. 2008. *The Yambo Ouologuem Reader.* Translated and edited by Christopher Wise. Trenton: Africa World Press.

Palmer, H. R. 1931. *The Carthaginian Voyage to West Africa in 500 B.C.* Bathurst: J. M. Lawani.

Parry, Milman. 1971. *The Making of Homeric Verse: The Collected Papers of Milman Parry.* Edited by Adam Milman. Oxford: Clarendon Press.

Person, Yves. 1968. *Samori: Une révolution dyula.* 3 vols. Dakar: IFAN.

———. 1976. *Samori: La Renaissance de l'empire mandingue.* Grandes Figures Africaines. Paris: ABC.

Piot, Charles. 1999. *Remotely Global: Village Modernity in West Africa.* Chicago: University of Chicago Press.

Poirier, Léon. 1940. *Brazza ou l'épopée du Congo.* Film. Société de Production du Film Brazza.

Pondopoulo, Anna. 2010. "Amadou Hampâté Bâ and the Writer Robert Arnaud (Randau): African Colonial Service and Literature." *Islamic Africa* 1 (2): 229–47.

Quint, David. 1993. *Epic and Empire: Politics and Generic Form from Virgil to Milton.* Princeton, NJ: Princeton University Press.

Quist-Arcton, Ofeibeia. 2010. "For Many in Senegal, Statue Is a Monumental Failure." NPR. January 5. http://www.npr.org/templates/story/story.php?storyId=122220923.

Raffenel, Anne-Jean-Baptiste. 1846. *Voyage dans l'Afrique occidentale.* Paris: Arthus Bertrand.

———. 1856. *Nouveau voyage dans le pays des nègres.* 2 vols. Paris: Imprimerie et librairie centrales des chemins de fer.

Ranger, Terence. 1993. "The Invention of Tradition Revisited: The Case of Colonial Africa." In *Legitimacy and the State in Twentieth-Century Africa,* edited by Terence Ranger and Olufemi Vaughan, 62–111. London: Macmillan.

Repinecz, Jonathon. 2015. "'The Tales of Tomorrow': Towards a Futurist Vision of Wolof Tradition." *Journal of African Cultural Studies* 27 (1): 56–70.

———. 2017. Review of *Ahmadou Kourouma, entre poétique romanesque et littérature politique. La Plume Francophone* (blog). April 14. https://la-plume-francophone.

com/2017/04/14/patrick-voisin-dir-ahmadou-kourouma-entre-poetique-romanesque-et-litterature-politique/.

Ricoeur, Paul. 1976. *Interpretation Theory: Discourse and the Surplus of Meaning*. Fort Worth: Texas Christian University Press.

Roberts, Allen F., and Mary Nooter Roberts. 2000a. "Artworks: Visual 'Literature' in Urban Senegal." *Public Culture* 12 (1): 285–88.

———. 2000b. "Papisto Boy." *African Arts* 33 (2): 72–92.

———. 2002. "Visual Tactics in Contemporary Senegal." *Matatu* 25–26: 191–228.

———. 2003. *A Saint in the City: Sufi Arts of Urban Senegal*. Los Angeles: UCLA Fowler Museum Publications.

Roberts, Allen F., et al. 2005. "Voir la ville invisible, Seeing the Invisible City." *Politique africaine* 100: 175–97.

Robinson, David. 2004. *Muslim Societies in African History*. Cambridge: Cambridge University Press.

Rochat, Laure-Adrienne. 2011. *De l'épopée au roman: Une lecture de* Monnè, Outrages et Défis *d'Ahmadou Kourouma*. Lausanne: Archipel.

Roth, Molly. 2008. *Ma parole s'achète: Money, Identity and Meaning in Malian Jeliya*. Berlin: Lit Verlag.

Sa'di, Abd al-Rahman [Abderrahman]. 1900. *Tarikh Es-Soudan*. Translated by Octave Houdas. Paris: Ernest Leroux.

———. 2003. *Timbuktu and the Songhay Empire: Al-Sa'dī's Ta'rīkh Al-Sūdān Down to 1613, and Other Contemporary Documents*. Edited and translated by John Hunwick. Leiden: Brill.

Sadji, Abdoulaye. 1936. "Ce que dit la musique africaine." *L'Education africaine* 94: 119–72.

———. 1958. *Maïmouna*. Paris: Présence africaine.

———. 1985. *Ce que dit la musique africaine*. Dakar: Présence africaine.

Sadji, Amadou Booker. 1997. *Abdoulaye Sadji: Biographie*. Paris: Présence Africaine.

Schiavone, Cristina. 1994. "A Propos de 'Le Jujubier du Patriarche': Entretien avec Aminata Sow Fall." *Francofonia* 27: 87–95.

Schulz, Dorothea. 1997. "Praise without Enchantment: Griots, Broadcast Media, and the Politics of Tradition in Mali." *Africa Today* 44 (4): 443–64.

———. 2001. *Perpetuating the Politics of Praise: Jeli Singers, Radios and Political Mediation in Mali*. Cologne: R. Köppe.

SCOA [Fondation SCOA pour la recherche en Afrique noire]. 1977. *Deuxième colloque international de Bamako (16 février–22 février 1976). Actes du colloque*. Paris: Fondation SCOA.

Seck, Fatoumata. 2018. "Goorgoorlou, the Neoliberal *Homo Senegalensis*: Comics and

Economics in Postcolonial Senegal." *Journal of African Cultural Studies* 30 (3): 263–78.

Serbin, Sylvia. 2004. *Reines d'Afrique et héroïnes de la diaspora noire*. Saint-Maur-des-Fossés: Sépia.

Seydou, Christiane. 1982. "Comment définir le genre épique? Un exemple: l'épopée africaine." *Journal of the Anthropological Society of Oxford* 13 (1): 84–98.

———. 1983. "The African Epic: A Means for Defining the Genre." *Folklore Forum* 16 (1): 47–68.

———. 1988. "Epopée et Identité: Exemples africains." *Journal des africanistes* 58 (1): 7–22.

———. 1998. "Musique et littérature orale chez les Peuls du Mali." *L'Homme* 148: 139–57.

———. 2010. *L'Epopée peule de Boûbou Ardo Galo: Héros et rebelle*. Paris: Karthala.

Seye, El Hadji Amadou. 2003. *Walo Brack*. Dakar: Editions Maguilen.

Sherman, Mark. 1995. "Problems of Bakhtin's Epic: Capitalism and the Image of History." In *Bakhtin and Medieval Voices*, edited by Thomas J. Farrell, 180–95. Gainesville: University Press of Florida.

Sidikou, Aïssata G. 2001. *Recreating Words, Reshaping Worlds: The Verbal Art of Women from Niger, Mali, and Senegal*. Trenton: Africa World Press.

Sidikou, Aïssata G., and Thomas A. Hale, eds. 2012. *Women's Voices from West Africa: An Anthology of Songs from the Sahel*. Bloomington: Indiana University Press.

Soares, Benjamin. 2004. "Islam and Pubic Piety in Mali." In *Public Islam and the Common Good*, edited by Armando Salvatore and Dale Eickelman, 205–26. Leiden: Brill.

———. 2014. "The Historiography of Islam in West Africa: An Anthropologist's View." *Journal of African History* 55 (1): 27–36.

Sôh, Siré-Abbâs. 1913. *Chroniques du Foûta sénégalais*. Translated by Maurice Delafosse and Henri Gaden. Paris: Ernest Leroux.

Sora Wade, Mansour. 1992. *Aïda Souka*. Film. Kaany Productions.

Sow, Alfa Ibrahima. 1970. *Inventaire du fonds du fonds Amadou Hampâté Bâ répertorié à Abidjan en 1969*. Paris: C. Klincksieck.

———. 1982. "Le Monde des subalɓe (vallée du fleuve Sénégal)." *Bulletin de l'IFAN* 44 (3–4): 237–320.

Sow Fall, Aminata. 1976. *Le Revenant*. Dakar: Nouvelles editions africaines.

———. 1993. *Le Jujubier du patriarche: Roman*. Dakar: Khoudia.

———. 2012. *L'Appel des arènes*. Paris: Edicef.

———. 1999. "Remarks on Yambo Ouologuem's *Le Devoir de Violence*." In *Yambo Ouologuem: Postcolonial Writer, Islamic Militant*, edited by Christopher Wise, 17–22. Boulder, CO: Lynne Rienner.

Stringer, Susan. 1996. *The Senegalese Novel by Women: Through Their Own Eyes*. New York: P. Lang.

Suret-Canale, Jean. 1962. *Afrique noire: L'ère coloniale, 1900–1945*. Paris: Editions sociales.

Sy, Abd-el-Kader Mademba. 1931. *Au Sénégal et au soudan français*. Paris: Emile Larose.

Sylla, Assane. 1978. *La Philosophie morale des Wolof*. Dakar: IFAN.

Tamari, Tal. 1991. "The Development of Caste Systems in West Africa." *Journal of African History* 32 (2): 221–50.

———. 1995. "Linguistic History for the History of West African 'Castes.'" In *Status and Identity in West Africa: Nyamakalaw of Mande*, edited by David Conrad and Barbara Frank, 61–85. Bloomington: Indiana University Press.

Tauxier, Louis. 1927. *La Religion bambara*. Paris: P. Geuthner.

———. 1937. *Mœurs et histoire des Peuls*. Paris: Payot.

Tedlock, Dennis, and Bruce Mannheim, eds. 1995. *The Dialogic Emergence of Culture*. Urbana: University of Illinois Press.

Thiers-Thiam, Valérie. 2005. *A chacun son griot: Le mythe du griot-narrateur dans la littérature et le cinéma d'Afrique de l'Ouest*. Paris: L'Harmattan.

Thioub, Ibrahima. 2002. "L'Ecole de Dakar et la production d'une écriture académique de l'histoire." In *Le Sénégal contemporain*, edited by Momar Coumba Diop, 109–53. Paris: Karthala.

Thoyer, Annik, ed. 1995. *Récits épiques des chasseurs bamanan du Mali de Mamadu Jara*. Paris: L'Harmattan.

———, ed. 1999. *Maghan Jan et autres récits des chasseurs du Mali*. Paris: L'Harmattan.

Traoré, Karim. 1999. "Jeli and Sere: The Dialectics of the Word in the Manden." In *In Search of Sunjata: The Mande Oral Epic as History, Literature and Performance*, edited by Ralph Austen, 171–88. Bloomington: Indiana University Press.

———. 2000a. "Kourouma's 'Monnè' as Aesthetics of Lying." *Callaloo* 23 (4): 1349–62.

———. 2000b. *Le Jeu et le sérieux: Essai d'anthropologie littéraire sur la poésie épique des chasseurs du Mande (Afrique de l'Ouest)*. Cologne: Rüdiger Köppe.

———. 2014. "Kourouma and the Hunters, Kourouma's Hunters." Unpublished conference paper. Modern Language Association, Chicago, January 11.

Triaud, Jean-Louis. 1998. "Haut-Sénégal-Niger, un modèle 'positiviste'? De la coutume à l'histoire: Maurice Delafosse et l'invention de l'histoire africaine." In *Maurice Delafosse: Entre orientalisme et ethnographie. L'itinéraire d'un africaniste, 1870–1926*, edited by Jean-Loup Amselle and Emmanuelle Sibeud, 210–32. Paris: Maisonneuve et Larose.

Tro Dého, Roger. 2011. "Ressources de l'oralité et traits postmodernes du roman africain: Du paradoxe à la connivence créatrice." In *Le Postmodernisme dans le roman africain: Formes, enjeux et perspectives*, edited by Adama Coulibaly et al., 145–79. Paris: L'Harmattan.

Urvoy, Yves. 1949. *Histoire de l'empire du Bornou*. Paris: Larose.

Van Vollenhoven, Joost. 1917. "Circulaire au sujet des chefs indigènes." *Journal Officiel de l'Afrique Occidentale Française* 633 (August): 466–73.

Vansina, Jan. 1965. *Oral Tradition: A Study in Historical Methodology*. Translated by H. M. Wright. London: Routledge & K. Paul.

Vidal, Jean. 1924. "La Légende officielle de Soundiata, fondateur de l'empire manding." *Bulletin du Comité d'études historiques et scientifiques de l'Afrique Occidentale Française* 8 (2): 317–28.

Vieillard, Gilbert. 1931. "Récits peuls du Macina et du Kounari." *Bulletin du Comité d'études historiques et scientifiques de l'Afrique Occidentale Française* 14 (1–2): 137–56.

Voisin, Patrick, ed. 2015. *Ahmadou Kourouma: Entre poétique romanesque et littérature politique*. Paris: Classiques Garnier.

Vološinov, V. N. 1973. *Marxism and the Philosophy of Language*. Translated by Ladislav Matejka and I. R. Titunik. Studies in Language. New York: Seminar Press.

Wane, Ibrahima. 2004. "Du français au wolof: La Quête du récit chez Boubacar Boris Diop." *Ethiopiques* 73: 1–12.

Warner, Tobias. 2016. "How Mariama Bâ Became World Literature: Translation and the Legibility of Feminist Critique." *PMLA* 131 (5): 1239–55.

Watt, Ian. 1957. *The Rise of the Novel: Studies in Defoe, Richardson, and Fielding*. Berkeley: University of California Press.

Willis, John Ralph. 1978. "The Torodbe Clerisy: A Social View." *Journal of African History* 19 (2): 195–212.

Wilson, Bryan, ed. 1970. *Rationality*. Evanston, IL: Harper & Row.

Wise, Christopher, ed. 1999. *Yambo Ouologuem: Postcolonial Writer, Islamic Militant*. Boulder, CO: Lynne Rienner.

Wynchank, Amy. 1991. "Wangrin, a Modern African Epic." In *Oral Tradition and Innovation: New Wine in Old Bottles? Selected Conference Papers*, edited by E. R. Sienaert, A. N. Bell, and M. Lewis, 228–38. Durban: University of Natal Oral Documentation and Research Centre.

Yapo, Louis P. 2008. "The Dynamics of Subversion and Resistance in Ahmadou Kourouma's Novels." PhD diss., University at Albany, SUNY.

Zabus, Chantal. 2007. *The African Palimpsest: Indigenization of Language in the West African Europhone Novel*. 2nd ed. Amsterdam: Rodopi.

Zanganeh, Lila Azam. 2010. "Une littérature de transition." *Le Monde*. April 15. http://www.lemonde.fr/livres/article/2010/04/15/une-litterature-de-transition_1333889_3260.html.

INDEX